Film and Television Scores, 1950–1979

Film and Television Scores, 1950–1979

A Critical Survey by Genre

Kristopher Spencer

McFarland & Company, Inc., Publishers
Jefferson, North Carolina, and London

Photographs are from the author's collection except as indicated otherwise.

LIBRARY OF CONGRESS CATALOGUING-IN-PUBLICATION DATA

Spencer, Kristopher.
  Film and television scores, 1950–1979 : a critical survey by genre / Kristopher Spencer.
      p.   cm.
  Includes bibliographical references and index.

  ISBN 978-0-7864-3682-8
  softcover : 50# alkaline paper ∞

  1. Motion picture music—History and criticism.
  2. Television music—History and criticism.   I. Title.
  ML2075.S72   2008
  781.5′409045—dc22   2008032756

British Library cataloguing data are available

©2008 Kristopher Spencer. All rights reserved

No part of this book may be reproduced or transmitted in any form or by any means, electronic or mechanical, including photocopying or recording, or by any information storage and retrieval system, without permission in writing from the publisher.

On the cover: *The Wild Angels* (MGM/AIP, '66) starring Peter Fonda *right with guitar* and Nancy Sinatra *standing left* (courtesy of the John Monaghan Collection).

Manufactured in the United States of America

*McFarland & Company, Inc., Publishers
  Box 611, Jefferson, North Carolina 28640
    www.mcfarlandpub.com*

To my wife Laura for her support and
encouragement throughout the creative process

Acknowledgments

A number of people have generously shared their learned opinions, knowledge and soundtrack collections as I conducted research for this book. I thank (in alphabetical order) Tim Ayres, Carlo Bagnolo, Thierry Balzan, Carlos Bes, Matthew Blake, Jim Blanchard, Josh Bloom, Jeff Bond, Godwin Borg, Dietmar Bosch, Col Boyter, Sascha Bretz, David Broussal, James Brouwer, Will Burns, Michael Canich, Cliff Chase, Allan Clark, Robert Conroy, Jeff Cornett, Daniele De Gemini, Thomas Deligny, Luca Di Silverio, Adam Dorn, Stelios Dracoulis, Michael Draine, Dave Eagle, Michael Engels, Robert Esterhammer, Michael Fishberg, Wolfgang Frank, Fabio Gasperoni, J. Max Gilbert, Alex Gimeno, Ed Godsall, Jeff Greer, Mark Hammond, Ross Harris, Christopher Hasler, Kirsty Hawkshaw, Carl Howard, Joshua Hultberg, Alexander Imiela, Valentina Imperi, Chris Joss, Brian Karasick, Lukas Kendell, Joe Kennedy, Kevin Lee, Shawn Lee, Herschell Gordon Lewis, James Lincoln, Rod Lott, Cary Madden, Craig Maki, John Mansell, Joseph McCallus, Scott McIntyre, Stephen McLaughlin, Luís Meleiro, Kenn Minter, John Monaghan, Money Mark, Stephan Moore, Owen Morgan, Dino Müller, Marco Nardo, Michael Nezis, Pierre Noblet, Rocco Pandiani, Alan Parker, Rich Patterson, Christophe Peiffer, Jon Pendleton, Brock Phillips, Stu Phillips, Mark Pritchard, Brian Raimy, Stefan Rambow, Vinod Sabnani, Martin Sander, Gak Sato, Dawn Schmelzer, Larry Schnake, John Schrivener, Doug Shipton, Joe Sikoryak, Jennifer Stevenson, Strictly Kev, Magnus Sundstrom, Anthony Tanita, Ollie Teeba, Chris Thomes, Nathaniel Thompson, Justin Thyme, Jonny Trunk, Raymond Tucker, Marco D'Ubaldo, Pierpaolo Valenti, Gustav Verhulsdonck, Kris Verschaeve, Chenard Walcker, Jake Wherry, Tane Williams and perhaps a few others whose identities remain a mystery to me.

I also want to acknowledge several record labels for generously providing promotional copies of soundtrack releases for review in this book and on www.ScoreBaby.com, the author's website. I thank (in alphabetical order) Aleph, All Score Media, Beat, Beyond/MGM, Black Cat, Brigade Mondaine, CAM, Capitol, Cinedelic, Cinesoundz, Cinevox, Crippled Dick Hot Wax, Diggler, DigitMovies, Easy Tempo/Right Tempo, El/Cherry Red, Escalation, Film Score Monthly, Fin de Siecle Media, Finders Keepers, Fresh Sound, Germanicus, Harkit, Intrada, Ipecoc, La La Land, Milan, Normal, Perseverance, Plastic, Potfleur, Pulp Flavor, QDK Media, Rhino, RPM, Ryko, SHADO, Silva Screen, Sony, Stax, Subterfuge, Trunk, Ubiquity, Vadim, Vanguard, Vampi Soul and Votary.

Table of Contents

Acknowledgments — vii
Preface — 1

1. Crime Jazz and Felonious Funk — 5
2. Spy Symphonies — 57
3. Sexploitation Serenade — 85
4. Staccato Six-Guns — 127
5. Sci-Fidelity and the Superhero Spectrum — 167
6. A Fearful Earful — 222
7. Rockin' Revolution — 282

Epilogue — 330
Bibliography — 337
Index — 341

Preface

This book is a selective survey of film and television soundtracks of the '50s, '60s and '70s—arguably the most fruitful and influential period of artistic and commercial development in the film music genre. While the focus is "Silver Age" film and television scores, some "Golden Age" film scores are included for the sake of comparison and contrast, and some Golden Age television scores merit inclusion due to stylistic similarities with contemporaneous film scores. Although defining the timeline of the Silver Age is an inexact science, the span of 1950–1979 is more than adequate for a thorough survey of the period's significant trends and milestones. Generally speaking, the Silver Age began in the early '50s when jazz, pop and rock started to influence film composers (and the filmmakers who hired them with the aim of releasing a movie and soundtrack album that would have popular appeal). Naturally, the Silver Age was preceded by the Golden Age (late '20s to late '40s) and theoretically followed by the Bronze Age ('80s to the present period). However, cinematic history demonstrates that these precious periods of film music do not adhere to firm timelines. Arguably, they merely reflect the generation of the composer or the artistic needs and commercial ambitions of the production. One might even argue that "Bronze Age" soundtracks merely feature an amalgamation of the styles developed during the earlier eras. That, however, is a subject for another tome.

By considering the influence of popular music on film scoring it can be argued that Alex North's jazz-tinged *A Streetcar Named Desire* (1951) is the first Silver Age soundtrack. Even so, *Streetcar*'s arrival did not bring a halt to the use of Golden Age film composers, nor did its brassy music discourage those composers from writing in the classically influenced style of previous decades. The well-established generation of mostly European-born composers such as Miklós Rózsa, Max Steiner, Franz Waxman, Erich Wolfgang Korngold and many others continued to compose in the sweeping symphonic style inspired by the Romantic classical composers of the 19th century. Great examples of Golden Age scores from the '50s and early '60s can be heard in *Lust for Life* (1956), *Ben-Hur* (1959), *Sodom and Gomorrah* (1962), all by Rózsa; *The Caine Mutiny* (1954), *Marjorie Morningstar* (1958), both by Steiner; and *Rear*

Window (1954), *Peyton Place* (1957) and *Taras Bulba* (1962), all by Waxman. However, by the late '50s the older composers found themselves increasingly in competition with younger composers for film assignments as well as television productions, and often struggled to deliver the modern sounds filmmakers demanded. Even a relatively young Golden Age composer like Bernard Herrmann resisted the trend toward more youth-oriented music styles.

Meanwhile, the younger generation of film composers, including North, Henry Mancini, John Williams, Elmer Bernstein, Jerry Goldsmith and many others, proved willing to experiment with various styles while occasionally writing more traditional scores, depending on the production. For example, Bernstein composed one of the great jazz scores for *The Man with the Golden*

Elmer Bernstein's *The Man with the Golden Arm* is not merely the best big-screen crime jazz soundtrack of the '50s; it also is a landmark score of the Silver Age. (CD cover appears courtesy of Fresh Sound Records; graphic design based on original album cover artwork by Saul Bass.)

Arm (1955), but later revived the grandeur of the Old West in Golden Age style for *The Magnificent Seven* (1960). North, having set the Silver Age in motion with *Streetcar*, also composed a suitably epic-sounding *Spartacus* (1960). Essentially, the younger composers had learned from the older masters of the genre, but weren't entrenched in the old ways.

As the '60s progressed, the symphonic style fell out of fashion as more and more filmmakers asked for soundtracks that would appeal to a younger audience. In 1964, the Beatles' soundtrack, or rather "songtrack," for *A Hard Day's Night* out-grossed the film's profits. It was hard to argue with the youth-oriented music's commercial viability. But it wasn't just rock and jazz that made the Golden Age style seem antiquated; it also was rhythm and blues, soul and funk. And, where popular forms proved inappropriate, Silver Age composers delivered orchestral scores that had more in common with avant-garde 20th-century classical movements of atonality, serialism and experimental electronics than the romantic 19th-century style favored by their forebears. As a result, the Silver Age period from 1950 to 1979 offered more stylistic variety than the Golden Age, and paved the way for the seemingly limitless variety heard in film and television soundtracks today.

But the old style proved resilient after all. Grand symphonic overtures and heroic orchestration roared back into favor in the late '70s with Williams' blockbuster *Star Wars* (1977). Since then, film soundtracks have incorporated elements from the Golden Age and the Silver Age. Contemporary film composers serve up epic scores (such as Howard Shore's Oscar-winning work on *The Lord of the Rings* trilogy) as well as experimental scores (such as Shore's jazz collaborations with saxophonist Ornette Coleman for *Naked Lunch*). However, the dominant legacy of the Silver Age is the commercialization of film and television soundtracks as a marketable item that is at once a souvenir of the theatrical release or TV program, and a creative, commercial work that can stand on its own merits.

Although a great deal of film music was recorded prior to the '50s, most of it wasn't released on LP or any other transportable commercial format. In other words, if one enjoyed hearing the music for a particular film, such as *Casablanca* (1942), one had to see the movie again to hear Max Steiner's wonderful score. Even *Streetcar*'s initial release was limited to select tracks on an extended play (EP) record and a set of 45 rpm records instead of a long playing (LP) format that would come to dominate the film music genre in decades to come. (In 1951, the LP format was still new and hadn't yet reached widespread household use.) Today we take it for granted that most major films (and many minor ones) receive soundtrack releases concurrent with their theatrical run. Sometimes these soundtracks actually contain legitimate film music (or at least re-recordings for the CD release), but just as often they contain a mix of commercially viable songs by popular recording artists that may or may not have been used in the film or TV show they supposedly represent. Purists tend to scoff at these so-called "music from and inspired by" collections, but such releases often outsell the actual film scores, which tend to favor orchestral instrumental music by composers who rarely have household name status. The movement toward "songtracks" has roots in the movie musical (sprouted with the movie-tie-in albums of Elvis Presley and the Beatles), which flowered in the late '60s with the hit soundtracks for *The Graduate* (1967) and *Easy Rider* (1969), and pollinated the genre with the blockbuster release of *Saturday Night Fever* (1977).

This book examines the evolution of the Silver Age soundtrack through a variety of film genres and musical styles. Not every film and television soundtrack release from that period is accounted for here, due in part to the limitations of the genre-specific chapter themes. Despite the inevitable gaps, it has been my aim as author to contextualize the development of various stylistic strains through specific types of film and television productions. From crime show and spy thriller to horror, sci-fi and beyond, this work aims to spotlight the best of each genre alongside the lesser entries, while calling attention to hidden treasures—soundtracks that outshine the productions they were composed to accompany. The book also examines many soundtracks for foreign films, which became increasingly popular and influential in Hollywood during the Silver Age. Moreover, the Epilogue examines the revival of interest in Silver Age scores and their influence on contemporary musicians within and outside of the film and television industries.

Although film and television soundtracks rarely sell in the quantities that qualify them as popular successes, the genre remains one of the richest in 20th-century music. Through the sophisticated formal disciplines of score composition and orchestration, soundtracks are capable of tapping into the infinite possibilities of drama, comedy, action and emotion—vicarious experiences—in a way that popular music generally cannot. It is music of the imagination.

Chapter 1

Crime Jazz and Felonious Funk

To enter the world of Silver Age crime soundtracks is to embrace the dark side of film and television entertainment—from post-war noir and the early days of TV crime shows to the gritty, cynical films of the Watergate era. The crime scores of the '50s, '60s and '70s mirror the evolution of the era's film music in general—notably the embrace of jazz and, later, funk, rock, soul and avant-garde classical.

Prior to the Silver Age of cinema and Golden Age of television, the crime genre made its transition from pulp magazine pages to radio programs, such as *The Shadow*, and movie serials, like *Dick Tracy's G-Men*. These hero-oriented productions were presented with rehashed orchestral scores only a few notes removed from 19th-century and early 20th-century classical works, such as Nikolai Rimsky-Korsakov's "Flight of the Bumble Bee," Modest Mussorgsky's "Night on Bald Mountain" and Gustav Holst's "The Planets." In each case, robust orchestrations accompany the epic struggle between hero and villain as violins soar triumphantly.

By the mid–1950s, however, the line between good and evil became increasingly tenuous. Do-gooder crime-fighters came with bad habits and dubious virtue. They didn't always "get their man," and dames often proved to be more trouble than even the most corrupt criminals. For this new era of moral ambiguity the only music that would prove apropos was jazz.

In the '50s jazz was still a fairly commercial music genre, though not nearly on the level of its dance floor incarnation better known as swing. To be considered a sophisticate in the post–World War II era often meant digging the sound of jazz, whether one was a beatnik or not. In the context of film noir and TV crime shows from 1950 to 1965, jazz perfectly accompanied the images of rain-drenched streets, smoky private eye consultations and backroom busts.

"[Jazz] represented something lean, tough, cynical, and intelligent—adjectives that applied easily enough to the detective heroes of these pictures. These guys weren't well described by a soft violin. Instead, the metallic-yet-soulful saxophone summed up this brave new world," wrote Skip Heller in the CD booklet notes of *Crime Jazz: Murder in the Second Degree* (Rhino, 1997).

That's not to say that jazz and the crime jazz of film and TV productions is the same beast. For one thing, crime jazz is mostly scripted and arranged for big bands, whereas the stylistically similar "cool" jazz and bebop of that period favored small group improvisation and long solos. Many West Coast musicians played crime jazz for the paycheck, not for the artistry. In fact, it wasn't until Johnny Mandel scored *I Want to Live* in 1958 that true jazz musicians were even granted an opportunity to compose a Hollywood score.

Swing for a Crime

The composer who usually gets credit for introducing jazz to the silver screen is Miklós Rózsa for *The Asphalt Jungle* (1950). A Hollywood veteran since 1937, Rózsa had scored many films, including *Double Indemnity* and *Spellbound*, before scoring John Huston's urban potboiler. While *The Asphalt Jungle* score contains jazz elements, it still leans heavily on the orchestral approach long favored by Hollywood studios. (It's worth noting that Rózsa's final film score—the noir spoof *Dead Men Don't Wear Plaid* [1982]—also favors the jazz sound.)

In 1951, a younger composer, Alex North, delivered a score that truly set the tone for iconic crime jazz. North, having written incidental music for the stage production of *Death of a Salesman*, followed its director, Elia Kazan, to greater success on the screen adaptation of *A Streetcar Named Desire*. On "Blanche," sultry horns smolder against fiery strings, transitioning into a cooler mood where shadowy piano and furtive horn figures dance against a spare cymbal ride. Although most of his scores favor the traditional orchestral style, North's contribution to the crime jazz genre proved inspirational to his younger colleagues, including Leith Stevens, Henry Mancini and Elmer Bernstein.

Stevens' *The Wild One* (1953) reinforced the idea of jazz being an unstoppable force in film music. As the orchestra bursts forth on the theme it's easy to imagine oneself a part of the biker gang as it wreaks havoc on a small town. The music is just that visceral. The motorcycle revving at the beginning of the theme also helps distinguish *The Wild One* as a thoroughly modern soundtrack moment. (For more on *The Wild One* see Chapter 7.)

A sure sign that jazz had found a home in Hollywood came in 1956 when Elmer Bernstein earned an Academy Award nomination for *The Man with the Golden Arm*. The film's gritty subject matter—heroin addiction—may have opened many eyes to the dangers hounding modern man, but the score opened audience ears to the high drama of hard-driving horn blasts, sultry woodwinds, rumbling bass and crashing percussion. No crime theme seems to swing harder than "Frankie's Machine." The brass screams against a backdrop of jackhammer percussion. On "The Fix," the same theme takes on a nightmarish urgency. On "Desperation," rumbling discordant piano and locomotive drums capture the single-minded obsession of the junkie. *Golden Arm* is simply one of the genre's most iconic scores.

A year later, Bernstein scored *Sweet Smell of Success*, a cynical drama set on New York City's Madison Avenue, where reputations are built up and torn down over cocktails. While Burt Lancaster and Tony Curtis exchange Machiavellian manipulations, Bernstein's score and additional jazz tracks by Chico Hamilton pour on sophisticated scorn. As Bernstein stated in cover notes for a 1962 LP of his *Movie & TV Themes*, "Jazz is contemporary ... [and] so are most films. Thus it seemed quite natural for me to utilize the elements of the jazz idiom in my work."

Also in 1956, Bernstein contributed jazz for a short-lived TV detective show, *Take Five*. "[It] failed," he noted, "but similar shows that followed did not, and jazz took a firm hold in television scoring."

Before the decade ended Bernstein would take another crack at TV crime with somewhat greater success, but first another young Hollywood composer would strike mainstream gold with his own take on TV crime jazz.

The claim came in 1958 when Henry Mancini, a long-time apprentice arranger at Universal, bumped into producer Blake Edwards in the studio barbershop. Edwards invited Mancini to score TV's *Peter Gunn* (1958–1961). Mancini's theme for the suave detective quickly became a standard of cool jazz (and eventually surf rock) repertoire. One could easily compile two or three discs worth of *Peter Gunn* variations by artists as disparate as Quincy Jones and Art of Noise. In the show, Gunn hangs out in the club Mother's where a jazz group plays underneath the dialogue.

"The idea of using jazz in the 'Gunn' score was never even discussed. It was implicit in the story," Mancini recalled in his autobiography *Did They Mention the Music?* (p. 87, Contemporary Books, 1989). "It was the time of so-called cool West Coast jazz," Mancini added. "That was the sound that came to me."

Walking bass and drums, smoky saxophones, and shouting trumpets were keys to the "Peter Gunn" sound, and the show also provided Mancini with his first opportunity to use bass flutes, an instrument that he used with great success throughout his career.

Peter Gunn was one of the first TV shows to receive a soundtrack LP release, which went to number one on the *Billboard* chart and held the position for 10 weeks—an astonishing feat for a jazz record, as well as a soundtrack. It stayed on the charts for more than two years and eventually sold more than a million copies. All of this made Mancini a bankable recording artist and one of the few film or television composers to ever become a household name.

The *Peter Gunn* score was only the beginning of what would prove to be an immensely popular and influential body of work. The "chilled-out sound-

Henry Mancini works with the stars of *Peter Gunn*, Craig Stevens and Lola Albright. His theme song for the TV show (NBC/ABC, 1958–1961) is arguably the most recognizable piece of crime jazz ever written. (Photograph courtesy of the Henry Mancini Estate.)

track"—as Steely Dan co-founder and jazz aficionado Donald Fagen called it (*Premiere*, 1987)—spawned two LPs and other related releases. Ten years later, Mancini scored the relatively unsuccessful *Gunn ... Number One* movie with a somewhat updated sound (check out the fuzz-tone guitar on "The Monkey Farm").

While *Peter Gunn* was hardly the first show of its kind, its soundtrack helped to popularize the crime jazz genre through the biggest mass medium ever. Other shows of the era that touted hard-boiled brass were *M Squad*, *77 Sunset Strip*, *Mike Hammer*, *Perry Mason*, *Richard Diamond*, *Naked City* and *Staccato*—the last of which features a Bernstein score.

If *Staccato* appeared to be a calculated response to *Peter Gunn*, its score was simply a reiteration of the sound Bernstein had already explored on the big screen. Johnny Staccato is a private eye who moonlights as a piano player in a jazz combo at a hip nightclub. *Staccato*'s theme aptly evokes an urban jungle's sweltering atmosphere. The rhythm section prowls along like a panther on the hunt, while brass and woodwinds soar above in the canopy of night. The show didn't enjoy *Peter Gunn*'s longevity, but its theme is nearly as iconic.

Earlier in 1958, Mancini scored Orson Welles' *Touch of Evil* at Universal Pictures, where the composer spent six years as an apprentice working on dozens of B-pictures. For *Evil*, Mancini worked closely with score supervisor Joseph Gershenson to meet Welles' demand for music that would only emanate from visual sources, such as a musical instrument, jukebox or radio.

"[Welles] truly understood film scoring," Mancini wrote in his autobiography (p. 79). "Since he was making a grimly realistic film, I think he reasoned that even the music had to be rooted in reality."

As *Evil*'s CD booklet notes explain, Welles wanted "musical color, rather than movement—sustained washes of sound rather than tempestuous, melodramatic,

Warren Barker's jazz score for *77 Sunset Strip* (Warner Bros., 1958–1964), starring Edd Byrnes as "Kookie," is as swinging and suave as the show's private detectives.

or operatic style of scoring." An old-fashioned cinematic symphony would have made the film's seedy proceedings absurd. On the other hand, Mancini's Afro-Cuban jazz and rock 'n' roll instrumentals provide the movie—in which Charlton Heston infamously plays a Mexican—an element of authenticity.

"*Touch of Evil* was one of the best things I did in that period of my life," Mancini later recounted (p. 82). "It's one of the best things I've ever done."

One of Mancini's next forays into crime jazz came on *Experiment in Terror* (1962). The composer experiments by blending rock 'n' roll "twist" elements with crime jazz. On its gorgeously sinister theme music, he uses an auto harp to create a mysterious atmosphere; in the composer's autobiography, he praised the instrument for its "great natural decay" and how its sound "seems to last forever." Listening to it conjures the sense of being stalked in a fog-enshrouded Golden Gate Park by San Francisco Bay. Displaying his great versatility, Mancini also delivers a catchy twist version of the track.

The Mancini crime theme that is more in keeping with his work on *Peter Gunn* is undoubtedly *The Pink Panther* (1963). Needless to say *The Pink Panther* was a massive success and spawned six sequels (all featuring Mancini music). The theme is—bar none—the ultimate in big screen crime jazz. From the opening notes on piano, bass and vibes, it oozes danger and intrigue, not to mention feline grace. A smoky saxophone states the bluesy theme, and an absolutely smoking big band responds. Then the piano, bass and vibes return, accompanied by woodwinds and saxophone to restate the theme. Pure perfection.

In 1963, Mancini scored the romantic, comedic crime thriller *Charade*—one of the highlights of his most protean period. The main title, "Megeve" and "Mambo Parisienne" are irresistible Latin grooves of the swinging '60s. And slower tracks, such as "Bateau Mouche" and "Latin Snowfall," offer listeners that distinctive Mancini romanticism. The truth is *Charade* suffers the same fate of so many Mancini soundtrack releases in that the demands of commerce dictated that only the melodic orchestral pop was worthy of LP release, and the more serious underscore—such as tension-building cues and action tracks—were left off the LP.

Mancini then scored another European-set crime thriller, *Arabesque* (1966). Again, Mancini makes memorable use of the exotic-sounding auto harp for the theme and the proto-psychedelic "Zoo Chase." The other unusual elements include a mandola, a detuned piano, three percussionists and tape-delay echo effects. It may not have much in common with Mancini's earlier, more straightforward crime scores, but it certainly demonstrates the adaptability of the genre.

While many crime scores barely qualify as genuine jazz, there are a handful from the era that come closer than most. One of the best belongs to *I Want to Live!* (1958), a true story about a murderess on death row. Johnny Mandel's sexy smoky score is a classic. The 26-piece All-Star Jazz Orchestra burn through the main theme, "Poker Game," "Stakeout," "Gas Chamber Unveiling" and other hot-blooded and emotionally wrenching tracks. Also featured are half a dozen cuts played by Gerry Mulligan's Combo. The legendary baritone saxophonist leads veteran jazz greats, such as Shelly Manne (drums), Art Farmer (trumpet), Bud Shank (alto sax, flute), Red Mitchell (bass), Frank Rosolino (trombone) and Pete Jolly (piano) on "Night Watch" and "Black Nightgown." Mulligan's inclusion is significant. The original LP cover notes by William Johns describe how the film's main character "moves through an atmosphere in San Francisco and San Diego where jazz hovers constantly in the background. One of the few stabilizing things in her life is her interest in jazz and, particularly, in the music of Gerry Mulligan." Mandel penned the tracks specifically for Mulligan's group, and they're peppered throughout the film as source cues.

"We'd been through a lot of bands together," Mandel said of Mulligan in a 1998 interview with Patrick McGilligan for the Rykodisc reissue. "I first ran into Gerry when he was with Gene Krupa and I was with Buddy Rich. This was in 1946. 'Disk Jockey Jump' had just come out and somehow Mulligan and I ... were thrown together in the New York nightclub and session scene. We remained good friends, right to the end."

The bits composed for the larger group are highly experimental and were daring for the era. Among the unusual instruments employed are contra-bass clarinet, contra bassoon, bass trumpet, bass flute, and E-flat clarinet. In addition, there is a wild assortment of percussion, such as scratcher, cowbells, Chinese and Burmese gongs, rhythm logs, chromatic drums and claves, as well as bongos and conga drums—collectively representing "the forces of law and order always hovering in the background," as McGilligan observed.

More importantly, *I Want to Live* stands apart from most crime jazz scores in that it is genuine jazz featuring improvisation, and not merely "scripted" jazz.

"I was really very nervous," Mandel told McGilligan, "until I realized, after I learned the language and how to sync everything, that essentially it is what I'd been doing for a long time and just didn't know it. It married all the things I'd been doing previously."

Mandel went on to win an Oscar for "The Shadow of Your Smile" from *The Sandpiper*, and scored many other popular movies, but his boldly inventive *I Want to Live* is among the best of the crime genre and of the era.

A year later, another undisputed jazz genius scored in Hollywood. Duke Ellington—arguably the most influential composer and bandleader of the big band era—contributed a Grammy Award–winning score for *Anatomy of a Murder* (1959). Although Ellington had occasionally composed music for low-budget musicals and short films prior to World War II, this courtroom drama offered him a unique opportunity. The music—with its rich harmonic shadings and intuitive use of soloists—is unlike any other crime jazz soundtrack,

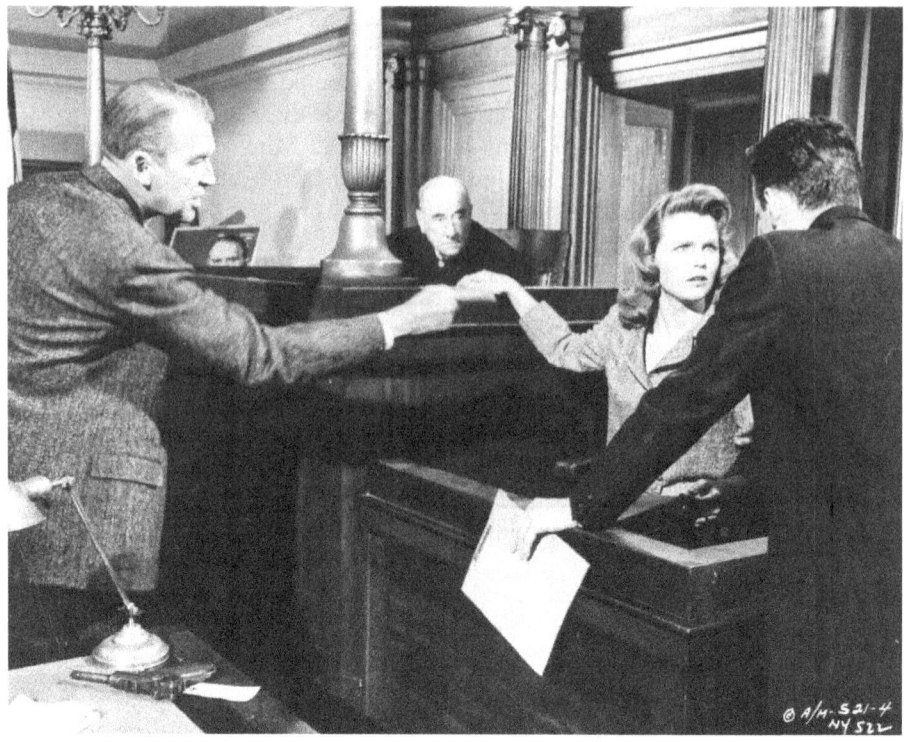

Duke Ellington's Grammy-winning score for *Anatomy of a Murder* (Columbia, 1959), starring James Stewart and Lee Remick, is as gripping as Otto Preminger's courtroom drama. (Photograph courtesy of the John Monaghan Collection.)

and many of the individual tracks would not sound out of place on other Ellington records of that period.

To his credit, Ellington provided the requisite array of moods and variations on theme to complement the film's characters and scenes, rather than merely recording variations of pre-existing music, to which he fittingly resorted for *Paris Blues* a year later.

Miles Davis, another jazz innovator, also scored in the crime genre—this time in Europe. Considering the immense popularity of jazz in France during the period, it comes as no surprise that filmmaker Louis Malle wanted to have an American jazzman provide music for his thriller *Ascenseur pour l'échafaud* (*Lift to the Scaffold*, 1958). Unlike most film music, Davis' score was improvised in the studio. According to the soundtrack CD booklet notes, it was an informal gig for the trumpet player and his mostly French sidemen; in fact, the film's star, Jeanne Moreau, played bartender in the studio while Malle screened selected scenes to the musicians. A rookie to the soundtrack game,

Davis took little to no control over the selection of final takes for the film, letting Malle call the shots. Davis used a few tracks on his *Jazz Track* LP.

Back in Hollywood, a number of brash bandleaders, including Pete Rugolo, David Amram, Kenyon Hopkins, Billy May and Hugo Montenegro, cut crime jazz soundtracks.

Long-time Stan Kenton arranger Rugolo proved to be a good fit for such crime shows as *Richard Diamond* (1957–1960) and *The Fugitive* (1963–1967), both starring David Janssen. Rugolo's penchant for dynamic, supercharged orchestration is well represented on both shows. The theme for *Richard Diamond* is nearly as memorable as "Peter Gunn." It's actually two themes in one. The brassy primary melody embodies Janssen's private detective, and the sexy bass line captures the criminal element whenever a villain is onscreen. Jazz greats, such as Shank, Mitchell and Manne, are among the players on the brash alluring main theme, percussion-peppered "Diamond on the Move," breathless "Teaser," sassy jukebox number "Teenage Rock" and wistful flute-filled "I'm Always Chasing Butterflies."

Rugolo also composed a tough, propulsive, albeit less memorable, theme for *Thriller* (1960-62), which also served as the show's "villain" theme. Among the other criminally cool numbers are the exotic, percussive "Voodoo Man," mysterious "The Guilty Men," two-bass spotlight "The Purple Room," Latin-tinged "Twisted Image," the sax-less swinger "Worse Than Murder" and genre-busting "Finger of Fear."

The Sicilian-born composer hooked up with his friend Janssen again for *The Fugitive*, which was one of the most popular crime shows of the '60s long before it became a big-screen hit in 1993. Again, Rugolo composed a memorable opener that, like James Bernard's themes for the Hammer horror pictures of the '50s and '60s, bears a melody that seems to "state" the show's title. "I always tried to get the name of the series, whatever it was called, into my themes," Rugolo recalled in the Silva Screen's CD booklet notes.

Rugolo, like many composers, recorded many variations on the theme for use as suspense, action and romance cues throughout the series. "I wrote an awful lot of chases, because I knew he'd be running a lot," Rugolo said of the approximately 90 minutes worth of music recorded in England to save on union costs.

The other memorable crime jazz tracks include the imposing "Lt. Gerrard," the sneaky "On the Run," the tense "Kimble vs. the One-Armed Man" and the percussive "Hand to Hand."

Another big band arranger known for his brassy attack was Billy May, who was one of Frank Sinatra's favorite bandleaders. May composed for several crime shows, including *Naked City* (1960–1962), *The Green Hornet* (1966–1967), *Batman* (1967–1968) and *The Mod Squad* (1968). May's rare opportunities to score were usually on Sinatra-related projects. The most notable is *Johnny Cool* (1963), which was produced by fellow Rat Packers Peter

Pete Rugolo's scores for TV's *Thriller* (1960–1962) and *Richard Diamond* (1957–1960) demonstrate the composer's brash, propulsive style. (CD cover appears courtesy of Fresh Sound Records; graphic designer unknown.)

Lawford and Sammy Davis, Jr. Wearing a stylish eye patch and van dyke beard, Davis also had a role in the movie and performed two vocal numbers on the soundtrack. The score is quintessential May, ranging from hard swinging ("The Lizard") to sw-elegant ("The Coolest Pad").

May also scored Gordon Douglas' *Tony Rome* (1967), starring Sinatra as the titular private eye. Nancy Sinatra sang the theme song.

Best known for his cover albums of *The Man from U.N.C.L.E.* and Ennio Morricone's "spaghetti western" music, Hugo Montenegro delivered a thoroughly swinging '60s sound for *Lady in Cement* (the *Tony Rome* sequel). "Ba-ba" vocalisms, intriguing harpsichord, sultry flute and a fat bass guitar riff make the theme a classic of the late '60s crime scene. Distorted guitar, Hammond organ and rampaging drums kick it up a notch on "Sugar Seymour," "Jilly's Joint" and "Yale's Pool Room." Montenegro incorporates psychedelic studio trickery on several tracks that heightens the groovy vibe. He cools the mood down a touch with "The Shark," without losing the trippy effects. Another highlight is "Tony's Theme," which brings the brass and "ba-ba" boys back into the mix, with harmonica and vibes along for the ride. Interestingly, there isn't a Sinatra vocal in earshot, and he fails to make an appearance on the LP cover. (Notably, Montenegro's Rat Pack connections extend to two scores for Dean Martin's Matt Helm spy flicks.)

Another jazz legend turned soundtrack artist was Kenyon Hopkins, a frequent collaborator of Creed Taylor (producer of the atmospheric concept albums *Nightmare!*, *Panic!*, *Lonelyville*, etc.). Hopkins delivered jazz-tinged scores for several movies, including *The Hustler* (1961), *Baby Doll* (1956) and *The Fugitive Kind* (1960). One of his best belongs to *Mister Buddwing* (1965). Hopkins' tough, swinging sound keeps cool even when incorporating Latin percussion and soulful Hammond organ. It isn't a crime jazz score in the strictest sense—the movie is more of a melodrama—but the feeling on many tracks, including the theme, isn't far removed.

Another borderline crime jazz soundtrack comes from *The Young Savages* (1961), with music by David Amram, who also worked on the political thriller *The Manchurian Candidate* (1962). The score ranges from the Latin jazz of "Las Muchachas Delicadas" to the Spanish-tinged theme with its solo harmonica to tension-filled polytonal underscore ("Switchblades on Parade," "The Last Taco," etc.).

Neal Hefti took inspiration from *Golden Arm* for another junkie drama, *Synanon* (1965). The jazzy, organ-led theme seethes with sadness and desperation. "A Perfect Beginning" is far more optimistic, with lively sax, warm guitar and gurgling organ tones playing over a crackling beat. "Blues for Hopper" is buzzy and hyperactive. Hefti also cooks up some choral pop tracks ("Main Street" and "The Whiffenpoof Song") that are comparatively "squaresville."

Funky with a "Bullitt"

A Hollywood composer who infused his crime (and spy) soundtracks with stabs at funk as well as jazz was Lalo Schifrin. The Argentinean-born composer had made his name with the greatest TV spy theme ever for Mission: Impossible (1966). The show's soundtrack demonstrates Schifrin's mastery of funky soul, as well as crime jazz, bossa nova and lounge. "Jim on the Move" combines elements found in many of Schifrin's recordings, principally a throbbing electric bass line, prominently mixed Latin percussion, bluesy piano fills and soulful horn arrangements—elements commonly heard in funk and rhythm & blues. "More Mission" boasts a lean, hard opening groove. And "Mission

Blues" swaggers. All evince Schifrin's Mission-period fascination with black music.

As if one great TV theme weren't enough, Schifrin delivered another in the same year for *Mannix*, adding an electric charge to the classic crime jazz sound. With muscular bass lines and a bigger backbeat, tracks like "The Shadow," "Hunt Down," and "Turn Every Stone" further demonstrate that Schifrin was anything but a one-hit wonder. He also contributed funky themes for TV shows in the '70s, including *Medical Center, Planet of the Apes* and *Starsky & Hutch*.

On the big screen, Schifrin continued to explore funky sounds on *Bullitt* (1968) and *Dirty Harry* (1971). For the Steve McQueen vehicle, the sound melds funk and swing. The hard and lean *Bullitt* theme rumbles forth on a muscular bass line and insistent beat, with jazz guitar taking the lead. Elsewhere in the score ("Hotel Daniels," "Ice Pick Mike," "Shifting Gears") Schifrin continues to work the groove with an orchestra as revved up as the muscle cars used in the film's legendary chase scene. Schifrin re-recorded the score in 2000 (and the *Mannix* score as well) without losing much intensity.

For Clint Eastwood's *Dirty Harry* films Schifrin toughened up his approach, absorbing the jazz-funk elements into an avant-garde orchestral sound. At the release of the first film many critics praised the score for its edgy abstraction. Listening to tracks like "Scorpio's Theme" (later sampled by rap group NWA) and "Dirty Harry's Creed," it is readily apparent that the mean streets of San Francisco in the '70s were far removed from the flower-power days of Haight-Ashbury. Schifrin's penchant for Latin percussion and throbbing bass lines provide a restless bed upon which tense orchestration writhes. Distorted guitar, angry brass and angular string sections riddle the eardrums like sonic shrapnel. Schifrin scored three of the *Dirty Harry* sequels, including the excellent *Magnum Force* (1973), *Sudden Impact* (1983) and *The Dead Pool* (1988).

Jerry Fielding scored the third *Dirty Harry* film, *The Enforcer* (1976), as well as several other Clint Eastwood films, including the crime thriller *The Gauntlet* (1977). On *Enforcer*, Fielding is at his most vital and vivacious. He makes no attempt to reinvent the *Dirty Harry* sound, and shrewdly follows Schifrin's established style for the series through the deft use of throbbing electric bass, wah guitar rhythms, percolating percussion, dissonant strings, brash brass and keyboard atmospherics. "Rooftop Chase" is the requisite bit of cop funk, but "Warehouse Heist" and "Alcatraz Encounter" are tenser and exercise Fielding's mastery of texture and ambience. The sound he's cooked up is by turns lean and mean, funky, swinging and—most surprisingly for a hard-as-nails cop drama—emotionally poignant. That's because he builds the score around Harry's new, ill-fated partner, Inspector Kate Moore. This feisty female cop provides Fielding with an emotional focal point. That's not to say *The Enforcer* is soft—it's compellingly tender when it needs to be, but otherwise just as tough as anything on the series' first two soundtracks.

Harry Callahan wasn't the only tough cop to hit the big screen in 1971. Gene Hackman played Popeye Doyle in *The French Connection* (1971). Eschewing conventional funk in favor of avant-garde jazz, Don Ellis' theme immediately puts the listener on edge by using siren-like horn blasts and Morse code woodwinds. For instance, "Copstail" busts out a funky beat, but interrupts it with abstract piano fills and tape-delay weirdness. Ellis' methods perfectly complement Hackman's eccentric portrayal of the hard-nosed cop. Like Popeye Doyle, Ellis never plays it safe—he's always pushing the sound into new territory with experimental techniques. Ellis also scored *The French Connection II* (1975).

Don Ellis' *The French Connection* (1971) is hard-hitting jazz-funk with an avant-garde sensibility. (CD cover appears courtesy of Film Score Monthly; graphic design by Joe Sikoryak.)

Also in 1971 was the neo noir *Klute*. The score by Michael Small features the psychedelic funk of "Bree's Abandon (Take It Higher)" and "Club Scene," but also offers some eerie, disturbing cinematic moods. The spine-tingling theme ("The Tape") blends exotic percussion with piano to create a spooky atmosphere of mystery—like something from Krzysztof Komeda's *Rosemary's Baby* (1968). It segues beautifully into the hypnotic "Rooftop Intruder," which sounds like something from a Morricone or Bruno Nicolai *giallo* soundtrack, due in part to female vocalism. Perhaps the more impressive track is "Goldfarb's Fantasy." With its mysterious Eastern European flavor (provided by a cimbalom), it is reminiscent of John Barry's *Ipcress File* or Mancini's *Arabesque*. With its deep bass and spacey funk, "Checking Leads" wouldn't sound out of place on a Roy Budd soundtrack.

Elmer Bernstein also tried his hand at funky crime scores, most notably with *McQ* (1974), starring cinema's least funky tough guy, John Wayne. Having regretted passing on the role of Harry Callahan, Wayne jumped at the

Elmer Bernstein at work in 1974, the year he scored *McQ*, a modern police thriller starring John Wayne, whose work he frequently scored. (Photograph courtesy of the Elmer Bernstein Estate.)

chance to trade in his 10-gallon hat and Winchester for a cop's badge and service revolver. Bernstein, who had worked on a number of the Duke's latter-day movies, climbed aboard for *McQ*. While his score stylistically diverges from his crime jazz scores of the '50s, it boasts in-your-face orchestration, with a barrage of percussion, including bongos, rock drums, claves, vibra slap, flapamba and bass marimba. Along the way, cool electrified flute, wah guitar and E5 organ add the requisite urban flavor.

A year later, Wayne starred in *Brannigan* (1975), a crime drama that sends an American cop to England to retrieve a mobster. Dominic Frontiere's score is funky, but also makes excellent use of strings and brass to build tension. Angular guitar lines and insistent percussion add a modern edge to Frontiere's energetic action sequences, such as the four-part "Ransom" suite and "Stampede Along the Thames." *Brannigan* is an underrated crime funk gem.

Perhaps the ultimate funky crime jazz album is David Shire's *The Taking of Pelham One Two Three* (1974). It has no love themes or lounge numbers to slow it down, just a relentlessly hard-driving, take-no-prisoners score. Shire set out to create a sound that would be "New York jazz-oriented, hard-edged" but with a "wise-cracking subtext to it." He turned to the 12-tone method of composition, which Arnold Schönberg developed decades earlier. (The disconcerting angularity of the Austrian's compositions occasionally caused fistfights between the audience and the musicians.) Something so naturally tense definitely fit the bill for this gritty, unsentimental drama about a hostage situation on a subway train. The music is diabolically calculated and pulsating, yet swings like a big band in hell. Electric bass, drums and tons of percussion provide the undercurrent for abstract horn, string, guitar, woodwind and keyboard lines. The theme gets restated again and again, but with such relentless variety it never becomes stale, only more intense.

Another outstanding crime score by a legit jazz musician is *Death Wish* (1974) by Herbie Hancock, whose first feature soundtrack was Michelangelo Antonioni's quasi-crime film *Blow-Up* (1966). For the Charles Bronson vigilante flick, Hancock cooked up a jazz-funk stew peppered with his harmonically rich keyboard textures and thick, hearty rhythms. The scintillating six-minute theme blends a rock solid bass line, soaring strings, chirping electric guitars and interwoven keyboard lines against a shimmering rhythm bed. Based on the theme alone, *Death Wish* is a classic '70s crime score.

On the small screen in the early '70s it seemed that every cop or private detective show had jazz-funk theme music. Pounding drums, wah guitar, Hammond organ, electric bass and brash brass were on display for *The Streets of San Francisco, Kojak, S.W.A.T., Baretta, The Rockford Files, Police Woman, Hawaii Five-0, Police Story* and many others. The composers behind this music included veterans like Mancini, Goldsmith and Morton Stevens, and relative newcomers like Mike Post. Many of these recordings owe a debt to movie and TV scores that preceded them.

David Shire's *The Taking of Pelham One Two Three* (1974) blends riveting jazz-funk with the 12-tone method pioneered by Arnold Schönberg decades earlier. (CD cover appears courtesy of Film Score Monthly/Retrograde Records; graphic design by Joe Sikoryak.)

Blaxploitation Beat

The funky soundtrack style heard everywhere in the '70s—from TV shows and big-budget thrillers (e.g. *Live and Let Die*) to porn flicks (e.g. *Deep Throat*) and foreign cinema (from CineCittá to Bollywood)—is most evident in blaxploitation movies. The influence of the genre and its music continues to be felt today, whether in films such as *Jackie Brown* (1997) and *Baadasssss!* (2003), or in hip-hop culture, whose deejays sample its soundtracks and whose emcees draw inspiration from its swagger and spirit of self-empowerment.

Blaxploitation cinema's cultural legacy is debatable to say the least. Consider its controversial history. Before it blossomed in 1971, blacks were typically relegated to lowly, patronizing and often humiliating roles in Hollywood movies. In the '60s the studios tentatively began to integrate non-threatening black characters into otherwise white cinema (e.g. *Guess Who's Coming to Dinner?*).

Before blaxploitation came into being, African-American Quincy Jones equaled Lalo Schifrin's effort in introducing funk to movie audiences in the mid-to-late '60s. Q—as he's known to many—made his reputation in the '50s and early '60s as a talented arranger and composer for jazz legends such as Lionel Hampton, Count Basie and Dizzy Gillespie, and for such singing stars as Frank Sinatra, Billy Eckstine, Sarah Vaughan and Dinah Washington. Beginning in the early '60s, Q composed numerous big-budget crime movies, including four starring Sidney Poitier, Hollywood's original black leading man.

Jones constantly experimented with style, incorporating swinging jazz, cool bossa nova, funk, soul and pop into big band or orchestral settings. His classic crime jazz highlights of the period include "Harlem Drive" and "Rack 'em Up" (from *The Pawnbroker*), "Blondie Tails" (from *The Deadly Affair*) and "Shoot to Kill" (from *Mirage*).

Lalo Schifrin's jazzy, funk-infused work for film and television during the '60s helped to pave the way for blaxploitation and action movie soundtracks of the '70s. (Photograph courtesy of the Lalo Schifrin Estate.)

Although it is in no way a blaxploitation film, the Academy Award–winning *In the Heat of the Night* (1967) was influential because it features not only a black actor in the leading role but also a score infused with black music. The most telling example is the Ray Charles–sung theme song, which is soulful, funky and swinging. Tracks like "Peep Freak Patrol Car" and "Cotton Curtain" feature an unexpected blend of orchestral tension, bluesy piano fills, moaning Ellington-esque horns, throaty flute squeals and vocal scats; their funk is as potent as moonshine. On "Where Whitey Ain't Around" a mean wah guitar solo joins an already volatile vibe. Elsewhere, Jones displays his great versatility with passages of pure orchestral movie music ("Shag Bag, Hounds and Harvey"). Taken in its entirety, *Heat* is but one of Jones' proto-blaxploitation outings, and not a pure example of what would be heard in the '70s.

Two other Jones scores from this period also qualify as proto-blaxploitation: the heist flick *The Lost Man* (1969) and *Heat*'s sequel, *They Call Me Mister Tibbs* (1970)—both starring Poitier.

The Lost Man theme blends African percussion, an angular melodic motif and a singsong chorus of chanting children to mysterious, hypnotic effect. The theme's disconcertingly unresolved scraps of melody resurface in more satisfying form on "Main Squeeze" and "Up Against the Wall," where complicated experimental arrangements are propelled by funky rhythms and electric instrumentation. On "Slum Creeper" a funky clavinet keyboard pushes the rhythm forward with slow deliberation as electric guitar competes for the sonic turf. The most straightforward track on the album may be "Sweet Soul Sister," a catchy mid-tempo number featuring a smooth vocal performance by Nate Turner, with backing vocals by the Mirettes.

While *The Lost Man* remains Jones' edgiest score, his work on *Tibbs* proved much more popular. Although the movie isn't considered pure blaxploitation, its theme created the template for many title tracks to come, including Hayes' *Shaft* and Schifrin's *Enter the Dragon*. Its hard-driving rhythm section, screaming organ blasts, punchy brass, chicken scratch guitars and vibrato-colored keyboard line set the standard for cinematic funk in 1970. Elsewhere in the score Jones continued to exploit the electric charge he'd harnessed on the theme song. "Fat Poppadaddy," with its catchy organ lick, screaming guitar solo and fatback drum break, pushed the funk harder and faster. He busted out the blues on "Side Pocket," with its saxophone solo, and call and response between the organ, guitar and horns. *Tibbs*, like *Heat* and *Lost*, is chock-full of intense, virtuoso arrangements that call upon funk, blues, soul and jazz. Without Jones' influence, the blaxploitation sound might never have come together so quickly and so potently.

In addition to the groundbreaking work of Jones and Schifrin, two other significant funky scores set the stage for blaxploitation. In 1968, Booker T. Jones and his MGs scored *Uptight*. The soulful, organ-led quartet burns through "Cleveland Now," "Children, Don't Get Weary," and "Blues in the Gutter."

The LP's cover notes state that director Jules Dassin's "breakthrough film ... is concerned not with just the militant and non-violent forms of black American protest, but also with the devastation of a human being cowed and pressured into submission by a society seemingly indifferent to his cries for help." The theme remains relevant today, but the score does little to illustrate *Uptight*'s message, aside from lending it a sometimes gospel-tinged uplift. The score also includes a version of the group's hit, "Time Is Tight."

More than any other pre-blaxploitation film, *Cotton Comes to Harlem* (1970), which is based on African-American Chester Himes' hard-boiled novel, set the template for blaxploitation movies to come. The original LP cover features a proto hip-hop painting by Robert McGinnis that includes a gold Rolls Royce, bikini-clad babes and the movie's heroes brandishing huge handguns. Ironically, the artist is white, and so is the funky score's composer. Galt MacDermot, a Canadian who spent some of his youth in South Africa, provided an excellent high-energy score for *Cotton* that blends big band funk with flower power groove and gospel-tinged soul—sometimes shifting between these styles unexpectedly within a single track. According to the booklet notes of *Cotton*'s CD reissue, even MacDermot's sidemen considered his funk sensibility unorthodox in comparison to, say, James Brown. But MacDermot credits the experience of playing in the Broadway pit of his rock musical *Hair* for his ability to play "flat out-loud and hard." MacDermot's outstanding abilities as a composer and arranger are in evidence on such tracks as the theme song, sung by George Tipton, and the instrumentals "Man in Distress" and "Harlem Medley."

To break down the racial wall entirely it took a film made by a black person for a black audience. Melvin Van Peebles, an African-American who cut his filmmaking teeth in France during the '60s, bucked the Hollywood system where he was under contract. Using money he earned making *Watermelon Man* (1970) for Columbia Pictures, he made the scandalous, X-rated, audaciously titled feature, *Sweet Sweetback's Baadasssss Song*. As the film's writer, director, producer, soundtrack composer and star, Van Peebles almost single-handedly activated the genre that would later be dubbed blaxploitation. In order to avoid industry union rules, he claimed to be making a porno. It became the highest grossing independent film up until that time, pulling in $16 million with extremely limited distribution. Unlike today's "indie" hits, however, it did not garner the filmmaker any big-studio offers. The film's gritty subject matter and provocative marketing tagline ("Rated X by an All White Jury") served to alienate mainstream Hollywood from the brash auteur. (In fact, Van Peebles has claimed to have never submitted the film to the ratings board, a move that—in those days—automatically earned any film with sexual content an "X" rating.)

Being the vision of a true auteur, *Sweetback* features a soundtrack composed by the filmmaker himself. Brer Soul and an early incarnation of Earth,

Melvin Van Peebles scored *Sweet Sweetback's Baadasssss Song* (1971), a film he also wrote, directed, produced and starred in. (CD cover appears courtesy of Stax Records/Concord Music Group; graphic designer unknown.)

Wind & Fire perform Van Peebles' unconventional, rambunctious score. Peppered with outrageous dialogue and unconventional vocals, the Stax soundtrack is raw and raucous. When compared to later, more conventional blaxploitation soundtracks, *Sweetback* is as unique as it is funky. For evidence, look no further than song titles like "Sweetback Getting It Uptight and Preaching It So Hard the Bourgeois Reggin Angels in Heaven Turn Around."

Hollywood's response to *Sweetback*'s stunning success was to transform a fairly generic crime thriller about a private detective named John Shaft into a genre-busting box-office smash. Directed by another African-American, Gor-

Isaac Hayes' soundtrack for *Shaft* (1971), starring Richard Roundtree, was a tremendous commercial and critical success, earning Hayes an Academy Award. (CD cover appears courtesy of Stax Records/Concord Music Group; graphic design by Tony Seiniger.)

don Parks, the success of *Shaft* (1971) generated two sequels and a TV show, not to mention dozens of copycat productions. Isaac Hayes' soundtrack, which was originally released as a double album, is a slick, radio-ready production. The award-winning theme song ranks alongside Quincy Jones' theme from *They Call Me Mister Tibbs* for setting the standard for all funky theme songs to come. Even without the theme, the soundtrack would still be solid. From "Bumpy's Lament" to "Café Regio's" to the 19-minute "Do Your Thing," *Shaft* remains a high water mark for the soul superstar, and the blaxploitation genre.

Based on *Shaft*'s commercial success, more than 200 other blaxploitation films were made over the course of the decade. Some followed the independent route established by Van Peebles, but many more would not have been bankrolled without the arguably exploitive interests of white Hollywood insiders. Regardless of intentions, the black action genre and the term "blaxploitation" were born.

Film scores have always reflected contemporary musical styles, and blaxploitation scores are no exception. Although blaxploitation soundtracks simply adapted pre-existing music styles—primarily the funky soul of '60s artists like James Brown and Sly & the Family Stone, as well as the Motown sound—they also expanded on those styles substantively. It's no exaggeration to say that the use of funk and soul in the cinematic context redefined the role of pop music in film. Although blaxploitation's use of vocal numbers differed insignificantly from what had come before, its use of the funky instrumental as an underscore for action was revolutionary. While the use of big band jazz in '50s and '60s cinema paved the way for the funky underscore, the latter form's emphasis on rock-like energy and youth-oriented electric instrumentation pushed what would have previously been background music into the foreground. Instead of merely reinforcing the action like a traditional score, the funky instrumental, with its primal rhythms and off-the-cuff jamming, became a character itself.

Furthermore, blaxploitation films represented an opportunity for black musicians and composers to reach a broader audience than they might have with an ordinary release. At a creative level, the soundtrack format offered such artists as Willie Hutch and Curtis Mayfield the opportunity to record songs of social consciousness with excellent production values and achieve broad distribution. In an extreme case, namely *Shaft*, the recording artist reaped not only the financial rewards associated with a smash hit movie, but two Grammy awards and an Oscar for "Best Song." Consider also that Isaac Hayes, the first African-American to win such an award, performed his "Theme from Shaft" at the Academy Awards ceremony before a television audience of many millions—albeit in a notoriously thick fog due to a defective dry ice machine.

Following the success of *Shaft*, there was a torrent of similar films and TV shows. The earlier success of *Cotton Comes to Harlem* prompted the making of the sequel in 1972, *Come Back Charleston Blue*. Donny Hathaway, Roberta Flack's frequent duet partner, scored the picture under Jones' expert supervision. This time the requisite funk cues are joined by ragtime jazz, Basie-esque blues and, quite unexpectedly, a bit of stripped-down electronic atmospherics. Like *Cotton*, *Charleston* distinguishes itself through sheer stylistic diversity. It may have been Hathaway's project, but the arrangements and experimental passages show Jones' unmistakable influence.

One of the best soundtracks of 1972, and of the blaxploitation era, is *Across 110th Street*, featuring music by legendary jazz trombonist J.J. Johnson, and songs performed by Bobby Womack & Peace. Hit-maker Womack's theme song boasts a memorable hook, a sweeping arrangement and a lyrical message that doesn't pull punches about organized crime and the drug epidemic. Womack also contributes a tender ballad ("If You Don't Want My Love"), an uptempo pop number ("Quicksand"), a bit of hard funky rock ("Do It Right") and raucous feel-good soul ("Hang on in There"). Johnson performs instrumental versions of most songs, but his contribution is most noticeable on "Harlem Clavinette," which raised the bar on cinematic funk with its pulsating rhythm and bubbly mix of brass, wah guitar, clavinet keyboard, percussion and electronics.

The "black dick who's a sex machine to all the chicks" returned in 1972 for *Shaft's Big Score*. Returning director Parks composed and recorded the score in about two weeks, and, unfortunately, it shows. Featuring vocal performances by O.C. Smith (of "Little Green Apples" fame) and the trumpet playing of jazz great Freddie Hubbard, Parks' score often apes the melodic motifs set forth by Hayes on the first film's soundtrack. It's telling that the compiler of Universal Music's *The Best of Shaft* included nothing from *Shaft's Big Score*, favoring instead Hayes' original and Johnny Pate's outstanding *Shaft in Africa* (1973). The best thing one can say about the second movie's soundtrack is that it features a fantastic action painting by John Solie that is reminiscent of McGinnis' paintings for James Bond soundtracks and movie posters.

If *Shaft's Big Score* falls short of the mark, then *Superfly* transcended it. For the Parks film, Curtis Mayfield, of the quintessential Chicago R&B band the Impressions, recorded the greatest blaxploitation soundtrack ever—and certainly one of the greatest song-based scores, regardless of genre. The film was a smash hit, but it may not have had such a substantial impact without Mayfield's emotionally stirring score, released on his own Curtom Records. Already well known for his socially observant songwriting, Mayfield elevated *Superfly* by providing songs that comment on the film's content—a feat that most blaxploitation soundtracks (and soundtracks in general) fail to accomplish—at least beyond the requisite title track or love theme. Songs like "Little Child Runnin' Wild," "Pusherman" and "Freddie's Dead" hit hard lyrically and with a melodic groove that never fails to hold the listener's attention. "Curtis took Fenty's script and composed sharp character studies for each primary player, making every song essential, and thus securing his soundtrack as the genre's finest work," states A. Scott Galloway on Rhino Record's essential 25th anniversary *Superfly* reissue.

Mayfield composed and performed on several other blaxploitation scores, but none measure up to his masterpiece. Few blaxploitation soundtracks match *Superfly*'s high standards, but its producer, Johnny Pate, went on to cut two blaxploitation classics himself (more on those later).

Motown legend Marvin Gaye also recorded an excellent soundtrack in 1972 for *Trouble Man*, with the help of genre regular J.J. Johnson. Recorded between his two masterpieces, *What's Going On* (1971) and *Let's Get It On*

Marvin Gaye and J.J. Johnson's soulful soundtrack for the underappreciated *Trouble Man* (20th Century–Fox, 1972), starring Robert Hooks, is just as dynamic as the film's shattering climax. (Photograph courtesy of the John Monaghan Collection.)

(1973), *Trouble Man* only occasionally features Gaye's trademark voice. The mostly instrumental score mixes jazz-tinged funk with laidback ballads. The cues benefit from unusual juxtapositions, such as the Herrmann-esque opening of "T Plays It Cool" launching into a mellow groove where smoky saxophone dances between jamming clavinet and Rhodes keyboard lines, fatback drums and hand claps—it's funk at its most effortless. The tight arrangements, solid musical performances and cinematic sweep of the Top 10 title track and instrumental cuts, like "The Break In," help *Trouble Man* stand out from the pack. (On a lighter note: It's unknown whether Laurence Tureaud drew any inspiration from *Trouble Man* song titles like "Don't Mess with Mister T" and "There Goes Mister T" when he created the like-named alter-ego of *A Team* fame.)

Coffy, the lively vigilante picture starring blaxploitation queen Pam Grier, features an outstanding Latin jazz-funk score by vibraphonist Roy Ayers. Tracks like "Coffy Is the Color," "Priscilla's Groove" and "Aragon" percolate with irrepressible rhythms, dynamic keyboard figures and a relentless groove.

One would be hard pressed to name a more high-energy blaxploitation score. "King George," with its lowdown funk and two-channel "dialogue" celebrating a certain pimp's powers of persuasion, may be the coolest mack daddy theme ever. There is even a bit of psychedelia mixed in ("End of Sugarman").

Another film to feature a black action heroine in 1973 was *Cleopatra Jones*, starring Tamara Dobson as a special government agent. Johnson's score is a solid outing for the jazz trombonist, and will satisfy fans of his other outstanding scores for *Across 110th Street* and *Willie Dynamite* (1974). This superb slab features compelling vocal performances by Joe Simon (on the theme) and Millie Jackson. An outstanding instrumental, "The Wrecking Yard," features percussive textures that evoke a tense game of cat and mouse amidst jagged metal junk heaps. On "Airport Flight" the frantic pace suggests action pushed into the red zone as the hero races against time to stop the villain's getaway. The film's popularity warranted a sequel, *Cleopatra Jones and the Casino of Gold* (1975), featuring a score by Frontiere.

Roy Ayers' score for *Coffy* (MGM/UA, 1973) is as funky and sexy as its star, Pam Grier—the queen of blaxploitation films.

The Mack, one of the legendary blaxploitation productions due to its lethal behind-the-scenes politics and its fact-as-fiction footage of the notorious Player's Ball, features one of Willie Hutch's bold blaxploitation scores. Hutch got the job when the filmmakers offered a cameo appearance to the Hutch-produced singing group Sisters Love. Motown released the soundtrack and, as was the label's habit, saw fit to feature the artist's portrait on the cover instead of movie artwork. The score features some of Hutch's best songs, including the affirmative soul number "Brothers Gonna Work It Out," the stirring ballad "I Choose You" and the hard-driving theme. Hutch display's his gift for nuance on "Mack's Stroll—The Getaway," where the first part's shimmering bittersweet strings segue into a frantic rhythm guitar workout. Hutch went on to score *Foxy Brown* the following year, but *The Mack* remains his, and one of the era's, best score. (For *The Mack*'s home video release in 1983, the studio foolishly replaced Hutch's score with an R'n'B-lite soundtrack by Alan Silvestri that pales in comparison.)

Another Motown soundtrack from 1973 was Edwin Starr's *Hell Up in Harlem*, the sequel to *Black Caesar*. James Brown, who scored *Caesar*, was originally asked to do *Harlem* as well, but the film's director, Larry Cohen, rejected his efforts in favor of the Starr vehicle, featuring songs written by Freddie Perren and Fonce Mizell (who, along with Berry Gordy and Deke Richards, formed the Corporation, the production team behind the Jackson 5). *Harlem*'s outstanding tracks include the rousing, electrically charged theme song and "Easin' In," which boasts an often-sampled, finger-snapping intro. The song could have been a hit, but Motown neglected to promote the score—a mere contract fulfiller for Starr.

After Cohen rejected Brown's *Harlem*, the "godfather of soul" released the music separately on a double album, *The Payback*, which is generally regarded as one of his best efforts; some fans insist it's better than his actual soundtracks. Prior to recording that album, Brown scored *Black Caesar* and *Slaughter's Big Rip Off*, which were released just six months apart in 1973. The former earned Brown the moniker "Godfather of Soul," and featured one of his best tracks ever, "Down and Out in New York City." The single charted at number 13 on the R&B chart and at number 50 on the pop chart. The other single "Mama Feelgood," which is sung by Lyn Collins, charted at number 37 on the R&B chart. The other funky standouts include "Sportin' Life" and "Like It Is, Like It Was," but overall the soundtrack isn't particularly memorable or cinematic.

Brown's *Slaughter's Big Rip Off* is more richly orchestrated but stylistically similar to his *Black Caesar*; the film itself is the sequel to *Slaughter*, which features a soundtrack by Luchi DeJesus. *Rip Off*'s theme song lacks a strong melodic hook, but a few of the instrumentals (arranged by J.B.'s bandleader, Fred Wesley) have a strong cinematic sweep. Tracks like "Transmograpfication" have a free-wheeling jazz quality, while vocal tracks like "Sexy, Sexy, Sexy" offer the sort of vibe one expects from the funky soul brother who gave the world "Sex Machine."

Brown may have been the "hardest working man in show business" in 1973, but he wasn't the only artist to release two scores that year. Johnny Pate scored the outstanding *Shaft in Africa*, and the excellent *Brother on the Run*.

Africa is a favorite among blaxploitation fans and hip-hop deejays alike. It's a truly cinematic soundtrack with memorable vocal tracks, but is also "sample-worthy" thanks to its effective use of spare instrumentation and African percussion. Closely associated with Curtis Mayfield's Impressions and the Chicago soul scene, Pate brings his fine-tuned arranger's sensibility to funky big band tracks like the theme and "You Can't Even Walk in the Park," and an adventuresome spirit to the exotic-tinged "Headman" and "Truck Stop."

J.J. Johnson's score for *Cleopatra Jones* (Warner Bros., 1973), starring Tamara Dobson, is as action-packed as the movie. (Photograph courtesy of the John Monaghan Collection.)

Laid-back tracks like "Aleme's Theme," "Jazar's Theme" and "Aleme Finds Shaft" display Pate's melodic gift, and the pensive "El Jardia" suggests the film's exotic location. The best known tune here, however, is the stirring anthem "Are You Man Enough," written by Dennis Lambert and Brian Potter, and sung by the Four Tops.

Brother is nearly as great. Featuring Pate's slick orchestration and a theme song sung by Adam Wade, *Brother* offers up its share of wah-fueled chase music and steamy love themes. Pate finds a perfect balance between a funky rhythm section, jazzy horns and strings on two versions of the theme. On "Auto Chase," African percussion drives the action, much as it did on *Shaft in Africa*.

Doo-wop dynamo Don Julian (of Meadowlarks fame) also scored two films in 1973, but only one was released at the time. For *Savage! Super Soul* Julian balances the hard-edged masculine sound of stripped-down funk with the sweetly feminine timbres provided by flute and acoustic guitar. There even is a "peace, love and understanding" spoken word track about cross-cultural friendship and musical fusion, featuring a Spanish-tinged musical backdrop. But when things get funky, the playing is raw and aggressive. While some numbers are complete unto themselves, others have a fragmented quality suggesting that a few short cues were edited together to make single tracks.

Julian's *Shorty the Pimp* is more noteworthy. The film was never released, and the soundtrack wasn't issued until 1998, the year Julian died. In the movie, Julian and the Larks star as a funk group, the Blue Flamingos, who get mixed up in some trouble. The *Shorty* soundtrack is interesting in the way it draws from such blaxploitation classics as Mayfield's *Superfly* score and the soul hits of the period. Since the group performs in the movie as a lounge act, the soundtrack features workmanlike covers of hit songs by Mayfield, Gaye and Stevie Wonder, and a better-than-average cover of Burt Bacharach's "The Look of Love." Among the better Julian originals are the jazzy "Brother What It Is," the lowdown funky "Vato's Brew" and the Temptations-like "Schoolin' and Foolin'." While Julian's "Superfly" knock-off, "Super Slick," is dispensable stuff, his "Shorty the Pimp" theme is arresting.

Other blaxploitation soundtracks of 1973 include Osibasa's ill-advised afro-beat outing for *Superfly T.N.T.*, and Badder Than Evil's well-executed but otherwise formulaic platter for *Gordon's War*. To Osibasa's credit, they didn't resort to Mayfield mimicry, but the end result proved too far left of field to catch on. *Gordon's War*, on the other hand, doesn't offer enough surprises to differentiate itself from the pack. Nonetheless, it has a killer chase theme, aptly titled "Hot Wheels."

Hit-maker Hayes returned to blaxploitation in 1974 with two solid scores for *Truck Turner* and *Three Tough Guys* (a.k.a. *Tough Guys*). Hayes also starred in both movies, the latter of which was an international production co-starring fellow badass Fred Williamson. Both scores offer Hayes' trademark slick production and hooky grooves. An overview of the track titles goes a long way toward filling the mind's eye with exciting imagery. *Tough Guys* features "Kidnapped," "Buns O'Plenty" and "Run Fay Run," which was later used in Quentin Tarantino's *Kill Bill Vol. 1* (2003). Meanwhile, *Truck Turner* features

After scoring big with *Shaft*, Isaac Hayes went on to score and star in *Truck Turner* and *Three Tough Guys* (both 1974). (CD cover appears courtesy of Stax Records/Concord Music Group; graphic design by Linda Kalin, based on original Stax album cover art.)

"Breakthrough," "A House Full of Girls," "Hospital Shootout" and the centerpiece "Pursuit of the Pimpmobile."

It was the same year Motown songwriting ace Hutch scored the grindhouse epic *Foxy Brown*, which nearly matches *The Mack*. "The Chase" is one of the most exciting opening tracks imaginable, built from layers of percolating rhythm and pulsating instrumentation. The main theme follows suit, adding soulful vocals to the mix. Hutch slows things down for romantic moods on "Hospital Prelude of Love Theme" and "Give Me Some of That Good Old Love." The groovy psychedelic appeal of the echo-laden "Out There" is intoxicating, and the sexy strut of "Foxy Lady" is guaranteed to inspire some dance moves. When it comes to naming Hutch's best soundtrack, it's a photo finish between *Mack* and *Foxy*.

An essential blaxploitation score that is often wrongfully overlooked is Johnson's *Willie Dynamite*. Featuring fine vocal performances by Martha Reeves (of Martha & the Vandellas), Johnson's score is nearly as good as *Across 110th Street*, and certainly on par with *Cleopatra Jones*. On the rousing title track and others, unexpected instruments like the twangy Jew's harp and a variety of harmonicas (such as the resonant bass harp) join more traditional funk instrumentation for an exciting sound driven by a cacophony of exotic percussion that includes tympani and tabla.

Speaking of dynamite, one of the most psychedelic blaxploitation soundtracks is Charles Earland's *The Dynamite Brothers* (1974), a little known flick about a black former football player and a Chinese black belt who join forces against a drug kingpin. The score prominently features the synthesizer experiments of Patrick Gleeson in combination with a crackling jazz-funk groove. "I was combining pop music with space music," Gleeson explains in the booklet notes of the Prestige release that pairs *Dynamite* with Donald Byrd's *Cornbread, Earl & Me* (1975), which was originally released on Prestige's sister label, Fantasy.

While *Brothers* was largely ignored upon theatrical release, *Cornbread* is considered a classic of the genre. In comparison to *Brothers*, Donald Byrd's score, as performed by his group the Blackbyrds, is relatively conventional, but it still packs a smokin' groove. The hooky theme song frequently turns up on compilations, and members of the original Blackbyrds (who were students of Professor Byrd's at Howard University back in the day) still play selections from the score in concert today. Many of the tracks were created from 20- or 30-second grooves, looped together and stretched out by arranger Mitch Farber and engineer Val Christian Garay. The recordings also feature session musicians who filled in when members of the Blackbyrds were hitting the books.

Monk Higgins and Alex Brown's *Sheba, Baby* (1975), which is one of the less popular Grier flicks, is an underrated gem, full of funky instrumental grooves and Philly soul numbers sung by Barbara Mason. The title track, sung by Mason, has an infectious hook wrapped around the line "She's a dangerous lady." Mason also shines on "A Good Man Is Gone," a mid-tempo blues that will have you singing along. The instrumentals hold up their end of the bargain, too. The brassy "Get Down Sheba," the sleazy "Three Hoods," and the strutting "Who the Hell Is That?" wouldn't sound out of place on a Hayes soundtrack. Other jazz-funk big band numbers include "The Shark," "Breast Stroke" and "Speedboat."

Another solid blaxploitation score is Luchi De Jesus' *Friday Foster* (1975). De Jesus scored several films of the era, including *Detroit 9000* and *Slaughter*, and he also arranged and produced Chet Baker, Sarah Vaughan and Peaches & Herb. Outstanding tracks include the theme, sung by Ward L. Chandler, and the Vocoder-enhanced scat funk of "Skin City." While a number of tracks have required premature fade-outs due to dialogue that has been wisely left out of the mix, the score has compelling cinematic passages, and wildly funky ones to boot.

Another later blaxploitation film is *The Monkey Hu$tle* (1976), featuring an upbeat funk score by Jack Conrad, who had a varied Hollywood career. In the '30s and '40s he acted in several B-movies, and then much later became a director, producer and composer. *Hu$tle* is a solid, workmanlike example of later-era blaxploitation scores. The disco influence is felt on tracks like "Roller Rink" and the title track, but doesn't overwhelm the vibe of good-time funk.

No discussion of blaxploitation soundtracks is complete without *Disco Godfather* (1976). Rudy Ray Moore's last '70s movie features slick funky disco played by session musicians performing under the moniker Juice People Unlimited. Even with Moore's outsized personality attached to it, however, *Disco* is still a minor entry.

One of the latter-day blaxploitation soundtracks of any substance is Mayfield's *Short Eyes* (1977), a film about a white child molester who receives rough justice at the hands of Latino and black inmates. As with his previous efforts, *Short Eyes* (which is slang for a pedophile) is full of topical lyrics, electrifying grooves and Mayfield's soulful vocals. The soundtrack nearly measures up to *Superfly*, but the film's unconventional subject matter has relegated both the album and movie to relative obscurity. Nevertheless, songs like the wah-drenched "Do Do Wap is Strong in Here" and the tense title track are some of Mayfield's finest movie tracks. Interestingly, Mayfield quotes from "Scarborough Fair" on the gently meandering "Father Confessor."

The influence of blaxploitation on contemporary musical tastes cannot be overestimated. Survey the tracks sampled by such hip-hop artists as Cypress Hill and Wu-Tang Clan, and you'll find dozens of blaxploitation beats and kung-fu movie cuts. There have even been imaginary soundtracks inspired by the genre, including *The Revenge of Mister Mopoji* (1994), *Soul Ecstasy* (1999) and *Super Chase* (2001).

The importance of music to black crime films can't be overstated. Bear in mind that radio spots for films like *Shaft* and *Superfly* often call attention to the soundtrack artist, practically in the same breath as the movie's star. This emphasis on the music further reinforces the idea that in blaxploitation films the music is as much a character as the flesh and blood men and women who populate the frame. Outside of Hollywood's classic movie musicals, no other genre can truly claim that distinguishing feature. What stirred the audience's soul back in the day continues to do so 30 years later. To quote the Godfather of Soul: "Like it is, like it was."

Kung-Fu Cuts

Black action movies of the '70s often played side-by-side with kung-fu flicks (and in the case of a film like *Black Belt Jones*, the two genres merged). The most popular martial arts movies of the early '70s starred the legendary Bruce Lee, including *Fists of Fury*, *The Return of the Dragon*, *Game of Death* and, most famously, *Enter the Dragon*. While not crime films in the usual sense, the action often revolved around organized crime and vigilante justice. Some of these movies have legitimate original soundtracks by such heavyweights as Schifrin and Barry, and others feature "needle drop" soundtracks falsely attributed to Joseph Koo.

Falling in the latter camp is *Tang Shan Da Xiong* (*Fists of Fury*, or *The Big Boss*, 1971). Another Koo-attributed soundtrack is featured in *Meng Long Guojiang* (*The Way of the Dragon*, or *Return of the Dragon*, 1972).

Schifrin came closest to blaxploitation with his excellent *Enter the Dragon* (1973), the Bruce Lee blockbuster directed by Robert Clouse. By then, the blaxploitation sound was enjoying great success with audiences, regardless of skin tone. The evidence of comfortable assimilation was on the screen—as the movie's Chinese hero (Lee) teams up with an African-American (Jim Kelly) and a Caucasian (John Saxon)—as well as on the soundtrack. The theme, with its chugging wah guitar rhythms, "Shaft"-like rhythm and ultra funky keyboard and brass lines, make it a classic of the blaxploitation genre. Elsewhere in the score, the mellow groover "Headset Jazz," and lean creepers "Into the Night" and "The Human Fly," also have funky appeal. The score remains a touchstone for fans of Schifrin, blaxploitation and classic kung fu. Rap group Wu Tang Clan paid homage to it with its debut album, *Enter the Wu Tang* (1993). And *Rush Hour* (1998) director Brett Ratner requested a *Dragon*-style score from Schifrin to accompany the high-kicking, crime-fighting, comic antics of Jackie Chan and Chris Tucker. Simply put, *Dragon* is a notable and influential entry in the blaxploitation soundtrack genre, even if the movie barely qualifies.

Director Clouse's next film, *Black Belt Jones* (1974), starring *Dragon*'s Jim Kelly, features music by Detroit funk guitarist Dennis Coffey and De Jesus. The score boasts a catchy, fast-paced theme and action cues that are funky, hard-driving and occasionally psychedelic.

The only other notable Bruce Lee soundtrack is *Game of Death* (1978) by John Barry, which favors an orchestral sound more in keeping with the composer's work on James Bond movies.

More Classic Crime Films of the '60s and '70s

Although jazz and funk styles dominated the crime sound of the late '60s and early '70s, a number of crime films of the era featured other styles of

John Barry's score for *Game of Death* (1978) uses Bruce Lee's kung-fu vocalisms to accent the music. (CD cover appears courtesy of Silva Screen Records.)

music. *Bonnie & Clyde* (1967) is one of the most famous genre entries. Charles Strouse's score can best be described as a blend of modern classical (with an occasional jazz tinge) and American folk music, namely bluegrass. It's no surprise considering Strouse studied with Aaron Copland, the so-called "dean of American composers," who was instrumental in developing the "Americana" style in major works such as *Appalachian Spring*, *Billy the Kid* and *Rodeo*.

Considering Johnny Mandel's prolific big band credentials, one might expect a straight jazz score from him for *Point Blank* (1967), based on a Donald Westlake novel. But the soundtrack ambitiously explores 12-tone serialism—a style not so much hard-boiled as it is scrambled. Soundtrack collectors who associate Mandel with his warm, sensuous Oscar-winning song "The

Shadow of Your Smile" (1965) will be surprised by the cold modernity of the composer's work on this crime thriller. Ponderous, dissonant orchestration with intermittent percussion accents and subtle use of the genre's standby keyboard, the harpsichord, cast an icy disposition over the proceedings, rarely offering reassurance through crime jazz conventions. However, there are smooth lounge jazz source cues, such as "This Way to Heaven" and, most enticingly, "I'll Slip Out of Something Comfortable," that are almost jarringly accessible next to such disquieting tracks as "Nightmare" and "Unquestioned Answers."

The Outfit (1973), another Westlake adaptation, features a score by Fielding whose approach to the genre is often unconventional. The composer balances his dark avant-garde sensibilities ("Taxi in the Rain") with tense, dissonant action jazz ("Office Scuffle/Kenilworth Heist/Casino Heist") and country western vocal tracks ("Quentin Blue," sung by Steve Gillette).

There is no crime theme as instantly recognizable as Nino Rota's tragic, nostalgic music for *The Godfather* (1972), which earned the "Best Picture" statuette at the Academy Awards. Rota's score also earned an Oscar nod, but was withdrawn due to the fact that Rota had recycled music he'd written for an earlier film, Eduardo De Filippo's *Fortunella* (1958). The film features not one but two famous themes. "The Godfather Waltz" opens starkly with solo trumpet, stating a plaintive melody punctuated by low discordant chords on piano and strings. With the trumpet silenced, a sad violin takes up the melody, joined by lilting guitar rhythms, accordion and woodwinds. This intimate instrumental ensemble elicits the exclusivity of mafia family life. Even more recognizable is the film's lush, timeless "Love Theme," a haunting, heartbreaking melody that unfolds with the inevitability of a tragic romance. Overall, Rota's *Godfather* score (on which he collaborated with Carmine Coppola, father of the director) exhibits considerable orchestral polish and a great love for the Italian heritage. If it weren't so famous, however, one wouldn't necessarily associate its beautiful music with the crime genre.

Another memorable Mob-related film from 1973 is *Serpico*, which tells the true story of a New York City cop who famously exposed police corruption and its ties to the mafia. With the help of arranger and commercial jazz legend Bob James, Greek composer Mikis Theodorakis (*Zorba the Greek*) scored the film with a blend of warm, easygoing jazz, "Big Apple" cop funk and, most unusually, a lilting, slightly sad theme. Although the title character's background is Italian, Theodorakis chose to use a balalaika on the theme, which gives it a strong, stately Greek flavor. It is an unusual choice, but the melody lingers in one's mind afterward. The lightweight jazz of "Honest Cop" and "Alone in the Apartment" are like precursors to smooth jazz, but "Meeting in the Park" adds tension to James' super-smooth arrangements.

If *Serpico* seems a little stuck in the '70s, Goldsmith's *Chinatown* (1974) is timeless. Goldsmith creates an entrancing film noir atmosphere with unconventional orchestration that uses four pianos, four harps, two sets of percussion and a solo trumpet. According to the composer, who had a mere 10 days to create the score, he resisted producer Robert Evans' suggestion that the music should have a period feel. "I said, 'No. If what you see on the screen is perfect, why make it sound like the '30s?'" Goldsmith recounted in Mark Russell and James Young's *Film Music Screencraft* (RotoVision, 2000).

Despite the resolute logic of that statement, there are period touches in the soundtrack, such as the source cue Bunny Berigan's "I Can't Get Started," as well as piano solos of the standards "Easy Living" and "The Way You Look Tonight."

Following a disquieting glissandi and vaguely Oriental note cluster, the melancholic and undeniably noir-sounding "Love Theme," featuring solo trumpet and strings, describes the rain-swept romanticism of a '40s Los Angeles fit for Bogey and Bacall. From there Goldsmith explores more modernistic moods where melodic fragments from the theme mesh with discordant avant-gardist touches that underscore the Oscar-winning story's perverse and disturbing twists.

Jerry Goldsmith's noir score for *Chinatown* (Paramount Pictures, 1974), starring Jack Nicholson, uses discordant avant-garde touches to connote the film's perverse and disturbing twists.

Hollywood legend Bernard Herrmann's final score accompanies the gritty *Taxi Driver* (1976), about a cabbie turned vigilante. The jazz-tinged orchestral score harkens back to the early years of crime jazz film and television scores, but with a darker sensibility rarely heard in the soundtracks of the '50s. The track "Diary of a Taxi Driver," featuring Bickle's monologue about the "scum" on the streets, is a mini-masterpiece of brooding menace, with pulsating snare and cymbal echoing the cabbie's restlessness like a ticking time bomb. (The trip-hop group Journeyman sampled the track on its 1997 album *National Hijinx*.) The "Main Title" juxtaposes this tense motif with a more romantic jazz theme for saxophone, piano, bass and vibraphone as if to emphasize the delusional thinking of the main character. According to Steven C. Smith, author of *A Heart at Fire's Center: The Life and Music of Bernard Herrmann* (University of California Press, 1991), Herrmann received some compositional help on the jazzier bits from arranger Christopher Palmer.

> Palmer took the first four bars of the soprano solo "As the Wind Bloweth" from *The King of Schnorrers*, then continued the melody line in a piece he titled "So Close to Me Blues." Herrmann was so delighted with the result that the theme became a key part of the score [*AHFC*, p. 351].

Smith also notes that director Martin Scorsese credited Herrmann for supplying the psychological background for the film.

Although the original soundtrack LP of *Taxi Driver* felt neutered by the inclusion of Dave Blume's "lite jazz" renditions of the master's melodies, the CD reissue restores Herrmann's potent score.

International Crime Wave

Like jazz and funk, their cinematic equivalents caught on with film composers and audiences around the world, particularly in Europe.

Any discussion of crime jazz from the U.K. must include Roy Budd, a former child prodigy who scored more than one dozen movies during his brief film career (he died in 1993 from a brain hemorrhage).

"You talking to me?" Bernard Herrmann's score for *Taxi Driver* (Columbia Pictures, 1976) provides a perfect backdrop for the violent ruminations of anti-hero Travis Bickle (Robert De Niro).

Most of Budd's scores are in the crime thriller vein, and are characterized by the use of spacious arrangements and bottom-heavy grooves.

Budd's most stunning theme music came on his second feature of 1971, the original *Get Carter*, a film about a hit man turned avenging angel. It's one of the era's most exotic and evocative of crime jazz themes, as it features tablas, a hypnotic double bass figure, and reverb-treated keyboards, plus the sounds of locomotion and crashing waves. Unfortunately, much of the soundtrack is taken up by dispensable rock and soul tracks of the period.

A year later Budd scored *Fear Is the Key* (1972), an Alistair Maclean–penned thriller. His fourth score overall, *Fear* is best known for its riveting theme and its ten-minute "Car Chase" number. This latter

Roy Budd is best remembered for the arresting theme heard in *Get Carter* (MGM, 1971), starring Michael Caine. Budd scored several thrillers starring Caine.

track features the sounds of tire squeals, honking horns, crashing cars and police sirens over the top of Budd's jazzy orchestral funk. It is powerhouse stuff. Legend has it that the musicians—the cream of the British library scene—that played on the session erupted into applause for each other's performances after each extended take. Elsewhere in the score, Budd explores Louisiana rhythm 'n' blues ("Louisiana Ferry"), jazzy blues ("Bayou Blues"), orchestral tension ("The Hostage Escapes") and climactic action ("Breakout!"). With its blend of jazzy interludes and dynamic cinematic centerpieces, *Fear* is an archetypal Budd soundtrack.

Budd's music for *Something to Hide* (1972) may surprise those who know the composer through scores like *Fear Is the Key*. Instead of the usual crime thriller music, we get Budd, the prodigiously talented pianist, playing "Concerto for Harry," a sprawling piece that displays his love of the Romantic movement, particularly Liszt, Rachmaninov and Tchaikovsky. It's impressive in isolation, but differs so much from Budd's other crime thriller work that it can barely be thought of as movie music.

Budd's *The Stone Killer* (1973) is true to the style he'd forged on *Fear Is the Key*, and would continue to develop in spy thrillers like *The Black Windmill* and *The Marseille Contract*. The theme starts gently before surging and settling into a funky groove with solo synth and brass counterpoint. Many of the intrigue and action cues are typical of Budd's crime work: strident strings, low bass, intimidating brass, dynamic keyboard fills, psychedelic accents, electronic stings, and shimmering percussion underpinned by intermittent rock drumming. An argument could be made that such cues are interchangeable from movie to movie, but that's more a reflection of Budd's stylistic consistency than a critique of his range. One need only hear the jazzy interludes (usually source cues), such as the gentle piano jazz of "In the Shadows," the mid-tempo soul "Black Is Beautiful," the groovy instrumental "Jazz Source" and the breezy Latin jazz of "Cool Bossa Source," to appreciate the diverse sounds at play on *The Stone Killer*.

Budd's *Tomorrow Never Comes* (1978) begins on a melancholy note with the Matt Monro–sung ballad "Alone Am I," but thereafter wastes no time in pumping up the orchestral tension. However, more often then not, Budd opts for gentler passages. Broad swathes of string textures abound, accented by woodwinds, acoustic guitars, electric piano and gentle harp flourishes. He also finds time to funk it up on the strutting "Manhunt" and the easygoing "Hanky Panky."

Another notable British crime score is Stanley Myers' broodingly funky, psychedelic *Sitting Target* (1972). Not unlike Budd's work, *Sitting Target* blends slow-mo beats, thick bass lines, spare string parts that twist and turn alongside spacious keyboard chords, solo horn and moody synths. There is a fair amount of repetition, but the lean, mean theme certainly invites it, lending itself to subtle variations. Like Budd, Myers used the cream of the U.K. library music scene, but this isn't like the flashy commercial power rock that seemed to dominate the British library funk of the '70s. In fact, it's almost minimalist at times and certainly jazzy in that meditative electric Miles Davis vein, though occasionally Myers offers upbeat passages to break the tension.

While the British favored secret agents (*Secret Agent*, a.k.a. *Danger Man*; *The Prisoner*; *The Avengers*) to police officers, one TV show, *The Sweeney*, is a notable exception. The show revoled around two of Britain's toughest cops, Regan and Carter, though it started in 1974 with a TV movie, *Regan*. Like the TV series that would follow, the movie distinguished itself from traditional British crime shows by revealing the ugly side of law enforcement and the alcoholic dysfunctional lives led by the main characters. *The Sweeney* soundtrack is a rarity of the genre: a legitimate funky crime score made up almost entirely of production music from specialist music libraries like KPM, DeWolfe, Bruton and Chappell. These tracks were composed and performed by seasoned session musicians such as Johnny Hawksworth, Keith Mansfield, Peter Reno and many others. In the case of *The Sweeney*, the library tracks are predominantly funky jazz-rock. The theme, by Harry South, is a brassy updating of the traditional crime show theme, bolstered by virtuoso electric guitar, rumbling bass guitar and an electric piano solo that wouldn't be out of place on a jazz fusion record. Elsewhere—as on "Flying Squad," "The Big Fuzz" and "Funko"—the mood favors action. As far as funky cop show scores go, *The Sweeney* is outstanding, especially as an introduction to the British sound library scene.

Another outstanding entry in the British crime funk genre is *The Hanged Man* score by Alan Tew, and performed by Bullet. Like *The Sweeney*, this is a '70s era show that uses library tracks—this time from Themes International. This score, which has been sampled by several hip-hop and electronica artists, is funky to a fault. The theme, with its high-flying synthesizer, is worthy of inclusion in any funky crime mix. Other tracks, like "Contract Man" and "Road Runner," are as lean and mean as anything heard on a blaxploitation score; but taken as a whole this rocking all-instrumental score offers little to distinguish it.

Across the English Channel in France, jazz and film noir both were beloved, yet there are surprisingly few French crime movie scores in the pure crime jazz vein. Such classic crime films as *Rififi* (1955) and *Bob Le Flambeur* (1955) reserve jazz for nightclub scenes only, favoring melancholic orchestral scoring for theme music and so forth.

Michel Magne is one of the notable French composers who embraced crime jazz as a style for such films as *Compartiment tueurs* (*The Sleeping Car Murders*, 1964), *Johnny Banco* (1967) and *De la Part des Compains* (*Cold Sweat*, 1970). His soundtracks from this period blend catchy crime jazz, swanky lounge and funky library-style cues, and display an inventive streak. For example, on an intriguing track like "The Killing Train" from *Compartiment tueurs*, Magne lends the Hammond-fueled groove a surreal quality due to electronic sound effects that suggest locomotive rhythms and—oddly—a mewing cat.

Vladimir Cosma is another outstanding proponent of French crime jazz. His *L'Affaire Crazy Capo* (*The Affair of Crazy Capo*, 1973), a French-Italian coproduction, is dramatic, but occasionally groovy. Analog keyboards—like the unmistakable sound of the Moog—are a notable feature. Some tracks receive a distinctively "French" treatment, as they prominently feature an accordion. Many tracks are lushly orchestrated, but never to the point of sappy melodrama; the score always is at the service of the suspenseful story. At times the music is incredibly spare, featuring little more than percussion. Other times a fuzztone guitar spikes the sonic cocktail. While the overall effort is more formal than funky, the end result is satisfying in a most unexpected way, almost resembling a Morricone soundtrack.

Speaking of Morricone, Italian composers excelled at crime soundtracks during the late '60s and '70s. Along with Morricone, the most prolific crime funk composers were Franco Micalizzi, Francesco De Masi, and Guido and

The main theme from Ennio Morricone's *Le clan des siciliens* (a.k.a. *The Sicilian Clan*, 1969) is among the composer's most haunting. (CD cover appears courtesy of CAM Original Soundtracks; graphic designer unknown.)

Maurizio De Angelis. Known as *poliziotteschi*, the most famous Italian crime films reflected the influence of gritty American movies such as *Dirty Harry* and *The French Connection*. The music exudes rock 'n' roll swagger and flash, along with hot-blooded Mediterranean melodrama, fueled by fuzz-tone guitar, soulful organ, rumbling electric bass, and crashing drums. Among the outstanding *poliziotteschi* are Morricone's elegiac *Il clan dei siciliani* (*The Sicilian Clan*, 1969), Piero Umiliani's jazzy *La legge dei gangsters* (*Gangster's Law*, 1969), Gianni Ferrio's melancholic *Tony Arzenta* (*Big Guns* or *No Way Out*, 1972), De Angelis' high octane *La polizia incrimina la legge assolve* (*High Crime*, 1973), De Angelis' emotive *Milano trema: la polizia vuole giustizia* (*The Violent*

Professionals, 1973), De Angelis' lean and mean *Il cittadino si ribella* (*Street Law*, 1974), Micalizzi's haunting *Hold-Up—istantanea di una rapina*, 1974), Albert Verrecchia's trippy *Roma drogata* (a.k.a. *Hallucination Strip*, 1975), De Angelis' *Roma violenta* (1975), Pulsar's psychedelic *Milano violenta* (1976), Micalizzi's classic *Italia a mano armata* (*A Special Cop in Action*, 1976), De Masi's dark *Napoli spara* (1977), Goblin's funky *La via della droga* (1977), Micalizzi's aggressive *La banda del gobbo* (*Brothers Till We Die*, 1977), and Lallo Gori's disco-influenced scores for *Ritornano quelli della calibro 38* (*Gangsters* or *Return of the 38 Gang*, 1977) and *Il commissario di ferro* (*The Iron Police Inspector*, 1978).

Guido and Maurizio De Angelis' *Roma violenta* (a.k.a. *Violent Rome*, 1975) is one of the exciting funk-rock crime soundtracks to come out in Italy during the '70s. (CD cover appears courtesy of Beat Records; graphic design by Daniele De Gemini.)

In Germany, the crime jazz soundtrack is closely associated with Peter Thomas and Gert Wilden. Both composers scored for the Edgar Wallace "krimis" of the late '50s through the early '70s, and Wilden for Jesus Franco's trashy Fu Manchu potboilers of the same period. (Martin Böttcher, Nora Orlandi and others also scored for the Edgar Wallace films.)

Edgar Wallace was a popular British pulp writer whose novels were adapted to the screen by Constantin Film, Germany's most successful film distributor at the time. Thirty-two B-grade flicks were produced over little more than a decade, with titles like *The Hound of Blackwood Castle*, *The Monster of Soho*, *Double Face* and *The Spell of the Sinister One*.

Peter Thomas is probably the most creative German film composer of his generation. His arrangements for the Edgar Wallace films feature gunshots, screams, explosions, primitive electronics and maniacal laughter. The music crosses big band with surf rock and Esquivel-style lounge. Thomas also scored the Jerry Cotton spy films of the same period.

Gert Wilden's crime jazz also blends big band and rock 'n' roll sounds. The evidence can be heard in the definitive collection of Wilden's Edgar Wallace/Fu Manchu phase, *I Told You Not to Cry*. The opener, "Rolf Törring," oozes danger and intrigue. The exotic percussion, wailing brass and hot-wired Hammond organ set the standard for beat jazz for the criminal set. Elsewhere, on tracks like "Hong Kong Twist," the sound is irrefutably pop rock. But on a track like "Murder Beat" the sound is jazz.

Crime and sex prominently figure in Germany's "Reeperbahn" movies of the '60s and '70s. These crime flicks take place in Hamburg's "red light" district, and revolve around prostitution, smuggling, drug running and the like. The music lies somewhere in between crime jazz and funk, favoring a rockin' "now sound" sensibility of the period. The drums and electric bass lay down a groove, as fuzz-tone guitar, organ, brass and sax wail away. Occasionally, a moaning female scat infiltrates the mix as a reminder of what awaits each listener in the seediest cinematic neighborhood. The best introduction to this music is the CD compilation *St. Pauli Affairs*, which features Thomas, Peter Schirmann, Roland Kovac, and several others.

Spain also got into the act. Take one look at the pulpy cover of the Fresh Sound Records' compilation *Jazz en el cine negro espanol 1958–1964* and one knows what one is in for—Spanish film noir crime jazz of the same era as *Peter Gunn*, *Johnny Staccato* and *Touch of Evil*. The package's luridly illustrated bilingual insert explains how the crime films of Julio Coll, Juan Bosch and other directors broke significant stylistic ground by delving into the seedy side of life in Franco's Spain through such films as *Un vaso de whisky* (*A Glass of Whiskey*, 1958) and *A sangre fria* (*In Cold Blood*, 1959). *Jazz en el cine negro espanol* delivers a riveting 79-minute program of hard-boiled brass, vulgar organ tones, well-chilled vibes and smoky atmosphere. Most of the music is by Jose Sola, with additional tracks by Augusto Alguero, Enrique Escobar and

Federico Martinez Tudo, who are relatively unknown to film music fans. Although one might expect frequent use of percussion and Latin rhythms, there is a fair amount of stylistic experimentation here. Some of the best passages employ the frenetic percussive style to depict dramatic action far from the dance floor. Other tracks favor swing and jazz styles that wouldn't sound out of place in a typical Hollywood production of the era. There's even a bit of rollicking rock 'n' roll featuring jangling electric guitar rhythms and wailing saxophone. Reinforcing the Hollywood influence is the presence of American singer Gloria Stewart on the slow, sultry "Manhattan Blues." Peppered with dialogue and the sounds of onscreen action, the listening experience is akin to playing a video just for the aural atmosphere. About half of the tracks exceed the 10-minute mark as multiple cues flow one after another.

Caper Concertos

The caper, or heist, film—like the mob movie, courtroom drama or prison picture—is a popular sub-genre of the common crime film. Its distinguishing feature is its sometimes gritty, sometimes glamorous preoccupation with the criminal mind. Instead of focusing on a law enforcer, the caper movie subverts the traditional crime story by concentrating on a charming, sophisticated thief or motley band of thieves. While a bank, casino, museum or jewelry cache provides the requisite motivation, the ultimate goal often is the promise of retirement from the life of crime, a conceit designed to capture the audience's sympathy.

Some caper films strive to comment on the immorality inherent in a life of crime by bringing about the culprit's ultimate capture or demise. Just as often, the crook improbably gets away with the loot to live and love another day of outlaw fantasy. Regardless of the denouement, caper movies are designed to electrify the audience with the vicarious thrill of living outside of the bourgeois constraints of acceptable, law-abiding behavior. Since the original modern caper film, *The Asphalt Jungle* (1950), hit the silver screen, the genre has enjoyed box office clout.

Musically speaking, caper flicks follow the stylistic evolution of crime films in general, from the noir jazz scores of the '50s through the colorful spy sound of the '60s to the funky soul soundtracks of the '70s. The evolution is as intuitive as it is canny. Jazz characterizes both the seedy underworld and improvisatory methods of the outlaw. The spy sound lends their crimes sophistication and glamour. And the funk serves as a not-so-subtle reminder of how hip and sexy the antihero must be to buck the system in style.

Caper films really took off during the spy-crazy '60s, and European locations proved popular, particularly along the "exotic" Mediterranean coast from Turkey to Spain. *Topkapi* (1964), helmed by *Rififi* director Jules Dassin, took advantage of Istanbul's mystique. The Greek composer Manos Hadjidakis penned a sprightly, suitably near-Eastern-sounding score for the film, which is set in Istanbul, using instruments like the zither and bouzouki to impart the character of the place as well as the story's comedic spirit. With titles like "Master Thief," "Turkish Security" and "The Sultan's Dagger," one might expect a lot of action, but Hadjidakis keeps the mood light and fairly romantic.

Over in Italy, Armando Trovaioli scored *Sette uomini d'oro* (*The Seven Golden Men*, 1965) and its sequel, *Il grande colpo dei sette uomini d'oro* (*The Seven Golden Men Strike Again*, 1967). As with other Italian crime and spy scores of the '60s, the mood is light-hearted, romantic and swinging. This is especially the case with the tracks for the first movie, which offers a catchy, brassy theme and numbers that feature wordless female vocals backed with walking bass and intriguing percussion fills. It's easy to imagine the folly of a foolish gang of robbers as they bungle the perfect crime. On the second soundtrack, however, the mood changes, with tracks that feature an almost gloomy male chorus (directed by Alessandro Alessandroni), and Brazilian numbers by another composer, Nilo Sergio. What appears on paper to be a logical soundtrack double feature ends up sounding like two unrelated scores.

Also filmed in Italy, *Caccia alla volpe* (*After the Fox*, 1966) features a charming score by Burt Bacharach, whose ear-catching music for *What's New, Pussycat?* earned the composer a fair amount of hip cache (later acknowledged with a cameo in the first *Austin Powers* movie). *Fox*'s title track, performed by the Hollies (with a spoken part by star Peter Sellers), is one of the oddest and funniest movie themes of the '60s; and the instrumental version features fine Hammond B-3. Fans of groovy movie funk will clamor for "Italian Fuzz" and "Bird Bath." Piero Piccioni scored the Italian release of *After the Fox*.

Set in Spain, *The Caper of the Golden Bulls* (a.k.a. *Carnival of Thieves*, 1967) fits the classic caper profile to a tee. Vic Mizzy, who scored a string of Don Knotts comedies during the late '60s and early '70s, delivers an ultralight, Latin-tinged *Caper*. While the music doesn't offer much in the way of explosive action, its buoyant dancing spirit is irrepressible. There are tracks named for the bolero, meringue, samba and waltz, not to mention "The Dancing Safe Crackers." For intrigue, look to the harpsichord and low flute of the sultry "Senorita with the Mini-Skirt," and the crisp percussion and punchy riffing on "Waiting for Frenchy." The Spanish setting is best exploited on "Jota Waltz," which features multiple guitars and castanets.

Back in Italy (but with scenes set in Istanbul, Madrid and London) is *Kriminal* (1966), a caper based on *fumetti neri*, or Italian crime, mystery or spy comic books. Italians love their comic book anti-heroes. *Diabolik*, *Satanik* and *Kriminal* are among the most famous, and each has been translated to film. Roberto Pregadio and Romano Mussolini's *Kriminal* features a swinging beat jazz theme—heard in two instrumental versions. There are other similarly styled tracks, featuring chugging rhythm guitar and bass with organ, or horns

Satanik (1968), which features a jazz score by Roberto Pregadio and Romano Mussolini, is one of several movies based on Italian adult comic books. (CD cover appears courtesy of Beat Records; graphic design by Daniele De Gemini.)

and crisp drumming. Other jazzy tracks offer intrigue, sex appeal and action, occasionally taking a lush lounge approach. The intrigue numbers sound like Barry's music for *Thunderball*, which was released a year earlier, but overall the music can be described as noir crime jazz. Pregadio and Mussolini also provided a jazz score for *Satanik* (1968), which isn't a caper flick.

Morricone's psycho beat score for *Danger Diabolik* (1967), orchestrated by the composer's frequent collaborator, Bruno Nicolai, features wild electronic abstractions, avant-garde trumpet solos, mystical sitar-laden intrigue cues and surf rock guitar-driven action cues that rival Neal Hefti's "Batman" theme. The music electrifyingly complements the comic book dynamism of Mario Bava's wildly colorful film, making *Diabolik* one of the essential crime soundtracks of the period.

For *Colpo maestro al servizio di sua maesta britannica* (*Master Stroke*, 1967), De Masi collaborated with Alessandroni on the theme, while De Masi is credited for most of the score. It is reprised frequently in this ultra-cool score, which also offers smoky lounge themes as well as intrigue and action cues along the way. Brass, percussion and De Masi's beloved Farfisa organ are prominently featured, as is Alessandroni's legendary I Cantori Moderni. Although most of the score supports a modern setting, a couple of tracks are in the spaghetti western style due to a clever plot element (the hero is an actor in sagebrush sagas). De Masi, who scored many Italian westerns, cooks up a saloon piano piece, and a bit of mariachi brass and vigorous acoustic guitar strumming on the side.

Another caper film set in Spain is *Deadfall* (1968), about a cat burglar who falls in love with the wife of the man who hires him for an elaborate jewel heist. It's a prime example of a score that outshines its movie. John Barry scored *Deadfall* between two of his best Bond scores (*You Only Live Twice* and *On Her Majesty's Secret Service*), and it certainly earns its place as one of his finer, if lesser known, efforts. Like any good Barry score, this one has many suspenseful passages, using streamlined arrangements and distinctive instrumentation (deep clean brass flares, harp glissandi, luxurious strings swells). Due to its setting, there are some Spanish accents, such as the percussion on "Statue Dance" and Renato Tarrago's classical guitar on the 14-minute "Romance for Guitar and Orchestra," which is truly the album's centerpiece. The score also boasts a fine Shirley Bassey vocal performance on the title track "My Love Has Two Faces." There also is a "Thunderball"-esque performance by an unknown male singer. Drawing comparisons to Barry's 007 scores is inevitable, as there are numerous passages that wouldn't sound out of place in films like *Diamonds Are Forever*.

When it comes to sophisticated '60s scores, Michel Legrand's "jazz-influenced symphony" for *The Thomas Crown Affair* (1968) is the real deal. Legrand's score contains one of the most memorable theme songs ever: the Academy Award–winning "The Windmills of Your Mind," sung by Noel Harrison, son of screen star Rex Harrison. Legend has it that, after watching a five-hour rough cut of the film, Legrand took a six week vacation during which he wrote 90 minutes of music that the film, in turn, was edited around (very unconventional, to say the least). As the story goes, if Legrand's experiment had failed he would have been obligated to write a second score for free. Beyond the haunting theme, Legrand provided a subtly balanced score that combines playfulness with tenderness. The score is at its grooviest with "Cash and Carry" and "The Boston Wrangler." Up-tempo and brassy, "Cash and Carry" catches fire with scat vocals, rumbling bass line and irresistible hook. Electric bass also

The centerpiece of John Barry's *Deadfall* (1968) soundtrack is Renato Tarrago's classical guitar performance on the 14-minute "Romance for Guitar and Orchestra." (CD cover appears courtesy of Film Score Monthly/Retrograde Records; graphic design by Joe Sikoryak.)

fuels "The Boston Wrangler," which features some intricate polyphonic textures and feedback zaps from a Hammond organ. For sheer instrumental brilliance, "Playing the Field" and "The Crowning Touch" can't be beat. On the former, lightning fast keyboard runs balance with slow passages of creamy lounge jazz. On the latter, classical piano runs cascade like waves on a beach, highlighted by chiming percussion accents. It's a gorgeous score, probably more so than most crime scores.

Another Hollywood caper movie soundtrack with European flair is *The Biggest Bundle of Them All* (1968). The fantastic album cover painting depicting the movie's vivacious sexpot star Raquel Welch in a bikini is enticing enough, but Riz Ortolani's score is not so much sexy as it is merely charming. There are tracks that go for groovy Italian style, but are more about delicacy than decadence. Crooner Johnny Mathis gets the platter started with the ballad "Most of All There's You." Fittingly, Ortolani serves up light orchestral and even lighter jazz. "The Dance on the Terrace" suggests romance under Mediterranean moonlight. "The Train Robbery" is the token action track, and "In the Night Club" is the requisite Italian go-go number; but these modest thrills aren't enough to save *The Biggest Bundle*. Even the soundtrack closer, the title song performed by Eric Burden and the Animals, fails to leave a lasting impression.

For every Hollywood-financed caper that takes place in Europe there is the rare European-made heist flick set in America with a mixed cast. Exhibit number 1: *Las Vegas—500 millones* (*They Came to Rob Las Vegas*, 1968). The booklet notes for the Harkit CD reissue makes the claim that it belongs in the "blaxploitation" genre, comparing it to *Superfly* and *In the Heat of the Night*. The comparison to *Superfly* is misleading, since *Superfly* is a song-based score and *Las Vegas* is not. Although *In the Heat of the Night* is not a true blaxploitation movie, the comparison to Jones' score is a bit more apt. Greek composer George Garvarentz's *Las Vegas* is an ambitious, highly polished exercise in orchestrated crime jazz. There's plenty of creativity in the arrangements, which favor brass, organ, piano, guitar, electric bass and lots of percussion. The opening track, "Inspector Douglas' Trick," recalls Mancini's work on *Touch of Evil*— which is impressive enough, but the appeal doesn't stop there. "Last Trip of the Truck" grooves like a Jones track, with loose melodic riffing over a swaggering beat. "Attack of the Truck" cranks up a frenzied tempo with a blur of quick bits from brass, strings and organ.

Of his 30-odd scores, *The Italian Job* (1969) is one of Quincy Jones' most creative and varied works, getting an eclectic though fairly non-funky treatment. It opens with the romantic ballad "On Days Like These," sung by Matt Munro. "Something's Cookin'" simmers in a mellow vibe that blends acoustic guitar with organ. From there, the score continues along its unpredictable trajectory, covering Baroque chamber music, moody orchestral, and quiet bossa nova, among other styles. The most curious concoctions are "It's Caper Time" and "Getta Bloomin' Move On!" Both tracks are jolly square dance-style numbers featuring vocals by the Self Preservation Society (Noel Coward's cons in the movie), and accompany action sequences like the movie's famous Mini Cooper car chase. According to Ben Raworth's booklet notes for the MCA CD reissue, the Self Preservation Society tune became an all-purpose anthem for rowdy Brits during the period.

During the '70s caper movies took many forms, ranging from the World War II–set *Kelly's Heroes* (1970) to the Victorian England–set *The Great Train Robbery* (1979). When it comes to wolfish Vietnam-era war movies masquerad-

1. Crime Jazz and Felonius Funk   53

George Garvarentz's score for *They Came to Rob Las Vegas* (1968) is an ambitious, highly polished exercise in funky crime jazz. (CD cover appears courtesy of Harkit Records; graphic designer unknown.)

ing in the sheep's clothing of an earlier, more "honorable war," *M*A*S*H* remains the ultimate example. However, *Kelly's Heroes*, with its subversively ironic comic caper storyline and nonconformist characters, also follows suit. *Kelly's Heroes* concerns a U.S. Army tank outfit that connives to steal Nazi gold. Contributing to *Kelly's Heroes* postmodern sensibility is Schifrin's rangy score, which includes militaristic funk pop, country western, folk, breezy vocal pop and a spaghetti western pastiche. Although *Kelly's Heroes* isn't likely to rank among Schifrin's most popular soundtracks, it possesses many of the qualities one looks for in a late '60s/early '70s Schifrin score: Pulse-pounding rhythms, rumbling electric bass lines, lean mean orchestral passages, memo-

Quincy Jones' score for *The Italian Job* (Paramount Pictures, 1969) features vocals by "the Self Preservation Society," essentially the gang Michael Caine's character leads on a heist.

rable melodies, and a bit of rock 'n' roll spirit. The infectious theme, with its "River Kwai" whistling and funky militaristic drumming, is well used. And the Morricone-inspired "Quick Draw Kelly," with its ringing bells, lonesome harmonica, acoustic guitar strumming and rattling percussion, captures the satirical nature of the "gunslinger" showdown. Elsewhere, the use of country western balladry (courtesy of Hank Williams Jr.) and breezy '60s pop chorus (courtesy of the Mike Curb Congregation) seems too anachronistic for its own good.

Loot (1970), which is based on a play by the legendary Joe Orton, is a much different take on the caper genre. It is an unusual entry, as the soundtrack favors brassy, upbeat pop instead of jazz, rock or funk. Written and arranged by library session ace Keith Mansfield, *Loot* features vocals by Steve Ellis, the soulful voice of the underrated Love Affair. Much of the soundtrack functions like a concept album about two bank robbers who hide their ill-gotten pounds in their mother's coffin. With titles like "More, More, More" and

"Loot's the Root," the song cycle follows a criminal's humorous obsession with money.

Dollar$* (1971) is one of Quincy Jones' funkiest and most satisfying soundtracks. Featuring vocal performances by Little Richard, Roberta Flack and Q's frequent collaborator, the Don Elliott Voices, the *Dollar$ score is an inventive blend of experimental jazz and rhythm and blues. The track "Snow Creatures" is as funky as it is unconventional. Taking the Don Elliott Voices through a series of avant-garde rhythmical motifs, Jones proves that the best way to create an atmosphere of mystery and tension is to embrace experimentation. Elsewhere, he employs a distorted, frenzied locomotive violin part (played by Doug Kershaw), funky Clavinette keyboard rhythms (on "Money Runner"), and spare, lowdown jazz abstractions ("Candy Man" and "Kitty with the Bent Frame") that ooze intrigue; those latter tracks clearly served as inspiration for David Holmes when he scored *Ocean's Eleven, Twelve* and *Thirteen*. *Dollar$* sits alongside *They Call Me Mister Tibbs* (1970) as his best funky soundtrack work.

A staple of cinema is the director/composer relationship. Some famous examples come to mind: Hitchcock and Herrmann, Spielberg/Lucas and Williams, Burton and Elfman. The relationship between Sam Peckinpah and Jerry Fielding was fruitful and sometimes volatile (which is no surprise given S.P.'s legendary forceful personality). Among their collaborations are *The Wild Bunch* (1969), *Straw Dogs* (1971)—both of which earned Fielding an Oscar nom—and *Bring Me the Head of Alfredo Garcia* (1974). The duo worked with Steve McQueen and Ali McGraw on *The Getaway* (1972), one of two movies Peckinpah, Fielding and McQueen made together that year (the other being the modern western *Junior Bonner*). Unlike with the cowpoke picture, the caper movie gig ended badly for Fielding when power player McQueen fired the composer in favor of using Jones, who previously scored the 1965 McQueen gambling drama *The Cincinnati Kid*. Naturally, Fielding was devastated, having already completed the score, which Peckinpah reportedly liked very much. Film Score Monthly resurrected Fielding's unused score—a move that Jones is said to have supported. The score itself is up to Fielding's usual high standards, blending tensely atmospheric, sparely orchestrated and percussive passages with naturalistic source music (in this case, country western). When the tension lifts for the end credits, Fielding lays down a cheerful wah countryjazz number.

Another Q-scored caper flick is *The Hot Rock* (1972). Compared to the excellent *Dollar$* soundtrack, this one is a bit uneven and not as immediately satisfying. The sporadic funky bits blend Afro-beat percussion with avantgarde jazz and electronics.

One of the best caper soundtracks is Budd's *Diamonds* (1975). It is evenly balanced between fully orchestrated easy listening themes and tense funky cues that are so stripped down they anticipate contemporary drum 'n' bass music. Soul singers Three Degrees (best known for the number one hit "When Will I See You Again") perform on three tracks, including the theme. Some tracks fall in between the aforementioned camps, including the highly atmospheric "Tel Aviv" and bubbling easy-groover "Beauty and the Bass."

The last great caper score of the '70s recalls a much earlier time period. *The Great Train Robbery* dramatizes the infamous first hold-up of a moving locomotive in Victorian England. Goldsmith scored the picture at the height of his powers, the same year he provided classic scores for *Alien* and *Star Trek: The Motion Picture*. *Robbery* captures the film's period and setting, but also suggests the clever thinking and forceful action required to stage a heist in motion. The theme, like much of this action-oriented soundtrack, lunges forward with propulsive orchestral force but never loses sight of the charmingly well-mannered melodies. There's plenty of pomp in such tracks as "No Respectable Gentleman" and "The Gold Arrives..." but Goldsmith never lets the listener forget that it's all exciting escapist fun.

Summary Judgment

Regardless of the culture, the universal language of jazz provides perfect translation for both criminal activity and investigation. For jazz musicians, con artists and private eyes alike, improvising means to live by one's wits, using evidence (like chord changes) to root out something real, something true. When the crime sound got funky in the '70s, it was not merely a reflection of popular tastes; it was a change of attitude as well. The influences of Vietnam, drug culture, racial tensions and the sexual revolution—not to mention the electrification of jazz itself—called for a new crime sound, a new plan of action that is still being imitated today.

12 Essential Crime Soundtracks

The Man with the Golden Arm (1955)—Elmer Bernstein
Peter Gunn (1958–1962)—Henry Mancini
I Want to Live! (1958)—Johnny Mandel
Bullitt (1968)—Lalo Schifrin
Danger Diabolik (1968)—Ennio Morricone
They Call Me Mister Tibbs (1970)—Quincy Jones
Dirty Harry (1971)—Lalo Schifrin
Shaft (1971)—Isaac Hayes
The French Connection (1971)—Don Ellis
Superfly (1972)—Curtis Mayfield
The Taking of Pelham One Two Three (1974)—David Shire
Diamonds (1976)—Roy Budd

Chapter 2

Spy Symphonies

When the swing revival of the mid–90s sparked a cultural re-appreciation for lounge music and exotica, it also ignited renewed interest in spy movie soundtracks. With the "go-go '90s" in full swing, the trendy cigar and martini crowd stocked their CD changers with one or more of the nostalgic compilations released at the time. No cocktail party could be complete without a 007 wannabe suavely requesting a vodka and vermouth concoction "shaken, not stirred." A newsstand fixture of the era, *Spy Magazine*, released a collection for the oh-so-ironic bandwagon jumpers simply called *Spy Music*. And as recently as 2002 the International Spy Museum in New York City released a similarly kitschy compilation—*Music to Spy By*.

The fad climaxed with the first *Austin Powers* movie (1997), a '60s spy spoof featuring an onscreen musical performance by *Casino Royale* composer and '60s icon Burt Bacharach. That film's soundtrack boasts a needle-drop theme ("Soul Bossa Nova") by Quincy Jones, which he recorded in 1962. Most of the score (and those of its two sequels) by George S. Clinton pay homage to Barry's classic work on the '60s James Bond epics, as well as period spy spoofs like *In Like Flint* (score by Goldsmith) and *The Silencers* (score by Bernstein).

Irony-clad nostalgia trippers aside, the renewed interest in spy soundtracks (and the oft-confused crime jazz) led to the release and re-release of many fine scores that sound great with or without the faux hipster trappings of cigar smoke-choked cocktail soirees.

While it would be tempting to start with Barry's James Bond scores, it's more appropriate—if only for the sake of chronology—to begin with *British Agent* (1934). Yes, the birthplace of the ultimate secret agent also produced the first spy film. The score by Bernhard Kaun and Heinz Roemheld is true to the "Hungarian" operatic scores of Golden Age Hollywood. This can be said of the many spy films that followed, including such classics as *The 39 Steps* (1935) and *The Lady Vanishes* (1938).

More Spies Please ... We're British

Britain began its love affair with espionage entertainment with the TV show *International Detective* (1959–1961), which blended a traditional police show with international intrigue. Edwin Astley, who went on to score *Secret Agent* and *The Saint*, contributed music, along with Leroy Holmes, Sidney Shaw and Harry Booth. The soundtrack is in the crime jazz vein of Bernstein's *The Man with the Golden Arm*, but occasionally eases into Mancini-esque Latin lounge. Of the 22 tracks, seven are variations on the theme, including charmingly dated vocal versions with a burly male chorus singing about how crime doesn't pay as long as the international detective is on duty.

Before the James Bond movie series brought spies to the largest audience ever, another series struck an equivalent coup on the small screen. The UK television series *Danger Man* (better known as *Secret Agent* Stateside) starred Patrick McGoohan as "Drake ... John Drake." *Danger Man* premiered on UK television in 1960, two years before the first James Bond film, *Dr. No* (1962); though Ian Fleming's first Bond novel, *Casino Royale*, appeared in 1953. Edwin Astley provided the music for *Danger Man* during its collective broadcast run from 1960 to 1966.

Like most '60s spy TV shows, *Danger Man*'s music is in the same jazzy vein as most crime-fighting programs of the era. On the show's original theme, big band brass engages in a call-and-response over a chugging locomotive rhythm. It's effective, but doesn't really distinguish itself from other crime jazz themes. Later, in 1964, Astley penned a new, catchier theme—"High Wire." It prominently features harpsichord in a more sophisticated arrangement that re-invents the crime jazz sound, and the featured instrument became a hallmark of the spy sound throughout the '60s. When the show debuted Stateside, yet another Astley-penned theme, recorded by Johnny Rivers, was used. *Secret Agent* proved to be a hit for CBS, and Rivers' "Secret Agent Man" reached number 3 on Billboard's singles chart. "Danger Man," "High Wire" and "Secret Agent Man" were released on 45s during the mid–1960s. (Notably, at least one version of "Secret

Patrick McGoohan's sophisticated spy John Drake is well served by Edwin Astley's lounge jazz score in ITC TV's *Secret Agent* (a.k.a. *Danger Man*; ITC, 1960–1966).

Agent Man" recorded by Rivers features an opening that apes "The James Bond Theme.") Stylistically, most of the music in *Secret Agent* could be described as baroque chamber jazz, with occasional exotic touches for foreign settings. The harpsichord imparts some of its essential "spy" character, but Astley's arrangements favor sophisticated cocktail moods rather than action, danger and intrigue.

Following his compelling depiction of agent John Drake, England's highest paid actor took a sympathetic role on a show of his own creation, *The Prisoner* (1967). He played "Number 6," a burnt-out and bitter agent who resigns, only to be kidnapped and imprisoned in a mysterious village. *The Prisoner* was

The Prisoner (1967), Patrick McGoohan's follow-up to *Secret Agent*, features an exciting main theme by Ron Grainer. (CD cover appears courtesy of Silva Screen Records.)

not an official sequel to *Secret Agent/Danger Man*, but is generally accepted as such in light of McGoohan's real-life frustration with *Secret Agent/Danger Man*'s increased predictability. *The Prisoner* lasted just one season, but maintains a strong cult audience to this day.

Regardless of behind-the-scenes intrigue, the soundtrack for *The Prisoner* is quite different from *Secret Agent*. Using the show's surrealistic setting as a creative springboard, the score's contributors (including Ron Grainer, Wilfred Josephs, and Alfred Elms) forego the usual spy stuff in favor of stylistic variety. Grainer—who also penned the theme for that other UK cult classic, *Doctor Who*—is credited with *The Prisoner*'s brassy theme. Most notably, it features the guitar playing of Vic Flick, whose work on "The James Bond Theme" is legendary. It also uses sound effects, such as thunderclaps, typewriter chimes and automobile growls, heard in the program's opening. Josephs and Robert Farnon unsuccessfully submitted themes for consideration. McGoohan considered Farnon's piece to be too Western. And Joseph's frantic and ambitiously modernist piece was used elsewhere in the first episode. The show also used classical pieces by Vivaldi, Bizet and Radetski, as well as instrumental tracks from the Chappell Recorded Music Library by Johnny Hawksworth, Jack Arel, Roger Roger and others. Much of this music captures the whimsical character of the village itself—particularly the marching band numbers—but a few tracks venture into territory as disparate as exotica, Moog electronica, sitar psychedelia, funky soul and groovy pop.

Naturally, not every UK TV spy show starred Patrick McGoohan. Let's not forget *The Avengers*. John Dankworth wrote the original theme for the series that debuted in 1961, but Laurie Johnson's theme music is more famous. It is lushly orchestrated, yet propulsive, swinging and memorable. One might even call it the perfect groovy theme music for London in the '60s.

While McGoohan had been one of the first choices to play James Bond, another UK TV actor eventually landed the role. Several years prior to his 007 debut in *Live and Let Die* (1973), Roger Moore played Simon Templar, a.k.a. *The Saint*, a playboy adventurer whose exploits lay somewhere between that of a private eye and an amateur spy. The show debuted in 1962 and ended in 1969. In the late '70s and '80s, other TV programs attempted to revive the character, which Leslie Charteris created in the '20s. Many popular *Saint* novels and short stories were published and reprinted between 1928 and 1982. Plus, more than two dozen movies have been made, including a pair for TV starring Moore, and the 1997 Hollywood reinvention starring Val Kilmer.

Edwin Astley's *Saint* theme, with its catchy, high-pitched melodic line, is an elegant spin on the crime jazz standard set by such Hollywood composers as Mancini and Bernstein. Jazzy moods like Latin lounge, exotic intrigue and gentle Debussy-isms dominate the show.

Following his successful run as *The Saint*, Moore joined Tony Curtis on a similar program, *The Persuaders*, which debuted in 1971 and lasted just one season. The characters played by Moore and Curtis are wealthy playboys working as amateur agents in the charge of a retired judge to right an assortment of wrongs—usually entailing a lighthearted competition for the favors of a young woman whose life or livelihood is at stake. John Barry's theme music outclassed the show. It opens with stately keyboard chords, followed by a Hungarian cimbalom, which the composer had used to great effect on the spy film *The Ipcress File* (1965). The theme also uses cool analog synth tones and throbbing bass guitar that emphasize the orchestration's spiraling effect.

Roger Moore's suave turn as the dashing Simon Templar, a.k.a. *The Saint* (ITC, 1962–1969), does good deeds to the lounge jazz sounds of Edwin Astley.

License to Score

As good as *The Persuaders* theme is, rarely has a discussion of John Barry's phenomenal spy scoring begun with anything other than his James Bond scores. *From Russia with Love* (1963), *Goldfinger* (1964), *Thunderball* (1965), *You Only Live Twice* (1967), *On Her Majesty's Secret Service* (1969) and *Diamonds Are Forever* (1971) all rank as essential classics. Although Barry went on to provide fine scores for five other Bond films—*The Man with the Golden Gun* (1974), *Moonraker* (1979), *Octopussy* (1983), *A View to a Kill* (1985) and *The Living Daylights* (1987)—the earlier work remains the most admired. None of it would have happened had the producers, Albert Broccoli and Harry Saltzman, reportedly not been dissatisfied with portions of Monty Norman's *Dr. No* (1962) score. Norman still gets credit for the influential theme due to contractual agreement, but it was Barry who wrote and recorded it. The track, which features the distinctive guitar playing of Vic Flick, is indisputably a Barry number.

"You can see how it develops from my earlier work," Barry said in an interview from *Film Music*, a book in RotoVision's Screencraft series. "'The James Bond Theme' has the same rhythms as 'Bees Knee,' the signature tune of the John Barry Seven, and the opening of *Beat Girl*, which had a similar guitar riff, which the orchestra then builds on."

Drawing on the influences of Stan Kenton and Dizzy Gillespie, Barry delivered the perfect Bond theme without ever having read one of Ian Fleming novels or even seeing a rough cut. The rest, as they say, is history. The producers were so impressed they asked Barry to stay on for what would prove to be the most influential movie series of the '60s and the longest running movie series ever.

On *From Russia with Love*, Barry contributed all but the theme, which was written by Lionel Bart (and sung by Matt Monro). According to Eddi Fiegel's *John Barry: A Sixties Theme* (Pan Macmillan, 1998), someone connected with the production wanted Bart to compose the entire score, but Barry was given the go-ahead (p. 106). He delivered an exciting score that cemented his place in the franchise. Most importantly, Barry wrote the action cue, "007," which would prove very adaptable in subsequent scores as an action alternative to "The James Bond Theme." Over a pulse-quickening snare and bass drum beat, whiplash strings and staccato trumpets announce imminent danger as trombones counter melodically on the hero's arrival. Then the orchestra reiterates the assurance of victory, building to a triumphant crescendo. With all due respect to Sean Connery's animal magnetism and macho heroics in the title role, the Bond craze wouldn't have been nearly as potent without music like "007."

On *Goldfinger*, the 007 franchise truly hit its stylistic stride, with Barry contributing an iconic spy soundtrack; it even bumped the Beatles' *A Hard Day's Night* from the top of the charts. In fact, Barry has said that it's his favorite. With the help of lyricists Leslie Bricusse and Anthony Newley, he composed one of the series' greatest theme songs, the first of three sung by the inimitable Shirley Bassey (excluding the rejected theme for *Thunderball*, "Mr. Kiss Kiss Bang Bang"). Amazingly, producer Saltzman didn't like the song at all, implying that it wasn't youth-oriented enough to attract the lucrative kid contingent (Pan Macmillan, p. 141). Co-producer Broccoli and director Guy

Sean Connery's legendary run as the sophisticated and dangerous James Bond defined "action hero" for the '60s, and John Barry's dynamic, exciting 007 scoring style reinvented the action movie soundtrack.

Hamilton loved it, though, and made certain it stayed in the picture, and within weeks of its release there were three cover versions in circulation.

The *Goldfinger* score offered Barry the opportunity to swing ("Into Miami"), foment with intrigue ("Teasing the Korean"), build tension ("Dawn Raid on Fort Knox"), and rock out surf style ("Goldfinger"—the instrumental). The *Goldfinger* score also offered Barry the opportunity to explore evocative sounds through unusual instrumentation. He used finger cymbals to supply a metallic "ting" to connote the gold element. He would achieve something similar on the *Diamonds Are Forever* score through the use of "twinkling" keyboards.

For the fourth 007 epic, the production team pulled out all stops for a bonanza of bombs, boats and bikini-clad babes. *Thunderball* is Barry's most action-oriented Bond score, and benefits from the movie's Caribbean location in that percussion is always close at hand. And considering the frequent underwater passages, Barry provided suitably heavy and undulating underscoring, accented by a hypnotic harp motif that perfectly suits the aquatic setting. Pro-

John Barry's explosive score is a perfect accompaniment for the climactic scene in *Goldfinger* (MGM/UA, 1964) when James Bond (Sean Connery) battles Oddjob (Harold Sakata) before defusing a bomb as the timer clicks to "007." (Photograph courtesy of the John Monaghan Collection.)

duction of the *Thunderball* soundtrack had a couple of hiccups—one that required an immediate remedy and one that persisted for many years. Barry had twice recorded "Mr. Kiss Kiss Bang Bang" (the Japanese nickname for 007 at that time)—with Shirley Bassey and Dionne Warwick. The song, which remained in the score as an instrumental, fit the bill musically, with its sultry saxophone, muted brass and flirty woodwinds. In the eleventh hour, however, United Artists requested a theme song that fit the bill lyrically as well, to maximize exposure. Having struggled with the general concept of a "thunderball," Barry and Don Black rushed to complete the explosive theme in time for the movie's release. Singer Tom Jones delivered in one take and blacked out after belting the final high note (Pan Macmillan, p. 189).

The aforementioned production hold-ups came as a result of the rushed release schedule. When the theatrical release date rolled around, only half of its music had been recorded for the LP release. Until the 2003 release of the remastered, extended CD edition, *Thunderball* only featured music from the movie's first half. With bonus tracks accounting for the movie's explosive climactic action sequences, the extended CD is the long-awaited complete version—making it one of the best action movie soundtracks ever.

Although some critics accused the 007 franchise of running out of steam on *You Only Live Twice* (Connery himself was experiencing spy fatigue), Barry surely was exempt from that failing, as his score is one of the series' best (and certainly its most romantic). It boasts a gorgeous theme featuring Bricusse's lyrics, and vocals by Nancy Sinatra that would later be sampled for the late '90s pop hit "Millennium" by Robbie Williams. Aretha Franklin was briefly considered to sing the theme, but Barry thought her style wrong for the song.

"Casting a song is terribly important," he's quoted as saying in Fiegel's Barry biography. "It's like casting a movie. You could have a good song, but if you get the wrong person doing it, you're dead." (Pan Macmillan, p. 200)

For the score, Barry was clearly inspired by the movie's Japanese setting, as he peppers his arrangements with indigenous instrumentation. Tracks like "Tanaka's World," "The Wedding" and "Mountains and Sunsets" are prime examples of Barry-style exotica. *You Only Live Twice* also features another outstanding 007 track, "Capsule in Space" (a.k.a. "Space March"). This ponderous cue for an ominous satellite was refined for a similar scene in *Diamonds Are Forever* (and much later it got the trip-hop remix treatment as "Timber" by Grantby for the 1996 "new crime jazz" compilation *Pop Fiction*). It also inspired similar cues by George S. Clinton in the first *Austin Powers* movie, and by Michael Giacchino in *The Incredibles* (2004). Overall, *You Only Live Twice* was Barry's most lushly orchestrated 007 score, and clearly one of the most influential.

Barry's creative direction for 007 scoring took a brief detour on the sixth installment, *On Her Majesty's Secret Service*. It should also be noted that, by then, Barry had won three Academy Awards (two for *Born Free* and one for

The Lion in Winter) and scored *Midnight Cowboy*, the only X-rated film to ever win the "Best Picture" Oscar. In other words, he was at the top of his profession. With Connery out of the picture and newcomer George Lazenby taking over (however briefly), Barry opted to pump up the sound with more electric instruments and a more aggressive sound.

"What I felt was: Well, we've lost Sean, and we have this turkey in here instead," Barry said. "And I have to stick my oar in the musical area double strong to make the audience try and forget that they don't have Sean ... to do Bondian beyond Bondian." (Pan Macmillan, p. 219)

For *OHMSS*, Barry composed a high-octane instrumental for the beginning of the film, placing the poignant, albeit non-thrilling, vocal theme "We Have All the Time in the World" (Louis Armstrong's final studio performance) elsewhere in the film. The instrumental introduced synthesizer to the Bond world, and to memorable effect. It even replaced the already familiar guitar in stating the Bond theme. A similar approach was taken on "Ski Chase" and "Battle at Piz Gloria."

The series' most sensitive installment (Bond falls in love and marries) also features a fair amount of the romantic style of scoring Barry had emphasized in *You Only Live Twice*. Often times it works beautifully (as on the Armstrong performance), but other times it is most unwelcome (such as the lounge snoozer "Try"). Most unwelcome is the flowery Nina number "Do You Know How Christmas Trees are Grown?"

For Connery's return on *Diamonds Are Forever*, Barry returned to the brassy orchestral approach he'd mined earlier on *Goldfinger*. Emphasizing the return to form further still, Barry brought back Shirley Bassey to sing the elegant, unsentimental theme music (with lyrics again by Don Black). The song caused friction between Barry and Saltzman, who reportedly hated the lyrics, and was partially responsible for Barry's subsequent absence on *Live and Let Die* (Pan Macmillan, p. 234). On the theme, Barry used electric bass and electric keyboard, and even mixed in some subtle funky wah effects, but still managed to maintain his classy creative direction.

For *Diamonds Are Forever*, Barry delivered his most exquisite 007 score. His ever-imaginative orchestrations made excellent use of already familiar themes and motifs (such as the aforementioned "Capsule in Space" as "007 and Counting," and the ever-popular "007" as "To Hell with Blofeld"). Although his work on later Bond pictures is respectable, one could stop at *Diamonds* and feel satisfied in the knowledge that nothing to come would top it or its predecessors.

During the '70s Barry would trade off with other composers to score Bond movies starring Moore (who'd been one of Fleming's early picks to play 007 in 1962). With Barry unable to work on *Live and Let Die* (1973), the producers selected two veterans of the Beatles—Paul McCartney for the theme song and producer George Martin for the score. The theme song, of course, was a massive hit. McCartney bridged the gap between the pop sentimentality of his group Wings and the fiery bombast of prior Bond themes, particularly "Thunderball."

Meanwhile, Martin handled the score like a seasoned pro, following in Barry's footsteps but also updating the sound with funky touches like the skittering rhythm guitar scratches so popular in blaxploitation scores of that era. Certainly the plot—with scenes set in Harlem and New Orleans—influenced Martin's decision to funkify the score. *Live and Let Die* remains one of the better non–Barry 007 scores.

Barry made a return engagement for *The Man with the Golden Gun* (1974), which is generally acknowledged as the cinematic low point in the series. Despite its kinky flaws, it displays a few campy charms, such as the white-suited Christopher Lee and Herve Villechaize unmistakably prototyping TV's *Fantasy Island* concept. Although he was given only two weeks to compose and record it, Barry's score outclassed the picture. His rollicking, rocking theme (written with Don Black, and sung by period pop star Lulu) can't be called a classic, but its melodic motif served the underscore effectively enough on tracks like "Let's Go Get 'Em." Barry also experimented with ragtime ("Scaramanga's Fun House") and the oriental motif ("Chew Me in Grisly Land").

Barry skipped *The Spy Who Loved Me* (1977), which proved to be a massive commercial hit without his aid. Marvin Hamlisch stepped in, co-authoring the memorable hit theme song "Nobody Does It Better" (lyrics by Carole Bayer Segar, and sung by Carly Simon). Unfortunately, his disco-influenced score has not aged well, making the soundtrack spotty at best.

Barry returned for *Moonraker* (1979), a movie so calculated it brought back the popular metal-mouthed henchman from the previous 007 blockbuster. Barry's score was hardly that crass. Given the inscrutable Ian Fleming title, the composer relied on lyric master Hal David to make sense of it (somewhat), and brought in Shirley Bassey one last time to give voice to it. Thankfully, Barry mostly eschews the disco sound used on the previous film in favor of his usual orchestral approach (the exception is the theme reprise at the end of the film). Atmospheric use of synthesizers adds a subtle updating touch.

Barry continued to score the series (*Octopussy*, 1983; *A View to a Kill*, 1985; and *The Living Daylights*, 1987), but following his departure from the series the Bond scores have been arguably less distinctive, less memorable. For the real deal, one must always return to the series' relatively purer days—those spy-crazy '60s.

Our Man in T.V. Land

During the mid–1960s several TV shows were created to capitalize on the spy craze. Among the most popular were *The Man from U.N.C.L.E.*, *I Spy*, *Get Smart* and *Mission: Impossible*.

During *U.N.C.L.E.*'s 1964–1968 run, Hugo Montenegro, RCA's go-to-guy for orchestral pop, recorded two LPs featuring music from the show, including compositions by Jerry Goldsmith, Morton Stevens, Walter Scharf, Lalo Schifrin and others. (Teddy Randazzo recorded an equivalent album for the show's spin off, *The Girl from U.N.C.L.E.*)

It wasn't until 2002 that *Film Score Monthly* released the first of three double-CD volumes of original music from *The Man from U.N.C.L.E.*, followed by a single-CD volume of music from the eight *Man from U.N.C.L.E.* movies that repackaged two-part TV episodes for the international market. These volumes feature dynamic jazz-influenced themes and cues by the afore-

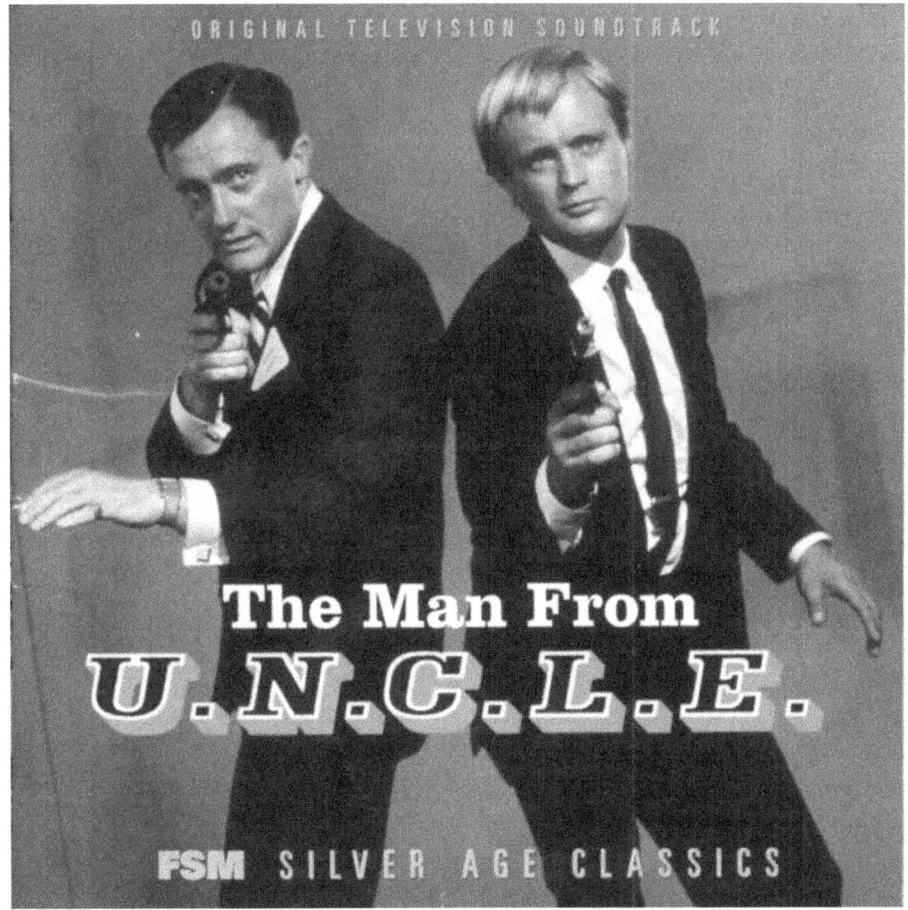

Many Hollywood composers contributed to *The Man from U.N.C.L.E.* (1964–1968), with Jerry Goldsmith delivering the dynamic main theme. (CD cover appears courtesy of Film Score Monthly; graphic design by Joe Sikoryak.)

mentioned artists, as well as Gerald Fried, Robert Drasnin, Richard Shores and Nelson Riddle. Credit for the main theme goes to Goldsmith, who had already become a top-flight composer on the Hollywood scene. Using a speedy 5/4 rhythm, Goldsmith combined militaristic percussion with the brass attacking the theme's stealthy melody. Drawing material from such episodes as "The Very Important Zombie Affair" and "The Dippy Blonde Affair," the composers never failed to score the show's ridiculous plots with a sound that is seriously engaging and frequently adventurous.

One year after *U.N.C.L.E.* was introduced, NBC debuted *I Spy*, a series about two globetrotting agents working undercover as a tennis pro and his trainer. The show was shot on location in Hong Kong, Japan, Mexico, Europe, North Africa and the USA. The exotic locations offered key composer Earle Hagen (along with Carl Brandt, Hugo Friedhofer, Nathan Van Cleave and Robert Drasnin) the opportunity to explore various musical styles and orchestration options. Hagen, whose "Harlem Nocturne" was used as the theme for Mickey Spillane's *Mike Hammer* TV program (1984), characterized his scoring style as "semi-jazz," with passages in the operatic or avant-garde styles. The theme, which is in ¾ time and features electric bass, pizzicato strings, woodwinds and brass, was precisely arranged to accompany the title sequence's combination of live action, animation and graphic art.

A veteran of *U.N.C.L.E.* (and author of its associated dance hit "The Man from T.H.R.U.S.H."), Schifrin went on to score *Mission: Impossible* for CBS. In so doing, he composed TV's greatest spy theme. Taking rhythmic inspiration from Goldsmith's *U.N.C.L.E.* theme, Schifrin cranked up the tension with an arrangement that lives up to the title sequence's burning fuse. Over a dense layer of percussion, the Eastern-tinged melody plays on piccolos, electric harpsichord, throbbing electric bass, blasting brass and economically arranged strings. He also delivered pop-funk swagger ("Jim on the Move" and "Wide Willy"), romantic strings ("Operation Charm"), Eastern intrigue and instrumentation ("The Sniper"), cool jazz ("Barney Does It All"), funky blues ("Mission Blues"), *Peter Gunn*-type crime jazz ("Self Destruct"), Spanish now-sound pop ("Affair in Madrid") and so much more. Fans of the trip hop group Portishead will recognize the loop from the group's first single, "Sour Times" (1996), that opens Schifrin's "Danube Incident."

Big Screen Spies—Beyond Bond

Matt Helm, Harry Palmer, Derek Flint, and Modesty Blaise are just a few of the big-screen spies who rode James Bond's coattails in the box office phenomenon that ruled the '60s. Many had strong-selling soundtrack releases. Popular interest was so intense that record companies also released spy-themed cover albums, such as *Music to Read James Bond By* and Hugo Montenegro's *Come Spy with Me*.

2. Spy Symphonies

Earle Hagen's music for *I Spy* (1965–1968) evokes the show's many exotic locales. (CD cover appears courtesy of Film Score Monthly; graphic design by Joe Sikoryak.)

In 1965, two notable spy films were released to compete against Bond at the peak of his popularity. One of them, *The Spy Who Came in from the Cold*, attempted to inject some reality into the spy craze. Sol Kaplan's score boasts noir-like atmosphere, but it didn't prove particularly popular.

Landing halfway between *Thunderball* and *The Spy Who Came in from the Cold* in terms of filmic tone was *The Ipcress File*, about the bespectacled agent Harry Palmer. Like Bond, Palmer had the benefit of spying to a John Barry score. Along with *The Quiller Memorandum* (1966), *The Ipcress File* represents Barry's only significant non–Bond spy scoring. The composer made a distinct effort to differentiate the Palmer sound through mood and, most noticeably, instrumentation. Barry avoids the bombast of a typical Bond score by using smaller scale orchestration featuring vibes, piano, guitar, and, most notably, a cimbalom (a melancholy-sounding stringed instrument traditionally played by Hungarian Jews or gypsies).

"*The Ipcress File* was like my homage to *The Third Man*," Barry recounted. "I knew that was how I wanted to do it from the start, but obviously I wasn't going to use a zither." (Pan Macmillan, p. 170)

Some of *Ipcress*' quieter passages that rely on trombone, French horn and the piano's lower register would not sound out of place on *Thunderball*, but

For *The Ipcress File* (1965), composer John Barry creates a more intimate, mysterious sound than he typically used for the James Bond movies. (CD cover appears courtesy of Silva Screen Records.)

the general absence of shock and awe rhapsodies helps differentiate *Ipcress* from the Bond scores. In fact, some of the jazzier sections wouldn't sound out of place on one of the crime jazz scores of the '50s. And, years later, some of the murkier cues turned up on the exemplary trip-hop compilation *Coffee Table Music*. Among that album's contributors was Grantby, a British production duo named for the villain in *The Ipcress File*. The score is the most memorable of the three Palmer soundtracks.

The second Palmer film, *Funeral in Berlin*, featured a score by Konrad Elfers, whose filmography is relatively sparse. Elfers' score is more traditional in approach than Barry's. As Barry adapted Herrmann's modernist method of brief and repetitive melodic patterns, Elfers leaned heavily on the romantic classical style that pre-dated Herrmann. That's not to say *Funeral in Berlin* sounds antiquated. At times, Elfers breaks from straight orchestral to incorporate swinging jazz passages and unexpected instrumentation. There are hints of 20th-century dissonance, but just as often the score exhibits the pure-toned tendencies of the 19th century.

The third and final Palmer film, *Billion Dollar Brain*, features another relatively schizophrenic score. The opening bars of its theme, by Richard Rodney Bennett, sound like something from Stravinsky's "Le Sacre du Printemps." But then a swelling piano motif interjects an emotional feeling akin to Tchaikovsky. Bennett used three grand pianos with orchestra to achieve the grand sound. Adding an additional unexpected wrinkle, he also employed a French electronic instrument called an ondes martenot throughout the score. It sounds very much like the ghostly theremin (although it employs a keyboard, whereas the theremin does not).

Unlike the Palmer movies, *Our Man Flint* (1966) and *In Like Flint* (1967) satirized the Bond films, but their scores by Goldsmith are not simply spoofs of Barry's work. The music is appropriately cartoonish and satirical in tone. The guitar-driven surf 'n' samba theme music—as *Guitar Player* magazine put it—only loosely sends-up "The James Bond Theme." Otherwise, Goldsmith's scores are lighter and jazzier than the 007 scores, which were almost always deadly serious and heavily orchestral. Aside from guitars, Goldsmith makes great use of percussion and keyboards (with weird electronic effects produced on a Solovox and Thomas organ). Many fine jazz soloists were also employed, including crime jazz drummer Shelly Manne, Red Mitchell (bass) and Dick Nash (trombone).

Another crime jazz veteran, Elmer Bernstein, delivered a thoroughly swinging score for *The Silencers* (1966), the first of the Matt Helm spy spoofs. Crooner Dean Martin stars, but Vikki Carr sings the swinging title song, as well as "Santiago." Bernstein's score is a descendent of his earlier crime jazz scores (e.g. *The Man with the Golden Arm*), but instead of a gritty urban tone, *The Silencers* lands between Barry's worldly seriousness and Goldsmith's Hollywood playfulness. On a track like "Blast-off Minus 3," the orchestration is spare and foreboding, like a 007 score, but when the percussion kicks in it's more reminiscent of the fun, frolicking *Flint* scores.

Schifrin scored the first sequel, *Murderer's Row* (1966), displaying the musical style that would become unmistakable to millions on his *Mission: Impossible* soundtrack. The exuberant orchestrations, the bold use of rumbling electric bass and pulse-pounding percussion, and the clear affinity for Latin lounge numbers are all on display. While the score is not essential Schifrin, it's clear that it served as a training ground for his TV work in particular.

The same can be said of *The Liquidator*, which features Schifrin's iconic use of low flute over bass, bongos and muted brass on "The Killer." Schifrin

Although *The Liquidator* (1965) was released to take advantage of the 007-fueled spy craze, Lalo Schifrin's score doesn't imitate John Barry's James Bond sound. (CD cover appears courtesy of Film Score Monthly; graphic design by Joe Sikoryak.)

was just becoming a name in Hollywood scoring circles when he was sent to London on a mission: Score *The Liquidator*. The 1966 spy spoof about a reluctant assassin-slash-playboy-spy was filmed in 1964/1965, but needed a score quickly to take advantage of the spy movie craze. According to the booklet notes in Film Score Monthly's CD reissue, the composer decided to steer clear of penning a Barry-esque Bond score in favor of something jazzier, but still with action-packed sequences.

After *Murderer's Row*, two more Matt Helm pictures were made: *The Ambushers* (1967) and *The Wrecking Crew* (1969), with comedic action scores by Hugo Montenegro.

Long before it became a legitimate James Bond movie, *Casino Royale* (1967) was one of the more famous spy spoofs. Taking its title (but little else) from the original Ian Fleming novel, this star-studded dud features a slick comic score by hit-maker Bacharach, with help from Herb Alpert & the Tijuana Brass (on the theme) and Dusty Springfield ("The Look of Love"). On instrumental tracks like "Money Penny Goes for Broke" and "Hi There, Miss Goodthighs" Bacharach provides some of the most memorable pop scoring of the '60s. The combination of muted brass, swirling violins, frisky percussion and sexy come-hither mood perfectly captures the era of the easy lay. Elsewhere, the mood is exuberantly comic, and could convince a listener to think that the movie is actually funny.

In 1966, yet another spy reached the silver screen, and this time it was a woman, *Modesty Blaise*. Based on the long-running British cartoon character created by Peter O'Donnell, *Modesty Blaise* is a wildly psychedelic take on the spy genre. John Dankworth, whose other "spy" work includes *Fathom* (1967) and *Salt & Pepper* (1968), provided a lively jazz-pop score. The theme song, with vocals by David & Jonathan, has that distinctive British '60s feeling that mixes wistfulness and whimsicality. The score rarely strays into seriousness or true tension, favoring cartoon-like excitement and picturesque cheer. For the climactic action sequence, Dankworth breaks out the military brass and drum rolls to comic effect, but the long-time Melody Maker Jazz Poll winner soon returns to the jazzier vibe to which he is better suited.

On *Salt & Pepper*, Dankworth hooked up with one of the film's stars, Sammy Davis Jr., for a couple of upbeat vocal numbers, including the swinging title track. Davis and Peter Lawford play mod nightclub owners who moonlight as secret agents. Dankworth's score focuses on big band jazz, eschewing the jazz pop experimentation of *Modesty Blaise*. Tracks like "Fine Flavour" and "Chase in a Mini Moke" are dashing bits of comic spy scoring. "Submarine Chase" relies on the simple yet insistent interplay of piano and percussion to build tension. And the suite-like "Flight for an Island" features the requisite military march motif for the action climax, but later exchanges the snare drums for congas and a modern jazz approach. The ragtime styling of "Fine Trad Flavour" acts as a reminder that the plot to hold England hostage with a

John Dankworth's somewhat cartoonish score for *Modesty Blaise* (1966) evokes the film's comic strip origins. (CD cover appears courtesy of Harkit Records; graphic design by Tim Creasey, based on original artwork by Bob Peak.)

nuclear submarine was all in fun. The flick spawned a sequel, *One More Time*, two years later.

Movies that combined espionage and comedy were difficult to avoid in the late '60s. Surprisingly, when comedian/composer Steve Allen scored such a picture, *A Man Called Dagger* (1967), the tone was anything but comedic. Although "The Swingin' Dagger Theme" riffs on a countermelody based on "The James Bond Theme," most of the score steers clear of satire. Allen's score takes most of its inspiration from Mancini's use of jazz combo on *Peter Gunn*, with occasional lapses into Barry-esque use of low flutes and muted brass during tension-building passages. The arrangements and orchestration by B-movie specialist Ronald Stein are lean, nimble and highly effective.

A sporadically effective but otherwise less satisfying spy score is Bert Kaempfert's *A Man Could Get Killed* (1966). While the composer of such hits as "Danke Schoen" and "Bye Bye Blues" occasionally delivers a compellingly spy-like passage, he often resorts to Latin-tinged romantic balladry using "Strangers in the Night" as inspiration. Fans of that tune will probably enjoy Kaempfert's seemingly endless variations, but fans of spy scores are likely to become frustrated with the erratic mood. The orchestration—complete with Kaempfert's prominent use of electric bass, pizzicato strings and high brass—is pleasant albeit underwhelming.

While spy movies of the '60s often went for laughs, this escapist genre struggled to be taken seriously during the '70s. A popular non–Bond espionage thriller of that decade is *Three Days of the Condor* (1976), which features a smooth jazz score by Dave Grusin. While this super-slick soundtrack has its fans, it also serves as an example of why the '70s wasn't a great period for spy scores. The theme's soothing lounge atmosphere fails to elicit the thrills one associates with near-miss assassination attempts (a plot feature). Cues such as "Flight of the Condor" and "Out to Lunch" blend slapping bass, soaring strings, cool key textures, wah guitars, funky drumming and soulful horns to pleasing effect, but there isn't even a hint of intrigue or danger in it.

Roy Budd faired better in creating a compelling spy sound. He scored a handful of British spy thrillers in the '70s—including three in 1974 alone—that are stylistically consistent with his work on crime films in general. Although Budd's *Get Carter* features a more memorable theme, his dark and moody *The Black Windmill* (1974) is a more rewarding opportunity to hear him contribute an entire score without the distraction of guest artists. On the opening track, "Kidnapped," the music establishes a strong sense of drama and action by eschewing a straightforward melodic structure, and relies on restless rhythm to move the cue forward. Low bass and exotic percussion provide solid support for somewhat unresolved melodic fragments from brass, strings and piano with electronic embellishments. The end result is the sound of pulsating tension and desperate action. Like Schifrin, Budd's prominent use of bass and percussion over spacious orchestral textures is a hallmark of the '70s thriller sound. The use of electronic embellishment serves as a precursor for the style of thriller scoring that predominates in contemporary entertainment. Although electric bass frequently figures in the mix, Budd also makes use of acoustic bass in both dramatic passages ("The Plant") and jazz club settings ("Cassette Jazz"). The latter track is an outstanding showcase for Budd's piano virtuosity; the former child prodigy was named best pianist five years in a row in a UK jazz poll. While that track is exemplary of his masterful jazz chops, the soundtrack is full of outstanding examples of his ability to compose and orchestrate highly listenable spy soundtracks. On "Diamonds" Budd uses deep bass sonorities created by orchestra, electronics and gong to create a cavernous sound space in which trumpet flares flutter out of the darkness. Underpinned by a strong drum beat and percussion, and moved forward by an acoustic bass solo, darkness turns to light as string textures shimmer and explode into a shower of glittering light. Budd would employ variations on the dark to light/light to dark motif on several other crime and thriller scores. A similar effect is created on *The Black Windmill*, but at a much quicker tempo, on the action-oriented "The Chase" and "Free Tarrant."

Engineer Paul Fishman recollected in the booklet notes of the CD reissue how Budd's music (which is co-credited to producer Jack Fishman on several key tracks) "was the creation of a musical identity, called the Drabble sound ... a bit like a musical version of Pavlov's Dog theory but for thrillers— chilling on demand." Fishman added that the musical idea convinced director Don Siegel to commission Budd.

Budd and actor Michael Caine "teamed up" again for *The Marseille Con-*

Roy Budd scored several Michael Caine thrillers, including *The Black Windmill* (Universal Pictures, 1974). His distinctive action scores are edgy and atmospheric, with jazzy interludes.

tract (a.k.a. *The Destructors*, 1974). It stands up as one of the best spy soundtracks of the '70s. The theme is propulsive and sweeping, with tense passages highlighted by percussionist Chris Karan's tablas, cimbalom and electronic warbling. The standout track is a slick bit of up-tempo action funk, with effects-laden saxophone and percolating proto-techno flourishes, called "Jazz It Up." *Contract* may not be a classic spy film, but its soundtrack is timeless, as it seamlessly blends jazz sensibility, ethnic instruments and electronics with powerful orchestral sounds.

Budd's score for *The Internecine Project* (1974) wouldn't have sounded out of place in *The Black Windmill* or *The Marseille Contract*. Strident strings, subtle electronics, conga- and tabla-spiced rhythm sections, cimbalom accents and thick rolling bass lines make for tense moods of intrigue that threaten to erupt into violent action. This musical recipe stirs one's appetite for mystery and danger, and has made Budd among the most sampled film composers by today's imaginative electronic music artists.

Budd also scored *Foxbat* (1977), a Hong Kong–set action flick co-scripted by 007 veteran director Terence Young. The haunting theme incorporates "Oriental" musical inflections for Cantonese flavor, and cimbalom for spy credibility, as strings carry the vaguely romantic melody. Other cues embrace blaxploitation style, with wah guitars alongside heavy percussion and orchestra. Even with its wall-to-wall action intensity, *Foxbat* also has room for heady atmospherics and psychedelic flourishes. It may not have the name recognition of soundtracks like *Get Carter* and *Diamonds*, but *Foxbat* features some of Budd's best work.

Just as Barry was the U.K.'s musical gift to spy cinema in the '60s, Budd was licensed to thrill in the '70s.

Continental Ops—The Spy Craze in Europe

Although Great Britain originated the spy craze, Hollywood was not alone in capitalizing on its popularity. Germany got into the act with several films about—of all things—an FBI agent in New York City. Eight "Jerry Cotton" movies—from *Schüsse aus dem Geigenkasten* (*Jerry Cotton G-Man Agent C.I.A.*, 1965) to *Der Tod im Roten Jaguar* (*Death in a Red Jaguar*, 1968)—were filmed in New York between 1965 and 1968, but received very limited distribution in the U.S. The ever-imaginative Peter Thomas scored them all.

To hear Thomas' music for the first time is to feel giddy with the discovery of a singular talent. The German composer's wild big band arrangements are peppered with an assortment of bizarre stylistic jolts and sonic surprises. Gunfire, revving motors and screams are just some of the elements heard in Thomas' spastic beat music concoctions. Blaring brass, jangly guitar rhythms, organ fills and scat vocals all have their place in the Jerry Cotton scores. In a way, Thomas' short attention span theater of the ears was perfect for the New

Peter Thomas' scores for the "Jerry Cotton" spy movies are dynamic and cartoonish, and excellent examples of the European spy soundtracks of the '60s. (CD cover appears courtesy of Crippled Dick Hot Wax; graphic design by Töni Schifer.)

York setting. Every element competes for attention and never lingers long enough to become boring.

Stylistically, the Cotton scores have less in common with the spy sound of London or Hollywood than Rome, where CineCittà Studios churned out a steady stream of lighthearted, romantic spy spoofs such as *Agente speciale LK, Agente 077—dall'oriente con furore, Missione morte molo 83, Due mafiosi contro Goldginger, Kiss Kiss Bang Bang, Supercolpo de sette miliardi* and *Kill!*

Piero Piccioni scored *Agente 077—dall'oriente con furore* (*Agent 077— Fury in the Orient*, 1965) and *Missione morte molo 83* (*M.M.M. 83*, 1965). Lydia Macdonald sings the English-language, Latin-esque theme "Before It's

Too Late" and the swinging "You Wonderful You." The instrumentals compellingly blend moody crime jazz brass and piano with restless exotic percussion. Jazzy, Latin and orchestral variations on the theme are heard in nightclub and mystery cues.

Piccioni's music for *Missione morte molo 83* takes a different approach. With its prominent solo trumpet and acoustic guitar, the theme sounds more like a jaunty spaghetti western, not a spy theme. Other cues, like "Mission Death at Dock 83," "The Chase" and "Investigations," are thoroughly crime jazz.

Despite its rather obvious name, Piero Umiliani's *Due mafiosi contro Goldginger* (*Two Mafiosi Against Goldginger*, 1965) has little in common with Barry's music of the period. Umiliani's score is typical of most Italian spy jobs in that the mood is breezy and easy or comically frantic, with occasional allowances for intrigue and drama. In *Goldginger*'s case, the serious passages draw considerable inspiration from exotic classical themes like "Bolero." Umiliani handles the balance admirably, investing each mood with the melodic ingenuity that would mark his work throughout the '60s and '70s. Umiliani also scored the sequel *Due mafiosi contro Al Capone* (*Two Mafiosi Against Al Capone*, 1966).

Umiliani's work also is heard in *Requiem per un agente segreto* (*Requiem for a Secret Agent*, 1967). His jazz guitar-driven score frequently depends on the melody of the theme "Don't Ever Let Me Go" (sung by Lydia MacDonald). Yet, there is plenty of variety in the score, even if the melody rarely changes.

Bruno Nicolai's *Upperseven* (*The Man to Kill*, 1965) features an elegantly swinging theme that serves as the basis for several intrigue and chase cues. Sultry woodwinds float over cool organ and vibraphone tones as reverb-drenched guitar notes ring out the theme. Elsewhere, electric bass replaces guitar for even murkier moods of surveillance and subterfuge.

Nicolai also provided a jauntily psychedelic score for *Agente speciale LK* (*Lucky the Inscrutable*, 1967). Most of Nicolai's cheerful arrangements are built around organ, jangly guitar rhythms and monosyllabic male and female vocals. The go-go "party" music—with stroboscopic organ effects—is lively and irresistible. Like so many Italian scores of its era, *Agente speciale LK* sidesteps seriousness in favor of fun. For example, "Spy Chase" comes off as a playful lark. In fact, Nicolai's score often recalls the soundtracks that accompany action comedies of the silent film era. Melancholic accordion or spry piano runs of a distinctly Italian character can be heard, accompanied by staccato guitar rhythms, thumping bass counterpoint and a quick drum beat.

Nicolai also scored *Kiss Kiss Bang Bang* (1966), delivering a jazzy, elegant score that features an ingratiatingly catchy theme and smoky moods of intrigue and romance.

A close associate of Nicolai—none other than Ennio Morricone—also scored his share of Italian spy flicks. Among his best efforts is *Slalom* (*Snow Job*, 1965). The score features fab vocal work by Alessandroni's chorus that chants "Slalom" on the surf-spy-ski theme song. Elsewhere, Morricone provides Arabian parlor music, bongo suspense and lush orchestral moods punctuated by flitting musical gestures, probably meant to personify the movements of downhill skiers.

Nicolai and Morricone teamed up on *OK Connery* (a.k.a. *Operation Kid Brother*, 1967), which is a pretty weak novelty act of a '60s spy movie starring

Ennio Morricone and Bruno Nicolai's score for *OK Connery* (a.k.a. *Operation Kid Brother*, 1967) outshines the gimmicky movie, which stars Sean Connery's brother Neil. (CD cover appears courtesy of Digitmovies Alternative Entertainment; graphic design by Claudio Fuiano.)

Sean Connery's real brother Neil and several James Bond regulars (like Bernard Lee and Lois Maxwell). The score is among the best non–Barry spy scores ever. The up-tempo theme, "Man for Me," builds like a Bond theme, but its big band rock feel, staccato rhythm and background vocal chorus make it sound distinctively Italian, despite the English vocal by Christy. On the cue called "Connery" the composers employ a counter melody that obliquely quotes "The James Bond Theme." Aside from the rocking yeah-yeah dance number "Allegri Ragazzi" and a couple of lush love themes, most of the score is jazzy, rhythmic, intriguing and action packed.

Another terrific Italian spy soundtrack is *Troppo per vivere ... poco per morire* (*Too Much for Living ... Little in Order to Die,* 1967). Composer Francesco De Masi employs the services of vocalists Raoul and Lara Saint Paul, as well as trumpeter Cicci Santucci, flautist Gino Marinacci, and Alessandroni's Cantori Moderni, for a blend of slinky lounge jazz, fuzz-toned crime jazz, and orchestral action and intrigue.

Another Morricone spy score of note is *Il serpente* (*Night Flight from Moscow,* 1972). The mostly atonal music for this Italian/French movie is a perfect example of Morricone's thriller work during the '70s. Full of turgid, jagged orchestration, the composer balances *Il serpente* with a romantic theme, "Tema Per Una Donna Sola"; a pop instrumental, "Nadine"; and a vocal performance by Italy's most famous soundtrack female singer, Edda Dell'Orso.

Italian spy films often were multinational productions. Another notable entry was the Italian-French-Spanish production of *Colpo grossa a Galata Bridge* (*That Man in Istanbul,* 1965), about a jet-setting playboy who helps a female FBI agent save a nuclear scientist from a megalomaniac and rival Chinese spies. George Garvarentz provided a Turkish-tinged score, using a full orchestra. On tracks like "Fight at the Turkish Bath" and "Chase on the Calatma Bridge," the composer's zest for Eastern flavor is fully on display. By using plenty of percussion, including kettledrums and tympani, Garvarentz cooks up a good deal of tension that threatens to explode when churning brass and strings enter the mix. On tracks like "The Bulldozer Leads the Dance," the orchestra sounds like an angry earthmover as it plows through a typically robust arrangement. The composer lightens up for the song "Love Was Right Here All the Time" (Buddy Kaye's lyrics sung by Richard Anthony), but the song is disposable in comparison to the relentlessly tense score.

Another multinational production, *Kill!* (1971)—about an Interpol agent on the take from international drug rings—has a (pardon the pun) killer score by Berto Pisano and Jaques Chaumont. The theme sticks in one's mind like an ice pick. Its stabbing rhythm, pounding congas, death ray electric guitar and stroboscopic orchestration are brilliantly executed. There are several tracks based on this theme, including the famous vocal version featuring Doris Troy (who went on to provide backing vocals on Pink Floyd's *Dark Side of the Moon*).

What's even more impressive about the *Kill!* score is the fact that it offers much more than the theme. It is rife with mysterious melodies, superb abstract orchestral cues, psycho beat, sitar exotica and a sexy whispered vocal performance by actress Jean Seberg. *Kill!* is a critical Italian soundtrack.

Another contemporary of Umiliani, Nicolai and company is Luis Bacalov. Probably his best spy score is *Rebus* (1968), featuring two sultry vocal performances by star Ann-Margaret. Set in Beirut, Bacalov's score delivers the expected Middle Eastern flavor, but does so with a surf-beat flair. Organ, electric guitars, brass and strings, backed by a crackling rhythm section, are often accompanied by native instruments such as the oud, setar, daf and tanbur. This is sometimes juxtaposed with hillbilly banjo and double bass. Listeners won't know whether to smoke a hookah or reach for the moonshine. Taken out of context, the stylistic stretch is pretty odd and pretty funny. The unexpected mix of styles, however, makes *Rebus* one of the most entertaining Italian spy soundtracks.

Another outstanding Italian entry is *Dick Smart 2.007* (1967). The score sets itself apart by favoring the South American sounds of bossa nova and samba, with loads of thrilling percussion. With titles like "My Name Is Smart ... Dick Smart" and "Kiss Kiss Girl Girl," it's clear that the movie doesn't take itself too seriously. The Spanish-born Mario Nascimbene also scored *Where the Spies Are* (1965) and *Operazione paradiso* (*Kiss the Girls and Make Them Die*, 1966).

On one of the few occasions when an Italian composer scored a British spy film, the soundtrack proved to be hard-edged and dark compared to the music featured in all–Italian productions. Piccioni's intense music for *Alistair Maclean's Puppet on a Chain* (1971) suited its subject matter (drug trafficking) and its gritty era. The film, which boasts a speedboat chase often compared to the car chase in *Bullitt* (1968), offered Piccioni yet another opportunity to deliver a Hammond-heavy score with psychedelic atmospheres and funky action. The theme is bustling big band funk situated somewhere between Bernstein and Isaac Hayes. Often times the sonic palette is limited to rumbling bass and crackling drums, intermittently joined by spacious organ chords and acid-tinged guitar solos. The track list reads like an Amsterdam police report: "Drug Dealers," "Psychedelic Mood," "Narcotics Bureau," "Drugs Hypnosis" and "Night Club"—all of which live up to their seedy promise.

Spies were slightly less popular in France, with a few notable exceptions. OSS 117 is the code name for Hubert Bonisseur de la Bath, a freelancing American secret agent of French origin. The character originated in paperback novels during the '50s, but didn't receive a successful film translation until the early '60s. In fact, the actor who provided the voice (but not the physical embodiment) of OSS 117 (Jean-Pierre Duclos) also provided the voice for the French-dubbed Bond films. In terms of cinematic thrills, the OSS 117 films fall somewhere between the 007 films and the fly-by-night copycat spoofs made in Italy. Four films were released between 1963 and 1966, and all featured Michel Magne's playfully imaginative scores befitting such settings as Thailand, Japan and Brazil. Along the way there are traditional crime jazz cues, pop vamps with scat vocals, brassy big band jams, cacophonous carnival numbers, furious samba dances and stately oriental overtures. The OSS 117 scores aren't likely to remind anyone of Barry's 007 work or Goldsmith's *Flint* scores. They're more in keeping with the comical Italian spy sound, but not to the point of mimicry.

Around the same time, Magne scored the *Fantomas* film trilogy (1964, 1965 and 1966). The villainous title character pursued by agents of Scotland Yard had been around since 1911; in fact, the early French "pulp" stories were adapted to the screen during the silent film era. The '60s version seemed to draw inspiration from the James Bond villain Blofeld by dressing the character in a monochromatic Nehru-collared suit. Magne's approach is orchestral, with occasional jazzy elements, and resembles in tone Goldsmith's *Flint* scores. Notably, Universal's CD release doesn't contain the original soundtrack, but a re-recording designed to sound like the original, even using the same instrumentation. The original tapes and manuscripts were lost in a fire, so arranger/composer Raymond Alessandrini recreated the score based on how it is heard in the movies.

Another standout French spy film (actually French-Italian) is *Le Magnifique* (*The Magnificent One* or *How to Destroy the Reputation of the Greatest Secret Agent*, 1973), about a second-rate spy novelist and his fictional creation. Claude Bolling's score is suitably light-hearted, yet sophisticated. Bolling uses Latin rhythms, but plays it for romantic effect. The best tracks, like "Karpoff," provide a sense of danger and intrigue to the high-flying fantasy sequences. The grooviest track is "Pop Mod," a laidback go-go number.

Conspiracy Theories

In this glancing review of the enormous spy genre it quickly becomes clear that naming every related film and television score is a near impossibility. The craze was so widespread during the '60s that one could devote an entire book to the soundtracks and novelty hits alone.

So, what makes spy soundtracks so appealing? Undoubtedly, the music owes its enduring attraction to the larger-than-life character of the subject itself. Who hasn't wondered what it would be like to infiltrate an underground lair with fantastic gadgets in hand and a quip on one's lips? The fantasy of single-handedly saving the world from a power-mad lunatic is as powerful today as it was during the Cold War, which provided a potent breeding ground during those "spy-crazy '60s."

While spy soundtracks helped to romanticize espionage during the age of imminent nuclear apocalypse, they also provided a bit of tongue-in-cheek sophistication during the retro '90s. Today, in the post–9/11 age of reality angst, the spy soundtracks of the '60s, in particular, offer a nostalgic reminder of a more innocent era. Like the song says: "You only live twice, or so it seems.... One life for yourself and one for your dreams."

12 Essential Spy Soundtracks

Goldfinger (1964)—John Barry
The Man from U.N.C.L.E. (1964–1968)—Jerry Goldsmith and others
Thunderball (1965)—John Barry
The Ipcress File (1965)—John Barry
Our Man Flint / In Like Flint (1966/1967)—Jerry Goldsmith
The Silencers (1966)—Elmer Bernstein
Mission: Impossible (1966–1973)—Lalo Schifrin
You Only Live Twice (1967)—John Barry
OK Connery (1967)—Ennio Morricone and Bruno Nicolai
Diamonds Are Forever (1971)—John Barry
Kill! (1971)—Berto Pisano and Jaques Chaumont
The Marseille Contract (1974)—Roy Budd

Chapter 3
Sexploitation Serenade

Sex sells. The motion picture medium—like any other visual art form—encourages the exploration of sexuality. In fact, salacious nudity in motion pictures is nearly as old as the format itself. It took less than a year for early filmmakers to realize that there is no subject more alluring than sex, or at the very least the female nude. In 1896, actress Louise Willy reportedly stripped for the French film *Le Bain* (*The Bath*). The same year saw the exhibition of *The May Irwin Kiss* (a.k.a. *The Kiss*, or *The Irwin-Rice Kiss*), which featured a scandalously prolonged close-up of a man and woman locking lips. Once the film industry really kicked into gear, the first Hollywood female stars to appear nude were swimming and diving champ Annette Kellermann (in *Daughter of the Gods*) and a 16-year-old June Caprice (in *The Ragged Princess*). Both films were released during the same week in 1916 by pioneer studio Fox Film Corporation. All through Hollywood's silent era there were numerous films featuring naked or half-naked females. From epics like *The Birth of a Nation* (1915) and *Intolerance* (1916) to flapper flicks like *Lover's Island* (1925) and *Hula* (1927), skin was most definitely in.

Although the first known pornographic film (the little seen but suggestively titled *A Free Ride*) screened in 1915, explicit sex acts weren't shown in early Hollywood films, despite the frequent baring of flesh. Nonetheless, early exploitation films like *Inside of the White Slave Traffic* (1913) and *Damaged Goods* (1914) promised sex in their advertising campaigns. Not surprisingly, decadent content shocked enough audience members to inspire the creation of a prohibitive production code (a.k.a. the Hays Code) by the early '30s, which restricted the depiction of nudity, sexuality, violence, drug use and other "morally offensive" activities. Until the Code was in full effect in 1934, many Hollywood productions challenged the morality crackdown with a parade of pictures that brazenly depicted the pursuit of sex, if not the act itself. Whether a film featured a liberated Joan Crawford parading about in her underwear (*Dance, Fools, Dance*, 1931) or a brazen suggestion from the ever-wanton Mae "I'm No Angel" West, Hollywood filmmakers made a point of challenging the Hays Code. It only served to hasten the censure. In fact, the Code blocked the U.S. distribution of the Czechoslovakian film *Ecstasy* (1933), which was the first feature film to depict sexual intercourse (though not in the graphic sense common to modern porn). It remains famous for its seemingly aroused performance by future Hollywood star Hedy Lamarr (then known as Hedwig Kiesler). The Hays Code squashed the Jazz Age's sexual revolution on screen, just as the Great Depression and World War II inhibited it on a broad social scale.

Not surprisingly, the Hays Code was abolished in 1967, due in part to a new sexual revolution ushered in by Elvis Presley's swiveling hips, the pin-up culture cultivated by World War II G.I.s, the advent of the birth control pill, Hugh Hefner's *Playboy* lifestyle revolution, the groundbreaking "Kinsey Report," a rising counterculture (courtesy of the Beats and Hippies), and a shift in the status quo (thanks to the Civil Rights and Feminism movements). Like seduction itself, one thing led to another, climaxing with a controversial little film called *Deep Throat* (1973).

So what is the soundtrack for sex and seduction? Is it a sultry Latin dance number, smoky torch song, the bump and grind of funky soul, or the vivacious shake of rock and roll? The short answer is: all of these things and more.

Skin-dependent Films

To see nudity and sexual situations in legitimate Hollywood features, one is generally limited to the pre–Code and post–Code eras of filmmaking. While the Hays Code imposed limits on the big studios, outlaw independent impresarios like Dwain Esper, Kroger Babb and David Friedman road-showed the grindhouse circuit during the '30s, '40s and '50s, exhibiting their low-budget exploitation flicks for the more daring moviegoer. By selling sin in the guise of seemingly well-intentioned sex hygiene scare films and vice racket exposés, the legendary "Forty Thieves" and their progenitors managed to show audiences a bit of bare thigh, breast or bottom before hastily packing up and hightailing it to the next town. When the raincoat crowd got their fill of one type of exploitation flick—such as the natives-gone-wild "goona-goona" pictures—the skin-dependent filmmakers produced pasty and g-string burlesque shorts or not-so-naughty nudist camp docudramas.

Needless to say, such skid row cinema was too low-profile to warrant legitimate soundtrack releases, not to mention an actual score. In fact, most striptease and stag films of the period featured canned recordings of generic jazz, nameless lounge exotica or incognito big band blues. Short of sitting through campy but quaint video reissues like *Teaserama* (starring Tempest Storm and Bettie Page) or *Love Moods* (starring Lili St. Cyr), the grind-curious must resort to retro rockin' strip club compilations like *The Las Vegas Grind* and *Jungle Exotica* series, or *Take It Off: Striptease Classics*. These feature long-forgotten groups with cheeky names like the Genteels, the Lushes and the Whips who cut 45s of stroll, jive and slop for seedy joints with names like Louie's Limbo Lounge and the little films they subsidized.

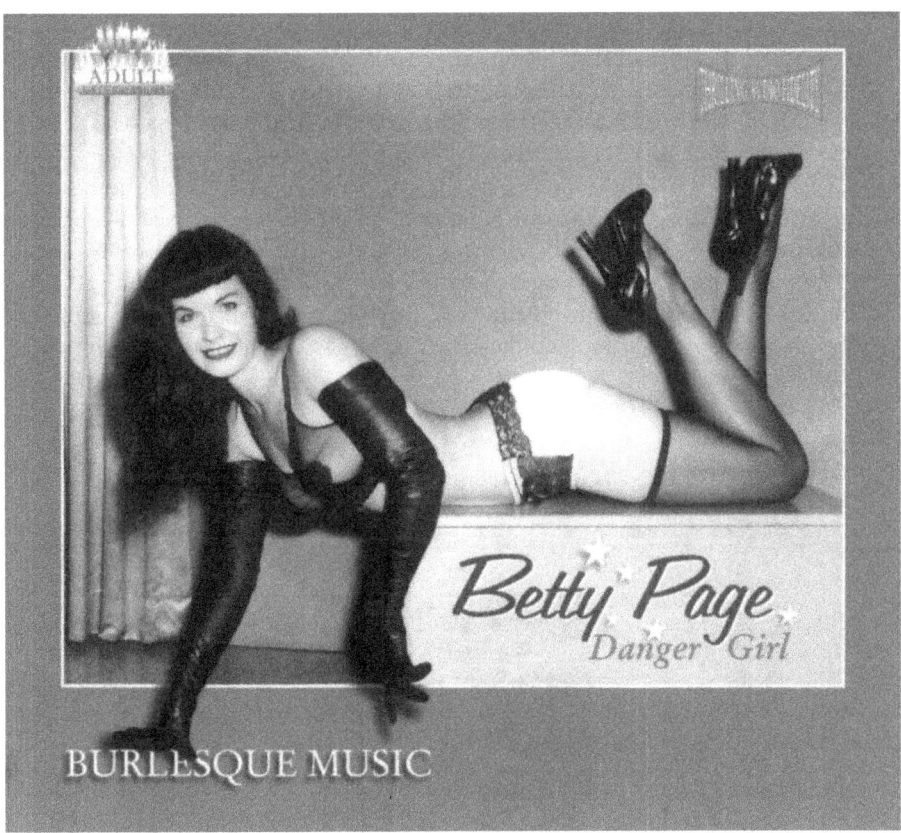

Bettie Page (a.k.a. Betty Page), the legendary pinup queen and star of sexploitation films, did much of her cheesecake and bondage shtick to the sounds of library music—like the jazzy numbers heard on the *Danger Girl* compilation. (CD cover appears courtesy of Normal Records/QDK Media; graphic design by Thomas Hartlage.)

To round out any respectable striptease "soundtrack" collection are three compilations released by Normal Records' QDK Media subsidiary during the height of the Bettie (or Betty) Page revival in the mid-to-late '90s. Subtitled *Danger Girl*, *Jungle Girl* and *Private Girl*, these high-concept imaginary soundtracks for the black-banged beauty promise "burlesque," "exotique" and "spicy" tunes, respectively. Not surprisingly, each collects late '50s and early '60s production library music for hire. Naturally, the *Danger Girl* comp favors crime jazz by such artists as a pre–Bond John Barry, Johnny Hawksworth and Robert Farnon. The *Jungle Girl* comp features exotica by library legends Nino Nardini, Roger Roger (a.k.a. Cecil Leuter) and Jack Arel, as well as more Barry, Hawksworth and many others. The *Private Girl* set is a mixed bag of lounge jazz and sultry swing by the same assortment of musicians featured on the other comps. While none of these comps scream strip-o-rama, their enclosed photo books show Bettie in all phases of dress and undress to aid the imagination.

QDK also paid homage to another icon of skin-dependent sleaze, the maverick filmmaker (and former *Playboy* photographer) Russ Meyer. The label's four-CD series features music and dialogue from 12 of the bosom maniac's soft-core features made between 1964 and 1979. (A fifth release backtracking to pre-1964 titles, like the original "nudie cutie" *The Immoral Mr. Teas*, *Wild Gals of the Naked West* and *Eve & the Handyman*, never materialized.) A handful of composers contributed to the scores of Meyer's movies, among them Igo Kantor, Bert Shefter, Paul Sawtell, William Loose and Stu Phillips (who

A number of versatile second-tier composers contributed to Russ Meyer's outrageous sexploitation films, including Paul Sawtell, Bert Shefter, Igo Kantor, William Loose and Stu Phillips. (CD cover appears courtesy of Normal Records/QDK Media; graphic design by Thomas Hartlage.)

went on to score Meyer's mainstream masterpiece *Beyond the Valley of the Dolls* in 1970).

A prolific team throughout the '60s, Sawtell and Shefter scored Meyer's *Motor Psycho*, an early entry in the '60s violent biker genre. The combustible combination of psychedelic rock and steamy jazz provides the perfect accompaniment for the road movie's saga of lawlessness and revenge.

Shefter and Sawtell perfected the *Motor Psycho* sound on Meyer's "roughie" masterpiece *Faster, Pussycat! KILL! KILL!* (1966). This time, they worked with Kantor, who scored Meyer's underground X-rated hit *Vixen*, the success of which convinced 20th Century–Fox to bring Meyer on board for *Beyond the Valley of the Dolls*. The intro from *Pussycat* is the iconic Russ Meyer soundtrack number. It combines a sublimely twisted monologue about sex and violence with a walking bass line and Philly-licked cymbal ride that lurches into a rollicking rock ode to "Pussycat's" rebellious ways—complete with "go, baby, go" taunts from the strip club patrons featured in the film's frantic opening montage. The medley-like track lurches from keyboard-fueled rock to smoky saxophone jazz to tension-building crime jazz and back again before leaning into a beat jazz vamp that wouldn't sound out of place in Mancini's *Touch of Evil*. The frenetic style-hopping perfectly complements the director's virtuoso editing style.

Loose was Meyer's main man during the '70s, providing over-the-top style-jacking splendor on *Up!*, *Mega Vixens* and *Beneath the Valley of the Ultra Vixens*. Featuring a "Greek Chorus," *Up!* comes on with a feel-good Broadway overture before resorting to clichéd comedy and melodrama cues, along with somber, classical-inspired passages. *Ultra Vixens*, which Loose scored with Paul Ruhland, embraces goodtime rock and funk along with more traditional tension-building dramatic cues and a bit of stripper sleaze.

Loose also contributed to Meyers' *Finders Keepers Lovers Weepers* (1968). The title track's frantic pace cooks up a head of steam before segueing into a nerve-rattling cue that briefly intercuts with a hard-swinging vamp. Notably, a sample of that catchy brass lick was put to good use on "History Repeating," a minor, late–1990s hit by the short-lived big beat sensation Propellerheads. The track also featured a comeback performance by the legendary James Bond theme diva Shirley Bassey, and was used in a Jaguar TV commercial.

Without a doubt, the ultimate Russ Meyer–related soundtrack is *Beyond the Valley of the Dolls* (a.k.a. *Hollywood Vixens*, 1970), but more about its terrific soundtrack in Chapter 7.

Big Budget Seduction

While Hollywood was still under the watchful eye of the Catholic Church's Legion of Decency, filmmakers nudged the envelope of acceptable onscreen sexuality with innuendo (like Lauren Bacall suggesting to Humphrey

Bogart that he "put his lips together and blow" in *To Have and Have Not*, 1944), or with symbolic imagery (like frothy waves splashing over the semi-clothed Burt Lancaster and Deborah Kerr in *From Here to Eternity*, 1953).

During the '50s, certain filmmakers pushed the boundaries of subject matter. Elia Kazan transplanted Tennessee Williams' melodrama *A Streetcar Named Desire* (1951) from Broadway, complete with its original cast. The film's hothouse atmosphere of sexual frustration is made all the more palpable by Alex North's influential jazz-tinged score.

A few years later, Kazan made a film that was even more brazen in its suggestive sexuality, as one of its characters is a "child bride." *Baby Doll* (1956) concerns a cotton gin owner married to a *Lolita*-esque teenager who is holding out on her hubby sexually until she turns 20. Another man attempts to seduce the girl and steal her husband's business. Kenyon Hopkins' sultry score, as orchestrated by Ray Heindorf, lends *Baby Doll* an atmosphere of decadent Southern charm. The lush score is like a jazz symphony, with occasional lapses into small group jazz and blues, featuring soloists on harmonica, saxophone, trumpet and guitar. The only break in musical character comes when Smiley Lewis, the legendary New Orleans R&B artist, is featured on the rollicking "Shame, Shame, Shame." The Legion of Decency condemned the film, though that hardly hurt its box office.

Another film that stirred up the gossip among genteel filmgoers was *Peyton Place* (1957), a tremendously successful melodrama based on a once-notorious bestseller. Among the film's scandalous attributes is a couple of "fast" teenage girls and another that is raped by her stepfather. Franz Waxman, a veteran of Hollywood's Golden Age, scored the picture with lush orchestration, but there isn't anything particularly "sexy" about the waltz-like main theme.

While Hollywood's '50s melodramas treated sex as a sin, the era's racy comedies poked fun at the pursuit of sex, and occasionally busted taboos, too. One of the best from the era is *The Seven Year Itch* (1955), starring Marilyn Monroe in all her skirt-blowing glory. Alfred Newman contributes the flirty, jazz-tinged score where lilting violins mingle with tinkling piano and insinuating brass, "The Tomato Upstairs" being a ripe example.

A year later came *The Girl Can't Help It* (1956), starring one of Monroe's blonde bombshell rivals, Jayne Mansfield. The giddy rock 'n' roll musical satire features a score by Lionel Newman and songs by Bobby Troup, who contributed similarly to Mansfield's next comedy, *Will Success Spoil Rock Hunter?* (1957), which is another classic sex comedy of the era. *Girl* features cameos by early rock 'n' roll legends such as Fats Domino, Little Richard, Eddie Cochran and Gene Vincent; legend has it that Elvis Presley was courted to make an appearance, but he allegedly asked for too much money. The theme song was a smash for Little Richard. Film auteur John Waters later used it on the soundtrack of his notorious trash classic *Pink Flamingos* (1972).

The most celebrated sex comedy of the '50s remains *Some Like It Hot* (1959), which the American Film Institute later named as "the funniest film ever made." Music is integral to the film's charm, as Tony Curtis and Jack Lemmon play musicians who have witnessed the Valentine's Day Massacre, and in an effort to avoid the mob, doll themselves up and join an all-female traveling jazz band featuring Monroe. The movie relies on innuendo, the cheeky kink of its cross-dressing heroes, and Monroe's undeniable sex appeal for much of its illicit kicks. Composer Adolf Deutsch supplies a mix of '20s hot jazz and pop, including period hits like "Sweet Georgia Brown" and "Down Among the Sheltering Palms." Monroe delivers memorable vocal performances on "Runnin' Wild," "I Wanna Be Loved by You" and "I'm Thru with Love."

Next to *Some Like It Hot*, the best sex comedy of the '50s must be *Pillow Talk* (1959), which stars Rock Hudson, Doris Day and Tony Randall. It was the first of three pictures the trio made. Music-making factors in this storyline, as well. Hudson plays a playboy theatrical composer who shares a telephone party line with his high-rise apartment neighbor, an interior designer

Composer Adolf Deutsch favored hot jazz and pop songs of the '20s for the soundtrack of *Some Like It Hot* (MGM/UA, 1959), Billy Wilder's sex comedy starring Jack Lemmon and Marilyn Monroe as members of a traveling "all-girl" big band. (Photograph courtesy of the John Monaghan Collection.)

(Day) who is dating his best friend, the ever-neurotic Randall. Hudson sets out to seduce Day's sexually frustrated single workingwoman, with hilarious results. To accompany Rock and Doris' onscreen sexual tension, composer Frank DeVol delivered the light-hearted pop score, which features a flirtatious duet by Hudson and Day.

In 1961, Mancini scored *Bachelor in Paradise*, a satire about a noted, jet-setting authority on romance. When the best-selling author of "How the Swedes Live" is sent to a California suburb to research "How the Americans Live," he's soon suspected of philandering with every married woman in his neighborhood. Long story short, he ends up in love with the local bachelorette.

Henry Mancini's swinging score for *Bachelor in Paradise* (1961), starring Bob Hope, evokes the film's wry examination of suburban cocktail culture. (CD cover appears courtesy of Film Score Monthly; graphic design by Joe Sikoryak.)

Despite its suggestive title, *Bachelor* fails to deliver titillation. It merits a mention, however, as an example of a Hollywood movie that promises to depict the free pursuit of sex only to settle for the ultimate entrapment of the protagonist in the marriageable arms of the leading lady. As the theme song comically suggests, the longing in the eligible bachelorette's eyes is for more closet space. Mancini's score is among his most charming cocktail concoctions.

With the arrival of the early '60s, studios became increasingly daring about making mass-market movies about prostitutes and strippers after European directors had art house hits with films like *The Nights of Cabiria* (1957) and *Never on Sunday* (1960). Among the notable Hollywood examples are *Walk on the Wild Side* (1962), *Irma La Douce* (1963) and *The Stripper* (1963).

Walk on the Wild Side is a "new kind of love story" set in and around a Depression-era New Orleans brothel, the Doll's House. Elmer Bernstein's score derives inspiration from the Big Easy's jazz traditions, but steers clear of predictability by mixing Dixie-style brass and woodwinds with the kind of full orchestration heard on Bernstein's *The Man with the Golden Arm*. The theme music, a swaggering blues number, is up to Bernstein's high standards. On a few tracks, like "Hallie's Jazz" and "Exit Kitty," Bernstein opts for the jazz combo approach. Regardless of the size of orchestration, Bernstein's jazz themes are effective at capturing the seedy allure of what the LP cover refers to as "tempestuous encounters" and "a perverse and possessive madam." Judging from Bernstein's balance of tender love themes and up-tempo jazz numbers, the film is more concerned with love among sexy trappings than sex for its own sake.

Irma La Douce, about an overzealous Parisian policeman (Jack Lemmon) who falls in love with a popular prostitute (Shirley MacLaine), was another sexy smash hit. However, the director, Billy Wilder, considered it a misfire, in part because it was a poorly conceived non-musical adaptation of the French musical using American actors. In other words, it tries to hard to be something it's not. Andre Previn's thoroughly French-sounding orchestral score transcends the film's shortcomings. The music sounds as if it's modeled on the classic musicals of M-G-M, only without the songs. While few music fans are likely to think the sound of Parisian accordions and sentimental violins are sexy, one can hardly blame Previn for taking that creative approach—especially since he won an Academy Award for his efforts.

The Stripper is a downbeat drama about a down-on-her-luck woman who starts stripping for conventions that come through her Midwestern town. Most significantly, it was the first theatrical collaboration between director Frank Schaffner and composer Goldsmith. Later, they made three powerhouse films together: *Planet of the Apes* (1968), *Patton* (1970) and *Papillon* (1973). Interestingly enough, *The Stripper* does not feature the popular David Rose song of the same title. Instead, one gets light and lively jazz numbers and more sentimental orchestral passages underscoring the main character's seedy plight.

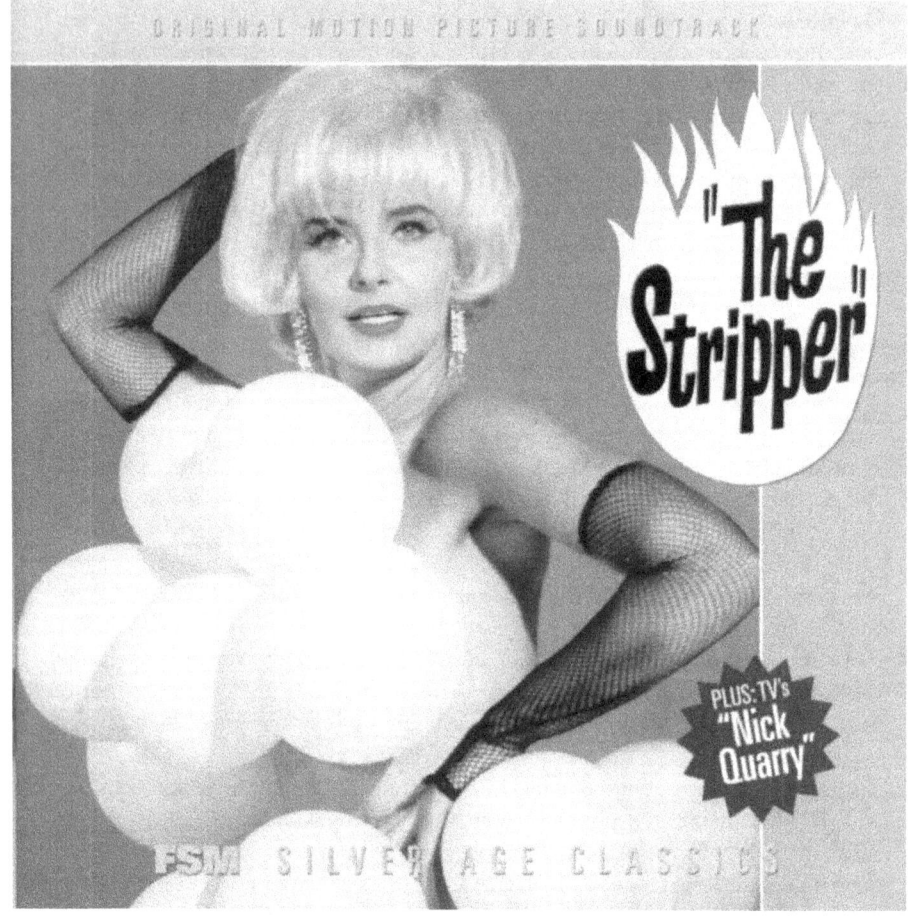

Jerry Goldsmith's *The Stripper* (1963) features a jazzy score, as well as rock 'n' roll and blues source cues. (CD cover appears courtesy of Film Score Monthly; graphic design by Joe Sikoryak.)

Goldsmith also provided a bit of randy rock 'n' roll and raunchy blues that is heard on a radio in the movie.

Six years after *Baby Doll* stirred debate by presenting an innocent teenage girl as the object of desire for unscrupulous men, maverick filmmaker Stanley Kubrick brought to the screen in 1962 Vladimir Nabokov's "unfilmable" novel *Lolita* (published in 1955). Here, the male protagonist is ostensibly a respectable and sophisticated intellectual who falls for a sexually promiscuous teenager. Although Kubrick's dark comedy is ostensibly about sexual perversion, it lacks purely exploitive sex scenes or nudity.

For *Lolita*, Nelson Riddle delivers a "pitch"-perfect score that also comments wryly on the era's clichés. Riddle proved to be an appropriate choice, given his pedigree of having made several mood music albums for postwar seduction. The sappy "Theme (Love Theme)" by Bob Harris (Stanley Kubrick's brother-in-law), which accompanies the opening image of masculine hands gingerly applying polish to the nails on a nymphet's foot, suggests that a soap opera is about to begin. The composer shows his stylistic range throughout the score. "Quilty's Theme" features intriguing harpsichord and woodwind cadences in contrast with dissonant strings that connote imminent danger. Such a piece wouldn't have sounded out of place in a spy thriller from the period. "Ramsdale" captures the bright optimism and bustling energetic character of small-town U.S.A. "Quilty's Caper" brings the swing. And "Shelley Winter's Cha Cha" presents a slightly stiff arrangement of the Latin dance to accompany Charlotte Haze's awkward seduction of the rhythmically challenged and romantically disinterested Humbert. The most recognizable number is undoubtedly "Lolita Ya-Ya." The tune, with its nubile bounce and saccharine strings, embodies the film's virginal nymphet as the ultimate candy-coated trophy in a male-dominated postwar culture of glorified youth and sexual awakening. *Lolita* stands as one of Riddle's best scores.

Two years after her debut as *Lolita*, Sue Lyon starred in *The Night of the Iguana* (1964), which placed her in a similar but abbreviated sexual situation with a defrocked preacher (Richard Burton). While the May–September dalliance is short-lived and unrequited, Burton also has erotically charged encounters with Ava Gardner, who isn't shy about keeping a pair of maraca-shaking native boys around for midnight swims. Benjamin Frankel's score for the Tennessee Williams–written film is lush and moody, but doesn't exude much of the eroticism underlying the character-driven drama. When precocious Lyon is seen cavorting with the native boys at a beachside café, it's to a quaint mariachi tune played on a phonograph. When the fiercely independent Gardner is seen cavorting with the native boys in the surf, it's to the erotically suggestive sounds of crashing waves and shaken maracas.

While *Iguana*'s exploration of

Nelson Riddle's sweet, bouncy "Lolita Ya-Ya" perfectly describes the innocently sexy *Lolita* (as played by Sue Lyon) in the film by Stanley Kubrick (MGM/UA, 1962).

sexual themes focuses on specific individuals, another film from 1964 promises to explore sexuality as a cultural force. *Sex and the Single Girl* concerns a magazine writer who attempts to expose as a fraud the author of a best-selling pop psychology book about emancipated sexuality. Neal Hefti's flirty but tame jazz score features lush pop ("Legs") and an up-tempo tune ("City Style") reminiscent of his later theme for *The Odd Couple* (1968), and the faddish "yeah-yeah" tune titled "Midnight Swim." The film's title song by Richard Quine (sung by Fran Jeffries) captures the film's moral that sex is merely a means to love and marriage. Notably, *Sex and the Single Girl*, along with *Pillow Talk* and *Lover Come Back*, served as inspiration for the 2003 pitch-perfect retro sex comedy *Down with Love*.

Another classic sex comedy of the swinging '60s is *What's New, Pussycat?* (1965), which concerns a playboy fashion editor who narrowly dodges the amorous advances of a bevy of babes as he struggles to become a one-woman man for his fiancée. The chick magnet enlists the dubious help of a longhair psychologist who'd rather get in on the action than help his patient commit to monogamy. A smash hit, *Pussycat* boasts one of the era's most memorable soundtracks by iconic '60s songwriter Burt Bacharach. Already well known for penning pop hits for such artists as the Shirelles and the Drifters, Bacharach broke into movies by contributing songs to Jerry Lewis' *Sad Sack* (1957) and portions of the score for the classic sci-fi horror movie *The Blob* (1958). After contributing catchy theme songs to the satire *Send Me No Flowers* and the romantic comedy *Promise Her Anything* (both in 1964), Bacharach earned the opportunity to score a genuine sex comedy. Bacharach and his loyal lyricist Hal David delivered their strongest theme song yet—well described in the Rykodisc booklet notes as a "lecher's waltz." It became a hit thanks to a bodacious vocal performance by Tom Jones, the Welsh heartthrob who'd hit the pop charts the same year with his trademark number "It's Not Unusual." The movie theme reached number three on the U.S. pop chart and received an Academy Award nomination, but lost to "The Shadow of Your Smile" by the Sandpipers. The movie's other standout tracks include the love theme "Here I Am," sung by Bacharach regular Dionne Warwick, which reached number 65 on the pop chart. The English group Manfred Man performed "My Little Red Book," but had little success with it (the psychedelic California band Love had better chart success with it a year later). The instrumental standouts are few, but "High Temperature, Low Resistance" and "Stripping Really Isn't Sexy, Is It?" are the epitome of cinematic savoir-faire.

Johnny Mercer, the celebrated lyricist, lends his easygoing croon to the buoyant, swinging "Big Beautiful Ball" on Johnny Williams' *Not with My Wife, You Don't* (1966). The sweet and lovely "My Inamorata" serves as the love theme. With swooning winds and reverberating electric guitar, "Arrivederci Mondo" is smooth and sexy in that mid–1960s Mancini-esque manner. "Hey Julietta" is a "la-la-do-do" wonderland of easy-listening vocals. An inventive brass arrangement and wailing Hammond organ make "Trumpet Discotheque" the epitome of groovy '60s Hollywood nightclub soul. The surf pop track "Not with My Wife, You Don't," with Beach Boys–style harmonizing, is serviceable but uninspired. Probably the best track here is "Hungarian Jungle Music," which features deep, fuzzy electric bass, a fantastic exotica beat, clanking metallic rhythm guitar, a fleet-fingered jazz guitar solo and sultry woodwinds. Among the other '60s sex comedies featuring swinging scores by Williams are *John Golfarb, Please Come Home* (1965), *Penelope* (1966) and *A Guide for a Married Man* (1967).

A much darker take on sex provided the inspiration for *Psychedelic Sexualis* (a.k.a. *On Her Bed of Roses*, 1966), which takes its title from Krafft-Ebing's 1886 study of aberrant sexual behavior. The "case study" that Zugsmith presents concerns a violent sociopath who has an odd floral fetish. Songwriter/composer Joe Greene's soundtrack is a bizarre concoction of proto-psychedelic jams ("The Boozer"), beat jazz ("The Bar Fly"), and experimental percussive abstractions ("Theme" and "Walk to Hell"). The only track that's conventionally sexy is, perversely, "Mother's Blues."

For sexy '60s camp, nothing beats *Valley of the Dolls* (1967). Based on the best-selling novel by Jacqueline Susann, *Valley* is the sordid story of a trio of ambitious young women wrestling with the trappings of fame and fortune in New York while popping a steady stream of "dolls" (uppers and downers). *Valley of the Dolls* may be unintentional camp on the screen, but its soundtrack is pure easy listening, with a bit of Broadway mixed in. Williams composed *Valley*'s lush pop score, and Dory and Andre Previn contributed several spirited show tunes. The mildly druggy intro of the film's theme hints at the high melodrama to come. Although Dionne Warwick is heard singing the song twice in the film, she does not appear on the soundtrack due to contract stipulations. Much of Williams' instrumental cues epitomize the swanky easy listening of the period. On "Chance Meeting," cascading harps and swirling strings accompany gently strummed acoustic guitar and bossa nova rhythms. "Neely's Career Montage" plays like a boisterous Broadway overture. And the era's attitude toward sex without marriage is perfectly summarized in the lyrics to "Come Live with Me."

A more serious landmark in sexually liberated cinema circa 1967 is *The Fox*. Adapted from a novella by D.H. Lawrence, the Canadian film is one of the first forays into serious gay and lesbian cinema, and it revolves around an uncomfortable love triangle between a lesbian couple and the man who comes between them. Schifrin contributed the subtle and elegant score, which will surprise anyone who exclusively associates the Argentine composer with crime and action soundtracks. The mood alternates between the soft, sweet, almost blissful tones of woodwind or strings, and the darker dissonant tones created by piano, percussion and winds. As Nicolas Saada points out on the Aleph edition booklet notes, "Schifrin manages to convey an incredible sense of emo-

Lalo Schifrin's score for *The Fox* (1967) captures the emotional conflicts at the heart of this film about two lesbian lovers and the man who comes between them. (CD cover appears courtesy of Aleph Records; graphic design by Theresa Eastman.)

tional conflict" with just a few musical motifs that seem to pay homage to both Herrmann and Claude Debussy.

A more mainstream example of the sexual revolution's influence on Hollywood can be found in a satire about what happens to bourgeois proto-yuppies when they attempt to embrace the "free love" movement. "Consider the possibilities" was the tag line for *Bob & Carol & Ted & Alice* (1969), wherein a hapless attempt at spouse swapping ends up leaving everyone involved feeling self-conscious and embarrassed. Quincy Jones, who composed and recorded eight scores in 1969, plays it cool on *BCTA*, relying on other composers' work. For the theme, he simply jazzes up Handel's "Hallelujah Chorus" with a bit of slide guitar and a rockin' backbeat. He also adapts Handel's "Messiah Part 3," using jazz vocalist Sarah Vaughan for an uncharacteristically straight classical reading. The instrumental versions of both Handel pieces are in a contemporary vein. Then there are rather bland vocal (Merrilee Rush) and instrumental versions of Burt Bacharach and Hal David's "What the World Needs Now." The remaining original pieces are fairly disposable by Quincy Jones standards. "Giggle Grass" and "Sweet Wheat" are slow blues. "Flop Sweat" is up-tempo roadhouse blues. And "Dynamite" is lively up-tempo blues, but it fails to distinguish itself. All things considered, *BCTA* is a lesser Q effort.

While *Bob & Carol & Ted & Alice* tried swapping partners, a far more remarkable pairing took place in *Midnight Cowboy* (1969). Although it's been re-rated with an "R," this squalid drama was one of the first major Hollywood pictures to receive an X-rating—more for its frank, sexually charged situations than its minimal nudity or specific sex acts. The story follows a hustler wannabe and his misfit friend as they try to survive on the gritty streets of New York City. The film was as successful and influential as it was controversial, and became the first and only X-rated film to win the Oscar for "Best Picture."

Barry's *Midnight Cowboy* is among his best non-spy soundtracks. Standout tracks include the elegant "Fun City," which later appeared on a Ralph Lauren television commercial in the '90s, and "Science Fiction," which accompanies an ill-fated gay sex pick-up in a movie theater. Oddly, it is very much in the Bond vein (think "Space March"). The title track, however, is one of the most haunting and lovely theme songs from the era. Featuring harmonica and acoustic guitars, it is as far removed from the James Bond sound as one can get, but Barry's personal stamp remains palpable. Not unlike the composer's love theme for *On Her Majesty's Secret Service* or the theme from *You Only Live Twice*, the *Midnight Cowboy* theme offers a hauntingly melancholic melody that mixes lush orchestration with one or more unique-sounding instruments (i.e. the harmonica and acoustic guitars). In the case of *OHMSS*, it was the incomparable voice of Louis Armstrong. On "You Only Live Twice," it was the combination of Nancy Sinatra's voice, the Japanese koto and the electric guitar playing the exotic minor key scale.

Of the *Midnight Cowboy* theme, Barry has noted that "the counter-melody is much more important than the melody, in that it's going nowhere—it's just this repetitive thing. Like when you travel around New York and see the homeless and you see these people going nowhere. That's where the falling motif for Jon Voight's character comes from." He added that the theme was orchestrated to "fit into the musical language" of "Everybody's Talkin'," by Harry Nilsson, which had appeared on the singer-songwriter's 1968 solo album *Aerial Ballet*. It was re-recorded for the soundtrack (*Film Music Screencraft*, 2000).

Two bands that are loosely associated with John Lennon, the Groop and Elephant's Memory, perform the remaining tracks on the soundtrack. According to Barry, the director was insistent that each song in the movie serves the overall vision. "I totally structured the songs, including Nilsson's 'Everybody's Talkin'." (*Film Music Screencraft*, 2000)

While *Midnight Cowboy* earned its X-rating for its bold examination of sexual degradation, *The Minx* (1969) earned it for 10 minutes of gratuitous sex, something that became increasingly common in the decade that followed. The plot revolves around the toxic cocktail of corrupt businessmen, corporate espionage and sexual blackmail. Oddly, the reasonably clean-cut pop/folk/rock outfit the Cyrkle—with only a couple of other minor albums to its credit—provided the soundtrack for the sleaze. The song selection ranges from brassy easy listening to sitar rock to bubblegum pop to bossa nova and beyond, but never jells as a cohesive score.

Another neglected trash flick is *The Love Machine* (1971), which is based on a Jacqueline Susann novel about a "lover machine" TV anchorman who sleeps his way to the top. The soundtrack boasts a couple of songs by Mark Lindsay and Brian Wells, and sung by Dionne Warwick ("He's Moving On" and "Amanda"). First-timer Artie Butler provides a groovy score, particularly the psychedelic soul "House Party" cues. While "Farewell Amanda" employs moody strings and piano stings, most of the material is easy listening. "The White Fox" and "New Threads on Parade" feature acoustic guitar, swirling strings and solo brass punctuated by chimes and a summery mood. "Backstage—The Christie Lane Show" is big band schmaltz akin to something heard on an awards show of the era. Butler went on to score another sexploitation flick of the '70s, *The Harrad Experiment*, two years later.

One of the most famous sexploitation soundtracks came from jazz musician Gato Barbieri for *Last Tango in Paris* (1972), the notorious X-rated film about a bitter and moody widower who hooks up with a young woman for a steamy, somewhat kinky affair. For their erotic scenes, Argentinean-born, self-taught saxophonist Barbieri provides a suitably sultry score that uses Latin jazz, the sexy tango, the graceful waltz and melancholic ballad to explore variations on a passionate theme. The original LP soundtrack differed from the score in that the cues were more fully fleshed out. *Last Tango in Paris* is a classic of sexy scoring.

Deep Throat and Beyond

While *Tango*'s shock value came primarily from seeing Brando "butter up" his costar, another film from 1972 was doubly outrageous, not only for its explicit sex, but also for its success. *Deep Throat*, the most famous and most profitable X-rated film ever made, is also the most profitable motion picture ever made. Shot for a mere $25,000, *Deep Throat* has raked in about $600 mil-

Gato Barbieri's passionate, jazz-infused score for *Last Tango in Paris* (MGM/UA, 1972) evokes the torrid affair of the characters played by Marlon Brando and Maria Schneider.

lion over the years. For better or worse, it legitimized hardcore porn as a bankable film genre, and spawned countless imitators. The soundtrack is not what one expects from a porno soundtrack. Instead of wall-to-wall porno funk, one gets some surprisingly memorable melodies, an occasional passage that conveys a genuine cinematic mood, competent musicianship by anonymous musicians, awful singing and silly dialogue. What passes for a theme ("Driving with Linda")—with its cheerful hurdy-gurdy melody—sounds like it should accompany a family-friendly montage of amusement park attractions. In a way, that's what makes the *Deep Throat* soundtrack so charming—it seems too naïve and fun-loving to accompany hardcore porn. LPs of the original soundtrack were given away at the theaters that dared show the movie.

Wherever *Deep Throat* screened it accompanied another legendary hardcore film made in 1972, *The Devil in Miss Jones*; both were directed by Gerard Damiano and co-starred Harry Reems, which made them an especially apt double feature. It stars 37-year-old Georgina Spelvin as a woman who barters with the devil to experience all that sex has to offer before spending

The soundtrack for *Deep Throat* (1972) isn't what one expects from a hardcore porno—it has too much personality! (CD cover appears courtesy of Light in the Attic Records; graphic design by Kiki Ajidarma.)

an eternity in hell for committing suicide (hell turns out to have no sex whatsoever, of course). In comparison to the joking, jovial Linda Lovelace vehicle, *Miss Jones* is positively nihilistic in tone. If the *Deep Throat* soundtrack strikes listeners as idiosyncratic, the *Jones* score by Alden Shuman is a transcendent revelation of sensual orchestration. Favoring lyrical solo piano (played by Frank Owens), tastefully lean arrangements, and haunting, ponderous melodies, Shuman's score—like the movie itself—is the antithesis of typical porno in that there's no sense of fun in it. The featured instruments include electric piano, organ and acoustic piano, tuned percussion, brass and woodwinds, electric guitar and bass, drums and a subdued string section—but never all together. Most of the pieces—which were arranged and produced by Peter DeAngelis or Ron Straigis—are stripped down, slow and expansive. "Hellcat" and "Miss Jones Comes Home" are gorgeous examples of the score's minimalist tendencies. While fans of more energetic sexploitation soundtracks are likely to reject its mournful introspective tone, it is an impressive and consistently well-crafted score that deserves to be heard—but presumably not as a prelude or accompaniment to sexual activity. The one funky track is "The Teacher," but with its almost baroque arrangement it distinguishes itself from the simple-minded porno funk that would turn up in countless other adult movies.

A better than average example of iconic porno funk can be found in the first black porno film, *Lialeh* (1973). Recorded by legendary funky drummer Bernard "Pretty" Purdie (his first credit on record as a composer), *Lialeh* is an unpretentious mix of mid-tempo soul balladry and head-nodding, foot-tapping grooves. Horace Ott contributes some tasty Fender Rhodes keys, and Sandi Hewitt brings a sassy sensual confidence to her lead vocals on tracks like "Touch Me Again" and "All Pink on the Inside." It isn't subtle, but the musicianship and production is warm and welcoming.

With pornography thriving at the fringe of mainstream cinema, Hollywood responded with films like *The Harrad Experiment* (1973), about an experimental coed college program where students and faculty engage in skinny-dipping and naked yoga as part of the sexed-up curriculum. A pre–*Miami Vice* Don Johnson stars and sings a couple of cheesy ballads ("It's Not Over" and "Wait for Me," which features a laughable spoken word interlude of pure schmaltz). The better tracks belong to Artie Butler, who provides breezy folk pop ("Low Fat Yoga") and funk ("A Bird in the Hand"), along with mushy easy listening ("First Love"). The movie was a big enough success to warrant a sequel, Steven Hilliard Stern's *Harrad Summer* (1974), with an easy-listening score by Pat Williams (*The Mary Tyler Moore Show*).

A more notorious example of post-porn mainstream cinema is *Pretty Baby* (1978), which scandalously stars an occasionally nude 12-year-old Brooke Shields as a virginal sex object. The soundtrack presents Jerry Wexler's adaptations of ragtime piano tunes by Scott Joplin and "Jelly Roll" Morton that serve as source cues in the film's principle location, a seedy New Orleans Storyville brothel at the turn of the 20th century. The music is perfect for the film, but doesn't make for an especially compelling soundtrack listening experience.

One of the last notable sex-oriented mainstream movies of the '70s is the hit comedy *10* (1979), which made Bo Derek the era's iconic female sex symbol. The film is also well known for making Ravel's "Bolero" the soundtrack for seduction, but most of the score sticks to the soft sentimental pop of Mancini, with a brief detour into disco funk ("Get It On"). Stars Julie Andrews and Dudley Moore actually sing on a few of the tracks, but the overall effect is far too sentimental to qualify as sexy.

Sex, Continental-Style

It's no secret that Europeans are generally less prudish about sex and nudity than Americans. The aforementioned 1933 Czech picture, *Ecstasy*, which was banned in the U.S., provides the most apt example; but for further proof consider *Porno Pop*, a 1971 theatrical compendium of vintage smut made between 1900 and 1940.

Nevertheless, both regions developed an interest in seeing skin and sin on the big screen at about the same speed. And by the early '50s, many American grindhouse theaters had come around to the European sensibility in a big way, serving up spicy new imports with a shot of espresso.

The film that sparked feverish interest in continental cinema was Roger Vadim's *Et dieu créa la femme* (*And God Created Woman*, 1956), starring the

The ragtime music in *Pretty Baby* (Paramount Pictures, 1978), starring Brooke Shields, captures the seedy yet innocent allure of the film's Storyville brothel setting.

archetypal sex kitten, Brigitte Bardot. This film famously introduced American audiences to the sexy young blonde who was Vadim's wife at the time, but it was hardly Bardot's first film. Bardot appeared in an astonishing 19 pictures between 1952 and 1956, and *God* was the sweet 16th. Many of the earlier Bardot films were quickly released in the U.S. after *God* to cash in on her overnight celebrity. Vadim's movie proved to be popular and controversial, becoming the most profitable foreign film in the U.S. for many years to come. It was banned in some states; and in others, theater owners risked arrest for its exhibition.

God was only the first of several Gallic cream puffs to explode onto the American screen in the late '50s. Those that followed included *L'Amant de Lady Chatterley* (*Lady Chatterley's Lover*, 1957), based on D.H. Lawrence's famous novel, and *Les Amants* (*The Lovers*, 1958), which introduced another French beauty, Jeanne Moreau. Both films caused uproar by presenting the unthinkable to American censors: Cheating lovers who go unpunished.

Paul Misraki provided the jazzy pop score for *God* (and *Mademoiselle Striptease*). The composer makes effective use of Latin rhythms, particularly in the scene where Bardot gyrates to a fiery conga beat in a club owned by one of her suitors. As the drums beat to a crescendo, Bardot's jealous young lover shoots the club owner in a fit of misguided passion.

Vadim continued to make spicy art house fare well into the '60s, including his modern-day adaptation of Pierre Ambroise Francois Choderlos de Laclos' 18th century novel *Les Liaisons dangereuses* (*Dangerous Liaisons*, 1960). A rousing bebop score by Art Blakey's Jazz Messengers, with compositional contributions by Duke Jordan (who plays piano on the recording) and Thelonious Monk, accompanies the story of seduction and betrayal.

Hookers with hearts of gold figure prominently in European cinema of the period, including *Le notti di cabiria* (*Nights of Cabiria*, 1957), scored by Nino Rota, and *Ieri, oggi domani* (*Yesterday, Today and Tomorrow*, 1963), which features a Sophia Loren striptease scored by Armando Trovaioli.

Melina Mercouri's portrayal of a prostitute is perhaps the most famous in European cinema, as seen

Georges Delerue and Piero Piccioni both contributed sensual scores for *Le Mépris*, a.k.a. *Contempt* (Embassy Pictures, 1963), starring Brigitte Bardot, who rocked international cinema like a sex bomb during the '50s and '60s.

in *Never on Sunday* (1960). The soundtrack by Manos Hadjidakis won the Academy Award for the catchy title song. Mercouri delivers the vocal version in Greek. Hadjidakis makes use of the bouzouki, a stringed folk instrument, throughout the soundtrack. By favoring small group settings over full orchestra, the composer completely immerses the listener in the film's Greek seaside oeuvre. And while 35 minutes of straight bouzouki music will challenge more than a few soundtrack fans, *Never on Sunday* remains the ultimate Greek soundtrack (next to *Zorba the Greek*, which Hadjidakis' contemporary, Mikis Theodorakis, scored).

Keeping a Stiff Upper Lip

When considering European sexploitation, Great Britain probably isn't the first country that comes to mind (except for *The Benny Hill Show*, a saucy variety comedy hour that premiered in 1969 and ran for 20 years). Compared to relatively liberated countries like Denmark and Sweden, Great Britain hasn't been a particularly productive sexploitation film exporter. But there are several independent and mainstream British films of the '60s that reflect the influence of the sexual revolution.

An early example of sexploitation in the UK is *Beat Girl* (a.k.a. *Wild for Kicks*, 1960). The classic British juvenile delinquency film features one of the hottest strip club scenes to appear in a non-pornographic film before, during or after the decency code. It also features John Barry's first film score. The plot concerns a Bardot-like teen that rebels against her father and new stepmother by hanging out in rock 'n' roll clubs with "beatniks." She also gets a job at a strip club. When she first enters the club she sees an exotic beauty performing a scorching striptease. Barry provides music for this scene and many others that qualifies as transitional work between his pop career leading the John Barry Seven and his early 007 scores. Many of the film's cues are built around *Beat Girl*'s turbo-driven crime jazz theme, featuring Vic Flick's guitar playing, which would later make "The James Bond Theme" instantly recognizable. (In fact, the riff served as inspiration for the new wave tune "Rock Lobster" by the B-52s in the early '80s.) Period pop star Adam Faith, who appears in the film, also performs on the soundtrack, including a vocal version of the *Beat Girl* theme.

As the decade reached its halfway point and the sexual revolution began to really heat up, a British film that could have been nicknamed "Sex and the Single Guy" won the Palme d'Or at the Cannes International Film Festival. *The Knack ... and How to Get It* (1965) captures the era's youth movement, with a special emphasis placed on the pursuit of sexual relations. For the score, director Richard Lester turned to Barry, whose star was rapidly rising. The two men met when both were hired to work on a television commercial for Rowntrees' After Eight Wafer Thin Mints. With his E-type Jaguar, and model/actress Jane Birkin on his arm, Barry definitely had the "knack"—that intangible gift for acquiring luxury and lovelies with little apparent effort. He also had the knack for soundtrack commissions that year, among them *The Ipcress File*, *Thunderball*, *King Rat*, *Four in the Morning* and *Mr. Moses*, in addition to *The Knack*. He even found time to write a stage musical, *Passion Flower Hotel*.

Barry's jazzy pop score for Lester's movie is the maturation of the "string beat" sound he'd used with his early '60s pop group the John Barry Seven. Instead of Vic Flick's surf guitar, Barry employs Alan Haven's organ textures against a background of xylophone, brass, and female chorus, as well as the pizzicato strings that defined his early pop sound. There are even queasy moments that connote uncertainty and intrigue that wouldn't sound out of place in his Bond scores. The theme's breezy mischievousness plays out dreamily in ¾ tempo. A second theme, for the principle female character, also receives variations throughout the soundtrack. Former Barry Seven singer Johnny DeLittle performs a vocal version of the theme on the U.S. release of the soundtrack, though it is not heard in the film itself.

A more serious British film that deals with sex and the single man is *Alfie* (1966), which uses frank sexual content to examine the foibles of a promiscuous bachelor. Burt Bacharach and lyricist Hal David contributed the theme song, but much of the score belongs to Sonny Rollins and his conductor Oliver Nelson. The soundtrack release does not contain the Bacharach tune. Rollin's "Alfie's Theme" captures the main character's beguiling ways with women through its jaunty tempo and minor key. It's the sort of theme that winds its way through the listener's brain long after hearing it. Rollins' nine-piece band includes such veteran jazz greats as Kenny Burrell (guitar), J.J. Johnson (trombone) and Jimmy Cleveland (trombone). Heard within the film, this jazz score reinforces the sense that Michael Caine's incorrigible philanderer is constantly improvising his way in and out of trouble. Heard on its own, one might think that *Alfie* is merely a wonderful but not especially cinematic jazz record of the '60s.

Here We Go Round the Mulberry Bush (1967), a swinging London coming-of-age sex comedy, also features contemporary musicians doing their thing. This time, however, the filmmaker Clive Donner commissioned new tracks primarily from the British bands Traffic and the Spencer Davis Group. Donner did this in lieu of having a traditional score done. The theme song, by Traffic, hit the top ten, and the album was a best seller. Nearly every track is a catchy energetic rock vocal number with the groovy high '60s vibe. The notable exception is the spectacular Hammond organ showcase "Waltz for Caroline."

Much more of a musical mixed bag is Francis Lai's *I'll Never Forget What's 'is Name* (1967), which was the first mainstream film to feature an utterance of the word "fuck" (by Marianne Faithful), as well as the first depiction of oral sex. The film concerns a businessman who gives up his career, wife and three mistresses to pursue the simple life. The soundtrack befits the mod London setting. The grooviest bits are source cues, including two "party" tracks and "Radio Music." "Keep It Cool" is cheerful Carnaby Street pop. "Boutique Music" is Procol Harum–esque lounge. "Andrew Dreaming," which accompanies an LSD-inspired dream sequence, is trippy orchestral music. Other orchestral cues evoke the beauty of Cambridge, and the pomp and circumstance of a "School Reunion."

Sound library legend John Hawksworth scored *The Penthouse*, a sexy thriller that takes place "isolated in mystery at the pinnacle of an uninhabited world," or so the notes read on the back of the original 1967 soundtrack LP. The film's score offers a wide range of jazz styles, from swinging "now sound" to hard bop to Latin. There's even a recurring hurdy-gurdy track that suggests something very twisted, kinky and humorous. In addition, there are dialogue tracks, including a seven-minute monologue about baby alligators.

Perhaps the greatest single influence in erotically charged English cinema is D.H. Lawrence, a native son and influential author of controversial and sexually frank novels. In addition to the Canadian film of *The Fox*, at least five other Lawrence novels from the '20s have reached the big screen, including *Lady Chatterley's Lover* (1955; remade in 1981), *Sons and Lovers* (1960), *Women in Love* (1969), *The Virgin and the Gypsy* (1970), and *The Rainbow* (1989).

For *The Virgin and the Gypsy*, Patrick Gowers provides a "Charleston Hop" and "Charleston Rag," as well as lyrical, romantic orchestral pieces of delicate beauty ("The Dreamer" and "After the Flood"), and even a track of hypnotic near-minimalism ("Rain Ride"). Other composers associated with Lawrence adaptations include Georges Delerue (*Women in Love*), Mario Nascimbene (*Sons and Lovers*), Joseph Kosma (*Lady Chatterley's Lover*, 1955), Richard Harvey and Stanley Myers (*LCL*, 1981), and Carl Davis (*The Rainbow*, 1989).

Another unusual UK film stirred up erotic feelings at the box office—namely, *The Sailor Who Fell from Grace with the Sea* (1976), a drama based on the Yukio Mishima novel, and starring Kris Kristofferson (who contributed to the soundtrack). The film is notorious for the nudity of its stars and frank sexuality (including an Oedipal female masturbation scene). Johnny Mandel's score is intimate and tender without resorting to easy sentimentality. An air of mystery pervades tracks like "The Tower" and "The Knothole." Stark arrangements for electric piano, harp, chimes and occasionally solo trumpet convey mixed emotions by way of the oblique, open-ended melodies.

Doin' Their Thing

When it comes to '60s psychedelica, nothing beats *Barbarella* (1968). The movie, an ultra-sexy sci-fi fantasy, is a cult classic like no other. It earns a mention here (as well as in the chapter devoted to sci-fi soundtracks) due to its many erotically charged scenes, including Fonda's spacesuit striptease during the opening credits that leaves her totally nude. Complementing the film's ample visual charms is the incredible soundtrack by the Bob Crewe Generation Orchestra, with music and lyrics written by Crewe and Charles Fox, and songs sung by the Glitterhouse (French composer Michel Magne's score was rejected). The brilliance of the *Barbarella* soundtrack is how it combines pop hooks, psychedelic rock production and full-bodied, big-budget orchestration. Otherworldly sound effects made on flanged and reverb-drenched instruments echo through the production alongside the relatively restrained sounds of large-scale cinematic pop orchestration. *Barbarella* remains one of the best examples of psychedelic scoring, and is a must have for any fan of '60s cinema.

Another essential psychedelic soundtrack of the sexual revolution is *Candy* (1968). Based on a ribald novel by Terry Southern (who collaborated with Vadim on *Barbarella*), this satiric sex farce revolves around a baby-faced ingénue, played by former Miss Teen Sweden Ewa Aulin, who brings out the lecher in every man who crosses her path. Featuring tracks by the Byrds and Steppenwolf, one might assume that the rest is merely filler, but it is Dave

Grusin's psych rock score that is the main attraction. Last heard providing lounge music for *The Graduate*, Grusin delivers a wild set that features acid guitar freak-outs, rock drumming, rumbling electric bass, swirling keyboard textures and enough orchestration to push the sound into the stratosphere.

Another classic sex comedy of 1968 is *Bedazzled*, which features a seductive and clever score by star Dudley Moore, who plays a shy short-order cook who makes a Faustian deal with the Devil to become an irresistible ladies man. Pianist Moore displays a talent for sexy blues vamps ("Strip Club"), haunting mood pieces ("The Millionaire"), pop

Bob Crewe's groovy soundtrack is perfect for the psychedelic and sexy scenes in *Barbarella* (Paramount Pictures, 1968), starring Jane Fonda.

singing ("Love Me"), and psychedelic beat music ("Bedazzled," featuring co-star Peter Cook's deadpan vocal).

Mondo Melodies

One of the most flexible sexploitation subgenres is the mondo movie. Filmmakers Gualtiero Jacopetti and Franco Prosperi pioneered the "shockumentary" genre with the surprise hit *Mondo Cane* (*A Dog's World*, 1962). The film features, among other things, topless native women and strange sexual rites from around the world. The novelty of seeing such lurid exotica on the big screen (and not just in the pages of *National Geographic*) sold plenty of tickets, and launched the mondo film phenomenon. Plus, its Oscar-nominated hit song "More" ("Ti Guardero' Nel Coure"), by Nino Oliviero and Riz Ortolani, helped sell plenty of soundtracks (it was even covered by Frank Sinatra) and legitimize the genre. The cosmopolitan mix of lush balladry, swing, orchestral moods, Latin dance numbers and instrumental pop is charming—though not particularly cinematic, and more quaint than "shocking." Ortolani and Oliviero worked together or apart on several other "mondo" movie projects.

Armando Sciascia was another composer who contributed to plenty of globetrotting grindhouse spectaculars. His music is featured in the striptease-oriented featurettes *Mondo caldo di notte* (*Hot World at Night*, 1962), *Sexy ad Alta Tensione* (*Sexy High Tension*, 1963), *Per una valigia piena di donne* (*The Kinky Darlings*, or, literally, *A Bag Full of Women*, 1963), *Sexy* (1963), and *Europa—Operation Striptease* (1964). Sciascia's sleazy jazz exotica are superior to nearly anything else in the mondo genre. He infuses each striptease number with a sense of intrigue and danger through the use of conga beats, minor key chord changes and sultry horns. The libidinous heat of jungle love is palpable even without these films' gaudy Technicolor imagery.

While the collaborations between composers Ortolani and Oliviero, and filmmakers Jacopetti and Prosperi, were important to the early popularization of the mondo genre, a different collaboration proved nearly as fashionable, and even more musically memorable. Whenever Piero Umiliani teamed up with documentary and feature filmmaker Luigi Scattini—and they did on several occasions—the results were outstanding. Following his early mondo movies *Sexy Magico* (1963) and the Jayne Mansfield docu-comedy *L'amore primitivo* (*Primitive Love*, 1964), Scattini worked with Umiliani on a shockumentary *Svezia, inferno e paradiso* (*Sweden, Heaven and Hell*, 1968). The film documents the Scandinavian country's lesbian nightclubs, biker scene, incidents of drug abuse and alcoholism, wife swapping and porn shops. Umiliani's score elevates the subject matter from sordid to sublime on tracks like "Topless Party" and "Fotomodelle." Soulful organ tones accompany fuzzy electric guitars, rumbling bass lines and an insistent rock beat. On other tracks, Gato Barbieri, who scored *Last Tango in Paris* (1972), joins the jazzy vibe. *Sweden* also features a tender vocal performance by Lydia MacDonald on "You Tried to Warn Me," and wonderful wordless vocals by the legendary Edda Dell'Orso, as well as Sandro and Giulia Alessandroni on several tracks, most notably on the hit "Mah Na' Mah Na'." Pop vocal groups of the period frequently covered the latter song, which features a nonsense lyric and maddeningly catchy melody; and it even became popular in the U.S. thanks to its unexpected use on the children's show *Sesame Street*. The soundtrack's reissue in the mid–1990s helped fuel the retro soundtrack revival.

Umiliani also scored Scanatti's *Angeli bianchi angeli neri* (*White Angel Black Angel*, or *The Satanists*, or *Witchcraft*, 1970), a shockumentary about the occult fad that bubbled up during the counterculture revolution in the late '60s. Although the film did not focus on sex per se, it wasn't shy about showing beautiful nude young women participating in orgiastic satanic rites. Musically speaking, this is one of Umiliani's most spellbinding efforts, mixing lushly

The Original Complete Motion Picture Soundtrack
Composed, Arranged and Conducted by Piero Umiliani

Piero Umiliani's score for *Svezia, inferno e paradiso* (*Sweden, Heaven and Hell*, 1968) includes the catchy tune "Mah Na' Mah Na'," which later turned up on the children's TV show *Sesame Street*. (CD cover appears courtesy of Easy Tempo Records [ET901]; graphic design by Giulio "Jazzy Jules" Maini.)

orchestrated "Italian recordings" with spare, percussion-filled "Brazilian recordings." From the very first track, "Sweet Revelation," the score transfixes with melodies that suggest a romantic film rather than a documentary. Umiliani's swinging arrangement provides perfect accompaniment for Shirley Hammer's unbridled vocal performance. "La Foresta Incantata" maintains the magic, building from a shimmering intro to combine a Nora Orlandi–led female chorus with lush orchestral swells, backed by throbbing bass and uncluttered drum patterns. If there is one track anywhere that captures the romanticized hippie notion of pagan witchcraft, this is it in spades. Although the score couldn't possibly get better than its first two tracks, it delivers even more unexpected pleasures in the catchy pop numbers "Now I'm on My Own" and "The City Life" (performed by Mark David and Forever Ember, a short-lived British psychedelic group). The aura of pagan-witches-run-amok intensifies on the ritualistic abstraction of "Streghe a Convegno" (featuring Alessandro Alessandroni's modern chorus), and becomes downright whimsical on "Magical Children" (featuring a multi-tracked psychedelic vocal by Hammer). Umiliani's clear affinity for acoustic folk (particularly brightly-strummed 12-string guitars, chiming harpsichord and harmonica) becomes apparent on the aptly titled "Folk Time." Even as the score increasingly turns to sparely orchestrated Brazilian percussion numbers, Umiliani still surprises with imaginatively loose interpretations of Bach's "Toccata and Fugue in D Minor" and Beethoven's "Moonlight Sonata." As diverse in style as it is rich in melodic invention, *Angeli bianchi ... angeli neri* nearly outshines the excellent *Svezia, inferno e paradiso*.

For Scattini's *Questo sporco mondo meraviglioso* (*This Dirty Wonderful World*, 1971), which was co-directed by Mino Loy, Umiliani continued to capitalize on his stylistically limber scoring style. While there aren't any tracks as emotive as "Sweet Revelation," or as catchy as "Mah Na' Mah Na'," Umiliani continues to work wonders with both melody and arrangements. On the title track, Umiliani employs a soaring, sentimental melody to exploit his gift for lush pop romanticism. Elsewhere, Umiliani explores the country folk sensibility on several tracks by highlighting lively acoustic guitar ("Western Melody" and "Old Rock"), harmonica ("Young Time"), and high-toned "whistling" organ lines and bluesy electric piano ("La Nuova Frontiera"). There's even a jaunty fiddlin' cowboy variation on "Mah Na' Mah Na'." While *Questo* is certainly a little bit country, it is a little bit rock 'n' roll, too. For potent proof, check out the sexy, reverb-drenched "Love In," the ultra-funky psycho beat variations on the theme ("Dove Và il Mondo" and "Mondo Dove Vai?"), and the quirky blues funk of "Moderato Grottesco and Cantabile." Another side of this wildly inventive yet casually executed score gives Umiliani the opportunity to stretch into easy, breezy Latin jazz on tracks like "Pepito," "Luna di Miele" and "Holiday Inn." Overall, *Questo* doesn't enjoy the fame of *Svezia*, and fails to deliver a killer vocal track like those found on *Angeli*, but it's still an immensely enjoyable "mondo" score. Umiliani went on to score six more Scattini features during the '70s—mostly exotic erotic dramas.

Speaking of erotic dramas, there are no more apt examples in European cinema than those of Radley Metzger, whose work includes *The Dirty Girls* (1964), *Carmen Baby* (1967) and *The Lickerish Quartet* (1970). The distinctive Metzger style features slinky, sexy European models, swanky sets, arty cinematography, and cool jazz and lounge soundtracks. He eventually made hardcore features under the name Henry (or Harry) Paris, including *The Private Afternoons of Pamela Mann* (1975) and *The Opening of Misty Beethoven* (1976).

Piero Piccioni's score for *Camille 2000* (1969) contains some of the composer's most seductive work. (CD cover appears courtesy of Easy Tempo Records [ET905]; graphic design by Giulio "Jazzy Jules" Maini.)

One of Metzger's best, *Camille 2000* (1969), features an ultra-groovy score by Piero Piccioni that is the perfect accompaniment for the film's mod set design, stunning photography and scenes of soft-core erotic depravity. Piccioni's sparely arranged, bass-heavy score captures the detachment and ennui of the dispassionate jet-setters who populate the film.

Metzger also distributed erotic films by other filmmakers, including Swedish moviemaker Mac Ahlberg, who made a number of notable films that popularized Euro soft-core erotica. Ahlberg is best known for the *Jag en Kvinna* trilogy (*I, a Woman I, II* and *III*, in 1965, 1968 and 1970), featuring music by Sven Gyldmark (and Bertrand Bech on the third movie). With titles like "Sex

Happening," "Beguine Erotic" and "Strip-Tease Party," one might expect a fairly sleazy listening experience from a film score such as *I, a Woman II*; but while some of the music borders on exotica, most of it is actually very quaint. "Feelings in a Dive," for example, might as well be called "Merry-Go-Round" because that's what this jovial waltz suggests. "Forbidden Love" sounds like "In the Mood" or some other big band number that wouldn't offend the most prudish member of an old folk's home.

The same year, Ahlberg made *Fanny Hill* (1968), one of several films based on John Cleland's landmark ribald 18th century novel. The Swedish version of Ahlberg's movie features music by *Pippi Longstocking* composer Georg Riedel, but the film's American distributor, Cinemation, brought in an ambitiously orchestrated modern soul soundtrack by Clay Pitts, which wasn't released until 1971. The centerpiece is the 15-minute "Please Touch Me." Pitts went on to score *La mujer del gato* (*The Female Animal*, 1970).

Armando Trovaioli scored more than his fair share of European skin flicks in the late '60s. The comedy *Il profeta* (*The Prophet*, or *Mr. Kinky*, 1968), and the erotic drama *La matriarca* (*The Libertine*, 1969), capture two sides of '60s-style Italian sexploitation. In *The Prophet*, a groupie sets out to seduce her guru, adding him to her long list of sexual conquests. Trovaioli's score is, by turns, groovy in the Tijuana Brass fashion, funky in the raunchy rare groove mode, exotic in the psychedelic sitar sense, and just about everything else in between. In *The Libertine*, a young widow discovers her late husband's kinky bachelor pad and then adopts a kinky lifestyle in a voyage of self-discovery. Trovaioli's score favors gentle piano variations of the film's easy-listening theme music. It's lovely, but not kinky in the least.

For sexier sounds, listen to Stelvio Cipriani's imaginative score for *Femina Ridens* (*The Frightened Woman*, 1969). The film tells a story about a sadist who invites a young woman home for a weekend of domination, but ends up being dominated himself and cured of impotence in the process. Cipriani's score explores various styles that were fashionable at the time. These include avant-garde psychedelica ("Love Symbol" and "The Run in the Alley"), jazzy baroque chamber music ("Rendezvous in the Castle"), minimalist blues with breathy sighs ("Sophisticated Shake"), a brassy and hard-driving theme song, and dreamy easy listening ("Mary's Theme"). The most inventive piece is "Hot Skin"; it combines the discipline of baroque harpsichord and strings with a wordless female vocal that mimics the moans and cries of a woman under the whip, which is characterized by sharp percussion accents.

A discussion of kinky Euro-trash of the late '60s and early '70s would not be complete without mention of Jess Franco, one of the most prolific B-movie makers ever. Franco's films are a veritable catalog of sexual decadence and perversion.

Franco's *Succubus* (a.k.a. *Necronomicon*, 1967) is arguably his most surrealistically entertaining film, featuring a drug-fueled orgy with a dwarf, as well as several sadomasochistic nightclub scenes. Dutch jazzman Jerry Van Rooyen's swinging soundtrack is entrancing. "New York Is in China" features languidly caressing strings and smoldering sax before a jazzy tempo shift, with tinkling piano and walking bass, leads into a sweet striptease motif with sultry brass. "Death Walks in High Heels" is straightforward post-bop, and "Lisbon Sidewalks" blends bossa nova with swing.

The ultimate "Franco-phile" sleazy listening experience is found on the compilation *Vampyros lesbos: Sexadelic Dance Party*, which collects music by Manfred Hübler and Siegfried Schwab (a.k.a. the Vampires Sound Incorporation) that originally appeared on two rare LPs, *Psychedelic Dance Party* and *Sexadelic*. Hübler and Schwab's catchy psycho beat grooves were used in three

Vampyros lesbos is a compilation of music heard in three sleazy Jess Franco movies, and originally released on two LPs in 1969 by Manfred Hübler and Siegfried Schwab. (CD cover appears courtesy of Crippled Dick Hot Wax; graphic design by Töni Schifer.)

1970 Franco films starring the mysterious and lovely Soledad Miranda, including the sexy horror movies *Vampyros lesbos* and *Sie Tötete in Ekstase* (*She Killed in Ecstasy*), as well as the spy flick *Der Teufel Kam aus Akasava* (*The Devil Came from Akasava*). This influential compilation fueled the retro soundtrack craze of the '90s and inspired an electronica remix album. A soundtrack collection without it is nowhere near complete.

Of lesser cult stature are *Marquis de Sade's Justine* (*Deadly Sanctuary*, 1968) and *Marquis de Sade's Philosophy in the Boudoir* (*De Sade '70*, or *Eugenie*, 1970), which feature two very different Bruno Nicolai scores. It's worth noting that the two Franco titles are commonly mistaken for one another. *Justine* features a full orchestra playing melodies straight out of the Romantic school. Nicolai's effort shames Franco's blurry, zoom-maddening camera work, but it certainly befits the film's otherwise high production standards (the highest ever for a Franco film). In contrast, *Eugenie* is remarkably diverse in its musical styles, including psychedelic blues, calypso, dreamy erotic easy listening, nightmarish avant-garde experiments, breezy bossa nova and elegant waltz.

A Franco film with a strong onscreen music element is *Venus in Furs* (1970). Centered on a jazz musician haunted by a femme fatale, the film has little in common with the like-titled erotic novel by Leopold von Sacher-Masoch. For the soundtrack, Manfred Mann, featuring Mike Hugg, provided a mix of post-bop small-group jazz for the club scenes, and electronic/acoustic psychedelia for the kinky horror scenes. The significant differences in style and instrumentation between the jazz tracks and the underscore might lead one to think that another composer went uncredited. Regardless, both are of high quality. For the film's surreal scenes of erotic horror, Franco brilliantly uses two overlapping pieces of repetitive minor key music to hypnotic effect.

Another filmic version of *Venus in Furs* (*Le malizie di venere*, 1968) features a diverse score by G.P. Reverberi and G.F. Reverberi that blends easy listening, Latin jazz, groovy dance music and psycho beat.

It should come as no surprise that 1969 was a banner year for European sexploitation soundtracks. Among the notable entries are Morricone's *Metti una sera a cena* (*Love Circle*, or *One Night at Dinner*) and *L'assoluto naturale* (*She and He*). The first film is the European equivalent to Hollywood's *Bob & Carol & Ted & Alice*, which came out the same year. The film's married couple becomes sexually (and competitively) entangled with various guests at their dinner party. The theme is certainly among the most collected Morricone tunes, and deservedly so. This quick-tempo bossa nova features a haunting wordless vocal by Edda Dell'Orso, who can be heard on countless Italian movie themes. This one builds slowly by simply repeating one melody over a counter melody, using just a few notes. Once heard, it is not soon forgotten. Throughout the score, Morricone emphasizes intimacy by using an acoustic pop combo sound with subtle strings washes and brass accents. Drums, tuned percussion, bass, organ, keyboards, acoustic guitar and occasionally voice are the melodic mainstays. The easy-listening vocal trio the Sandpipers recorded the theme in English as "Hurry to Me" for an Italian 45.

For *L'assoluto naturale*, Morricone delivered yet another haunting melody, one that conveys the frustrated relations between a romantic purist (Lawrence Harvey) and a devotee of physical love (Sylva Koscina). Morricone's score elicits the tension between these characters and the connection they would fulfill, if only on conflicting terms. Nicolai's orchestrations are intimate and nuanced. Every track is a variation on this cyclical melody.

Another highlight of the era is *Il dio serpente* (*The Snake God*, 1970), which presents the Caribbean as a domain of voodoo sex rituals. Augusto Martelli's score (his first) is a surprisingly easy blend of calypso groove ("Siempre Cantando") and sinister-sounding tribal chant and percussion ("Zombie's Mood").

For something entirely different in erotic cinema, consider Morricone's emotionally complicated period score for *Addio fratello crudele* ('*Tis Pity, She's a Whore*, 1971), in which Charlotte Rampling plays a delectable young woman in an ill-fated incestuous relationship with her brother. Morricone's score is perfect for this medieval story of tragic romance. Morricone employs Alessandro Alessandroni's Cantori Moderni and a chamber orchestra featuring a variety of distinctive wind instruments, as well as layered string parts, acoustic guitar and harp. The themes are—like the story's central love affair—tender, intimate and emotionally complicated. Superficially, the score sounds "medieval," but the use of countermelodies and complex harmonies distinguish the music from mere pastiche, and educe the internal conflicts and emotional torture that ultimately rend the lovers apart.

Another study in dark eroticism is *La gatta in calore* (*The Cat in Heat*, 1972), which explores a housewife's affairs. Gianfranco Plenizio's complex and dissonant score is gloomy and sensuous. Titles such as "Obsessive Ecstasy," "Foul Sin" and "Crowded Solitude" capture the pronounced sense of fear trapped in these tangled arrangements. Softer pieces for piano and strings suggest languid lesbian lovemaking. "Grigio Perla" is lowdown and groovy. Vocalist Dell'Orso appears on three tracks.

After making a few shockumentaries together, filmmaker Scattini and composer Umiliani made several sexploitation films, including three that feature the stunning exotic beauty of model-turned-actress Zeudi Araya. *La ragazza fuori strada* (*The Girl from the Street*, 1971), *La ragazza dalla pelle di luna* (*The Sinner*, 1972) and *Il corpo* (*The Body*, 1974) all offer a satisfying mélange of funky grooves, sensual ballads, jazz-rock abstractions and fun-in-the-sun calypso ditties. The instrumentation is usually spare, making prominent use of the Hammond organ, choppy rhythm guitar, delicate acoustic guitar, repetitive bass figures and an assortment of drums and percussion. Some tracks are little more than solo piano or solo organ. Other tracks add fuller orchestration with strings, brass and woodwinds, but Umiliani—whose roots

Piero Umiliani's score for *La ragazza fuori strada* (*The Girl from the Street*, 1971) is a satisfying mélange of funky grooves, sensual ballads, jazz-rock abstractions and fun-in-the-sun calypso ditties. (CD cover appears courtesy of Easy Tempo Records [ET921]; graphic design by Giulio "Jazzy Jules" Maini.)

are in jazz—rarely resorts to a bloated orchestral sound. Taken as a set, this trilogy is a must for fans of the composer, and will appeal to fans of Euro-skin cinema in general.

Perhaps the ultimate Italian sexploitation movie theme is Armando Trovaioli's "Sesso Matto" from the 1973 movie of the same name (a.k.a. *How Funny Can Sex Be?* or *Crazy Sex*). During the go-go '90s, the Easy Tempo label revived the randy disco theme song on the first volume of its esteemed 10-volume series, and on a remix EP as well. The track's irresistible combination of disco funk and multi-tracked moaning, groaning, giggling female voices

Armando Trovaioli's *Sesso matto* (a.k.a. *How Funny Can Sex Be*, 1973) is most famous for its funky disco title track, which is widely acknowledged as one of the absolute classics of Italian sexploitation cinema. (CD cover appears courtesy of Beat Records; graphic design by Daniele De Gemini.)

(Dell'Orso, of course) predates Donna Summer's somewhat similar "Love to Love You, Baby" by two years. Aside from its titillating title track, the soundtrack features a variety of sounds, including lowdown groovy exotica, early rock 'n' roll pastiche, psych rock (played by Mario Bertolazzi's group Il Punto), sentimental balladry, Bacharachian easy listening, languid moods, quirky keyboard abstractions, traditional Italian and Spanish street music, Rota-esque Latin romanticism, comically sped-up bits, and a Moog version of a theme by Rossini *á la A Clockwork Orange*. None of it is as sexy as the theme music, but it is tremendous proof of Trovaioli's far-ranging musical talent.

Another Italian composer who scored sexploitation soundtracks is Alberto Baldan Bembo. Among his best are *L'amica di mia madre* (*My Mother's*

Friend, 1973) and *Lingua d'argento* (*The Silver Tongue*, or *Emmanuelle's Silver Tongue*, 1975). The first concerns a 17-year-old boy's sexual education with his friend's hot mom. The second follows a *ménage a trios* and features an opening scene in a sex club. Bembo's music for both films can best be described as cinematic Latin jazz-fusion with an ear for pop. Smooth brass, lean strings, rumbling bass guitar, precisely played rhythm guitars and jazzy keyboard fills meld easily with a flawless rhythm section. The slowly building "Pedro Come," and the lowdown mood of "Gonzalez Go," are highlights from *Mia Madre*, and the disco funk of "Trop's" and "Mubu" are among the best tracks on *d'argento*.

Franco Micalizzi scored *Adolescenza perversa* (1974), another *ménage a trios* story. Again we're treated to quasi-erotic vocalisms, care of Dell'Orso. This time the musical mood is less concerned with tension and more focused on mellow, occasionally melancholic moods and laidback psychedelic grooves. Acoustic guitar and electric keyboards intermingle like lovers, and occasionally a backbeat propels the pulse. When the mood takes a turn into darker emotional territory, it is still drop-dead gorgeous, thanks to Dell'Orso's vibrato-laden heavy breathing.

A more notorious entry in the soft-core art house genre is *Il portiere di notte* (*The Night Porter*, 1974), which explores a psychosexual relationship between a hotel porter (and former Nazi officer) and a hotel guest who was once his teenage sex slave in a concentration camp. Danièle Paris' claustrophobic score features a creepy, slow-motion tango theme with plodding piano patterns, off-kilter trombone notes and saxophones that simultaneously warns of imminent ruin and invites one to succumb to it. It's a perfect accompaniment for the twisted dance undertaken by the fateful lovers.

One of the most famous European sexploitation films is *Emmanuelle* (1974), Just Jaeckin's soft-core adaptation of Emmanuelle Arsan's erotic "memoir" about a diplomat's wife who seems to bring out lustful advances in everyone she meets. The film was immensely popular and

Charlotte Rampling as Lucia in *Il portiere del notte*, a.k.a. *The Night Porter* (AVCO Embassy, 1974), performing in a Nazi cabaret. Danièle Paris' darkly sensual score is fitting accompaniment for a film about destructive erotic obsession.

influential, spawning several sequels and a sleazier copycat series starring the exotic beauty Laura Gemser as *Emanuelle* (with one "m"). Pierre Bachelet and Herve Roy's soundtrack favors gently undulating jazz-rock that's generally on the soft side. However, for the more violent sex scenes they employ a harder, more aggressive variation that plays up the intricate arpeggios that underpin the melody, giving the music quasi-progressive rock flair.

Bachelet returned to score Jaeckin's immediate follow-up, *Histoire d'O* (*The Story of O*, 1975). If *Emmanuelle* tells the story of a woman encouraged by her philandering husband to take lovers, then *Histoire d'O* tells the story of a woman forced by her husband to be a sexual slave of other men. Bachelet's

Pierre Bachelet's theme for *Histoire d'O* (a.k.a. *The Story of O*, 1975) is sexploitation music at its most serious and sinister. (CD cover appears courtesy of CAM Original Soundtracks; graphic designer unknown.)

stately and sinister theme music is a seductive combination of slow-motion Pink Floydian pomp, multi-tracked and synthesized female vocalisms, a serpentine electric bass line, super-phased acoustic guitar, shimmering cymbal crashes, enough layers of synthesizer wash to make Rick Wakeman blush and the strangely psychedelic steel guitar to top it all off.

Serge Gainsbourg, the French pop star, songwriter and notorious lover of such cinematic sexpots as Bardot and Jane Birkin, also composed and recorded music for more than 30 films between 1959 and 1990. A number of them qualify as sexploitation (*Strip-Tease*, 1962; *Sex-Shop*, 1972; *Goodbye Emmanuelle*, 1978; etc.) Gainsbourg also acted in several films, and wrote and directed a few, too. For his first directorial effort, the erotic dramedy *Je t'aime, moi non plus* (*I Love You, I Don't*, 1975), he also contributed the screenplay and soundtrack. It is a notable effort because it capitalized on the pop chart success of Gainsbourg and Birkin's 1969 hit single of the same title, which was a smash in Europe, and fittingly reached number 69 on the U.S. hit parade. The soundtrack features a few instrumental variations on the hit song, but does not contain the vocal version itself, which appears on the studio effort *Jane Birkin et Serge Gainsbourg* (Gainsbourg also recorded an earlier version with Bardot). Disco queen Donna Summer recorded a 15-minute version of the song, which appears on *Thank God It's Friday* (1978). The remainder of the *Je t'aime, moi non plus* soundtrack features an unexpected but confident blend of easy rollin' country pop, pickin' and grinnin' bluegrass, and rip-roarin' country rock. This sort of range will come as no surprise to fans of the prolific composer, who confidently experimented with jazz, Latin, pop, rock, reggae, disco and everything in between during his lengthy career. Another erotic Gainsbourg soundtrack is *Madame Claude* (1977), which Jaeckin directed. Also of interest is his studio concept album *Histoire de Melody Nelson* (1971), about a *Lolita*-esque love affair, for which he made movie-like music videos with Birkin.

The success of the European soft-core film industry during the mid-to-late '70s owes a debt of gratitude to the original *Emmanuelle*. Among the film's numerous official and unofficial sequels, the most notable belong to a separate series beginning with *Emanuelle nera* (*Black Emanuelle*, or *Emanuelle in Africa*, 1975), starring the mixed-race beauty Laura Gemser. These films have a tendency to be raunchier and sleazier than the original *Emmanuelle*, offering viewers scenes of gore, violence, brutality, bestiality, and, in some versions, conventional hard-core sex. Nico Fidenco's *Emanuelle* scores are by turns sultry and serious, fun and funky. Generally, Fidenco works with a small combo led by keyboards and guitars, adding exotic percussion, woodwinds, brass and strings in small doses. The sound is sophisticated, groovy and melodically memorable, with occasional Latin rhythms, unusual electronic textures and production nuances that show the influence of proto-techno wizards Giorgio Moroder and Kraftwerk.

Next to *Vampyros lesbos*, the movie music compilation that has fueled the most interest in European sexploitation soundtracks has been *Schulmädchen Report* (*Schoolgirl Report*), featuring Gert Wilden's beat lounge and acid rock soundtracks for the famous series of 12 German soft-core films made between 1968 and 1978. These raunchy instrumentals (with occasional erotic female vocalisms) provide ample proof of Wilden's talent for creating catchy hooks, and ability to exploit his audience's twin interests in free love and acid rock. On tracks like "Soul Guitar" and "Dirty Beat" (which borrows a Led Zeppelin riff), Wilden's orchestra lays down a hard-rocking groove of heavy drums, throbbing electric bass, screaming Hammond organ and fuzz guitar. This is sex without subtlety or mystery, and the approach is hard to argue against. Elsewhere, on tracks like "Sexy Girls," the sound is decidedly easy listening, but the use of turned-on vocalisms and smoking saxophone offers a nudging reminder of the sleazy context.

Another German composer who scored his fair share of erotic films was Gerhard Heinz. The composer worked on several German-produced films between 1968 and 1979. The tracks can be heard on the compilation *Melodies in Love*, which starts promisingly with "All You Ever Need Is Beat" (from *Schamlos*, 1968). This wild theme song, which features the composer exchanging over-the-top vocals with Aniko Benkö, is the epitome of exciting, libido-charged beat music. A more orgiastic sound would be difficult to imagine. It is the only track from the late '60s on the compilation, which makes all that follows it relatively disappointing. Still, there are some excellent examples of '70s erotic scoring on display. "Bangkok at Night" (from *Drei Bayern in Bangkok*, 1976) and "I Need It" (from *Die Schulmädchen vom Treffpunkt Zoo*, 1979) feature emphatic moaning from the female singer Steffi Vinjak; and the multi-tracked vocal by Michael Scheikl on "Svenska Disco Machine" (from *Drei Schwedinnen auf der Reeperbahn*, 1979) captures the cocksure bravado of a guy's night out in the red light district. "Liebespiele" (from *Liebespiele Junger Mädchen*, 1972) is reminiscent of Bacharach's mid–1960s *Casino Royale* period. The suggestively titled "Come Shoot" (from *Die Nichte der O*, or *Julia: Innocence Once Removed*, 1974) features a gently pumping beat beneath muted horns, organ chords and the breathy voiced Background Studio Groupies, who simply chant the title.

Peter Scores, another compilation, focuses on the sexploitation scores and sex-inspired recordings of the brilliant Peter Thomas, another German. Among the movies covered by this release include *Happening in White* (1969), *Som Hon Bäddar Får Han Ligga* (*Do You Believe in Swedish Sin?* 1970) and *Engel, die ihre Flügel verbrennen* (*Angels with Burnt Wings*, 1970). Thomas' take on "sexy" can be fun-loving ("Panki") and tender ("Sweet Girl—Sweet Love"), cosmopolitan ("Surf with Gunter"), raunchy ("Oh, Oh, Oooh, Ei Ei Ei," "Modern Sex"), and wildly excited ("Coitus Crash"). According to the CD's booklet notes, written by Thomas, even when the composer was making a non-soundtrack recording he sometimes used sex as inspiration. For "Otran

Limited Respettivo," he screened some blue movies for his musicians in the studio.

Yet another German compilation of note is *Birds Do It*. It collects tracks from German sex education films of the '60s and '70s, including *Die Sexuellen Wünsche Der Deutschen* (*The Sexual Desire of Germans*, 1972), *Liebe in Drei Dimension* (*Love in Three Dimensions*, 1973), *Sex Pervers* (*Sex Perversity*, 1970) and *Hausfrauen-Report International* (*International Housewife Report*, 1973). Several tracks are from sex-ed films by Oswalt Kolle, whose experience as a magazine reporter covering sexuality translated to a run of films with titles like *Das Wunder Der Liebe 2* (*The Miracle of Sexual Partnership*, 1968) and *Dein Kind, das Unbekannte Wesen* (*Your Child, That Unknown Creature*, 1970). Featuring such heavy hitters as Thomas and Heinz, the selection swings with hooky, psychedelic sleazy listening from films that sought to guide young men and women in the techniques of love.

Another notable European filmmaker (and still photographer) of soft-core erotica is David Hamilton, who made three films at the tail end of the Silver Age, including *Bilitis* (1977), *Laura, Les ombres de l'ete* (*Laura*, or *Shattered Innocence*, 1979), and *Tendres cousines* (*Cousins in Love*, 1980). Francis Lai's pallid score for *Bilitis* is well suited for a film featuring Sapphic caresses, but its gauzy disco-era synth pop hasn't aged well.

Patrick Juvet's score for *Laura* holds up slightly better, as it

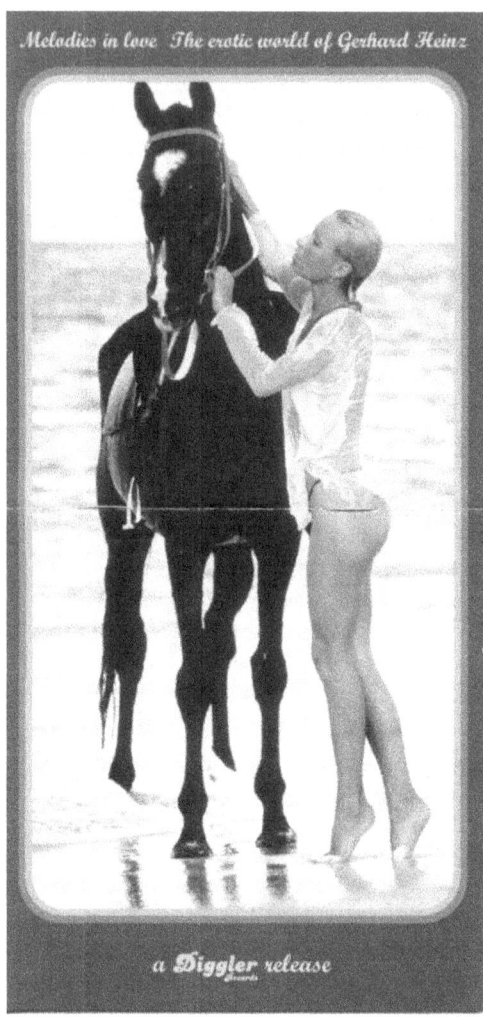

Gerhard Heinz's *Melodies in Love* compilation epitomizes libido-charged beat music of the swinging '60s and '70s. (CD cover appears courtesy of Diggler Records; graphic design by Alexander Imiela and Christiane Lüdtke.)

strikes a balance between soft and hard sounds. "Theme de la Statue" starts quietly, with piano and synth playing a gentle melody, before surging in volume with distorted rock guitar, thumping drums and crashing cymbals. Just as it seems ready to explode, the gentle keyboard melody returns, only to give way again to the rock motif before finishing the way it started. It captures the yin and yang of erotic scoring. Elsewhere, Juvet also works a propulsive disco groove ("Fire" and "Photo Session"), casts an atmospheric synthesizer spell ("Le Reve" and "Fascination") and provides soft-focus keyboard balladry ("Le Theme de Laura" and "La Tristesse de Laura").

Although the infamous *Caligula* (1979) is hardly the final word on European sex cinema, it marks a symbolic and chronological stopping point in the Silver Age's racy ride. Written by Gore Vidal, and financed by *Penthouse* magazine's motion picture subsidiary, Tinto Brass' ambitious film was altered by *Penthouse* publisher Bob Guccioni, who added hard-core footage shot on set after hours. Scandalized by the liberties taken with his film, Brass had his name removed from the final product at the time of the theatrical release. He wasn't alone in wanting to hide from the critical fallout over the project. Many of its stars—among them Malcolm McDowell, Peter O'Toole, John Gielgud and Helen Mirren—denounced the picture. Bruno Nicolai used the name Paul Clemente for his original score, which is gloriously dramatic, capturing both the decadent atmosphere of ancient Rome and the twisted tragedy of its true story. The score also uses additional music by Aram Khachaturian (from "Spartacus") and Sergei Prokofiev (from "Romeo and Juliet"). The soundtrack was released on LP, which included a disco version of the love theme "We Are One" that didn't appear in the movie.

Caligula is an apt example of how the sexual revolution of the late '60s and early '70s exhausted its creative potential, and its welcome in mainstream cinema, by the end of the decadent "Me Decade." The film's initial promise of depicting the depravity of ancient Rome with artistic integrity and historical accuracy was undone by the whims of a powerful man who—like the film's self-serving and delusional main character—squandered the good will of an empire, namely the moviegoing public. By the time *Caligula* hit theaters, filmgoers had discovered the advantages of home video and discreet viewing pleasure in time for a wave of new conservatism, at least in the United States, which had long been a major market for European sexploitation films.

By the end of the '70s many people were curbing their casual sex habits for fear of getting herpes; and the discovery of AIDS brought the sexual revolution to a screeching halt for many people. In a way, the age of sex-obsessed cinema came to an impasse, if not a dead end. Nonetheless, the age of sex in cinema—from the winking innuendo of *Some Like It Hot*, to the grindhouse sleaze of *Mondo Topless*, to the soft-core simulation of *Camille 2000*, and to the hard-core action of *Deep Throat*—had climaxed, rolled over and fell into a restless sleep.

12 Essential Sexy Soundtracks

Some Like It Hot (1959)—Adolf Deutsch
Lolita (1962)—Nelson Riddle
What's New, Pussycat? (1965)—Burt Bacharach
Barbarella (1968)—Bob Crewe
Candy (1968)—Dave Grusin
Sweden, Heaven and Hell (1968)—Piero Umiliani
Schoolgirl Report (1968–1978)—Gert Wilden
Vampyros lesbos (1969)—Manfred Hübler and Siegfried Schwab
Angeli bianchi ... angeli neri (1970)—Piero Umiliani
Last Tango in Paris (1972)—Gato Barbieri
The Devil in Miss Jones (1972)—Alden Shuman
Je t'aime, moi non plus (1975)—Serge Gainsbourg

Chapter 4

Staccato Six-Guns

The western is the most mythic film genre. Since the early days of cinema, the Old West has provided ample fodder for stories of good versus evil, of men against nature, and each other. Time and again the genre relies on familiar situations to convey deeper truths about human nature and about the desires to explore and conquer a new frontier. The familiar conflicts that arise from those goals (cowboys versus Indians, outlaws against civilization, the settler's struggle in an inhospitable land) are almost incidental in western films. As Robert Warshow noted in his essay "The Westerner," the genre is "an art form for connoisseurs" where the discerning viewer endures formulaic plots to savor its creative variations.

The history of the western film is literally as old as the medium itself. When Thomas Edison first began experimenting with motion pictures—Mutoscope and Kinetoscope minute-long peep shows—his subject was cowboys and Indians. Two years before the turn of the century, the Edison Company produced two simple western dramas, *Cripple Creek Bar Room* and *Poker at Dawson City*. Five years later, filmmaker Edwin Porter made the earliest version of *The Great Train Robbery*, which featured such iconic western elements as a shoot out, a posse pursuit, and, naturally, a train holdup. The popular appeal of the many silent westerns following *Robbery* come as no surprise, considering they depicted an era that was barely over (1850–1900).

Throughout the '20s, '30s, '40s and '50s, the western ran the gamut from gimmicky Tom Mix fantasies and cowboy musicals starring Gene Autry and Roy Rogers to ambitious widescreen epics by such Golden Age directors as John Ford and Howard Hawks.

During the early Silver Age, the Hollywood composers who worked in the genre with the most success were such Golden Age greats as Dimitri Tiomkin (*High Noon, Red River, Duel in the Sun, Rio Bravo*), Alfred Newman (*How the West Was Won, The Bravados*), Jerome Moross (*The Big Country*), and Max Steiner (*The Searchers, San Antonio, Dallas*). Their soundtracks capture the mythic grandeur of the Old West, of big sky vistas, spectacular natural wonders and the immense desire and fortitude of those who overcame substantial obstacles to settle in an untamed land. While movies with modern settings explored dark territory and moral ambiguity through the use of contemporary music styles, western scores continued to trot out old-fashioned music ideas that evoked an earlier age when you could tell good from evil by the color of a character's hat. In the hands of Hollywood's old school maestros, the western seemed resistant to change.

Listen to Steiner's score for *The Searchers* (1956)—the sentimental strings, soothing sonorities and cavalry brass—and one can easily imagine it accompanying a western from the '40s or even the '30s. The same can be said of Tiomkin's western works of the '50s, from *High Noon* (1952) to *Rio Bravo* (1959), and the early '60s as well (remember *The Alamo*, 1960). And for the most part, their musical approach was entirely appropriate, considering the traditional type of western (often starring John Wayne) for which they were scoring. Not surprisingly, the western—more than any other genre—got a relatively late start on Silver Age scoring trends.

Certified Silver Age composer Elmer Bernstein also favored a traditional sound when scoring for "the Duke." On *The Comancheros* (1961), strings swell like a mountain stream during the spring thaw ("The Wide Open"), and brass flares like a raging forest fire ("Texas Rangers"). Tiomkin would have been proud.

Perhaps Bernstein's greatest contribution to the genre is the best example of how the era's younger composers brought a relatively fresh, thoroughly American approach to a genre previously dominated by European-born composers. More than any other American western score of the Silver Age, *The Magnificent Seven* (1960) captures the best aspects of the genre's golden past, as well as the compositional trends of the 20th century. The marvelously rousing main theme is exuberantly heroic, and serves the score well through a variety of moods and orchestral treatments. On the rhythmically exciting main theme, the strings carry the memorable main melody as brass adds a propulsive countermelody. Quieter passages partner steadily strummed acoustic guitar with pretty woodwinds. On "Calvera," percolating percussion and staccato string strokes run headlong into Asiatic horn figures before dissolving into a brief section for meditative Spanish guitar, which hints at the danger waiting in the film's main setting, a Mexican village terrorized by bandits. What makes *Magnificent* different from Golden Age westerns, which tend to have "Hungarian" operatic scores, is its obvious debt to American folk music, particularly the influence of Aaron Copland.

"*The Magnificent Seven* score really benefited from the fact that for years I'd wanted to do an American type of theme, as it was something I knew a great deal about, partly because of my interest in American folk music, and also because of my relationship with Copland," Bernstein explained in Mark Russell and James Young's *Film Music Screencraft* (p. 40, Rotovision, 2000). "He invented American music to a great degree—a certain style, a certain sound, and I always found it very attractive."

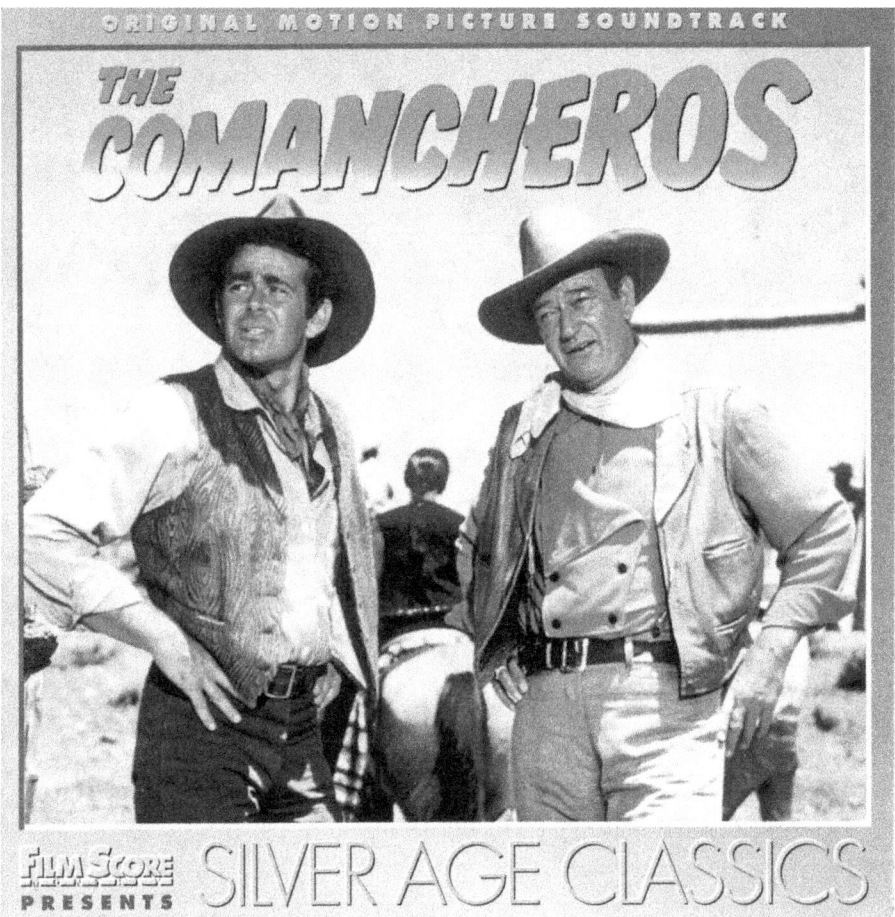

Elmer Bernstein's score for *The Comancheros* (1961), which stars the ultimate cowboy actor, John Wayne, is stylistically similar to earlier John Wayne movie scores. (CD cover appears courtesy of Film Score Monthly; graphic design by Joe Sikoryak.)

Bernstein added that Jerome Moross' score for *The Big Country* (1958) greatly influenced his score for *Magnificent Seven*.

"By the time I got to do *The Magnificent Seven*, all of this stuff that had been in my head for years and years had a chance to be set free," Bernstein explained. "And I think that accounts for the tremendous amount of energy and rhythmic intensity in that score."

Comparatively, Jerry Goldsmith brought a blend of traditional western style, as well as his serialist sensibility, to non–Duke westerns of the '60s such as *Rio Conchos* (1964). Melodious strings, staccato guitar strums and bright

Elmer Bernstein's rousing score for *The Magnificent Seven* (MGM/UA, 1960), starring Robert Vaughn (left) and Yul Brynner, captures the gun-slinging excitement of this classic western.

percussion details can be heard on the theme, but more modernistic treatments creep into the score. Darkness envelopes "The Intruder" as strings writhe and fall into the lowest register, and dissonant strings wash over "Chief Bloodshirt" as low percussion throbs and brass pulsates threateningly.

During the early-to-mid '60s, westerns proved particularly popular on the small screen (*Bonanza, Gunsmoke*, etc.), but the increasing popularity of more modern action genres (particularly spy thrillers) made it more difficult for westerns to corral moviegoers. That's not to say that Hollywood didn't make great westerns during the period. Classic oaters such as *The Man Who Shot Liberty Valance* (1962) and *Ride the High Country* (1962) continued to find a traditional audience. However, by the mid-1960s the genre clearly entered a period of stagnation in Hollywood, highlighted by the release of the western spoof musical *Cat Ballou* (1965). Parody and pastiche tend to be a sure sign that a genre is dead or dying, and the days of the traditional western had ridden off into the sunset.

How Europe Won the West

When a new day dawned for the genre, finding the western revived and refreshed, it was in Europe, not Hollywood. Between the early '60s and mid–1970s, approximately 600 westerns were filmed on European soil. While the vast majority were Italian/Spanish co-productions, the trend really started in the homeland of popular novelist Karl May. Although he never visited the American West, the German's evocative, albeit inauthentic, western novels set the stage for about a dozen frontier films. The first of these was *The Treasure of Silver Lake* (1962), which was a hit in what was then West Germany,

German-made westerns based on Karl May novels were popular during the '60s and '70s, featuring music that imitated both Hollywood and Italian western scores. (CD cover appears courtesy of All Score Media/Cinesoundz [www.cinesoundz.com]; graphic design by Thomas Gross.)

as well as France and Italy. *Treasure* and its sequel, *Winnetou the Warrior* (1963), were shot on the rugged terrain of Yugoslavia and starred washed-up American actor Lex Barker.

The rousing romantic scores by Martin Böttcher draw inspiration from Tiomkin's grand style and Bernstein's *Magnificent Seven* (1960). Peter Thomas, Riz Ortolani, Erwin Halletz and Raimund Rosenberger also scored late '60s German westerns.

West Germans weren't alone in their fascination with the Old West. The East German state-supervised film industry (Deutsche Film-Aktiengesellschaft, or DEFA) also produced its fair share of sagebrush sagas. The DEFA westerns made in the '60s and '70s mimicked the *Winnetou* films in so far as depicting Indians as noble (i.e. quasi-socialist) victims of the white man's colonial (i.e. quasi-capitalist) barbarism. Such movies as *Weisse Wölfe* (*White Wolf*, 1969), *Tödlicher Irrtum* (*Deadly Error*, 1970) and *Kit & Co.* (1974) were shot in Yugoslavia or Georgia, with—like some Golden Age Hollywood productions and the *Winnetou* westerns—Caucasians cast as Native Americans.

Although many of the DEFA horse operas were made after Italian westerns became popular, their soundtracks often favor the epic Hollywood style, but occasionally venture into more experimental territory (*á la* Morricone's spaghetti-isms or even non-western-sounding action funk). Among the composers who contributed to these films are Wolfgang Meier, Günther Fischer, Karl Ernst-Sasse, Hans-Dieter Hosalla, and Wilhelm Neef. Soaring strings, mighty brass, galloping rhythms, and bright acoustic guitar chords capture the spirit of big country adventure, while plaintive flute melodies and pitter-pattering percussion evoke the peaceful native way of life. On "Weitspähender Falke," Meier blatantly borrows from Bernstein's *M7* theme. At other times—often on suspenseful cues—the approach is more experimental. Sasse's primitive rhythm soundscape on "Klondyke" from *Kit & Co.*, and "Todesrennen" from *Blutsbrüder* (*Blood Brother*, 1975), are entrancing and suspenseful. Fischer's groovy spaghetti-inspired theme and funky action tracks for *Tecumseh* (1972) are exciting. Hosalla busts out mariachi brass, saloon piano and, unexpectedly, marimba and wah guitar. When Fischer employs a pulsing synth and distorted guitar lead on *Severino* (1978), it sounds like Goblin covering Morricone's music from *Once Upon a Time in the West* (1968).

Undoubtedly, German westerns display a number of anachronistic characteristics, such as favoritism toward Indians, the use of phony European-style guns, white men playing Indians, and Yugoslavia standing in for the "Wild West." Nonetheless, there is an impressive stylistic range in their soundtracks.

The Birth of the Italian Western

Although German-made westerns proved popular with audiences all over Europe, Italian westerns were successful worldwide. The sub-genre soon became known as "spaghetti westerns" (or "macaroni westerns" in Japan); but while the nickname was originally used as a slur, many fans now consider it an affectionate term. Italian westerns usually featured multi-national casts (typically with an American actor in the lead), had multi-national financial backers and often were filmed in Spain. (For what it's worth, Great Britain started the trend of shooting westerns in Spain with *The Sheriff of Fractured Jaw*, 1959.)

It wasn't until 1964 that the Italian western truly hit its stride with Sergio Leone's adaptation of Akira Kurosawa's samurai film *Yojimbo* (1961). Originally named *The Magnificent Stranger*, Leone changed the title to *Per un pugno di dollari* (*A Fistful of Dollars*, 1964), probably to avoid sounding too derivative of *The Magnificent Seven*, which had been popular in Europe. Leone, who cut his filmmaking teeth as a second unit director on sword-and-sandal epics, made *Fistful* for a mere $200,000, hiring Clint Eastwood (of U.S. TV's *Rawhide*) to star; European film productions often hired little known or even washed-up American actors as a way of appealing to audiences everywhere. As legend has it, he originally wanted the established film composer Angelo Lavagnino, but hired his old school chum Morricone instead, despite having been unimpressed with Morricone's film work up to that point. What convinced Leone was a pop single featuring a Morricone-arranged version of the Woody Guthrie song "Pastures of Plenty," as sung by Peter Tevis, an American singer who was working in Italy. The recording's lean arrangement features electric guitar, galloping rhythm, whip cracks and bell chimes that would soon distinguish Morricone's western scores. Leone loved it, but suggested using a whistler instead of a singer. Little did they know how influential the film and its soundtrack would become. In fact, they were so nervous about the film they used bogus names in the credit sequence: Bob Robertson for Leone and Dan Savio for Morricone (who was also known to use the pseudonym Leo Nichols).

Fistful opens with the acoustic guitar and whistling of Alessandro Alessandroni, who soon became a hired gun for dozens of western soundtracks (next to Morricone, A.A. is the most influential artist in the genre). *Fistful*'s theme builds slowly, adding elements like trills, whip cracks, bell rings, reverberating Fender Stratocaster and Alessandroni's grunting male chorus ("We defy"). Finally, galloping drums and a lean string arrangement join in. The sound is distinctively different from Hollywood western style, yet captures the character of the Old West in a way no other composer had managed to do up to that point. Morricone undoubtedly drew inspiration from Leone's habit of explaining his film's story in highly evocative terms, imitating the noises one would hear in a given setting. Also, Morricone and Leone agreed early on to provide main characters with a leitmotiv—a brief musical theme; in fact, Morricone quoted from his arrangement of "Pastures of Plenty" for the man with no name's leitmotiv in *Per qualche dollaro in più* (*For a Few Dollars More*, 1965). Of primary importance, Morricone wished to avoid creating a score

Ennio Morricone's scores for Sergio Leone's "Dollars Trilogy," including *Per qualche dollaro in più*, a.k.a. *For a Few Dollars More* (MGM/UA, 1965), starring Clint Eastwood, redefined the western sound.

that would sound like a Hollywood western, so he intentionally used instruments that weren't associated with Tiomkin, Bernstein, et al., such as electric guitar, maranzzano (Sicilian Jew's harp), flute and recorder, for unexpected sonorities. The *Fistful* theme would prove as influential to its genre as Mancini's "Peter Gunn Theme" or Monty Norman's "The James Bond Theme" to the crime and spy genres; though Morricone's theme for *Il buono, il brutto, il cattivo* (*The Good, the Bad, and the Ugly*, 1966) would eventually overshadow it in popularity. The rest of the *Fistful* score is equally evocative and effective. Suspenseful piano runs, mysterious woodwinds and queasy strings make "Almost Dead" by turns tense and soothing. "Square Dance" is the most traditional sounding piece on the score, but still fits in with Morricone's unorthodox aesthetic. Rumbling kettle percussion and a pulsating orchestral attack make for a riveting ride on "The Chase." On "The Result," honking harmonica accents the mounting tension, which gives way to the slow-starting climax of "Without Pity."

Fistful remains one of the most influential soundtracks of all time, though the composer has been known to dismiss it as one of his lesser works among his 30-odd western scores. Nonetheless, RCA's in-house orchestrator, Hugo Montenegro, recorded a top-ten LP of "pop" versions of music from the "Dollars Trilogy" shortly after *The Good, the Bad and the Ugly* became a box office hit in the U.S.

While popular history of the Italian western soundtrack usually begins with *Fistful*, it wasn't Morricone's first shot at the genre. He contributed scores for two other Italian westerns prior to that seminal film, including *Duello nel Texas* (*Gunfight at Red Sands*, 1963) and *Le pistola non discutono* (*Guns Don't Argue*, 1964). The music draws some inspiration from the classic Hollywood western sound (Tiomkin again, but also Bernstein's *M7* score is a clear influence, as *Gunfight*'s "A Gringo Like Me" features a similar repeating staccato countermelody). On *Guns*, Morricone embraces the movie's Mexico setting (which is common to so many Italian westerns since they were usually shot in Spain, using Spanish extras). Overall, *Guns* is still a transitional and traditional-sounding score for Morricone; "Lonesome Billy" is about as Coplandesque as Morricone ever sounded. The elements that would distinguish the bulk of Morricone's western work are not apparent on *Gunfight* or *Guns*.

The composer that Leone originally wanted to score *Fistful*, Angelo Francesco Lavagnino (who worked with Leone on *Il colosso di Rodi*, a.k.a. *The Colossus of Rhodes*, 1960), crafted his first western score for *Los pistoleros de Arizona* (*5,000 dollari sull'asso*, or *Five Thousand Dollars on One Ace*, 1965). The score sounds not quite like a Hollywood western and not quite like a spaghetti western, but a little bit of both. Fans of Lavagnino's work are likely to appreciate how he incorporates the western-style electric guitar, mariachi trumpet and throbbing electric bass into his otherwise traditional orchestral style.

On *Per qualche dollaro in più* (*For a Few Dollars More*, 1965) Morricone continued to refine his *Fistful* sound with chiming clockwork percussion, macho Spanish guitar fills and Grand Guignol pipe organ. The tracks that use the clockwork motif so effectively are "Sixty Seconds to What?" and "The Musical Pocket Watch." We also get a jaunty honky-tonk piano number ("Aces High"), slow burning fuses ("The Watchers Are Being Watched" and "The Showdown"), and solemn meditations on the main theme ("Goodbye, Colonel" and "The Vice of Killing"). The theme features Alessandroni's distinctive whistling alongside twangy Jew's harp, penny whistle bird calls, tolling bells, grunting male chorus, hand claps, galloping guitars and finally a rousing orchestral finish.

Aside from its revolutionary use of "natural" sounds within the music, what makes Morricone's "Dollars Trilogy" scores so amazing is how the composer perfectly captured the mood of Leone's pictures without the benefit of seeing even completed scripts, much less a rough cut of the films. It was as if the old school chums were tuned to the same creative frequency.

"I never show the final script to Ennio," Leone recounted in an interview quoted by Didier Deutsch in booklet notes for *The Legendary Italian Westerns*. Leone describes how he told Morricone what he had in mind, as if he were describing "some fairy tale." The filmmaker gave the composer an idea of the type of music he envisioned for each situation. Morricone then composed several short themes—one for each major character—and played them for Leone on the piano. When all the characters had been assigned their musical signatures, recording commenced.

"Then I take the recording to the set and use it while the actors go through their lines," Leone explained. "I find it gives striking results."

The key component to the Italian western sound—both for Morricone and other composers—is Alessandroni and his Cantori Moderni (Modern Singers). A boyhood friend of Morricone, the self-taught musician brings a distinctive sound, and Morricone arguably was the first to recognize it. Alessandroni later recounted (in a 1997 interview with John Mansell) how Morricone

Ennio Morricone composed the scores for Sergio Leone's films prior to filming, which allowed the director to play the music on set to inspire his actors, including Lee Van Cleef (seen here in *For a Few Dollars More*, MGM/UA, 1965).

had telephoned him during the development of *Fistful* and asked him if he would play guitar and whistle on the soundtrack. Alessandroni added that he expanded his choir for the project, giving it the name I Cantori Moderni. The modest virtuoso also told Mansell, "I am a performer, not a star. The stars are the composers," despite the fact that he went on to compose film scores as well.

A year later Morricone tracked the most famous spaghetti western of all, *Il buono, Il brutto, Il cattivo* (*The Good, the Bad and the Ugly*, 1966). It was this film that popularized the genre in the U.S. in particular; up until this film neither of Leone's previous "Dollars" films were released Stateside. *GBU* remains Morricone's most famous and beloved score, which is ironic considering he's been known to say that he doesn't even like the genre. The theme song is among the most quoted in film history (along with the "The James Bond Theme" and the theme from *Jaws*). As was Morricone's habit, each of the main characters got his own musical motif. For "the good," there is the famous "ah-ey-ah-ey-ah/wah-wah-wah" call-and-response. "The bad" gets the echoing arghilofono—the low-key version of the ocarina, a wind instrument in terra cotta from the region of the Abruzzi. And Alessandroni's Cantori Moderni gives "coyote" voice to the motif for "the ugly." In fact, Leone specified to the composer that each of the characistics (good, bad, ugly) was simply part of a single character, depending on the circumstances. So, Morricone used a single musical theme for each character, but altered the tone accordingly. Morricone's gift for creating dynamic variations on a single theme is particularly evident on *GBU*, as the various instrumental voices take turns bringing the melody to life, often with an appropriate feeling of wild desperation. Elsewhere, brass is used to solemn effect, capturing the sense of loss on the film's Civil War sets. Along with the theme, "The Ecstasy of Gold" is an outstanding achievement. Featuring Dell'Orso's solo voice against a backdrop of mounting grandeur, the track captures the desperate search in a military cemetery for the tomb allegedly containing the treasure. The presence of Morricone's score is so strong in the film that Leone later said that the composer was his "best dialogist," since the music often spoke for the actors when the actors weren't delivering lines. Although *GBU* was hardly the first spaghetti western, the effect of its popularity abroad spurred interest in previously made Italian westerns and lit the fuse for an explosion of other film productions.

That same year Morricone scored another western set during (or at least shortly after) the Civil War. *I crudeli* (*The Hellbenders*, 1966) finds Morricone working his magic on a slightly smaller scale and under the pseudonym Leo Nichols. Concerning a Confederate soldier for whom the war against the North is anything but over, *The Hellbenders* offers Morricone an opportunity to explore militaristic drum patterns and eloquent solos on trumpet (sometimes doubling as cavalry bugle). It was Morricone's first score to employ trumpet so extensively; legend has it that Morricone was quite adept at playing the instrument. The main melodic motif—delivered on electric guitar, with countermelody provided by piano, bass and chorale against a stuttering drum roll—recalls the questioning melody in *GBU* ("ah-ey-ah-ey-ah"), but is sufficiently different to be memorable in its own right. As is evident in most of Morricone's western soundtracks, many tense scenes are scored with minimalist flair, highlighting unusual instruments in unexpected combinations. It's worth noting that Morricone's music for *The Hellbenders* was lifted for uncredited use in a less known western, *Drummer of Vengeance* (1974).

Again working under the name Leo Nichols, Morricone scored *Navajo Joe* (*A Dollar a Head*, or *Savage Run*, 1966). With its primitive choral chants from I Cantori Moderni, a stomping tribal rhythm and Gianna Spagnolo's wordless wail, the title track is among Morricone's most striking themes. The theme's jagged guitar line, rolling piano and multi-tracked voices add to the rhythmic cacophony as the music builds to a shattering climax. Throughout the soundtrack Spagnolo's vocals and the drum-heavy arrangements lend the proceedings a primitive, highly ritualistic sensibility.

Morricone's work for Leone remains his greatest contribution to the genre, but he worked with other directors as well, notably Duccio Tessari, who'd contributed to the screenplay for *Fistful*. Morricone first scored *Una Pistoli per Ringo* (*A Pistol for Ringo*, or *A Ballad for Death Valley*, 1965), then its sequel, *Il ritorno di Ringo* (*The Return of Ringo*, or *Ringo Rides Again*, 1965), and shortly thereafter *7 pistoli per i MacGregor* (*Seven Guns for the MacGregors*, 1965). His new collaborator, Bruno Nicolai, orchestrated each of these scores and many other Morricone scores, until the two composers had a falling out in the mid–1970s.

The theme for the first *Ringo* movie is lush, dreamy and sentimental. A reverberating electric guitar, and then a string section, carries the haunting melody, while Cantori Moderni provides an intermittent but uplifting countermelody. The overall effect is mesmerizing. This is probably the first Morricone theme to warrant the description of drop-dead-beautiful. "Angel Face" reprises the melody, adding an English lyric by Gino Paolo and a clear, strong vocal by Maurizio Graf. On "Waiting," minimalist tick-tock guitar plucks provide tension as woodwind and brass make furtive movements toward danger, and strings radiate in the background like heat waves. On "The Massacre," Spanish guitar strums out a funeral march as a Mariachi trumpet, joined by orchestra and choir, mourns a grievous loss of life.

For the darker *Ringo* sequel, Morricone and his frequent orchestrator, Bruno Nicolai, continued to work their magic, particularly on the theme song, which is sung by Graf and the Cantori Moderni. Morricone's big hook melody, and Nicolai's rousing arrangement, make a perfect match for Graf's passionate singing of lyrics by Maurizio Attanasio.

Attanasio also contributed lyrics for *Seven Guns for the MacGregors*. Taking inspiration from Scottish drinking songs, "March of the MacGregors" combines a militaristic tempo with a whistling, happy-go-lucky male chorus.

"Santa Fe Express" is the B-side of this 45-only soundtrack release, with a reprise of the theme set to an energetic gallop.

As a result of the successful *Ringo* movies, a slew of *Ringo* knock-offs were quickly made and released. *Centomila dollari per Ringo* (*$100,000 for Ringo*, 1965) features a score by Nicolai that fits stylistically between Bernstein and Morricone. With its super vibrato vocal by Bobby Solo, a memorable hook and harmonica accents, the theme music ("Ringo dove vai?" or "Ringo Came to Fight") is as perfect a cowboy theme as they come.

Gianni Ferrio scored *Un dollaro bucato* (*Blood for a Silver Dollar*, 1965)—

Gianni Ferrio's score for *Un dollaro bucato* (*Blood for a Silver Dollar*, 1965) features the familiar sagebrush sounds of galloping rhythms, reverberating guitar chords, throbbing bass lines and robust brass. (CD cover appears courtesy of CAM Original Soundtracks; graphic designer unknown.)

one of the composer's better spaghetti western efforts. Featuring the familiar whistle of Alessandroni, the score is loaded with the sagebrush saga sounds of galloping rhythms, reverberating guitar chords, throbbing bass lines and robust brass. Much of it sounds as if it was recorded in an echo chamber, most noticeably when Lydia MacDonald sings on the sentimental and melancholy "Give Me Back."

Adios Gringo (1965) features an exciting and unusual score by Benedetto Ghiglia. Rumbling kettledrums, call-and-response arrangements and strange choral sonorities help to differentiate it. There is a vaguely psychedelic feel to the instruments; the guitars ring, chime and slide in spectacularly unexpected ways. An ocarina and low flute are also employed quite effectively. Although there are only a couple of melodies employed on the soundtrack, Ghiglia's creativity always makes for intriguing variations.

For *Un dollaro tra i denti* (1967)—the first of four *Stranger* films—Ghiglia continued creating idiosyncratic western movie music. Taking a stylistic cue from Morricone, Ghiglia incorporates natural sounds, like whip cracks and blacksmith anvil strikes, along with distorted electric guitar, primitive flute, and unrefined chorus yelps and hollers.

For *Johnny West il mancino* (*The Left-Handed Gunfighter*, 1966), Lavagnino took the opportunity to pair a square dance fiddler and banjo picker on "Disco Western III." Elsewhere, the composer relied on his usual and effective blend of brass, organ, guitar, bass and drums. The composer has self-deprecatingly dismissed his western scores.

"The music I wrote for westerns was similar to the scores written by other Italian composers," Lavagnino is quoted in the booklet notes of *Spaghetti Westerns, Vol. 1*. "The music itself reflected our own cultural heritage through the use of instruments like the guitar, the electric guitar, voices, the harmonica, the ocarina, the electric bass, and others. All those instruments reflected pretty well our country, as well as the way we imagined the cowboy way of life, horses, train robberies, gunfights, and the like. Of course, Morricone did it first and did it better, because he scored important westerns that had something new to say. I cannot say the same, as I did not have movies like that to do."

Armando Trovaioli's *I lunghi giorni della vendetta* (*Long Days of Vengeance*, 1966) captures the western sound with the usual blaring trumpets, guitars and orchestra. On the theme, the metallic rattling sound created on an electric guitar helps build the tension like a rattlesnake's warning.

Beginning with a delicate harp, Luis Bacalov's *Quien sabe?* (*A Bullet for the General*, 1966) opens like no other spaghetti western. But soon mariachi brass joins in, and then guitars, male vocal and orchestra, with an energetic tempo. Harp continues to play an integral part in the arrangements, which are often lean and spacious, allowing for single "voices" to be heard. Throughout, the south-of-the-border ambience is prevalent. The best track is undoubtedly the memorable theme, which smolders with quiet intensity.

On *Sugar Colt* (1966), Bacalov delivers one of his best westerns. Following a light-hearted theme song, the mood turns dark with tense orchestral intrigue. Morriconian bell-ringing drama and suspenseful moods dominate, bolstered by dissonant strings, trilling flutes and clattering percussion.

Bacalov's very best western score, however, belongs to *Django* (1966). With its ringing acoustic guitar and big hook melody, the theme (the instrumental version and Roberto Fia's vocal version) is among the most hummable western themes. The score also features orchestral passages of stirring intensity. Electric guitar, solo trumpet, dissonant strings, low piano notes and percussion predominate on a score that also boasts a lively mariachi number.

Django was a controversial success, and banned in several countries, including the U.K., due to its ultra violence. It spawned its fair share of official and unofficial sequels. Among the knock-offs are *Django, the Last Gunfighter* (1967), with a score by Roberto Pregadio and Walter Rizzati; *Django Shoots First* (1967), with a score by Nicolai; and *Django, Prepare a Coffin* (a.k.a. *Viva Django*, 1968), with a score by Gianfranco and Gian Piero Reverberi. The most famous (or rather infamous) sequel is the ultra-violent *Django Kill* (1967), with a score by Ivan Vandor.

While there are numerous examples of spaghetti westerns that copied the *Dollars* trilogy, the *Stranger* series is among the most obvious (with the "stranger" standing in for the "man with no name"). As mentioned earlier, Ghiglia provided the trippy Morriconian score for the first installment. Cipriani scored the psychedelic *Stranger* sequel *Un uomo, un cavallo, una pistola* (*The Stranger Returns*, or *Shoot First, Laugh Last*, or, literally, *A Man, a Horse, a Gun*, 1967), and the east-meets-west second sequel *Lo Straniero di Silenzio* (*The Stranger in Japan*, 1968). Franco Bixio, Fabio Frizzi and Vince Tempera scored the belated third sequel, *Get Mean* (1976). Cipriani's *The Stranger Returns* is a classic of the genre. It blends memorable melodies with classic spaghetti western instrumentation and fitting details, like screams, whip cracks and bells.

Carlo Savina scored *I due Ringos del Texas* (*The Two Ringos from Texas*, 1967), which explores the various sounds one can create with a mouth harmonica. Alongside throbbing electric bass, solo brass, rhythm guitar and vibes, a harmonica trills like some strange bird and later rises and falls like a heat wave.

The melancholy theme by Roberto Pregadio and Walter Rizzati for *L'ultimo killer* (*The Last Killer*, or *Django the Last Gunfighter*, 1967) is played stoically on acoustic guitars, electric bass and brushed drums before sullen strings and solo trumpet wash over them. Sad, lonely music like this is common to the genre, but this score actually has tracks called "Sadness" and "Loneliness," not to mention "Bitter and Violent." It is not cheery stuff, but it is melodically haunting.

Swirling strings and chiming percussion introduce *La più grande rap-

Stelvio Cipriani's score for *Un uomo, un cavallo, una pistola* (*The Stranger Returns*, 1967) blends memorable melodies with classic spaghetti western audio details like screams, whip cracks and bells. (CD cover appears courtesy of CAM Original Soundtracks; graphic designer unknown.)

ina del west (*The Greatest Robbery in the West*, or *Halleluja for Django*, 1967). What sounds, at first, like the beginning of a Christmas program soon turns into square dance fun with seesawing fiddles, banjo, guitar, comedic horns and lively percussion. Bacalov's theme (with variations "Saloon Polka" and "Square Dance") is quite a change of pace for the genre, but a welcome one. Beyond the main theme the tone becomes more suspenseful, with the composer making effective use of full orchestra, accented by rumbling percussion, mysterious flute trills and discordant guitar arpeggios. *Robbery* certainly shows Bacalov's flair for both the dramatic and the comedic.

Reverberi's strange *Una Colt in pugno al diavolo* (*A Colt in the Fist of the Devil*, 1967) makes the old west sound like the cowboys are on LSD, which turns out to be a good thing. While not all of the score is psychedelic, the use of whistling, with odd organ fills, plus flanged, detuned and distorted guitar and intermittent strings, makes for a trippy listen.

Dio perdona ... il no! (*God Forgives ... I Don't*, or *Blood River*, 1967) features a grandiose score by Carlo Rustichelli that incorporates an operatic male chorus with surging Wagnerian orchestration, but also includes passages rem-

Carlo Rustichelli's score for *Dio perdona... il no!* (*God Forgives... I Don't*, or *Blood River*, 1967) offers a range of musical styles, from Hollywood western to Wagnerian opera to New Orleans dirge. (CD cover appears courtesy of Digitmovies Alternative Entertainment; graphic design by Claudio Fuiano.)

iniscent of classic Hollywood westerns. It's an unusual approach, to say the least. The score also features a marching band number and a New Orleans–style funeral dirge with Dixieland horns and a clarinet solo.

Another unusual entry in the genre is Ferrio's jazz-influenced *Sentenza di morte* (*Death Sentence*, 1967). The theme song, "The Last Game," features a commanding performance by soul baritone Nevil Cameron, and easily distinguishes itself from the pack. Its unconventional arrangement adapts the spaghetti style of Morricone, but places considerable emphasis on the vocal, allowing the accompanying instrumentation to punctuate the melody in unexpected ways. The jazz influence is highly pronounced on "Midnight Game," where double bass, vibes and saxophones provide a foggy atmosphere of mystery. "The First and Last Game" also plays up the noir mood with turgid strings, bongos, jazz guitar and organ bits. Ferrio also delivers more traditional spag western cues, featuring mariachi brass ("Hot Mexico") and Spanish guitars ("Guitar Game" and "Hot Mexico").

For *Da uomo a uomo* (*Death Rides a Horse*, 1967), Morricone continued to experiment with the style he invented. Here he pairs dissonant acoustic guitars with chanted vocals by Cantori Moderni. The flute, which occasionally pipes up, sounds worthy of Ian Anderson of Jethro Tull. The score features an effective mix of rousing chase music and somber atmospheric pieces. The chase music is brutally intense, with electric guitars, panpipe and vocal chants. There are several variations on the theme, which was covered by spag western singer Raoul for a 45 release. Film music critic John Bender wrote that Raoul's version is the ultimate spaghetti western ballad. It's certainly one of the best. Notably, Italian film music fanatic Quentin Tarantino later used a selection from the *Death* score for his film *Kill Bill Vol. 1* (2003).

One of Morricone's most popular scores belongs to the politically charged *La resa dei conti* (*The Big Gundown*, 1967). Conducted by Nicolai and featuring the Cantori Moderni, the soundtrack sold well when originally released on LP, and for good reason. The theme song, "Run Man Run," galvanizes, thanks to its bravura vocal performance by Christy (a.k.a. Maria Cristina Branucci). The melody crops up repeatedly, but lends itself to many variations and moods, from solemn to energetic. Religious pieces are not uncommon on the score. For example, "Coro dei Mormon" is an outstanding *a cappella* showcase for Alessandroni's singers. Although instrumentation is rarely outlandish, occasionally the approach is quite unusual. On "La Corrida" Morricone's avant-gardisms reach a fever pitch as atonal woodwinds and piano jockey for position before racing off against a backdrop of squonks, rattles and honks into melodic territory that simultaneously suggests a mariachi band gone loco, and German theatrical songwriter Kurt Weill and *Looney Tunes* composer Carl Stalling collaborating on a New York street corner. On another track, a female member of Cantori Moderni provides a variety of birdcalls against a background of wheezing, panting noises from an indeterminate source. Probably the most famous track is "La Resa dei Conti (Seconda Caccia)," where an intricately played electric guitar joins the mounting instrumental charge to a fierce crescendo. Notably, New York avant-garde jazz artist John Zorn's Morricone tribute album *The Big Gundown* features a radical interpretation of *The Big Gundown*'s theme.

Nearly as memorable is Morricone's *Il grande silenzio* (*The Big Silence*, 1967). Stabbing keyboard lines, throbbing electric bass, pounding percussion, trilling woodwinds and the ubiquitous Alessandroni singers make tracks like "Crossing Through the Weather" a gripping ordeal. On the flipside, the gentle, intricate 12-string guitars and serenely swelling melody of "Journey," which is a variation on the film's theme, is Morricone at his most soothing. Legend has it that *The Big Silence* is Morricone's favorite western score outside of his work for Leone. For a composer noted for using unusual instruments, it should come as no surprise to hear sitar and tabla in the mix on this score.

That same year Francesco De Masi scored *Sette Winchester per un massacro* (*Seven Guns for a Killing*, 1967), again featuring his favorite western vocalist, Raoul. De Masi was never one to ape Morricone, as he always brings a distinctive bottom-end thrust to his western scores. Here, thick electric bass joins acoustic and electric guitars, as well as brass, strings and percussion, for a lean and tough sound.

De Masi's music for *Vado, L'ammazzo e torno* (*Any Gun Can Play*, or *For a Few Bullets More*, 1967) uses harmonica to good effect against a backdrop of acoustic guitar arpeggios, swelling strings, and clicking, rattling percussion ("Vento e Whisky" and "Riding and Whistling"). Franco De Gemini plays harmonica here and on countless other spag westerns. Like Alessandroni's whistling and guitar playing, De Gemini's harmonica is—as film music critic John Bender put it—as elemental to the genre as are "sweaty, squinty-eyed close-ups." Alessandroni's acoustic guitar again is set against the gentle backdrop of strings and thumping bass notes on the somber ballad "Mexico Western."

For *Ammazzali tutti e torno solo* (*Kill Them All and Come Back Alone*, 1968) De Masi wrote a virile theme song, "Gold," for Raoul to sing. "Clyde's Final Trick" reprises the theme in the most somber manner possible. "Challenge to Death" finds De Masi really pushing the genre's familiar stylistic conventions with a creative discipline and orchestral flair that elevates the material with high, bright notes punctuating the rhythmically dense melody and countermelody. The track should be enough to convince anyone that De Masi was among the genre's best composers. Part of the credit must go to Alessandroni, who plays guitar on *Any Gun* and *Kill Them All*, and gets a co-composing credit.

De Masi's work on *Quanto costa morire* (*The Cost of Dying*, 1968) is among his best efforts in the genre. The soundtrack begins innocently enough with a jaunty track for harmonica, banjo, bass guitar and light snare work. The theme "Who Is the Man?"—with its intricate guitar arpeggios, bongos and

Quanto costa morire (a.k.a. *The Cost of Dying*, 1968) contains one of Francesco De Masi's best western scores. (CD cover appears courtesy of Digitmovies Alternative Entertainment; graphic design by Claudio Fuiano.)

mariachi brass—is a solid example of a melodramatic Italian western theme song, though it avoids the sort of bombast that has given the genre a reputation for going over the top with emotion. Naturally, it features De Masi's favorite singer, Raoul. The suspense cues, which are quite effective, are sometimes subtly reminiscent of Barry's suspense cues for 007 movies in their use of low brass and sneaky percussion fills.

De Masi's music for *Ringo il cavaliere solitario* (*Ringo the Lone Rider*, 1968) signifies its post–Civil War setting—like so many war westerns—with militaristic snare drums. The mournful trumpet, electric guitar figure and harmonica capture the sense of living with loss in a long-suffering land.

De Masi's music for *Quella sporca storia nel west* (*Johnny Hamlet*, or *That Dirty Old Story of the West*, 1968) has a surreal bent, with psychedelic echo effects on tracks like "Suspence al Villaggio." Tracks like "Cercando un Fantasma" and "La Medaglia" have a suspenseful quality that reflects the film's Hamlet-inspired plot, complete with nightmare visions of the hero's dead father.

Another composer capable of creating a mysterious mood for a western was Coriolano (Lallo) Gori. His score for *Il winchester che non perdona* (*Buckaroo*, 1968) is outstanding. Gori, like De Masi, injects his music with a strong bottom-end presence, care of an electric bass. As a western specialist, he wasn't shy about using twangy electric guitar, lyrical Spanish guitar, harmonica (De Gemini again), and mariachi brass. He also was fond of inserting mysterious percussive sounds into suspenseful passages, where shuddering strings and descending plucks of a harp momentarily remind one of John Barry's creeping 007 suspense motifs until a solo trumpet confirms that this is a western and not a spy picture. The catchy theme crops up repeatedly. Dean Reed croons the late–1950s rock-a-billy ballad.

Among the jazziest Italian film composers to take a stab at a spag western was undoubtedly Piero Piccioni (though Piero Umiliani was another). On *Quel caldo maledetto giorno di fuoco* (*The Day of Fire*, 1968), Piccioni delivers a rumbling theme, with organ carrying the melody of "One More Time." The swinging, finger-snapping track wouldn't sound out of place on one of Piccioni's modern scores, like *Colpo rovente* or *Playgirl '70*.

Relative unknowns in the annals of Italian film music, much less the spaghetti western genre, are Vasco Vassil Kojucharov and Elsio Mancuso. Their work on *Una lunga fila di croci* (*No Room to Die*, or *Noose for Django*, 1968) is shockingly effective and memorable. The six-minute "Crossing the Border" is more like two tracks joined at the hip. The first half is an electrically charged suspense cue built on bongo beats, shuddering strings, and stings of harpsichord and electric guitar. After nearly three minutes of classic B-film chills, a brisk drum rhythm kicks in, propelling the track into full-gallop jazz flute trills, swirling stings, jazz guitar and harpsichord worthy of Lalo Schifrin. This second part is also the basis of the vocal theme "Maya" (a.k.a. "I Expect Nothing"), sung in English by Franco Morselli. As Bender noted for *Spaghetti Westerns Vol. 4*, "it's bursting at the seams with the wild and furious spirit of the mythical west."

Although many Italian composers scored westerns, Morricone's efforts always seem to be a cut above, even above the films for which he composed. *Tepepa* (*Blood and Guns*, 1968) is a fair example. As is his standard, Morricone delivers stirring themes, though the mood tends toward somber. Discordant strings weave a dark spell on tracks like "Una Povera Casa" and "Tradimento Secondo." Crunching percussive Spanish guitar chords, piano and harpsichord stings, and stuttering drums add to the drama. "Viva La Revolucion" reinforces the film's south-of-the-border setting with sleepy guitar arpeggios that chime in as keyboards and orchestra repeat the haunting melody in a steady, stoic fashion.

For fans of the genre, it always comes back to Morricone, and the reason is simple: no other composer matches his ability to reinvent the style with each successive score. Take the theme from *Faccia a faccia* (*Face to Face*, 1968). Here Morricone, who previously worked for Sergio Sollima on *The Big Gundown*, gets things going with rumbling drums and an angular melody played on pipe organ. Strings start to stir in the background until a guitar and harpsichord suddenly launch a relentless, frenzied riff over a pounding bass drum. Dell'Orso's soprano soars over the beat, and the high strings are briefly mimicked by brass. The piece is melodically dramatic, and the arrangement is gripping, but also avant-garde sounding—typical Morricone with Nicolai conducting. Later in the score, the melody returns on an electric organ. It also features De Gemini's harmonica and an organ piece that Morricone later adapted for the film *The Mission* (1986).

Although *Il mercenario* (*A Professional Gun*, or *Revenge of a Gunfighter*, or *The Mercenary*, 1968) is generally considered one of the best spaghetti westerns, the soundtrack by Morricone and Nicolai is not particularly memorable by Morricone's standards. With its emphatic brass and violin volleys, it is clearly more Nicolai than Morricone, though the latter occasionally receives sole credit for this score. The score's most outstanding contribution to the genre is its Rodrigo-inspired "bullring symphony," as Howard Hughes calls it in his insightful book *Once Upon a Time in the Italian West: A Filmgoer's Guide to Spaghetti Westerns* (I.B. Tauris, 2004). Hughes also points out that the movie's powerful theme is "almost identical" to Morricone's theme for *Guns for San Sebastian* (1968).

A far more serious sound is heard in Carlo Rustichelli's darkly romantic and suspenseful *L'uomo, l'orgoglio, la vendetta* (*Man: His Pride and His Vengeance*, or *Pride and Vengeance*, 1968). Spanish guitars play prominently against a backdrop of lush orchestration, which sometimes assumes a sinister disposition. It makes for an absorbing listen, but few would mistake it for a spaghetti western score. It is excellent nonetheless.

Another two Rustichelli scores belong to comedic westerns, *I quattro dell'ave maria* (*Ace High*, or *Have Gun Will Travel*, 1968) and *La collina degli stevali* (*Boot Hill*, or *Trinity Rides Again*, 1969), starring Terence Hill and Bud Spencer, who made a number of westerns together and apart. Master orchestrator Nicolai conducts the material on *Ace High*. Using chorus (I Cantori Moderni di Alessandroni) and orchestra, as well as solo instruments such as piano, organ and harmonica (De Gemini), Nicolai lends Rustichelli's music rich textures that tap into the story's adventure, suspense and comedic elements. Like *Boot Hill*'s score, the themes for *Ace High* sometimes display a bittersweet Italian sensibility backed with waltz-like cadence. At other times, the sound is much more in the traditional expansive western style that sug-

Franco Micalizzi's jaunty score for *They Call Me Trinity* (AVCO Embassy, 1970), starring Terence Hill (and Bud Spencer), captures the film's comedic spirit. (Photograph courtesy of the John Monaghan collection.)

gests big skies and windswept landscapes. On *Boot Hill*, Rustichelli starts with reverent strings and chorus on the theme, followed by circus and can-can music. Of the two scores *Ace High* has the stylistic advantage, thanks to Nicolai's considerable experience conducting numerous scores for Morricone. Notably, Hill plays a character named Cat Stevens in *Ace High*; the pop folk singer of the same name had debuted on record in 1967.

An essential soundtrack that is more likely to stir the passions of spaghetti western fans is Morricone's *C'era una volta il west* (*Once Upon a Time in the West*, 1969). Richard Corliss of *Time* magazine wrote that it was "arguably the richest in movie history." As was his habit on a Leone production, Morricone composed the score before the film was shot so that Leone could use the recorded music on location to inspire his actors. The film itself has been described as Leone's opera, and Morricone's music delivers the requisite grandeur. The theme, which is gently introduced on harpsichord, builds gradually with orchestral accompaniment. Dell'Orso's lends her angelic voice, and then Mahler-esque French horns and strings sweep in, lifting the listener like a bird over a vast western vista. This is Morricone film music at its most gorgeous. The theme is reprised on "Jill's America." From there, the composer does not hesitate to paint a more sinister picture by employing much more abrasive sonorities. "As a Judgment" uses a severely distorted electric guitar sound against screeching violins. The track that most resembles Morricone's earlier western efforts is "Farewell to Cheyenne," which features a loping clip-clopping rhythm, Alessandroni's whistling, a bit of restrained saloon piano and acoustic guitar. It's an iconic western cue from the master.

The instrument most memorably employed in *Once Upon a Time in the West* is De Gemini's raspy, echoing harmonica, which figures prominently in the onscreen action.

"One day while chatting with Leone I brought up the idea of a film that would boldly present the harmonica, symbolically, as the central character, and to my surprise he replied he thought this was a good idea," De Gemini recounted in his memoir, *From Beat to Beat* (Beat Records, p. 41, 2006). "When one considers the intense metaphorical importance of the harmonica in *Once Upon a Time in the West* it certainly seems Sergio followed through on my 'hint.'"

Ennio Morricone's epic score is a perfect fit for Sergio Leone's widescreen masterpiece *Once Upon a Time in the West* (Paramount Pictures, 1968). (Photograph courtesy of the John Monaghan Collection.)

In *West*, Charles Bronson plays "Harmonica," a gunslinger out to avenge the murder of his brother by the ruthless killer "Frank" (Henry Fonda). Late in the film, "Harmonica" remembers how years earlier Frank and his gang tied his hands behind his back, shoved a harmonica in his mouth and forced him to support his noose-ensnared brother on his shoulders under the desert sun. As the memory ends in the inevitable death of his brother, "Harmonica" outduels Frank, and then places his instrument in the mouth of the fatally wounded killer as a way of identifying himself and reminding Frank of his own cruelty.

"The aim was to perfectly simulate the famous 'last death-rattle' as sounded on the harmonica," De Gemini wrote in 2006. "Morricone, during the first recording session, told me to place three notes in a sequence that could evoke the horrible anguish of those scenes.... There were only three strange notes because in the movie the two tortured souls, one good, one evil, who were going to be breathing into a harmonica, could not move the instrument with their hands.... This eerie sound is so perfect for the movie." (*FBtB*, p. 43, 45)

De Gemini's harmonica and Dell'Orso's voice also are heard on Bacalov's *Il grande duello* (*The Big Showdown*, or *Storm Rider*, 1969). On the theme, Bacalov also makes excellent use of a human whistle (Alessandroni?) imitating wind, beautifully backed by harpsichord, acoustic guitar, throbbing electric bass, woodwinds and strings. Notably, Tarantino used the track in his trash cinema epic *Kill Bill*.

On Bacalov's *I quattro del pater noster* (*The Four Horsemen of the Pater Noster*, 1969), one hears in a brass fanfare a melody similar to one that was scored decades later by Howard Shore for Peter Jackson's epic *The Lord of the Rings*. Undoubtedly, this is merely a coincidence, but the similarity is striking nonetheless. The score's mood ranges from spry to suspenseful.

For *La notte dei serpenti* (*Night of the Serpent*, 1969), Riz Ortolani deftly combines big orchestra with south-of-the-border musical motifs. The theme opens mysteriously with echoing twin electric guitar lines that advance hesitantly like a snake across hot asphalt. Low brass, a deep bass drum and a shimmering cymbal provide intermittent evidence of heat waves along a lonely stretch of a desert two-lane. Elsewhere, the score rumbles forth like a Golden Age Hollywood western—all big-sky bravado, sometimes topped with mariachi trumpets. Ortolani occasionally dials down the mood for a Spanish guitar and strings, and on at least one track his wife, Katina Ranieri, sings a sleepy lullaby.

For a rather pleasant take on the spaghetti western sound, look no further than Angelo Lavagnino's soft and rolling theme for *Gli specialisti* (*The Specialist*, 1969). Woodwinds and harpsichord carry the lilting melody like a kite on a summer breeze, while the grounded rhythm section holds it steady and guides it to a safe landing. This is a far cry from the gun-toting savagery of most spag western scores. Another delightful track sprints along on similar instrumentation with the slightly frenzied pace of a youthful game of tag.

Gianni Ferrio also delivered an unconventional Italian western score with *Vivi o preferibilmente morti* (*Alive or Preferably Dead*, or *Sundance Cassidy and Butch the Kid*, 1969). With full-blown musical numbers, *Alive* offers a sentimental score worthy of *Oklahoma* that features such zany western sounds as buzzy paper and comb, and Jew's harp. The leadoff track, "Monty and Ted," is a rollicking country duet by John Ireson and Wayne Parham (a.k.a. the Wilder Brothers). Lilian Terry and Cantori Moderni sing on "Yes, Sir," which features dueling Dixieland clarinet and trumpet, along with handclaps. There also are tender themes like "Two Peaceful Brothers" and "Falling in Love with a Pretty Girl" that rely heavily on saccharine strings and lush orchestration.

Piero Umiliani's score for Mario Bava's comedic *Roy Colt & Winchester Jack* (1970) uses subtle psychedelic effects and a vocal performance on the theme by a group called Free Love. The composer tweaks audience expectations by mixing modern elements (bass guitar, Hammond organ) with traditional western sounds (acoustic guitars, banjo, whistling, fiddle, harmonica and solo trumpet).

Augusto Martelli's arrangements for *Sartana nella valle degli avvoltoi* (*Sartana in the Valley of Vultures*, or *Ballad of Death Valley*, 1970) flirt with rock. The song "A King for a Day" makes good use harmonica and Jew's harp, while the bass line and drumming lock into a funky groove. On "Sartana in Action," a throbbing rhythm and distorted guitar chords complement flute stabs and harmonica.

Augusto Martelli sets down a jazzy groove for "Still Water," the main song for *Ancor dollari per i MacGregor* (*More Dollars for the MacGregors*, 1970). An electric bass underpins a macho baritone delivering a heavily accented vocal over liquid piano and staccato brass. With its thumping bass drums and telegraph keys and woodwinds, "Happy Cowboys" almost sounds like the theme for some evening news program. On "Indian Dance," Martelli again displays his taste for percussion and a lone woodwind when evoking primitive rites.

On "Free," the theme song for *La collera del vento* (*Trinity Sees Red*, 1970), Martelli pairs a classic hippie sentiment (about being free to live life the way you want to) with a slightly funky banjo riff, accompanied by a bubbling bass line, vibes and percussion. Another standout track is "The Riot," which sounds suitably chaotic, with heavily distorted guitar stings and rumbling drums. "The Village" is yet another example of Martelli's version of native primitivism.

In the '70s, comedic westerns became increasingly popular, and Morricone scored his fair share, including *Vamos a matar, companeros* (1970). The catchy theme music features wailing harmonica, banjo and frenzied chanting

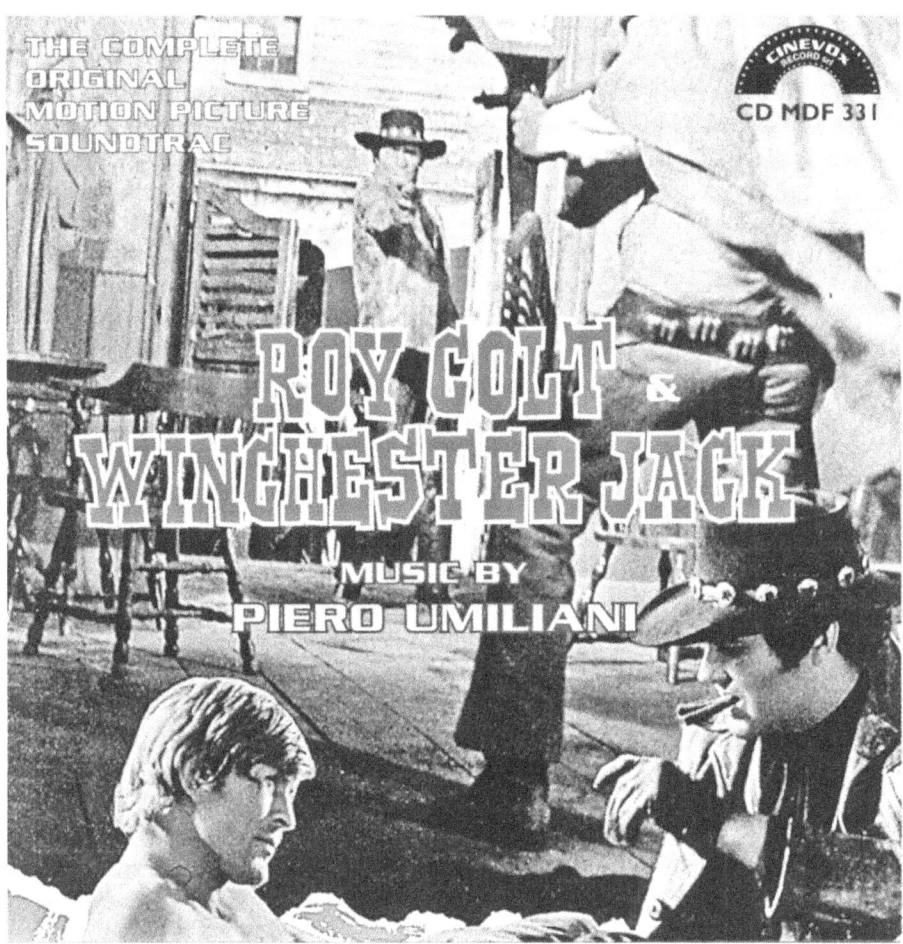

Piero Umiliani's score for *Roy Colt & Winchester Jack* (1970) uses subtle psychedelic effects and a vocal performance on the theme by a group called Free Love. (CD cover appears courtesy of Cinevox Records; graphic design by Fredrika Cao.)

chorus. While most of the other tracks on *Companeros* don't match the brilliant theme for sheer intensity, other highlights include the discordant and suspenseful "Un Uomo in Agguato," the folksy and laidback "Il Pinguino" and its fuzz-toned variation "Il Ringuino."

Bacalov was back in the saddle for *L'oro dei bravados* (*Gold of the Heroes*, 1970). It contains one of his most amazing western themes. Electric guitar stings, bright acoustic guitar and rattlesnake percussion provide a dust-blown backdrop for trilling keys and harmonica with Jew's harp accents, as well as bird call clarinet and whistled solos. Elsewhere on the score the composer uses rumbling bass, shivering strings, suspenseful harpsichord, clockwork harp notes, hoarse flute trills and occasional psychedelic effects.

Nicolai's *Buon funerale amigos, paga sartana* (*Have a Good Funeral, Sartana Will Pay*, 1970) is powerful stuff. With galloping rhythm and virtuoso guitar playing, one of its hard-charging themes is as relentless as a stampede until the coda, where swirling violins, electric guitar stings and horn blasts give way to acoustic guitar filigree and birdcall woodwinds. In just over two minutes it seems to have something for everyone. Of course, this being a Nicolai score, there are also tracks of serene strings and tender Spanish guitar.

Although Nicolai's score may be the best found in a *Sartana* film, De Masi's music for the sequel *C'è Sartana, vendi la pistola e comprati la bara* (*I'm Sartana, Trade Your Pistol for a Coffin*, 1970) also is outstanding. The theme features whip cracks, vibe accents, bright acoustic guitar rhythms and a hallucinatory midsection with swirling harp, intricate percussion fills and suspenseful bass guitar.

De Masi also works his strange magic on *La sfida dei McKenna* (*Challenge of the McKennas*, 1970), where an assertive electric bass meets a crisp beat. All of the instruments occupy a distinct place in the sound space, with unique flourishes, such as screeching violins, that suddenly propel the music forward.

Nicolai, having been the master orchestrator of many Morricone scores, brings that talent, along with his compositional chops, to *Un uomo chiamato Apocalisse Joe* (*The Man Called Apocalypse Joe*, 1970). The first sequence combines soft flute, solemn oboe, throbbing bass, stalwart guitar, militaristic drums and soaring strings. Later in the score, Nicolai throws a musical curveball with a piece that has one foot in the western motif and the other seemingly in a Renaissance fair. It's a remarkable juxtaposition to accompany the shenanigans of a gunman who doubles as a wayward thespian.

One of the most unusual and electrifying spaghetti western scores belongs to *Matalo* (*Kill Him*, 1970), by Mario Migliardi. Full of fuzz-toned guitar and aggressive hard rock drumming, *Matalo* has the genre's greatest acid rock theme, complete with snarling vocals. Echoing psychedelic atmospherics are heard throughout the score, particularly on the chase cues. On "Chase," the main theme is repeated and extended, connected with pulsing, ringing piano notes, hypnotizing like a desert heat haze. On "Chase #2" and "Chase #3," phased percussion and piano create a metallic locomotive pulse for a disorienting soundscape of anxious pursuit. On the cacophonous "Chase #4," discordant layers of percussion and fuzz-toned guitar clash with distorted voices and taunting woodwinds. On "Ghosts," the theme becomes completely fragmented and beatless, blowing like sand phantoms through an echoing slot canyon. On *Matalo*, Migliardi interprets Morricone's western aesthetic through the filter of psychedelia to create one of the genre's best soundtracks.

By the early '70s the peak era of spaghetti westerns was long past, but fans could rely on the genre's outstanding composers to deliver high quality

Ennio Morricone continued to experiment with his already innovative western sound on *Giù la testa* (a.k.a. *Duck You Sucker*, or *A Fistful of Dynamite*, 1971). (CD cover appears courtesy of Cinevox Records; graphic design by Fredrika Cao.)

soundtracks. Undoubtedly, Morricone's score for Leone's political western *Giù la testa* (*Duck You Sucker*, or *A Fistful of Dynamite*, 1971) is among the best soundtracks the genre has to offer from the '70s. By turns tender and quirky, *Duck* features sublime orchestration with choral accents (male and female), as well as whistling and other instrumentation typical of the genre. On the romantically tinged title track, Dell'Orso does what she does best while male singers chant what sounds like "shaun, shaun," but it probably represents the characters John and Juan. The overall effect is quite memorable. Another track, which was released as a single around the time of the film's release, is "March of the Beggars," which features a comically croaking male voice and mischievous melody played on alternating instruments over a spare snare drum rhythm. This deliciously inventive piece plays out with the inevitability of the classic works of Mozart and Bach, and is guaranteed to stick in one's memory. Odd sonorities always have been innate to Morricone's magic. Listen to the distorted keyboard notes at the beginning of "Scherzi a Parte." Alone they would become tiresome after a few bars, but used sparingly against more traditional instrumentation, the squonking cartoonish noise is a marvelous example of how well electronic sounds can mesh with acoustic sounds. The most amazing track on *Duck* is the nine-minute "Invenzione per John" (or "Inventions of John"), which deserves to be dubbed "Reinventions of Ennio." Morricone reprises his theme but extends it through free-form abstraction by overlapping melodic ideas where every element seems out of sync with the other. Morricone deconstructs his musical thoughts and, along the way, discovers countless variations on his theme. It's the most hypnotic nine minutes you're likely to find on an Italian western score. It's nothing short of brilliant. The nearly seven-minute track "Rivoluzione Contro" initially sounds like an outtake from Stravinsky's "Le Sacre du Printemps" before dissolving in discordant strings and electronic static from another world. It's the most sci-fi moment one is likely to hear on a western score, period. *Duck* is another classic western score by the master of the genre.

Maestro Bacalov scored several westerns in 1971, including the comic *Si può fare ... amigo!* (*The Big and the Bad*). Soul singer Rocky Roberts (of the Airedales) performs "Can Be Done" with a choir of children, making it an unusually adorable spag western song. Interestingly, Roberts sounds a bit like David Bowie on the track, particularly when he uses low vibrato. Bacalov makes great use of distorted guitar stings, and harmonica wails and warbles, on the score as well.

Bacalov's *Monta in sella, figlio di ...* (*Ride a Horse, Son of...*, or *Great Treasure Hunt*, 1971) is relatively traditional, with high shimmering strings and a sentimental melody played by solo horn, and later by a small ensemble. Some cues are more modern, relying more on repetitive keyboard figures and acoustic guitars, but more often than not the orchestra swells to "Big Country" effect.

Bacalov's *Lo chiamavano King* (*A Man Called King*, 1971) displays a more contemporary sound. Short bursts of machine-gun drum rolls riddle the theme, "His Name Was King," supported by booming bass guitar runs and a bit of distorted guitar. Soulful Ann Collin sings the vocal version. It's a tough-sounding score for a bounty hunter saga, with a few melancholy and suspenseful passages.

Nicolai's rousing, comedic *Gli fumavano le colt, lo chiamavano camposanto* (*Bullet for a Stranger*, 1971) contains one of his best themes. Built around a galloping tempo, the track features a lead whistler, a grunting male chorus, electric guitar spikes, ringing chimes, big hook melody and relentless rhythmic attack.

Stelvio Cipriani's *Il pistolero cieco* (*Blindman*, 1971), starring Ringo Starr, is one of the few Italian westerns with theme music featuring sitar. (CD cover appears courtesy of Digitmovies Alternative Entertainment; graphic design by Claudio Fuiano.)

Although he is better known for his *gialli* and *poliziotteschi* soundtracks, Stelvio Cipriani tracked a few westerns, including *Il pistolero cieco* (*Blindman*, 1971). It contains one of the few western themes to feature sitar, which is integral to several tracks without sounding like a gimmick. Cipriani also makes good use of singer/composer Nora Orlandi and her choir, who fit seamlessly into Cipriani's hard-riding East-meets-West pop orchestration. The eastern influence is appropriate since *Blindman* is *en homage* to Japanese cinema's blind samurai hero *Zatoichi*. The *Blindman* score has fantastic passages where 12-string guitar arpeggios mesh with sitar, flute, bass and drums to create a suspenseful atmosphere of imminent danger against a stark desert background.

The soundtrack also boasts a fair amount of lively mariachi music (sans sitar, of course). Throughout, Cipriani offers up big melodic hooks and thrilling, pulse pounding, near-rock arrangements without losing the western feel.

Always one to steer clear of western clichés, Piero Piccioni's *Una Colt in mano al diavolo* (*A Gun in the Hand of the Devil*, 1972) reflects the modern jazz sensibility he frequently brought to his western scores. The theme features a rumbling bass line and skittering trap work, as well as bluesy solo guitar and acoustic guitar rhythms. No whistling, no harmonica, no mariachi brass in earshot. Another track, "Mystery," wouldn't sound out of place in a *giallo* thriller from the same period. Ominous organ chords and a stealthy bass line connote imminent danger.

By the early '70s filmmakers were frequently toying with the genre to freshen it up. Comedy westerns were most common, but occasionally another hybrid reared its head, like the East-meets-West kung-fu western *Il mio nome e Shanghai Joe* (*My Name Is Shanghai Joe*, 1973). Nicolai provided the music, including the mesmerizing "La Partenza," which features a lovely electric guitar ostinato and lead organ against a steady beat, sounding a little like the '60s-inspired rock group Stereolab. However, for the theme he simply recycled his earlier title track for *Have a Good Funeral, My Friend ... Sartana Will Pay*.

Piccioni's penchant for jazzy grooves took to the dusty trail yet again on *Nel nome del padre, del figlio e della Colt* (*In the Name of the Father, of the Son, and of the Gun*, 1973). The theme features repetitive figures played in unison by brass, organ and guitar, as the rhythm section lays down a funky jazz groove. It sounds utterly contemporary and suggests in no way whatsoever that a western is taking place. One would think that the alternate "beat version" would further distance the score from the subject matter, but the use of solo trumpet actually lends the track a vague notion of sagebrush and six-shooters.

Morricone perfected the comic western sound on the theme for the hit *Il mio nome e Nessuno* (*My Name Is Nobody*, 1973). As on his classic western scores of the '60s, Morricone combines lean arrangements that highlight the genre's customary instruments (acoustic guitar, recorder, chorus). This time a squonky synthesizer adds a quirky twist. Elsewhere, Morricone employs another familiar element from his earlier efforts, a ticking clock. It is even accompanied by chimes, vigorous acoustic guitar picking and electric guitar stings (courtesy of Bruno Battista D'Amario)—it's a classic Morricone western sound. As is his habit, Morricone isn't shy about satirically quoting from a classical piece as well (e.g. "Flight of the Valkyries")—on synth, no less—for the showdown between Henry Fonda's old gunfighter and the army of outlaw riders known as the "Wild Bunch." The track also uses 12-string guitar (played by Silvano Chimenti), panpipes, Alessandroni's whistling and the background singing of his Cantori. It's an outstanding track from Morricone's last great western score.

Nicolai's music for *Lo chiamavano Tresette, giocava sempre col morto* (*The Man Called Invincible*, or *They Called Him the Player with the Dead*, 1973) is lively and delightful. The opening track is possibly the most happy-go-lucky, ridin' the range and lovin' it theme written for an Italian western. And the tango that uses solo violin and saloon piano, followed by harmonica, Jew's harp and acoustic guitar, is sublime stuff.

Another lighthearted entry is Rustichelli's *Tutti per uno, botte per tutti* (*The Three Musketeers of the West*, 1973). A clip-clop rhythm drives "Dart Theme," with accordion, harmonica, guitar and bass. The fiesta music injects new blood into the mix, with hyper, comic, synthetically modulated instrumental effects. It sounds like someone spiked the sangria with hallucinogens.

Umiliani returned to the western scene for *Dieci bianchi uccisi da un piccolo indiano* (*Blood River*, 1975). More than *Roy Colt*, *Blood River* adheres to the traditional western sound. Robust orchestration and a noticeable absence of the jazz influence make *Blood River* less discernible as an Umiliani score. That's not to say it's lacking in excitement. It's positively brimming with compelling, suspenseful music. "La Vendetta" is outstanding, with a Spanish-tinged hook and forceful, crisp execution. Above all, Umiliani injects the material with energy and creativity often lacking in scores by composers who worked on dozens of westerns.

A composing team that came on strong toward the end of the spaghetti western era was composer Bixio, lyricist Fabio Frizzi, and arranger and orchestrator Vince Tempera. For the comic *Carambola* (1974) the trio supplied a hypnotic, brooding theme that beautifully juxtaposes simultaneous electric guitar and trumpet solos. On the finale, the trumpet is replaced by a second guitar, which makes for an even better juxtaposition. On the sequel, *Carambola filotto tutti in buca* (*Carambola's Philosophy: In the Right Pocket*, 1975), Bixio, Frizzi and Tempera deliver guitar-oriented music that is more rambunctious and upbeat. They also show a fondness for solo fiddle on "Funny Town."

The next year, Bixio, Frizzi and Tempera worked on *I quattro dell'apocalisse* (*Four of the Apocalypse*, 1976). Some of the score has a mellow country folk feel, made particularly noticeable on sub–Simon & Garfunkel ballads by the virtually unknown Cook & Benjamin Franklin Group. Occasionally—like on "Slow Violence"—the music is more orchestral, and employs percussion, acoustic guitar, flute and harpsichord to create tension. When the trio resort to folk rock instrumentation—as on "Death's Song"—the result is usually quite compelling, and nearly makes up for the soft ballads one must endure along the way.

Bixio, Frizzi and Tempera's *Sella d'argento* (*Silver Saddle*, or *They Died with Their Boots On*, 1978) is similar, but there's more tension; and the guest singer, Canadian Ken Tobias (who also wrote the lyrics for the theme), is slightly less trying on one's patience. The instrumentation is again inspired by folk rock, but the execution has more bite. On a track like "Hot Lands," the ensemble playing (guitar, bass, banjo and percussion) is positively sizzling. The guys show a soft side on cuts like "My Name Is Silver Saddle," where strings swell and harmonica wails. The production quality is excellent and makes

Bixio-Frizzi-Tempera brings a folk-rock feeling to their score for *I quattro dell'apocalisse* (*Four of the Apocalypse*, 1976). (CD cover appears courtesy of Cinevox Records; graphic design by Fredrika Cao.)

every element pop. "In the Desert" vibrates with electric bass before a group of violins, and then full orchestra, jump in at a full gallop; "Part 2" replaces strings with mariachi brass. For a score that came along many years after the genre's peak, *Silver Saddle* is remarkably strong and positively electric.

Though there were spaghetti westerns made beyond *Amore piombe e furore* (*Gunfire*, or *China 9 Liberty 37*, 1978). It will serve as stopping point for this overview on Italian westerns. On one of Donaggio's few western scores one finds "Tema Di Clayton," a fitting track to close the survey. Its wailing harmonica nearly recalls Morricone's "Man with a Harmonica" music from

Bixio-Frizzi-Tempera also brings a folk-rock vibe to *Sella d'argento* (*Silver Saddle*, 1978). (CD cover appears courtesy of Digitmovies Alternative Entertainment; graphic design by Claudio Fuiano.)

Once Upon a Time in the West. Accompanied by acoustic guitar only, it captures the essential spirit of the European interpretation of the Old West, where moody men wander alone in a wasteland occasionally finding camaraderie by a fading campfire.

The Post-Dollars Hollywood Westerns

After Italian westerns became popular in the U.S. (starting with *The Good, the Bad, and the Ugly*) Hollywood filmmakers revived the genre Stateside with the help of its classic figurehead Wayne and, particularly, its new icon Eastwood. While some of the films (*Hang 'Em High*, 1968) imitated the Italian style, or even went so far as to use a Morricone score (*Two Mules for Sister Sara*, 1970), others digressed entirely (the musical *Paint Your Wagon*, 1969; or the cowboy as modern-day sheriff in *Coogan's Bluff*, 1968). The Italian western's penchant for brutality, violence and anti-heroes can be seen in numerous Hollywood productions, such as the Eastwood vehicles *High Plains Drifter* (1973) and *The Outlaw Josey Wales* (1976), as well as non–Eastwood pictures like *The Wild Bunch*. Not surprisingly, some of the American films were direct adaptations of Italian productions; for example, *High Plains Drifter* was based on *Django the Bastard* (1969). Furthermore, Hollywood even attempted to hire Leone to direct *Hang 'Em High*, following the box-office success of the *Dollars* trilogy (he turned down the offer to continue working on *Once Upon a Time in the West*).

Essentially, Hollywood filmmakers of the new era knew better than to fall back on nostalgic ideas of the Old West after American audiences had acclimated to the cynical Italian style. Moreover, they had to compete for box-office dollars with gritty modern-day crime dramas featuring tough anti-hero cops (like Steve McQueen's Frank Bullitt and Eastwood's "Dirty" Harry Callahan). Hollywood's revisionist westerns of the late '60s and '70s display boldness and daring that clearly took some inspiration from the ultra-violence and existential moodiness of Italian westerns.

The revisionist Hollywood westerns also managed to sound uniquely American despite the influence of the Morricone style, which was popularized by Hugo Montenegro's orchestral pop albums for RCA. While Morricone had clearly tapped into the elemental characteristics of the "Wild West" through the use of whip cracks, tolling bells and so on, the Hollywood composers imbued their western scores with an indigenous American melodic sensibility that the Italians could only imitate. The composers for the post–*Dollars* Hollywood westerns—among them Bernstein, Goldsmith, Dominic Frontiere, Lalo Schifrin and Jerry Fielding—sometimes took stylistic inspiration from Morricone (most noticeably on Frontiere's *Hang 'Em High*), but rarely as much as other Italian composers (and often times not at all). More often than not, post–*Dollars* Hollywood western scores have a style that is distinctly American, yet distinctly different from the Golden Age Hollywood western scores that were often composed—ironically enough—by transplanted Europeans like Tiomkin, Steiner and Rózsa.

For example, Goldsmith's *Hour of the Gun*, a revisionist Wyatt Earp saga that received its theatrical release just one month before *The Good, the Bad and the Ugly*, opens like a grand old Hollywood western with a rousing, expansive theme that stirs passion for the frontier. The "Main Title" adapts the melody in a spare arrangement that creates quiet tension by isolating the instrumental "voices." Overall, the score doesn't quite break with the old style of the Hollywood western, but aims to make a break for new territory.

Perhaps the first Hollywood production to "respond" to the spaghetti westerns was *Hang 'Em High*, featuring a score by Frontiere that shamelessly imitates the Morricone sound. Bells toll ominously and harmonica moans moodily as electric and acoustic guitars square off for a duel. Then brass bursts forth, kicking up dust with a galloping rhythm.

Hang 'Em High wasn't the only Hollywood western score to find inspiration in the Italian style. Goldsmith's *Bandoleros* (1968) also shows the Morricone influence, albeit blended with the American composer's serialist style. The lone whistler, Jew's harp, chirping/chiming percussion and electric guitar on the main theme are obvious references. But on dramatic passages, such as "El Jefe," the dissonant flares and throbbing bass line are more in keeping with Goldsmith's work from the period.

Bernstein's score for the "Duke" vehicle *True Grit* (1969), the first Wayne western to follow the widespread Stateside releases of the "Dollars Trilogy," resists the Italian influence in favor of a thoroughly American sound that is much more modern than Bernstein's earlier western scores. Brassy, propulsive and upbeat, *True Grit* eschews the Old West big sky grandiosity in favor of an easy-on-the-ears orchestral pop sound. Soothing strings, folksy harmonica and jazzy saloon piano harmoniously blend with rock drumming, tambourines and other percussion accents. Its groovy electric bass-driven modernity extends to the use of sitar, Hammond organ and punchy brass on "A Dastardly Deed," and harpsichord and organ on "Chen Lee and the General." Co-star Glen Campbell adds commercial value by singing the easy-listening title song.

Comparatively, Goldsmith's outstanding score for *100 Rifles* (1969) is very experimental and dynamic, and doesn't seem to have much in common with Hollywood's Golden Age westerns *or* Morricone's re-imaging of the sagebrush sound. As is his wonderful habit, Goldsmith pits cacophonous brass against clamorous percussion on the riveting "Escape and Pursuit." And who else but Goldsmith would use detuned guitar and bass, along with prepared piano, in a western? The effect is strangely sinister and mysterious ("The Church"), and highly suggestive of mounting danger ("Ready for Ambush"). It's an awesome display of the composer's ability to re-imagine the western sound in Morricone's wake. If one must limit their western soundtrack collection to a single Goldsmith score, *100 Rifles* should be the one.

The most famous—or rather infamous—film to arise out of the post–*Dollars* western revival was the ultra-violent *The Wild Bunch* (1969). Director Sam Peckinpah once acknowledged that his film might never have been made had it not been for spaghetti westerns. Although the film frequently takes place south of the border—a familiar conceit of countless Spanish-location Italian westerns—Fielding's score does not mimic the style of the Italians. And aside from the familiar harmonica element, *The Wild Bunch* doesn't sound particularly influenced by earlier Hollywood western scores. Like Goldsmith's post–*Dollars* western work, Fielding's score marks a break with the past and

Jerry Goldsmith's unusual score for *100 Rifles* (1969) uses detuned guitar and prepared piano. (CD cover appears courtesy of Film Score Monthly; graphic design by Joe Sikoryak.)

attempts to create a fresh interpretation of the genre. It has a grander sound than most spaghetti westerns—fuller orchestration, with less emphasis on individual sounds. The theme has a languid Spanish character and is lovelier than one would expect from such an unsentimental and violent film. Many tracks work purely as support for the Mexican setting, but the more formal passages carry a melancholic mood that easily turns toward slow-burn tension. On the whole, the score eschews old-school over-the-top emotion and big-sky grandeur in favor of subtlety.

Immediately after making *The Wild Bunch*, Peckinpah made the comedic western *Ballad of Cable Hogue* (1970), which features a folk-infused score by

Goldsmith. Lyricist Richard Gillis sings of self-sufficiency on "Tomorrow Is the Song I Sing," which features odd little embellishments like pizzicato strings, chirping crickets and discordant zither thrums. Lone acoustic guitar, banjo, fiddle, harmonica and zither lend the score a rustic, rural character, but a string section adds orchestral fullness and a melancholic subtext to the otherwise light-hearted folk-inspired passages.

Goldsmith's *Rio Lobo* (1970), starring John Wayne, offers more modernistic touches than the Duke's earlier films. The composite track "New Arrival/Unexpected Gun" offers the contrast of old and new techniques. Reassuring brass figures and strummed guitar make the "new arrival" seem innocent enough, but with the notice of the "unexpected gun" comes orchestral discord, distorted undulations and anxious brass flares that wouldn't sound out of place in the composer's score for *Planet of the Apes*.

Another terrific and unconventional Goldsmith western score can be heard on *The Wild Rovers* (1971). Again rustic folk melodies (some sung by Ellen Smith) factor in the score. The main theme incorporates the folk element (as well as banjo and saloon piano) into an expansive arrangement that flirts with the Americana style that can be traced back to Aaron Copland, Moross' *Big Country* and Bernstein's *Magnificent Seven*. On "Old Times," Goldsmith overlaps musical ideas like flitting reminiscences. Even more interesting is "Saturday Night," which starts with folksy strummed auto harp before introducing plaintive recorder, lively electric harpsichord, solo brass, accordion, and joyously swinging and sliding strings. It's a western score that is unabashedly traditionalist without sounding old school or routine.

Jerry Fielding scored several films for Eastwood during the '70s, including *The Outlaw Josey Wales* (1976). Like Goldsmith, Fielding also relies on folk music forms to establish the setting, but never at the cost of thematic complexity and orchestral richness. He calls attention to the film's post–Civil War setting by using militaristic fifes, drums and bugles, as well as accordion and occasional string washes, on the theme. On "Ten Bears," Fielding conjures the primitive world of Native Americans through the spare use of percussion and woodwinds. But on "The Final Revenge," he relies on dissonant strings, brass, woodwinds and percussion to create a passage of frenzied, anxious action that wouldn't sound out of place in one of his more modern crime scores.

As the '70s continued, fewer memorable westerns were made, as Eastwood and even Wayne diversified by making modern crime dramas. After starring in at least 10 westerns over the course of the '60s and '70s, Eastwood only made one in the '80s (*Pale Rider*, 1985) and one in the '90s (*Unforgiven*, 1992). Wayne's monumental western ride ended with *The Shootist* (1976), which features yet another magnificent big-sky score by Bernstein, who scored most of Wayne's later work. Simply put, the Silver Age western died with the Duke, but along the way it took a wildly unexpected ride that brought it back from the brink of extinction and reinvigorated its mythic appeal.

12 Essential Western Soundtracks

The Big Country (1958)—Jerome Moross
The Magnificent Seven (1960)—Elmer Bernstein
Rio Conchos (1964)—Jerry Goldsmith
A Fistful of Dollars (1964)—Ennio Morricone
For a Few Dollars More (1965)—Ennio Morricone
The Good, the Bad, and the Ugly (1966)—Ennio Morricone
Django (1966)—Luis Bacalov
Once Upon a Time in the West (1968)—Ennio Morricone
The Wild Bunch (1969)—Jerry Fielding
100 Rifles (1969)—Jerry Goldsmith
True Grit (1969)—Elmer Bernstein
Matalo (1970)—Mario Migliardi

Chapter 5

Sci-Fidelity and the Superhero Spectrum

Sci-fi cinema is as old as filmmaking itself. Science fiction has been a movie genre since at least 1897. It was in that year that Frenchman Georges Méliès made two proto-science fiction films—one involving a mechanical man (*Gugusse et l'automate*, a.k.a. *The Clown and the Automation*) and another (*Les Rayons Roentgen*, a.k.a. *A Novice at X-rays*) about a skeleton leaving a body after exposure to x-rays. Méliès went on to make *La lune à un mètre* (*The Astronomer's Dream, A Trip to the Moon*, or *The Man in the Moon*, 1898), and a year later the first film version of H. Rider Haggard's 1886 supernatural fantasy adventure yarn *She*.

During the early 20th century there would be numerous films that fall into the categories of sci-fi (*Aelita: The Revolt of the Robots*, 1924; *Metropolis*, 1926), scientific horror (the first *Frankenstein*, 1910; *Alraune*, 1918)) and fantasy adventure (*The Lost World*, 1925; *Mysterious Island*, 1929). During the '30s these related genres were further developed, with considerable success. Often the horror and sci-fi elements blur, resulting in such memorable entries as James Whale's *Frankenstein* (1931), *Dr. Jekyll and Mr. Hyde* (1932), *The Invisible Man* (1933) and *King Kong* (1933). As the decade wore on, several straight sci-fi films were made, including *Flash Gordon* (1936), *Things to Come* (1936), *Flash Gordon's Trip to Mars* (1938) and *Buck Rogers* (1939). The character of Flash Gordon returned in the early '40s to conquer the universe (as one film title suggests), but on Earth scientific horror and straight-up monster movies (*Frankenstein Meets the Wolf Man*, 1943; *The Invisible Man's Revenge*, 1944) were more common fare. Notably, the first film adaptations of *Batman* and *Superman* hero comics arrived in theaters in 1943 and 1948, respectively. In truth, the '40s marked a step backward in the development of sci-fi on the silver screen, as studios favored horror.

If the '40s left sci-fi fans starved for serious futuristic thrills, the '50s delivered more big-screen sci-fi than ever before, and remains to this day the Golden Age of the genre. The studios spawned dozens of movies that fed on the fascination and fears of paranoid filmgoers caught in the clutches of the "red scare" and the nuclear age. Such classics as *The Day the Earth Stood Still* (1951), *The War of the Worlds* (1953), *Godzilla* (1954), *Forbidden Planet* (1956) and many others are still viewed and admired today.

Sci-fi soundtracks are paradoxically among the most classically rooted of the genre scores discussed in this book, drawing inspiration from such works as Igor Stravinsky's *The Rite of Spring* and Gustav Holst's *The Planets*. Occasionally, they also incorporate early electronics, like the otherworldly theremin and the sonorously similar ondes martenot. Ironically, sci-fi scores rarely use electronics exclusively (Louis and Bebe Barron's *Forbidden Planet* is a notable exception).

The '50s: Us and Them

It's no secret that many sci-fi films of the '50s reflected and reinforced the national obsession with communism (the "red scare"), nuclear catastrophe and monstrous mutations born from radioactivity. The decade's sci-fi films also fueled the post-war audience's fascination with space exploration (and, more importantly, the conquest of distant worlds), which would continue into the '60s and ironically diminish once mankind actually reached the Moon.

The arrival of the '50s brought two space exploration pictures of note. With a tagline that stated "The Future is Here," *Rocketship X-M* was rushed through production and into release to beat the higher-budget *Destination Moon* in 1950. Ferde Grofé Sr., who is best known for his "Grand Canyon Suite," scored *X-M* using a theremin for the eerie scenes on Mars. Before X-M actually arrives on Mars, however, one gets pure Golden Age orchestration, with sweeping strings, boisterous brass and crashing cymbals. Although he rarely scored pictures, Grofé displays a knack for dramatic build-ups and atmospheric tension. The juxtaposition between the familiar, earthly sonorities of strings, brass and woodwinds, and the otherworldly warble of the theremin, echoes the scenes that find man in an ominous alien environment.

Comparatively, Leith Stevens' *Destination Moon* is firmly rooted in the modern classical tradition and does not feature electronics. The music still calls to mind the mysterious reaches of outer space, particularly during "In Outer Space," when Stevens uses vibes for a suspenseful tick-tock tactic, which Goldsmith later mimicked with woodwinds on the *Alien* (1979) soundtrack.

With its episodic pacing and grandly sweeping orchestration, Stevens' *When Worlds Collide* (1951) vividly describes Earth caught in the grip of imminent peril and the desperate attempt by mankind to avoid destruction. Like many Golden Age–style scores, *Collide* describes the onscreen action so closely that watching the film is hardly necessary. Heard today, the score sounds old-fashioned in its operatic complexity, unlike other sci-fi scores from the same year—namely Dimitri Tiomkin's *The Thing from Another World* and, more importantly, Herrmann's *The Day the Earth Stood Still*.

5. *Sci-Fidelity and the Superhero Spectrum*   169

Dimitri Tiomkin's *The Thing from Another World* (1951), which John Carpenter remade as *The Thing* (1982), employs a full orchestra, with theremin. Although it is a fair example of the Golden Age film composer's tendency toward symphonic complexity, the orchestration is unusual in that it eschews a heavy string sound. In fact, Tiomkin uses only double bass in addition to brass, woodwinds, timpani, two pianos, three harps, pipe organ, a Flexatone and wind machine. While there's no mistaking this eerie, angular, tension-mounting score for anything other than a sci-fi/horror spine-tingler, it's inter-

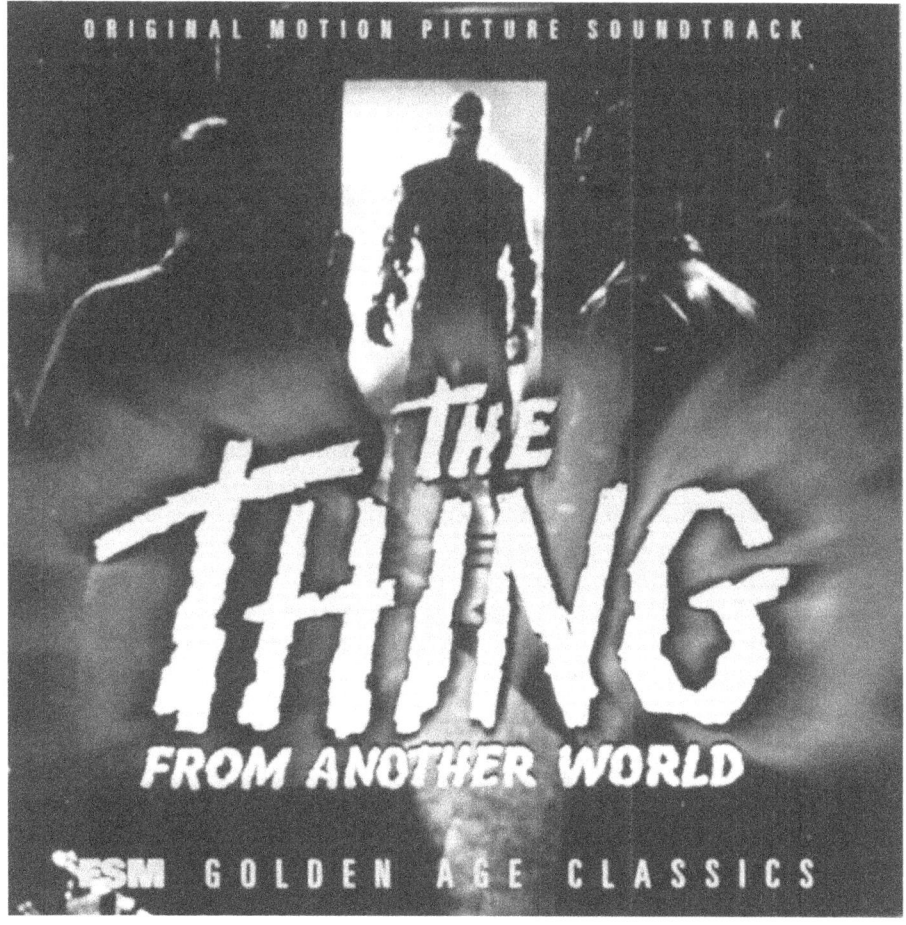

Dimitri Tiomkin's score for *The Thing from Another World* (1951) uses a theremin, but its bombastic operatic style clearly characterizes it as a holdover of the Golden Age. (CD cover appears courtesy of Film Score Monthly; graphic design by Joe Sikoryak.)

esting how its brash, brassy character mirrors the story's militaristic leanings. In the film, the military runs roughshod over the empirical curiosity of the film's scientists to destroy the alien invader. In that sense, Tiomkin's busy, hot-blooded score is perfectly suited to the conservative socio-political undercurrent of the story, while its use of theremin serves as a convenient aural metaphor for the alien threat hanging over mankind, or at the very least a remote arctic outpost. *The Thing from Another World* is a natural bridge between Stevens' *When Worlds Collide* and a sci-fi score that used theremin to even greater effect and raised the bar for all sci-fi scores to come.

Bernard Herrmann's *The Day the Earth Stood Still* (1951) is comparatively modern, unconventional and experimental. It tops Tiomkin's *Thing* score by stripping away needless orchestration at key moments. For instance, in both scores there is a low brass motif that lumbers forth like a monster; their similarity is striking. But in Tiomkin's theme the motif must compete with swirling orchestration that eventually overwhelms it. On Herrmann's "Gort," the motif is simply accompanied by theremin and slowly pounding drums. The isolation makes the motif far more threatening.

Day is not only a classic sci-fi score, it's also a fine example of why Herrmann is regarded as one of the most influential and groundbreaking film composers of the 20th century. Here he used a small orchestra, including two theremins, one reed organ, two Hammond organs, two pianos, electrically amplified violin, cello, bass, several percussionists and multiple brasses. Subtle and sparsely arranged, *Day* benefits from a less-is-more aesthetic. Without going into excessive technical detail, Herrmann's themes are symmetrical in structure and methodical in execution. Perhaps this is why he's now recognized as one of the forefathers of minimalism, a school that has since spawned such composers as Philip Glass, Steve Reich and John Adams, whose intricate, highly repetitive compositions are rarely as melodically memorable as Herrmann's film work. Simply put, on *Day* Herrmann threw down the gauntlet for a new style of film scoring, one that he continued to explore on other sci-fi films, as well as Alfred Hitchcock's thrillers.

Stevens delivered his best sci-fi score yet for the first film version of the legendary 1898 H.G. Wells novel *The War of the Worlds*. This like-named, lavish, full-color film from 1953 captures the heightened paranoia of the "red scare" era. With blaring horns and earnest strings, the theme churns forth on a robust Latin rhythm, which is an odd choice for an alien invasion picture but catchy nonetheless. Swirling, then shuddering, strings denote imminent trouble on "The Meteor." The music connotes otherworldly fear without resorting to the use of a theremin. Although some of these "Martian Heat Ray" effects sound as if created by an electric organ, it would be a stretch to consider them part of Stevens' otherwise conventional and sometimes melodramatic score. Nonetheless, the effects are mesmerizing and effective, even by today's standards.

Bernard Herrmann's *The Day the Earth Stood Still* (20th Century–Fox, 1951), starring Michael Rennie and Patricia Neal, is the first true Silver Age sci-fi score.

One of Elmer Bernstein's early efforts is an intermittently exotic *Cat Women of the Moon*. Bernstein later told Nick Joy in a 2002 *Music from the Movies* magazine interview that he had no regrets about doing a lowly sci-fi B-movie like *Cat Women*:

> *Robot Monster* and *Cat Women* were done during the period when I was under a political cloud and those were the only films I was offered to do. But I've always enjoyed the challenge of trying to help a film, and I had as much fun working on those films as I did on *The Ten Commandments*.

Guaranteed to thrill is the composite score for the classic *It Came from Outer Space* (1953). Irving Gertz, Herman Stein and Henry Mancini contributed to this sometimes sentimental, often times spooky theremin-enhanced soundtrack. Shrill strings, agitated brass and woodwinds, harp glissandi and otherworldly vibrato sounds on the organ and theremin make this one of the most effective sci-fi scores of the era. Gertz, who composed some of the more reassuring themes for the film, talked of his experience in an interview for the film's release on DVD:

Prior to becoming a household name, Henry Mancini helped score a number of "B" sci-fi and horror movies, such as *Creature from the Black Lagoon* and *It Came from Outer Space*. (Photograph courtesy of the Henry Mancini Estate.)

> *It Came from Outer Space* was an "eye opener." It was a wonderful challenge. It's modern, it's contemporary, it's outer space ... it gives the composer a lot of elbow room to write freely and unconfined.

David Buttolph's *The Beast from 20,000 Fathoms* (1953), one of the era's many movies about monsters born from nuclear testing, features spacious orchestration that evokes the deep blue sea. Harp glissandi suggests the mysteries swimming in its depths; but whenever angry brass blasts to the surface, all doubt is removed as to the ferocity of the titular beast.

Bronislau Kaper's *Them!* (1954), another atomic mutation flick, uses vibrato brass, shrill strings and crashing percussion in the theme. Elsewhere, shivering strings and spidery xylophone and marimba figures mimic the presence of giant ants.

Another giant radioactive "bug" movie is *Tarantula* (1955). Herman Stein's score (with contributions by Mancini) echoes Stravinsky and Mussorgsky during the suspenseful passages, but more often resort to the shrill cacophony befitting an attack by a gargantuan arachnid.

Mischa Bakaleinikoff's *It Came from Beneath the Sea* (1955), yet another atomic mutation movie, boasts bombastic brass, rumbling kettledrums, and string figures that rapidly ascend and descend like a monster from the deep. Bakaleinikoff scored several other sci-fi flicks, including *Earth vs. the Flying Saucers* (1956) and *Twenty Million Miles to Earth* (1957).

Next to Herrmann's *The Day the Earth Stood Still*, the most impressive sci-fi score of the '50s is Louis and Bebe Barron's groundbreaking "electronic tonalities" for MGM's memorable *Forbidden Planet* (1956). No conventional instruments were used, as the Barrons relied entirely on cybernetic circuits that they conceived, designed and built themselves. These warbling, gurgling, squealing electronic "voices" never convey a discernable melody, yet they still suggest dramatic activity—if only in the most abstract sense possible. The Barrons scored MGM's sci-fi extravaganza having previously only scored short experimental films, like *Bells of Atlantis* (1952) and *Miramagic* (1954). They'd even worked closely with avant-garde figurehead John Cage. Although the score was a critical success and earned the duo an Oscar nomination, they were unable to reap the credit and awards they deserved due to rules of the film composers union to which they did not belong. Sadly, they never composed for a major studio film again, though their influence can be heard in numerous film and television scores that followed. Although it lacks the melodic and rhythmic attributes that make music conventionally appealing, *Forbidden Planet* is a masterpiece of its kind.

Leith Stevens' *World Without End* (1956), a film that borrows from *The Time Machine* and anticipates *Planet of the Apes*, shows Herrmann's influence without sounding derivative. The theme pitches up and down a scale, with eerie, ethereal tones created by a combination of woodwinds, vibes and shuddering strings. It is among Stevens' most haunting and flexible themes, as he is able to adapt it for romantic sequences as well as scenes of high tension.

Carmen Dragon maximizes the tense rollercoaster ride of *Invasion of the Body Snatchers* (1956) with blaring brass, rumbling percussion and portentous strings. During the foot chase in the California hills toward the movie's end, a strange, alarm-like horn sounds at regular intervals as the orchestra charges forward, echoing the desperate flight of the main characters.

One of the era's most prolific B-movie composers was Ronald Stein. His first sci-fi score was *The Day the World Ended* (1956), which promised "a new high in naked screaming terror." His next hair-raising sci-fi score, *It Conquered the World* (1956), is a classic example of both Stein's creativity as a composer and of the sound of '50s B-movie thrills. It is the sound of a composer whose imagination is limitless, even if his budget and resources are constrained. He shows strong orchestration skills, employing simple effects (like the sneaky percussion fills) to mimic the action on the screen or simply add a sense of alien danger. Like Herrmann, Stein's arrangements display a lean muscularity and economy of style, though Stein's compositional style is more like Stevens than Herrmann in that it mirrors the action onscreen, not the psychological undercurrent.

On the comic *Invasion of the Saucer Men*, Stein lightened up enough to use a bit of "Flight of the Bumble Bee" xylophone (presumably for flying saucers), and melodic pastiche featuring isolated instruments that represent onscreen mischief. Occasionally, bluesy horn solos lend the proceedings a charmingly dated quality. Overall, the light, lean orchestration recalls the soundtracks of the Golden Age Warner Bros. cartoons, though it isn't as frenetic or bravura as Carl Stalling's *Looney* tunes.

Stein also scored *Not of This Earth* and *Attack of the Crab Monsters* (both 1957), as well as *Attack of the 50-Foot Woman* (1958).

According Eric Hoffman and Ted Newsom's booklet notes for the Stein compilation *Not of This Earth*, the theme for the eponymously titled film is a four-note musical pronunciation of the title. Generally, the score is eerie and foreboding. Cymbals shimmer forth like a specter at the beginning. A horn blast shatters the quiet, giving way to echoing vibraphone, furtive strings and timid woodwinds. On "Flight from Fear," more shimmering sounds (courtesy of vibes or organ) set the stage for anxious strings. On "The Eyes Have It," rumbling drums and low brass further build the tension. Seething fear courses through "Rapid Blood." And the "End Note" does little to alleviate the mood of fear and loathing.

For *Attack of the Crab Monsters*, Stein delivered a more aggressive sound, with stabbing brass attacks and shrill strings. Harp glissandi calls to mind the nautical setting. Fluttering organ and string tones add that distinctive B-movie vibe of unearthly excitation.

Stein provides a similar sound for *Attack of the 50-Foot Woman*, using marimba to lend the theme a newsroom teletype, "this just in" sense of anticipation. He also provides some lively rock 'n' roll for the club scenes, featuring catchy hooks, randy saxophone, flirty piano fills and vibes. On the more dramatic cues, brass sounds the alarm as strings and woodwinds shriek, and cymbals crash, in the background when the 50-foot female wreaks havoc.

A notable composing team during the '50s and '60s was that of Paul Sawtell and Bert Shefter. Their sci-fi scoring can be heard in *Kronos* (1957), *It! The Terror from Beyond Space* (1958), *The Fly* (1958), *Return of the Fly* (1959) and *Curse of the Fly* (1965).

While all three *Fly* scores are in the grand Golden Age style, *The Fly* is the most romantic (though *Curse* runs a close second in that regard). Soaring strings, coquettish woodwinds and virile brass provide passages ("Happy Couple/Matchbox") of country lane serenity and evenings-by-the-firelight tenderness. The sense of horror doesn't rear its ugly head until more than halfway through the score, and briefly at that ("The Claw"), which mutates from horror to heartbreak. Even late in the film, as the onscreen action becomes increas-

Paul Sawtell and Bert Shefter's score for *The Fly* (1958) is remarkably sentimental and a throwback to the Golden Age style. (CD cover appears courtesy of Percepto Records; graphic design by Joe Sikoryak.)

ingly hopeless, Sawtell and Shefter's score tends toward the sentimental. While *The Fly* may not strike listeners as an archetypal sci-fi score, it certainly befits the film's depiction of tragic love born from science gone horribly wrong.

Sawtell and Shefter's score for *Return of the Fly* outshines the movie. Compared to the first film's score, it is much less romantic, as its principal "love theme" is abandoned early on in favor of moods that reinforce the story's descent into terror. The flitting, high-pitched strings on "Fly Fright" befit the flight of a fly. Rapidly descending brass figures on "Rat Monster/Getting Rid of the Car" suggest imminent danger, while hypnotic harp arpeggios help conjure an air of mystery. *Return* is certainly a stronger example of sci-fi horror scoring than *The Fly*, though some listeners are likely to favor the first film's romantic overtones.

Shefter alone scored the third *Fly* film, as Sawtell was ill at the time. *Curse* balances the romantic tendencies of *The Fly* with the more conventional thriller scoring heard in *Return*. The use of piano makes the romantic themes sound vaguely like one of the European Romantics, such as Rachmaninoff. Naturally, the piano assumes a different, supportive role during the conventional tension-mounting cues like "London Lab." Lurching rhythms and frantic orchestration create excitement on "The Creature," while dissonant strings give the off-kilter piano lullaby a queasy lethargy on "Pat Drugged." Shefter recycles some of the themes heard in the first film, but there are enough variations and new ideas to differentiate the two. By quoting from the first film without overdoing the romance, Shefter makes *Curse* the best balanced and most fulfilling of the three *Fly* soundtracks.

Sci-fi wasn't exclusive to Hollywood. From Great Britain's Hammer Studios came *The Quatermass Xperiment* (a.k.a. *The Creeping Unknown*, 1955), which was based on a 1953 BBC mini-series. This space flight/alien invasion thriller features a string-heavy orchestral score by James Bernard that occasionally gives way to experimental passages of repetitive atonal motifs bolstered by rumbling percussion (as on "Cacti" and "Metamorphosis"). *Quatermass* features only strings and percussion, due in part to budget constraints.

"Hammer Films, though working on small budgets, always aimed at high quality in their music, as indeed they did in all their departments," Bernard wrote in his introduction to Randall D. Larson's *Music from the House of Hammer* (1996). Bernard added: "Hammer liked to have symphonic scores, written by classically trained composers, conducted by classically trained conductors, and performed and recorded by players and sound engineers of the highest caliber."

The sequel, *Quatermass II* (a.k.a. *Enemy from Space*, 1957) features tense, dissonant music by Bernard, who also scored the lesser known Hammer sci-fi flick *X The Unknown* (1957).

Tristram Cary's sprawling and complex *Quatermass & the Pit* (a.k.a. *Five Million Years to Earth*, 1967), the third and best film of the series, favors restless action cues where brass and strings attack in equal measure. The score also includes some startlingly minimalist electronic music that whirs and gurgles through nine lengthy cues on the tale end of the *Quatermass* collection. Cary provided both symphonic and electronic cues at the studio's request, but some weren't used at all, as Hammer opted to repurpose Carlo Martelli's music from *Witchcraft* when Cary became unavailable to write additional music. Cary later contributed electronic music for the *Doctor Who* television show.

Swords & Sorcery

Swords and sorcery may have little in common with sci-fi, but the two genres are frequently lumped together under the term sci-fi/fantasy. On film, there have been far fewer entries in the fantasy camp, but thanks to the enduring popularity of epics like *The Lord of the Rings*, and larger-than-life characters like Conan the Barbarian, fantasy continues to capture the imagination of filmmakers and movie audiences.

During the '50s and '60s the names most associated with swords and sorcery were sci-fi/fantasy film producer Charles Schneer and special effects wizard Ray Harryhausen, whose stop-motion animation techniques are legendary.

Schneer and Harryhausen's *The Seventh Voyage of Sinbad* (1958) features an imaginative, transporting Herrmann score that earns a spot alongside his more famous sci-fi scores. The overture is certain to quicken a listener's pulse with its adventurous spirit and syncopated rhythms. The inventive use of xylophone to conjure a sword-fighting skeleton on "The Duel with the Skeleton" is breathtaking and blood-chilling. "Baghdad" transports the listener to an ancient, mysterious, storybook city where magic and beauty are palpable. The intimidating brass chords that characterize the Cyclops fittingly recall "Gort," the single-vizored robot of *The Day the Earth Stood Still*. Herrmann also scored the classic *Jason and the Argonauts* (1963). Golden Age master Miklós Rósza scored *The Golden Voyage of Sinbad* (1974), and Silver Age maverick Roy Budd scored *Sinbad and the Eye of the Tiger* (1977).

Enzo Masetti's *Le Fatiche di Ercole* (*Hercules*, 1958) and *Ercole e la Regina di Lidia* (*Hercules Unchained*, 1959), the sword-and-sandal fantasies, are sturdy and purposeful, moving forth with a heroic purity of tone. This is Golden Age adventure music par excellence. Certainly there are somber moods when low brass threatens to pull the listener into murky, perilous depths. But then strings sweep in with magnificent, even romantic, earnestness to rescue you from the brink of some hideous fate.

Armando Trovajoli's *Ercole al centro della terra* (*Hercules in the Haunted World*, or *Hercules in the Center of the Earth*, 1961) is spooky and strange, delirious and disorienting, with one foot in the Golden Age of film scoring and one foot in avant-garde psychedelia. Using ominous woodwinds, shuddering strings, rumbling percussion and otherworldly effects, Trovajoli conjures the *Haunted World* with bewitching sounds of the beyond.

Lost Worlds

An enduring sci-fi subgenre commonly known as prehistoric fantasy or lost world holds a tenuous connection to sci-fi when science (e.g. time travel) or scientists are involved in the adventure.

Aside from the serial *Mysterious Island* (1951), the first major prehistoric fantasy flick of the '50s was *The Lost Continent* (1951), which promised "thrills of the atomic-powered future and adventures of the prehistoric past" on its movie poster. The soundtrack by Paul Dunlap is typical of the genre, with big, bold orchestral flourish as kettledrums rumble impressively.

Armando Trovajoli's score for *Ercole al centro della terra* (*Hercules in the Haunted World*, or *Hercules in the Center of the Earth*, 1961) features otherworldly sounds that are perfect for the film's underworld setting. (CD cover appears courtesy of Digitmovies Alternative Entertainment; graphic design by Claudio Fuiano.)

The most famous prehistoric fantasy picture of the '50s came at the tail end of the decade. Herrmann's *Journey to the Center of the Earth* (1959) is among his best in the sci-fi genre. Omitting strings from the orchestration entirely, the ever-experimental composer employs thundering pipe organ, mesmerizing harp, blaring brass, crashing percussion and a rare wind instrument known as the serpent that collectively evoke the cavernous journey into the bowels of the Earth. The serpent, which is related to the cornet, is named for its large serpentine shape. It dates from the late 16th century, and when played in the lower register could be mistaken for a sick trombone or tuba. In Herrmann's score it's positively ominous and monstrous, as it is used to characterize a giant chameleon.

Herrmann's *The 3 Worlds of Gulliver* (1960), which he started work on only three days after finishing *Psycho*, freely references the style of music typical of 18th and 19th century English composers. In fact, as director of the CBS Radio Symphony, Herrmann frequently programmed works by such period composers as Henry Purcell, Thomas Arne and Charles Avison. Still, one can hear Herrmann's touch—however briefly—in the spiraling vibraphone of "Clouds."

Herrmann's *Mysterious Island* (1961), one of nine filmic adaptations of the Jules Verne novel, is full of blaring brass, crashing cymbals and angular melodic motives. *Mysterious Island* never fails to draw the listener into the adventure, described in such track titles as "Escape to the Clouds," "The Giant Crab," "Pirates!"

Russ Garcia scored two sci-fi/fantasy films for George Pal in the early '60s—*The Time Machine* and the lost world adventure *Atlantis, the Lost Continent* (1961), which features crystal death rays, fish-shaped submarines and alchemical transformations of men into animals. Legend has it that Garcia's 1959 sci-fi concept album *Fantastica* led Pal to hire the composer. It's fair to say that Garcia's adventurous but still melodic score outshines *Atlantis*, which went into production with little known TV stars and a smaller-than-needed budget. Garcia blends full-blooded, triumphant orchestration with fanfares that evoke ancient pageantry, romantic strings and themes that flirt with the exotic but steer clear of clichés. A good example occurs during the love scene where a submarine approaching in the background is suggested by gentle but dissonant pulses created by harp and horns reminiscent of underwater sonar bleeps without being obvious about the reference.

She, the classic lost world adventure, returned after a 30-year absence in the 1965 Hammer Film production starring Ursula Andress. Hammer regular James Bernard provided the lush, sensual score that well serves the titular underworld empress "who must be obeyed." The music for the Bedouin attack is thrilling and pulse-pounding. Bernard, who scored a wide variety of Hammer films, from sci-fi (*The Quatermass Xperiment*, 1955) to its usual horror fare (*Dracula*, 1958), delivered his most haunting theme for *She*.

Hammer also produced a prehistoric trilogy consisting of *One Million Years B.C.* (1966), which stars that other '60s bombshell, Raquel Welch, *Creatures the World Forgot* (1970) and *When Dinosaurs Ruled the Earth* (1970). One of the trilogy's producers, Aida Young, selected Mario Nascimbene over Hammer's usual composers, having worked with him before.

In *One Million*, Nascimbene's primeval themes call to mind a primitive world where dinosaurs and men battle for survival. The juxtaposition between rattling, clattering percussion (courtesy of an ass jaw, necklace of chestnuts and something nicknamed a rastrophon) and atmospheric orchestra and choir is particularly effective on "The Pteranodon Carries Loana to Its Nest." The

Russell Garcia used three percussionists to create sound effects on his score for *The Time Machine* (1960). (CD cover appears courtesy of Film Score Monthly; graphic design by Joe Sikoryak.)

shuddering string section rises and falls like an ominous wind. Other highlights include "Cosmic Sequence" and "Eruption of the Volcano," both of which feature sound effects created by the composer using a 12-deck tape console of his own design called the "mixarama." According to Nascimbene aficionado Rafael Martinez, the composer used the device to add not only non-musical sound effects like dinosaurs, wind and rain, but also recordings of vocal and orchestral instruments and notes (that description makes the mixarama sound like a cousin to the mellotron). It's difficult to tell what was created by the mixarama and by a live orchestra. Martinez maintains that the composer did not use the mixarama on *Creatures the World Forgot* and *When*

Dinosaurs Ruled the Earth (1970), relying on live orchestra instead. The outcome is noticeably more conventional and arguably less satisfying, though still suitable for the prehistoric fantasy setting.

The '60s: The Final Frontier

Sci-fi of the '60s moved away from paranoia and alien invasions to embark on a more open-minded journey into time and space. Bolstered by the promising space race, filmmakers turned to telling mostly upbeat adventure stories of man journeying to strange worlds (sometimes within the human body itself) and through warps in time. The scores for these films are often couched in the familiar style of Golden Age Hollywood, but frequently expand the musical palette to summon a brave new world.

Mario Nascimbene's primeval themes for *One Million Years B.C.* (20th Century–Fox/Hammer, 1966) evoke a primitive world where dinosaurs and men—and women such as Raquel Welch—must battle for survival.

George Pal, the man who successfully brought H.G. Wells' *The War of the Worlds* to the silver screen during the '50s, convinced the late author's heirs to let him adapt *The Time Machine* in 1960. Russ Garcia's richly evocative and romantic orchestral score blends English folk-type melodies to capture the story's initial Victorian setting with more modernistic, Stravinsky-inspired passages for tension and action. The descending three-note theme for celesta is employed whenever "time travel" is involved. Garcia told interviewer Randall Larson in 1984 that aside from getting Pal's approval on the themes, he was left to his own devices. The California-born composer also indulges in sound effects creation for futuristic scenes and time machine operation. In 1987, Garcia explained to Matthias Büdinger in *Soundtrack!* magazine that he used three percussionists to create effects by "hitting a musical saw with a soft mallet and wavering it, hitting gongs and holding a mike in the center and gradually moving it out to the edge," among other things.

During the '60s one of the big names in film and television sci-fi fantasy entertainment was Irwin Allen, a producer and director. He made a big splash in the '50s with the documentary *The Sea Around Us* (1952), but is best known for a quartet of successful sci-fi and adventure TV shows. Allen launched his TV career with *Voyage to the Bottom of the Sea* (1961), a sort of take-off on Jules Verne's *20,000 Leagues Under the Sea*, which had been a big-screen hit for Walt

Paul Sawtell and Bert Shefter's score for *Voyage to the Bottom of the Sea* (1961) blends militaristic flourishes with nautical impressionism. (CD cover appears courtesy of Film Score Monthly; graphic design by Joe Sikoryak.)

Disney in 1954. For the *Voyage* film Sawtell and Shefter contributed a sweeping orchestral score, while a host of composers, including Goldsmith, Leith Stevens, Morton Stevens, Alexander Courage and Nelson Riddle, contributed to the subsequent TV show. Notably, Sawtell and Shefter previously scored Allen's *The Lost World* (1960). Their *Voyage* film score is romantic and enveloping, making great use of harp and piano. The influence of Claude Debussy's lush impressionistic "La Mer" ("The Sea") is palpable; however, the mood isn't always silky smooth, and frequently veers into tension or mystery on such cues as "Raw Nerves," "Rising Heat/Catastrophe," "The Squid Attacks" and "Lunatic Action/The Burnout Point." The Debussy influence also is heard on the Russell Faith–penned theme sung by movie co-star Frankie Avalon.

Sawtell and Shefter also scored the sci-fi horror film *The Last Man on Earth* (1964). The film is the first adaptation of Richard Matheson's classic novel *I Am Legend*, and it anticipates *Night of the Living Dead* (1968); Matheson's novel was later adapted for the screen as *The Omega Man* (1971). Sawtell and Shefter work in a vein they tapped on *The Fly* and *The Return of the Fly*, though the romantic element naturally is not an option. Tense moods and otherworldly sonorities predominate, and the duo employs a choir that sounds like a pack of vampire maniacs.

The film of H.G. Wells' *First Men in the Moon* (1964) features a score by Laurie Johnson, who is best known for his theme music for TV's *The Avengers*. The music for this lunar fantasy is by turns impressionistically lovely ("Love Theme"), comically playful ("Cavor's Experiments"), spectral ("The Sphere"), and raucously shrill ("Battle with the Selenites"). Brassy, with pounding percussion, Johnson's score isn't afraid to go for abrasive orchestral textures to pump up the drama.

The Satan Bug (1965) is an earthbound germ warfare thriller with a score by Goldsmith, who clearly drew inspiration from the title for his diabolically angular theme music featuring spidery staccato percussion. *The Satan Bug* sounds a bit like a rehearsal for *Planet of the Apes* (1968), which is one of Goldsmith's best sci-fi scores. *Bug* shares with *Apes* a penchant for exotic melodic motifs, which are—yet again—reminiscent of the ultimate sci-fi soundtrack classical reference: Stravinsky's "Rite of Spring." Other familiar elements are the layers of percussion and the spare arrangements featuring isolated voices that "talk" in turn, or over one another, without becoming cluttered. The score also reveals Goldsmith's interest in subtle electronic effects—disconcerting warbles here, a mysterious shimmer there. It is not only an interesting stepping stone in Goldsmith's development as a composer for sci-fi films, but also an entertaining and nuanced score in its own right.

Fantastic Voyage (1966) was a cutting edge film for its time, and Leonard Rosenman's score was fittingly edgy. With its heartbeat tempo, clicking teletype machines and synth pulses, the "Theme Sound Effects Suite" is musique concrete par excellence. This non-musical approach was employed because the

Leonard Rosenman's score for *Fantastic Voyage* (20th Century–Fox, 1966) is used primarily when the film's action takes place inside the human body. (Photograph courtesy of the John Monaghan Collection.)

filmmakers (Rosenman included) decided not to use music until the microsurgeons entered the patient's body in their tiny submarine. Once inside, Rosenman uses full orchestra and atonality to accompany the tense, surrealistic journey through veins and major organs. The score only becomes conventionally tonal once the microsurgeons have completed their mission and exited the body. With its rumbling lower register and skin-crawling upper register, the influence of the *Fantastic Voyage* score can be heard in many of today's sci-fi horror thrillers.

One of Herrmann's finest sci-fi scores is *Fahrenheit 451* (1966). The project came along at a difficult time in the composer's private life, as he'd just gone through a painful divorce. Then Alfred Hitchcock fired Herrmann from *Torn Curtain* (1966), their seventh big-screen collaboration, for failing to deliver a pop-oriented score. Ironically, it was Hitchcock disciple François Truffaut who hired the composer to score his adaptation of Ray Bradbury's *Fahrenheit 451*, a cautionary tale of a dystopian future where books are forbidden and burned by firemen. According to biographer Steven C. Smith,

Herrmann was attracted to the project in part due to his love of books and an admiration for Ray Bradbury. In fact, Herrmann had scored a few Bradbury-penned episodes of Hitchcock's popular TV show.

According to *Film Music Screencraft* (RotoVision, 2000), by Mark Russell and James Young, Truffaut wanted "his futuristic vision to be accompanied by music of clarity and almost neo-classical simplicity." When Herrmann asked him why he'd been selected when the director had access to younger, more avant-garde composers, Truffaut said that those composers would supply him with music of the 20th century, and that Herrmann would compose music for the 21st century. A documentary on the *Fahrenheit 451* DVD indicates that the collaboration wasn't always an easy one. For example, Herrmann's mechanical, repetitive music for the fire truck sequence features xylophones. Truffaut deemed them too comical and insisted they be removed during the recording process. Herrmann got the message, but refused to remove the xylophones. By leaving the xylophones in, Herrmann instilled childishness in the music, which served to reinforce the notion that a society that condones book burning is irresponsible and senseless.

Music critic Tony Thomas writes in *Music for the Movies* (Silman James, 1997) that Truffaut later thanked Herrmann for "humanizing" the film. The score delivers familiar Herrmann orchestral elements, like mesmerizing harp, tinkling xylophone, swirling strings and tense, nail-biting rhythmic passages ("The Books"). It also contains some of Herrmann's loveliest melodies that are full of bittersweet romance and wonder ("Valse Lente"), as well as some of his most diabolically possessed music ("Flowers of Fire"). The most romantic passages accompany scenes where the main character, a fireman who has realized the error of society's ways, is captivated by the written word in a way that another man might be by a lover. As Herrmann's lush strings wash over one scene, the protagonist is seen secretly reading *David Copperfield* by the light of a TV. *Fahrenheit 451* is one of Herrmann's best non–Hitchcock scores.

The most famous and influential sci-fi picture of the '60s is Stanley Kubrick's *2001: A Space Odyssey* (1968). The soundtrack for this landmark work is difficult to assess outside of its filmic context because much of it originated long before the film went into production. Although Kubrick hired Alex North, who had scored the director's *Spartacus* (1960), the filmmaker opted to use his temp track, a kind of soundtrack placeholder that many filmmakers use until an original score is finished. *2001*'s temp track cum final score consists of classical pieces by such disparate artists as Johann Strauss ("The Blue Danube"), Richard Strauss ("Also Sprach Zarathustra"), Aram Khachaturian ("Gayane Ballet Suite") and Gyorgy Ligeti ("Atmospheres," "Lux Aeterna" and "Requiem for Soprano, Mezzo Soprano, Two Mixed Choirs and Orchestra"). According to Robert Townson, in *Keeping the Score* by David Morgan, North naturally was devastated and demoralized by Kubrick's decision, but wisely had a clause put into his contract to let ownership of the compositions revert back to him after two years. North is rumored to have turned his score into a symphony, and he is known to have adapted selections for other soundtracks. Eventually his friend Goldsmith recorded North's powerful and modernist *2001* score with the National Philharmonic Orchestra. However, when most fans of the film (and detractors as well) think of *2001* they remember the anthem "Also Sprach Zarathustra," the graceful "Blue Danube" and the starkly terrifying and strangely beautiful Ligeti compositions. Paradoxically, despite having performance and recorded histories outside of *2001*, all of these pieces have become so closely identified with the film that it is difficult to hear them without thinking of *2001*. "Also Sprach Zarathustra" suggests planetary movements. "Requiem" conjures the god-like monolith. "Lux Aeterna" calls forth the lunar landscape. "The Blue Danube" brings to mind the space station. "Atmospheres" (and "Requiem" merged) hypnotizes with recollection of the section known as "Jupiter and the Infinite Beyond." For better or worse, Kubrick's decision to stick with the temp track is now part of *2001*'s monumental legend. Its success undoubtedly influenced the filmmaker's decision to follow suit on later films, like with Wendy (Walter) Carlos' adaptations of Beethoven classics for the director's next picture (another sci-fi masterpiece), *A Clockwork Orange* (1971).

North's original music for *2001* is an outstanding score by any standard and might have served Kubrick's film well, but trying to imagine *2001* with different music remains difficult. It's not surprising that Goldsmith was eager to record his late friend's score for the Varese Sarabande release—the recording often sounds like a Goldsmith soundtrack. The pounding percussion and dissonant horns on "Eat Meat and the Kill" reminds one of the Goldsmith's *Planet of the Apes* (1968) score. And the spooky atmosphere of "The Bluff" wouldn't sound out of place in *Alien* (1979), another influential sci-fi film that features a classic Goldsmith score. Fans of Kubrick's film may not be able imagine his sci-fi masterpiece with anything but the score he used, but North's rejected score is an important work worth discovering.

The film of Ray Bradbury's *The Illustrated Man* (1969) was considered an interesting failure upon release. Undoubtedly, Goldsmith's score is the interesting part. Even Bradbury thought it outshone the film. Because the film is episodic, the score shows some stylistic range. At times it is melancholy and lyrical, and at other times sterile and electronic. It goes from tunefully impressionistic ("Theme") to chillingly atonal ("Angry Child"). Goldsmith excels at atonality, being a self-described serial composer. But his themes aren't so much austere as they are formal and frequently haunting. The electronic bits are often subtle (like the use of an Echoplex on woodwinds), but on tracks like "21st Century House" the electronics branch out to constitute most of the sound. In fact, his use of electronics anticipates his work on *Logan's Run*.

The Ape Shuffle

The *Planet of the Apes* movie series (1968–1974) is one of the most ambitious, albeit uneven, film franchises ever. Goldsmith scored the first film and *Escape from the Planet of the Apes* (1971). Leonard Rosenman scored the second film, *Beneath the Planet of the Apes* (1970), and the final film, *Battle for the Planet of the Apes* (1973). Jazz legend Tom Scott scored for the fourth picture, *Conquest of the Planet of the Apes* (1972), and Lalo Schifrin contributed to the short-lived TV show (1974).

Musically speaking, the most consistent element in these scores is the reliance on tension-building modern orchestral motifs that wouldn't sound out of place in a concerto by Bartók or Stravinsky, all of which is gripping and truly cinematic. Goldsmith's Oscar-nominated score for the first film set the tone for the entire series. Dissonant orchestration conjures an "alien" world full of conflict and tyranny. Occasionally the pattern is broken, but always for the sake of experimentation.

Goldsmith's score for the first film, which marked Goldsmith's second collaboration with director Franklin Schaffner, stands as one of the greatest sci-fi scores ever. Eventually, Goldsmith and Schaffner worked together on *Patton* (1970), *Papillon* (1973) and *The Boys from Brazil* (1978). On *Apes*, the composer uses a wide range of primitive instruments, such as ram's horn, the Brazilian wind instrument cuika (to mimic the hooting of apes), and more wood percussion than one can shake a stick at. Such exotic instrumentation gives the abrasive, dissonant music a unique character—one that not only provides perfect accompaniment for the film's harsh environs and disorienting situations, but also makes for a compelling listen away from the viewing experience. On "The Searchers," intermittent and isolated musical phrases become increasingly vague with the use of echo. The use of metal mixing bowls on that track provides an eerie effect. Rapid arpeggios underlie the hooting horn blasts on "The Hunt." Restless piano and creepy rattling percussion pursue in "No Escape." Ominous bells and doom-laden atmosphere overhangs "The Trial." The cuika returns to taunt again on "The Intruders."

Goldsmith's *Escape* bolsters the atonal compositions with funky bass lines and tonal electric guitar fills. These contemporary touches are appropriate, because in the film the apes travel back in time to America circa the early '70s. While *Escape* is a strong score for a fairly cheesy second sequel, it's no match for the composer's first *Ape* effort.

Although 20th Century–Fox had originally assigned Goldsmith to score the first sequel, *Beneath*, he was working on *Patton* at the time, so Leonard Rosenman came on to score it. Rosenman was an inspired choice, since he'd already scored *Fantastic Voyage*, as well as Robert Altman's space exploration documentary *Countdown* (1968). Instead of merely aping the sound of the first *Apes* soundtrack, Rosenman carried over some elements (atonal compositions,

Leonard Rosenman's score for *Beneath the Planet of the Apes* (1972) memorably uses pipe organ and avant-garde choir for the climactic scene in an underground church where a nuclear missile is worshipped. (CD cover appears courtesy of Film Score Monthly; graphic design by Joe Sikoryak.)

crashing percussion, blaring horns) and added some of his own (metallic sonorities, brass pyramids, complex layers of tonal color and distorted animalistic sounds). The rambunctious, metallic-tinged, action cues recall the tense moments in *Fantastic Planet*, and also anticipate the composer's later work on animator Ralph Bakshi's *The Lord of the Rings* (1978). Rosenman's approach to the material may be consistent with Goldsmith's, but the end result is more dense and complex. Considering a plot that involves mutant humans who worship a nuclear weapon in an underground cathedral, Rosenman's use of avant-garde choir and pipe organ is fitting. The composer ironically uses the hymn "All Things Bright and Beautiful" as the basis for the mutants' perverse ode to apocalypse. Although it is less famous than the first film's score, it is among the best sci-fi scores of its era. Interestingly, the original LP release did not contain the original score, but a re-recording by a smaller orchestra with added rock instrumentation and spoken bits that tie the story to the music. With a fat David Axelrod–style backbeat, "March of the Apes" comes on like a classic slab of jazz-funk of the post–*Bitches Brew* era. The effect is particularly twisted on "Mass of the Holy Bomb."

Jazzman Scott's follow-up for *Conquest* is stylistically consistent with the scores penned by Goldsmith and Rosenman. Given little time, the famed saxophonist and arranger took his mentor Schifrin's advice to write a row of orchestral events that would connote dramatic development without the pressure of composing and orchestrating large-scale pieces. As a result, the score seems somewhat fragmented. However, the instrumentation is sufficiently imaginative to engage a close listener. As *Film Score Monthly*'s Lukas Kendall points out in the soundtrack CD booklet notes, the son of *Twilight Zone* composer Nathan Scott used prepared piano, and even built a hardwood xylophone-like dakadebello for use on the otherwise brassy score. Scott injects jazz into the circus-like "Simian Servant School," jaunty easy listening on "1991 Restaurant," and acid blues rock on "Subjugation Soul." Another standout track, the free jazz-like "Revolution," wasn't even used in the movie, but appears on *FSM*'s CD release. In fact, much of Scott's score was either not used or misused in the movie, according to Kendall's CD notes, and the filmmakers even resorted to using a Goldsmith cue from the first film in a critical scene.

Battle for the Planet of the Apes ranks as the least favorite film for the series' fans, so it should come as no surprise that Rosenman's score easily outshines it. Militaristic and brash, the theme marches forth with haughty intent. Brass figures are juxtaposed with pounding, saber rattling percussion. Atonal atmospheres of dread and disturbance dominate tracks like "March to the Dead City" and "Mutants March." The dirge-like "Ape Has Killed Ape" plays out with hypnotic rhythm. It's an intense score, but Rosenman's work on *Beneath* is more adventurous.

For the live-action TV show, Schifrin clearly made an effort to deliver music consistent with the big-screen series. The Argentinean composer provided a jarringly primitive, atonal, electronically accented theme, and scored several episodes (including the first). Taking a stylistic cue from Goldsmith and Rosenman, Schifrin created a percussion-heavy, action-packed sound. He uses orchestral dissonance to capture the alienation felt by astronauts lost in a dystopian and primitive future where apes rule over men. Shuddering strings, nervous woodwinds, strident brass and atmospheric keyboards create a persistent and nightmarish tension and sense of urgency. The closest Schifrin had

Lalo Schifrin's score for the short-lived *Planet of the Apes* live action TV show (1974) sticks to the jarringly primitive, atonal, electronically accented sound originated by Jerry Goldsmith on the first *Apes* movie. (CD cover appears courtesy of Intrada Records; graphic design by Joe Sikoryak.)

previously come to such a sound was on his *Dirty Harry* scores. Schifrin also recorded two funkified tracks—"Ape Shuffle" and "Escape from Tomorrow"—for a promotional 45 at the time.

The '70s: Dystopias & Death Stars

The early '70s—a time of political scandal and a protracted, unpopular war—was an interesting time for sci-fi films. Suddenly, space travel adventures were passé, or at the very least unfashionable, and cautionary tales were in vogue. The decade initially brought dispiriting tales of deadly viruses (*The Andromeda Strain*, 1971), ultra-violence and brainwashing (*A Clockwork Orange*, 1971), post-apocalyptic society and disease (*The Omega Man*, 1971), and totalitarian states and technology run amok (*THX 1138*, 1971). Only in the second half of the decade did space operas return to favor.

Having put his stamp on space exploration cinema in the '60s with *2001*, Kubrick's first film of the '70s reflected a more dystopian vision of the future right here on Earth with his satirical adaptation of Anthony Burgess' *A Clockwork Orange* (1971). As on *2001*, Kubrick used a classical score, this time featuring works by Henry Purcell, Gioacchino Rossini, and Sir Edward Elgar, but mostly Ludwig van Beethoven—the composer who is a central obsession of the film's main character, proto-punk Alex (Malcolm McDowell in a career-defining role). Giving the Beethoven pieces a "futuristic" edge is Wendy Carlos (originally credited as Walter Carlos), who performs movements from the "Ninth Symphony" on Moog synthesizers and introduces the Vocoder, which synthesizes the human voice. Carlos (along with producer Rachel Elkind) made her name in 1968 with the Grammy-winning *Switched on Bach*, which became the best-selling classical recording up to that time. The synthesizer pieces featured on the original soundtrack release (particularly "Timesteps," "Theme (Beethoviana)" and the title music, which is based on Purcell's "Music for the Funeral of Queen Mary") are particularly engaging, which brings us to the album originally released on LP as *Wendy Carlos's Clockwork Orange*, and later reissued on CD with additional music as *Clockwork Orange: Wendy Carlos's Complete Original Score*.

The story behind these three different releases is worth mentioning. Around the time when Kubrick was filming *A Clockwork Orange*, Carlos was developing an electronic piece called "Timesteps" as a way to introduce listeners to the Vocoder before foisting upon the era's virginal ears a Vocoder-enhanced version of the choral movement of Beethoven's "Ninth." Being fans of Burgess' novel, and having heard that Kubrick was making a film of it, Carlos and Elkind completed their work on these recordings and shipped them off to the director for consideration. Kubrick's response was favorable, and he hired the musician and her producer to complete more synth pieces for the soundtrack. Not all of the pieces made it into the film, and only a section of "Timesteps" was used, which opened the door for Carlos' version of the soundtrack, originally released by CBS Records mere weeks after the official soundtrack hit the stores. The studio album features the entire 14-minute version of "Timesteps," as well as other music Carlos developed for use in the movie, except for two pieces that simply didn't fit on the record due to space. "Orange Minuet" and "Biblical Daydreams," which appear as bonus tracks on the East Side Digital CD released in 1998, were developed for use in the movie's stage sequence and Bible fantasy sequence, respectively. Instead of using them, Kubrick stuck with his temp tracks for those scenes, Nicolai Rimsky-Korsakov's "Scheherazade" and Terry Tucker's "Overture to the Sun." Although the East Side CD doesn't contain all the temp tracks Kubrick used in the film (or perhaps because of it), it is a more satisfying *Clockwork Orange* listening experience, thanks to its stylistic consistency. Carlos worked with Kubrick again on the modern horror classic *The Shining* (1980).

The Omega Man (1971), starring the era's sci-fi action hero Charlton Heston, was an update of *The Last Man on Earth*, the first film adaptation of Richard Matheson's *I Am Legend*, about one man combating germ-infected vampire mutants. It features a fine rock and jazz-influenced score by Ron Grainer, who is best known as the composer of themes for various British TV shows, including *The Prisoner* and *Doctor Who*. The late Grainer had a gift for melodic hooks, but his work on *The Omega Man* is nuanced. Certainly there are memorable melodic themes ("The Omega Man"), up-tempo pop hooks ("Surprise Party") and jazzy grooves ("Needling Neville," "Swinging at Neville's"), but there also are tracks that blend experimental instrumentation with strong cinematic atmosphere ("The Spirits Still Linger"). On that last

Ron Grainer's score for *The Omega Man* (Warner Bros., 1971) evokes the film's central conflict that pits a lone survivor of a post-apocalyptic plague against diseased, vampire-like people. (Photograph courtesy of the John Monaghan Collection.)

track, and many others, one hears the decaying bell-like resonance of water chimes. Percussionist extraordinaire Emil Richards, who invented the instrument, creates the microtonal sounds by dipping a bell into water (the instrument also can be heard on Goldsmith's *The Illustrated Man* and Michel Colombier's *Colossus: The Forbin Project*, as well as other film scores). Grainer's rather carefully arranged score (that eschews trumpets and tuba, limiting brass to trombones and French horns, but never together) evokes the film's central conflict that pits a lone survivor of a post-apocalyptic plague against the diseased, vampire-like people. Keyboards also figure heavily in the score, but are so well incorporated into the small orchestral sound as to not seem heavy handed. In fact, the entire score benefits from Grainer's light touch. It is a little bit rock, a little bit lounge, and a little bit avant-garde.

In keeping with the theme of futuristic disease, composer Gil Melle provided a creepily effective atonal electronic score for *The Andromeda Strain* (1971), which deals with an extraterrestrial virus.

When it comes to dystopian sci-fi films, the name that doesn't exactly spring to mind is George Lucas, and the same can be said of dystopian sci-fi scores and Schifrin. But then *THX 1138* offers sufficient proof on both counts. The 1971 feature is an expansion of an award-winning short film by the future creator of *Star Wars* (1977). No one paid much attention to *THX 1138* when it was originally released, but when *Star Wars* reinvented sci-fi cinema, many fans sought out the earlier film, which is more of a curiosity than a crowd pleaser. Schifrin's score is certainly unusual, since it removes the composer from his comfort zone of crime jazz and anticipates his work on the *Planet of the Apes* TV show. Here, the man behind *Mission: Impossible* and *Dirty Harry* delves into atonal abstraction ("Theme," "Loneliness Sequence") and electronic atmospherics ("First Escape," "Second Escape"). Schifrin balances these disturbing moods with more accessible, melodically conventional tracks that employ pop ("Be Happy"), Latin jazz ("Source #1, #2, etcetera) and tribal percussion ("Primitive Dance," "Torture Sequence"). The plaintive love theme is pleasingly exotic, featuring alto flute and harp. There also are tracks that blend in Gregorian chant ("The Temple") and liturgical Baroque music ("The Hologram").

Douglas Trumbull, the effects specialist who worked on *2001: A Space Odyssey*, made his directorial debut with the environmental message film *Silent Running* (1972). The film features a gentle, light orchestral score by Peter "PDQ Bach" Schickele, and three vocal performances by his occasional collaborator, folk singer Joan Baez. Naturally, the Baez numbers have a strong folk feeling, and the instrumental version of the song "Rejoice in the Sun" has it as well. The rest of the pastoral score contains elements of folk in lean arrangements that favor solo instrumental voices in small acoustic ensembles. That's not to say the score is bereft of tension. Tracks like "No Turning Back" and "Saturn" have dark, atonal passages that interestingly transition back into Schickele's quasi-medieval accents.

Another notable sci-fi soundtrack featuring a figure from the classical world is the film of the Kurt Vonnegut Jr. novel *Slaughterhouse Five* (1972), featuring performances by Glenn Gould of music by Johann Sebastian Bach.

Probably the most unusual sci-fi soundtrack is *Space Is the Place* (1972) by Sun Ra and His Intergalactic Solar Arkestra. Sun Ra (formerly Herman Sonny Blount of Birmingham, Alabama), who famously claimed to be from another planet, recorded many jazz albums with a space age theme (*We Travel the Space Ways, Cosmic Equation, Love in Outer Space*, etc.). In fact, he recorded two different albums in 1972 with the title *Space Is the Place*—one for the jazz label Impulse, and the other as the film's soundtrack on Evidence Records. The film in question was part documentary, part sci-fi, part blaxploitation, and part revisionist Biblical epic. The film never received a theatrical release (even in that relatively adventurous cinematic era), but recently was released on DVD. With track titles like "Calling Planet Earth" and "Satellites Are Spinning," *Space Is the Place* is thick with the far-out sounds of Sun Ra's Arkestra. Chanted vocals, wheezing brass and woodwinds ride on intermittent Latin rhythms as Sun Ra lays down thick abstract note clusters on organ and Moog. As an album it isn't significantly different from Sun Ra's other work, but, like most of his music, it conjures otherworldly imagery more convincingly than most legitimate sci-fi soundtracks. At times, it even recalls Art Mineo's legendary Seattle World's Fair album *Man in Space with Sounds* (1962). A vocal track invites listeners "who find Earth boring" to sign up with "Outer Spaceways Incorporated," and it's difficult to resist while listening to Sun Ra and his band blast off for planet Jazz.

Soylent Green (1973) is the last in a line of early '70s sci-fi films starring Charlton Heston. Fred Myrow's soundtrack (with veteran TV composer Gerald Fried conducting) is by turn atonal orchestral ("Stalking the Pad"), off-kilter jazz-funk ("Tab's Pad/Furniture Party"), cheesy '50s-style pop ("Shirl and Thorn"), hallucinatory easy listening ("Home Lobby Source") and pastoral impressionism ("Sol's Music"). It may be stylistically tough to pin down, but *Soylent Green* (little green crackers made of people) is frequently compelling and suitably strange.

Another dystopian future film with a satirical edge is *Westworld* (1973), about an island resort that lets the rich live out their fantasies, such as participating in a Wild West shootout. For *Westworld*, Fred Karlin delivered Wild West and medieval-inspired source cues, as well as a dramatic underscore. Pastiche highlights include "Stagecoach Arrival" and "The Queen's Indiscretion." The more dramatic pieces, which echo the pastiche elements while reinforcing the futuristic story, combine abrasive sawing action on violins and dobro, scraping shaking percussion, electronics and pounding piano arpeggios. The methodically chaotic arrangements capture the madness afoot in a fantasy world gone horribly wrong. The "Chase" and "Gunslinger" cues are particularly effective at creating intense anxiety (the staccato piano figure on "Gun-

Fred Karlin's score for *Westworld* (1973) includes Wild West and medieval pastiche cues. (CD cover appears courtesy of Film Score Monthly; graphic design by Joe Sikoryak.)

slinger" is reminiscent of Morricone's spaghetti western work). Notably, Karlin took an innovative approach by recording much of the score in his home studio. The film's special effects may seem antiquated by today's standards, but Karlin's score is still a killer.

Three years later, Karlin scored *Westworld*'s sequel, *Futureworld* (1976). The soundtrack eschews pastiche in favor of a more satisfyingly dramatic score. Like Goldsmith's *Logan's Run* (also in 1976), *Futureworld* combines electronics with traditional orchestra. Instead of taking Goldsmith's conceptual approach (the use of electronics only for scenes in the city), Karlin's tactic is less specific and more integral to the overall electro-acoustic sound. Abrasive, pulsating synthesizers mingle with forceful string and brass sections, and rumbling rattling percussion. Staccato piano and guitar figures complement the precise electronic and percussive textures, particularly on action-oriented tracks like "The Chase" and "Samurai Fight."

Logan's Run (1976) is a classic dystopian sci-fi film that was quickly forgotten when *Star Wars* arrived in theaters a year later. Set in a far-off future of domed cities, holographic entertainments and sex without love, it's a chilling morality tale with disco-era fashions and feathered hair. Goldsmith's score

Jerry Goldsmith uses electronic music for the city scenes in *Logan's Run* (1976) and acoustic instrumentation for the scenes that take place in nature. (CD cover appears courtesy of Film Score Monthly; graphic design by Joe Sikoryak.)

is among the most electronic soundtracks to accompany a major movie of that era. For scenes inside The City, Goldsmith employs synths that gurgle, squeak and whoosh with atonal abandon. Elsewhere, particularly for scenes outside of the city, Goldsmith uses acoustic orchestration (strings, piano, woodwinds) to represent the natural world. The love theme and "The Monument" are warm examples of sweet tonality in a score dominated by dissonant, brilliantly executed sounds.

Andre Previn's *Rollerball* (1975) contains classical pieces (by Bach, Shostakovich, Tchaikovsky and Albinoni), but also features three Previn originals, including the chillingly electronic "Glass Sculpture," and the funky lounge "Executive Party" and "Executive Party Dance." There's a groovy, sleazy charm to these latter tracks, but they don't exactly sit well with the rest. Perhaps Jewison wanted to imbue his film with *2001* classicism, but acquiesced to his studio's need for something contemporary that radio stations might play.

Dino De Laurentis' *King Kong* (1976) presents one of John Barry's best action scores outside of the James Bond canon. Considering that the original film featured a spectacular score by Max Steiner, it's interesting to note how romantic Barry's score is for the remake. Tracks like "Maybe My Luck Has Changed," "Arrival on the Island" and "Arthusa" are lovely and tender. That's not to say that Barry's *Kong* is all hearts and flowers. Standout action tracks like "Sacrifice—Hail to the King" and "Breakout to Captivity" are brimming with excitement, thanks to intense tribal percussion, soaring strings and forceful waves of low brass. Speaking of low brass (which dominates this score), Barry builds enormous tension on tracks like "Incomprehensible Captivity," which captures the great ape's somber mood. More mysterious is "Full Moon Domain—Beauty Is a Beast," which segues from lush romanticism to eminent danger. The nadir is undoubtedly the disco pop instrumental "Kong Hits the Big Apple."

Jerry Fielding's *Demon Seed* (1977) is abstract and embraces avant-garde techniques that could be an extension of the fiendish supercomputer that rapes and kills in the movie. Fielding worked with synthesizer player Ian Underwood (a close associate of Frank Zappa during the '60s and early '70s), as well as jazz session guitarist Lee Ritenour, both of whom are credited with electronic performances that enhance an otherwise atonal orchestral approach. As Lukas Kendall and Jeff Bond observe in the booklet notes for the Film Score Monthly CD release that pairs *Demon Seed* with *Soylent Green*, Fielding's score "hovers in 'trapped with a killer' territory," relying on dissonance to convey the film's claustrophobic story of technology run amok.

1977 was a major year for big-screen sci-fi—perhaps the most significant in the history of the genre—with two films capturing the imaginations of viewers young and old. Stephen Spielberg's *Close Encounters of the Third Kind*, and George Lucas' top-grossing *Star Wars*, reinvented not only the marketability of sci-fi movies but also the notion of an "event" movie. Instrumental to the success of both films was the music of John Williams, who'd become the go-to composer for blockbusters since his work on Irwin Allen's star-studded disaster epics *The Poseidon Adventure* (1972) and *The Towering Inferno* (1974).

For *Close Encounters*, Williams delivered a score that is just as evocative and memorable as his *Jaws* score, but is fittingly more magical and otherworldly. Williams brilliantly combines experimental atonal orchestrations with romantic melodies that capture mankind's longing to discover if there is life "out there" and unravel the mysteries of the great unknown. Unlike *Star Wars*, which overshadowed it in popularity, *Close Encounters* lacks a grand major key fanfare or recurring theme. Perhaps viewers left the theater briefly humming Williams' five-note quotation from "When You Wish Upon a Star," but otherwise it's not a very hum-able score. Perhaps the most familiar cue for symphony audiences is the "End Title," which is frequently included in movie-themed orchestral programs. Instead of going for easy sentimentality (which he is often accused of doing), Williams brilliantly keys into the film's suspense and shock elements by writing turbulent, dense, atmospheric music ("Nocturnal Pursuit," "The Abduction of Barry," etc.) that conjures the mysteries that obsess and eventually confront the film's characters.

More than any other score of the Silver Age of cinema, *Star Wars* revived the epic style of the Golden Age with large orchestras, grand themes and sweeping imagination. Williams—who had worked through the '60s under the name of Johnny, penning pop and jazz-influenced scores in the Mancini vein—began to dabble in epic scoring with Allen's disaster flicks, and he really came on strong with *Jaws*. In an 18-month

Harrison Ford (Han Solo) looks like a Wild West gunslinger in *Star Wars* (20th Century–Fox/Lucasfilm, 1977). John Williams' heroic score is perfect for George Lucas' space western.

period spanning 1977 and 1978, however, Williams made his mark with *Close Encounters of the Third Kind*, *Star Wars* and *Superman*. The *Star Wars* score (like the movie itself) is a throwback to a more innocent age of sci-fi cinema—to the space operas of Buck Rogers and Flash Gordon. The *Star Wars* score sounds as if the paranoia of alien abduction horrors ('50s/'60s) and post-apocalyptic dystopian nightmares ('60s/'70s) never even happened. Williams' use of a prominent heroic title theme and several rousing leitmotivs proved refreshing after more than a decade of frequently discordant and sometimes disturbing sci-fi scores. That's not to say that Williams didn't provide a few discordant passages for *Star Wars*; he simply countered them with reassuringly ascending reprises of the courageous theme. Above all, Williams continues to demonstrate his absolute mastery of large-scale orchestrations, bringing imagination and classical discipline to the medium. Among the outstanding cues are "Imperial Attack," "The Last Battle," and "The Throne Room and End Title." The campy intergalactic ragtime jazz number "Cantina Band" is also a fan favorite. Given the amount of experimentation sci-fi scores have invited over the years, *Star Wars* isn't particularly innovative, but its crowd-pleasing qualities cannot be disputed.

For *Superman* (1978), Williams delivered another heroic score. The soaring, patriotic theme is the very embodiment of the film's superhuman hero. It is one of the finest "superhero" scores of all time, more memorable than the bombastic scores that accompany the superhero movies of the early 21st century. Following the rousing theme, the music for the sequences on planet Krypton are relatively austere, sometimes employing synthesizer accents. Once "Clark Kent" is on Earth, however, the music takes on an upbeat character. Even the gorgeous love theme exudes a heroic character. Williams further indulges fans of his famous flair for sentimentality on "Leaving Home," but balances it with the mysterious mood swings of "The Fortress of Solitude." Williams is at his most romantic on "The Flying Sequence" and the Margot Kidder showcase "Can You Read My Mind," but the remainder favors the action fans relish. Tracks like "Super Rescues" and "Superfeats" reprise the theme while building excitement for the film's action-packed conclusion. "Lex Luthor's Lair" is fittingly sinister, but with a vaguely comedic bent befitting Gene Hackman's over-the-top performance. "The March of the Villains" accomplishes a similar feat. "Chasing Rockets," "Turning Back the World" and the "End Title" do for *Superman* what similar tracks do for *Star Wars*—they build excitement for an explosive finale.

Leonard Rosenman's soundtrack for Ralph Baksi's animated version of *The Lord of the Rings* (1978) is difficult to judge in light of Howard Shore's subsequent work on Peter Jackson's blockbuster trilogy. While Shore's work on the trilogy ranks as a monumental effort in its own right, Rosenman's generally enjoyable score for the Bakshi flop is relegated to second rate in comparison. That's not to say that it is inherently inferior. There are memorable melodies and imaginative arrangements throughout. Typically, Rosenman, a protégé of the innovative Austrian composer Arnold Schönberg, uses atonality for the action sequences and tonality for the theme and its variations. This is a significantly different sound than Shore used on the live action trilogy. The low moaning voices and eerie atmospherics on "The Journey Begins: Encounter with the Ringwraiths" wouldn't have sounded out of place in one of Rosenman's *Planet of the Apes* scores, and the same can be said for music that accompanies Orc scenes. "Escape to Rivendell" and "Mines of Moria" bristle with frantic energy and spooky atmosphere. "The Battle in the Mines" is as exciting an action track as any that Rosenman composed for any of the sci-fi epics he's worked on, including *Star Trek IV: The Voyage Home* (1986). The doggerel chanting, churning rhythm and brass attack of "Helm's Deep," and the intense atonal orchestral action of "The Dawn Battle," further demonstrate the dark power of Rosenman's vision. On a lighter note, the composer enlists choirs of adults and children to sing lyrics by Mark Fleischer on "Mithrandir."

Another atonal sci-fi score of the late '70s is by then-rookie film composer Denny Zeitlin for *Invasion of the Body Snatchers* (1978). Because the film combines sci-fi with horror, its discordant, electronically embellished score diverges from the fashionable neo–Golden Age style popularized by Williams. When Zeitlin, an accomplished jazz pianist and psychiatrist, signed on at director Philip Kaufman's request, he anticipated writing a jazz score because Donald Sutherland's character was originally imagined as a musician. Then the script changed and the filmmakers decided that an avant-garde orchestral score with jazz highlights and electronic effects would be appropriate. In a lengthy interview recording presented on the Perseverance CD of *Body Snatchers*, Zeitlin talks of how he was ill prepared to take on such a project, but received the support he needed from conductor Roger Kellaway and orchestrator Greig McRitchie. In fact, the stress of working on a film score led him to reject all subsequent offers, despite the high praise he earned from Kaufman and in the press.

"*Body Snatchers* was so perfect because paranoia was so pervasive in the piece," Kaufman states in the booklet notes. "Denny was able to reach into his psychiatry practice and pull out notes and sounds. I know people at the time thought it was one of the best scores they'd heard."

According to the CD booklet, John Wasserman, the critic at the *San Francisco Chronicle*, called it "an Academy Award nominee job if there is any justice." (Zeitlin wasn't nominated, and Giorgio Moroder won for *Midnight Express*.)

Nominated that same year for *The Boys from Brazil*, Jerry Goldsmith was doing some of the best work of his storied career. Not exactly a sci-fi movie, but a thriller about a bogus manned mission to Mars, *Capricorn One* (1978) features a characteristically excellent and edgy Goldsmith from one of the

Danny Zeitlin originally intended to score *Invasion of the Body Snatchers* (1978) with jazz, but wisely switched to avant-garde orchestration to play up the otherworldly horror of the story. (CD cover appears courtesy of Perseverance Records; graphic design by Wolfgang Fenchel.)

composer's peak creative periods. Percussive and aggressive, the "Theme" sets the tone brilliantly, but counters the main section with a soft melodic theme (which re-occurs as "Bedtime Story") representing a family at the center of the action. Although the arrangements are dominated by percussion and brass, Goldsmith makes effective use of piano and occasionally synthesizer. Strings and low brass join piano and synth to lend an ominous tone to "The Message." Because the movie is a thriller, there are numerous passages that build tension (notably the nail-biter "Break Out"). The soft and mellow "Kay's Theme" is pretty but diffuses the drama.

Jerry Goldsmith's *Capricorn One* (1978) favors an aggressive brass and percussion attack befitting this tense sci-fi conspiracy thriller. (CD cover appears courtesy of Intrada Records; graphic design by Joe Sikoryak.)

Goldsmith's *Alien* (1979), Ridley Scott's influential space horror masterpiece, is another high mark for the composer, though it was misrepresented in the film itself. For the booklet notes that accompany Cliff Eidelman's re-recording of score selections on the Varese Sarabande compilation *The Alien Trilogy*, Goldsmith explained how the filmmakers had temp-tracked *Alien* prior to his signing on with selections that included Goldsmith's own music for *Freud* (1962). The score that finally accompanied the film included portions of Goldsmith's original score, in addition to music from *Freud* and music by Howard Hanson and W.A. Mozart.

"The whole score was eventually emasculated," Goldsmith said. "Half of the music didn't end up where it was supposed to go."

Goldsmith re-recorded the *Alien* score with the National Philharmonic Orchestra for the original soundtrack release. It is by turns gorgeous, gripping and sinister. Goldsmith relies on strings, brass and woodwinds, but also uses harp, chimes and vibraphone. He also employs unusual instruments, such as the serpent, didjerido, log drums and shaum. The style is starkly modernist, with avant-garde touches. The echoing four-note "time" motif suggests the deep, lonely reaches of outer space. A solo trumpet represents both outer space and the main character of Ripley. All in all, *Alien* is a haunting score of primordial power.

If *Alien* represents the dark side of Goldsmith's sci-fi scoring prowess, *Star Trek the Motion Picture* (1979) is the composer at his most wide-eyed and optimistic. It's also a classic example of a score that outshines its movie. The "Theme," which Goldsmith struggled to create, is as rousing and persuasive as Alexander Courage's theme for the original TV show (1966–1969) in evoking the spirit of grand galactic adventure. A version of it was later used for the long-running second TV series, *Star Trek: The Next Generation* (1987–1994). Another standout is "Klingon Battle," which pulses with anticipation as metallic stings and electronic accents add to the atmosphere. "Ilia's Theme" (for the bald female character) channels lush romanticism through soaring strings and piano. "Vejur Flyover" is another highlight, representing the mysterious and threatening Vejur invader. Craig Huxley's Blaster Beam lends the score a futuristic effect. It resurfaced for James Horner's subsequent *Star Trek* film scores.

Like the first *Star Trek* movie, which was subsequently out-performed by its sequels, *Mad Max* (1979) briefly spawned a franchise during the '80s (most notably the 1981 sequel *The Road Warrior*), which made an action star out of Mel Gibson. Both films feature tense orchestral scores by Australian composer Brian May, who should not to be confused with the Queen guitarist. For a post-apocalyptic, motor-headed film, it is surprising that it didn't get a more abrasive electronic or rock score. That's no criticism of May's music, which blends synthesizers with traditional instrumentation. Tracks like "Max the Hunter" and "Max Decides on Vengeance" are vigorously rhythmic and full of blustery machismo and action.

By Barry standards, *The Black Hole* (1979) is a minor entry in a career dominated by his work on the James Bond series. At times it sounds interchangeable with one of his later Bond entries, such as *Moonraker*, which he recorded the same year (and which also featured outer space action). The "Theme" is heroic, but fairly generic, perhaps because it has no strong central character to represent. The score is a bit more memorable when it strives for dark drama. Here its swirling violins and portentous brass promise imminent peril. But even this sounds like a job for Bond, James Bond. Notably, *The Black Hole* was the first soundtrack digitally recorded.

Among the last sci-fi movies of the '70s was *Time After Time* (1979), for which Miklós Rózsa composed one of his last scores (in the fifth decade of his illustrious career). Understandably, the H.G. Wells versus Jack the Ripper time travel story gets a Golden Age scoring treatment. The music describes the action with driving force. The Hungarian-born composer provides a blend of 19th-century romanticism and action cues suitable for a "ripping yarn." After all, this was the man who scored such grand old classics as *The Thief of Baghdad, Ivanhoe, Ben-Hur* and *El Cid*.

"Rózsa took to my film like syrup to wheatcakes," wrote director Nicholas Meyer on the original soundtrack LP's cover notes, "responding to its peculiarities as I had dreamt he would, to its odd mixture of fantasy and reality."

With its old-fashioned style it may seem an odd selection to close out the sci-fi '70s, but considering the neo–Golden Age style ushered in by Williams, it is indeed fitting. Like any time travel story, this one comes full circle.

Sci-fi from Europe

While Hollywood churned out a galaxy full of sci-fi pictures, European filmmakers ventured into the genre as well, albeit with much smaller budgets.

Angelo Lavagnino scored a series of four space exploration flicks by Antonio Margheriti: *I criminali della galassia* (*Wild Wild Planet*, 1965), *I diafanoidi vengono da marta* (*War of the Planets*, 1965), *Il planeta errante* (*Planet on the Prowl*, 1965) and *La morte viene dal planeta aytin* (*Space Devils*, 1965). Lavagnino uses a large orchestra to convey the adventurous spirit that pervaded the space age culture of the '60s, and evokes the mysteries of space exploration. That's not to say this is kitschy music. Actually, it's thoroughly cinematic, connoting action and drama with orchestration that wouldn't sound out of place in Gustav Holst's "The Planets." When Lavagnino goes romantic he ventures into Les Baxter territory, which isn't a bad thing, but these aren't the best bits. Classic sci-fi fans will be happy to know that electronic effects are often part of the mix, but they generally originate from an organ. This isn't as far out as Louis and Bebe Barron's *Forbidden Planet*, but it's still aspires to be "out there." There are a couple of pop-oriented tracks to lighten the mood when the organ takes a solo or two. "Galaxy Galore" is one such track, featuring a vibe solo over beat jazz backing. Another is "Space Devils," which sounds like a mid-tempo spaghetti western loungecore number.

Another Italian entry in this genre is Mario Bava's classic sci-fi horror film *Terrore nello spazio* (*Planet of the Vampires*, 1965), which has been known by at least a dozen different names, and famously served as a reference point for *Alien*. Gino Marinuzzi Jr.'s atmospheric and experimental score perfectly captures the movie's creepy mood. The score combines traditional orchestra (reminiscent of 20th-century masters Bartók and Stravinsky) with electronic sound effects that are otherworldly without sounding cheesy or dated.

Yet another Italian sci-fi film of 1965 is *La decima vittima* (*The Tenth Victim*). Set in a future society where war is outlawed and murder is sanctioned by the government as part of a televised, cash-prize awarding survival contest, *The Tenth Victim* has a "futuristic jazz" soundtrack by Piero Piccioni. Hammond-driven grooves and big band numbers enhanced by sporadic stroboscopic sound effects provide the retro-futuristic aural backdrop for "The Hunt." Among the highlights is the vocal track "Spiral Waltz" (lyrics by Sergio Bardotti), in which one-time pop princess Mina sings "My lips are on fire, but

Piero Piccioni's "futuristic jazz" score for *La decima vittima* (*The Tenth Victim*, 1965) is among the composer's best. (CD cover appears courtesy of Easy Tempo Records [ET923]; graphic design by Giulio "Jazzy Jules" Maini.)

they're made of ice." Also, on the theme she scats "die, die, die." It's as quirky and appealing as star Ursula Andress' "bullet" bra striptease.

Germany got into the act as well with TV's *Raumpatrouille* (*Space Patrol*, or *Orion 2000*, 1966), and Peter Thomas' score for this space opera is his small-screen masterpiece. The composer behind such big-screen Edgar Wallace schlock as *The Hunchback of Soho* and *The Curse of the Sinister One* found a perfect vehicle for his beat jazz experiments on *Space Patrol*. The brassy, bass-thumping theme music starts with a metallic-voiced countdown and takes off with wailing Hammond organ, which plays an integral part throughout the soundtrack. "Lancet Bossa Nova" features pulsating staccato organ textures, sultry sax and muted brass. "Bolero on Moon Rocks" is slow-motion make-out music that English rock group Pulp sampled for the title track on *This Is Hardcore* (1998) at the peak of the lounge music revival. Thomas employs improvisatory male vocalisms on "Take Sex." The quasi-baroque dirge "Jupiter's Pop Music" features jazzy flute and a sprinkling of harpsichord runs. On "Love in Space" the bluesy, spacious saxophone is jarringly interrupted by a vertigo-inducing descent into an instrumental maelstrom, only to return again to a sonorous meditation of sultry subway blues. "Orion 2000" reprises the theme music into a noir-like groove. Simply put, *Raumpatrouille* is Euro '60s sci-fi at its grooviest.

On the big screen, Germany (in a co-production with Spain and Italy) launched *Perry Rhodan—S.O.S. aus dem Weltall* (*... 4... 3... 2.. 1... Morte* or *Mission Stardust*, among other titles, 1967), featuring one of the most popular sci-fi adventure characters ever. The film boasts a semi-electronic score by Anton Garcia Abril, and a groovy pop theme courtesy of Marcello Giombini, who is better known for his spaghetti western scores. Thousands of novels and short stories have been published about the space explorer, but there seems to have been only one theatrical feature made. Giombini provided a catchy, upbeat theme, and Abril delivered an experimental, spacey, exotic score. Wordless vocals, jangling guitars, whistling woodwinds, splashy dance rhythms and cricket-like electronics intermingle for a classic '60s sci-fi sound.

Back on the small screen came the British-German production *Star Maidens* (*Die Mädchen aus dem Weltraum*, 1975), featuring an exciting disco-funk soundtrack by Berry Lipman. The proto-feminist space opera seems well suited for vamping synth melodies and hip-swaying rhythms of Lipman's library pop concoctions like "Sex World," "Highway Patrol" and "Starship Strut." Fittingly enough, while *Star Maidens* was being filmed, production on *The Rocky Horror Picture Show* was underway in the studio next door. The disco-era spirit of sexual liberation must have been palpable at Maidenhead Studios in 1975.

The now defunct East Germany (DEFA) also produced sci-fi films. Of course, most fans of the genre think of the utopian novels of Stanislaw Lem or the art house films of Andrej Tarkowskij (*Stalker*, 1979; *Solaris*, 1972) when they think of Communist Bloc sci-fi. But *Kosmos* draws attention to populist

Perry Rhodan—SOS Aus Dem Weltall (a.k.a. *4...3...2...1... Morte!*, 1967) features a semi-electronic score by Anton Garcia Abril, and a groovy pop theme by Marcello Giombini. (CD cover appears courtesy of Diggler/Cinesoundz [www.cinesoundz.com]; graphic design by Thomas Gross.)

B-grade sci-fi like *Der Schweigende Stern* (*The Silent Star*, or *First Spaceship on Venus*, 1960), *Signale—Ein Weltraumabenteuer* (1970), *Eolomea* (1972) and *Im Staub der Sterne* (1976).

First Spaceship on Venus (*Der Schweigende Stern*, or *The Silent Star*, 1960/1962), an East German/Polish co-production featuring a racially diverse international cast, was scored by Anrzej Markowski for the European release, and rescored by Leith Stevens and monster movie specialist Hans Salter for the U.S. release.

One of the most important composers in East Germany was Karl-Ernst

Barry Lipman's score for *Star Maidens* (*Die Mädchen aus dem Weltraum*, 1975) reflects the disco-funk fashion of the era. (CD cover appears courtesy of All Score Media/ Cinesoundz [www.cinesoundz.com]; graphic design by Matthias Kern.)

Sasse, who also scored many of the country's "Wild West" films. His music for the *2001*-influenced *Signale* leaps from experimental electronics (created with the use of noise generators, ring modulators and filters) to jazzy piano solo to jaunty big band dance music that sounds a lot like Peter Thomas' theme for *Space Patrol*.

Günther Fischer, another important figure in East German cinema, scored *Eolomea* using a bizarre combination of jazz, avant-garde orchestral and spacey psychedelic funk.

Sasse and Kolditz teamed up again for *Im Staub der Sterne*, with the director writing lyrics for the sublime psychedelic lullaby "Das Licht." Elsewhere,

Sasse cooks up psychedelia with jazzy electronics, beat guitars, echoing percussion and far-out synth solos.

The most famous "European" sci-fi film of the '60s is undoubtedly the sexy psychedelic sci-fi fantasy *Barbarella* (1968), featuring an incredible soundtrack by the Bob Crewe Generation Orchestra, with music and lyrics written by Crewe and Charles Fox, and songs sung by the Glitterhouse. (Crewe was selected after French composer Michel Magne's score was rejected.) The brilliance of the *Barbarella* soundtrack is how it combines pop hooks, psychedelic rock production and full-bodied, big-budget orchestration. Otherworldly

Bob Crewe delivered a hip, sexy and psychedelic score for *Barbarella* (1968) that is among the best of the era. (CD cover appears courtesy of Harkit Records; graphic design by Tim Creasey.)

sound effects made on flanged and reverb-effected instruments echo through the production alongside the relatively restrained sounds of large-scale cinematic pop orchestration. *Barbarella* remains one of the best examples of psychedelic scoring, and is a must have for any fan of '60s cinema.

That same year, Morricone provided a far more austere score for the post-apocalyptic thriller *Ecce Homo—I Sopravvissuti* (*The Survivors*). Morricone and his regular conductor, Nicolai, works small, employing Dell'Orso's haunting voice and several soloists, including two percussionists, to create a primitive atmosphere tinged with regret and sickness. This isn't what most listeners look for in a late '60s sci-fi soundtrack, but the overall effect is suitably chilling.

One of the best European sci-fi soundtracks belongs to the French-Czech co-production of the surreal animated *La Planète sssauvage* (*Fantastic Planet*, 1973), which won the Special Jury Prize at Cannes Film Festival that year. Serge Gainsbourg arranger Alain Goraguer's funky psychedelic score isn't likely to strike many listeners as a typical sci-fi score—and it certainly isn't—but it may be one of the most haunting scores to ever grace the genre. A lean orchestra made up of Fender Rhodes electric piano, vibes, flute, saxophone, guitars, bass, bongos, Hammond organ, strings, subtle electronics, vocal sighs, and drums do the trick. Sure, some genre purists are likely to sneer at the wah guitars, but Goraguer's gift for transforming a handful of hypnotic hooks into entrancingly trippy movie music can not be ignored. This isn't some eccentric variation on a blaxploitation soundtrack, but a genuinely creative, transporting soundtrack.

Big in Japan

Starting with *Gojira* (*Godzilla*, 1954), featuring a soundtrack by Akira Ifukube, Japan became a powerhouse sci-fi monster movie industry. The original cut of the film offers biting social commentary about the damage done by the hydrogen bomb on Hiroshima and Nagasaki particularly, with the giant lizard representing the catastrophic attack. *Godzilla* was only the beginning of what proved to be a long-lived cinematic phenomenon. Legend has it that Ifukube began work on the first *Godzilla* score before the film was even complete. His theme is among the most easily identifiable themes in the genre. With drums pounding and cymbals clashing, the string section marches forward with a vigorous riff that epitomizes the unstoppable force that is Godzilla, as well as the military that bravely combats the giant lizard. It also recalls one of the most common musical reference points for countless sci-fi soundtracks, Stravinsky's "Rite of Spring," which is famous for its unrelenting rhythms and jarring dissonances. The dirge-like "Godzilla's Rampage" eventually became the theme music for subsequent Godzilla movies, much in the way that Monty Norman's "James Bond Theme" and Barry's "007" became identifiable cues in so many James Bond pictures. Although Ifukube created new music for each of the films he worked on, he recycled "Japanese Army March" from *Godzilla* in later films, such as *Invasion of the Astro-Monster* (for its "Monster Battle March"). The catchy up-tempo march has undeniable appeal and a vaguely Russian pomp to it. The score reaches its operatic conclusion with a grimly gorgeous funereal piece featuring choir. Not only is this score tremendously appealing and effective, it also is one of the most influential sci-fi scores ever, and provided a touchstone for many sequels.

Ifukube's *Sora no daikaiju Radon* (*Rodan, the Flying Monster*, 1956) is perhaps less memorable than *Godzilla*. This portentous score emphasizes sustained note clusters in the lower register of a piano, and the threatening low brass that is a staple of the genre, as well as shrill flutes and vibrato-addled trumpets, screeching violins, swirling harp and piano glissandi. Tracks like "The Large Underground Cave" and "A Shadow Blankets the Sky" capture the sense of mystery and terror as well as any movie music ever could.

The sci-fi monster phenomenon took a human turn on *Bijo to Ekitai-ningen* (*The H-Man*, or *Liquid Man*, 1958), featuring a score by Masaru Satôh. A noir influence can be felt in the soundtrack, which has several jazz tracks for the nightclub scenes. Some of them are sung by a sweet-voiced English-speaking female, such as the off-kilter Latin-tinged vocal track "The Magic Begins" and the foggy ballad "So Deep Is My Love." The non-jazz tracks, like "The H-Man Appears" and "The Living Liquid," are downright creepy, and minimally arranged around skin-crawling string textures, serpentine flutes, high-pitched electronic pings and sustained organ tones.

The Denso Ningen (*Secret of the Telegian*, 1960), featuring a score by Sei Ikeno, is a futuristic crime film wherein the villain uses a teleporter (like on *Star Trek*) to transport himself to the locations of his intended victims. Ikeno's score combines traditional thriller music, nightclub jazz and noir mood music. The best tracks—like "Telegian in the Warehouse District" and "Sudo, Fiend of Vengeance"—are the suspense cues that interject discordant orchestral outbursts with avant-garde jazz horn vamps and gong blows. It's busy and abstract stuff, but definitely delivers white-knuckle suspense.

Kunio Miyauchi provided a Herrmann-esque score for *Gasu Ningen Dai Ichigo* (*The Human Vapor*, 1960), which is one of a handful of Toho Studios' human transformation sci-fi horror films. The restless theme music combines pulsing strings (as in *Psycho*) with occasional vibrating electric organ accents, crashing percussion and separate, overlapping horn statements. Like the other scores in this loose series, this one features a batch of Latin-tinged jazz dance tracks. They add ambience, but the dramatic cues—like "Horror of the Human Vapor" and "The Shadow"—are the standouts.

Yuji Koseki scored *Mosura* (*Mothra*, 1961). The notable track here is "Mothra's Song," with lyrics by Tomoyuki Tanaka, Shinichi Sekizawa and Ishirô Honda. The harmonizing female singing group the Peanuts sing this catchy, bouncy bubble-gum exotica in Malay.

Yosei Gorasu (*Gorath*, 1962), featuring a score by Ken Ishii, is an unusual entry in the Japanese sci-fi genre, as it actually involves outer space (an asteroid threatens to destroy Earth). The score is among the best of the genre. Electric guitar stings, organ drones, sweeping and stroking strings, ponderous brass and cool vibes combine to make for a richly atmospheric and sometimes unsettling listening experience. Some of the tracks verge on jazz, but still manage to be highly cinematic and melodically memorable—not merely generic nightclub source cues.

The psychedelic *Matango* (*Attack of the Mushroom People*, 1962), another title in the human transformation subgenre, features a score by Sadao Bekku. Like the other pictures in this series, *Matango* has its share of jazz numbers, but the real attraction is the dramatic score. With evocative titles like "An Isolated Island Shrouded in Mist" and "Inside the Flames of Disaster," the score captures the hallucinatory qualities of this horrific *Gilligan's Island* prototype. Creepy skeletal xylophone, shuddering strings and ominous ostinatos run rampant.

The undersea sci-fi adventure *Atragon* (*Atoragon Flying Supersub*, 1963) features an exotic score by Ifukube. "The Prayer of the Mu Empire" is a ritualistic processional that sounds straight out of the Arabian Nights. While the three-part "Test Maneuvers of the Undersea Warship" is stern and militaristic, "Makoto's Theme" is luminescent and lovely. Shuddering strings and low piano rumblings represent undersea mysteries and danger on "The Submarine Returns." Middle Eastern sonorities, backed by jungle drums, return on "Warning from Mu." Echoplex-effected piano and strings enhance tracks like "The Submarine Surfaces" with an underwater atmosphere.

Ifukube's *San daikaiju chikyu saidai no kessen* (*Ghidorah, the Three-Headed Monster*, or *The Greatest Giant Monster Battle on Earth*) uses ominous low brass to announce the monster's arrival, suggesting certain doom for everything in its way. The short trumpet solo almost has a jazz-like flare, but the orchestra crushes it beneath a heavy heel. Theremin-like female singing can be heard on "The Flash," "Magnetism" and "Discovery of the Meteorite." Raspy, groaning brass makes its presence known on "Fury of the Gravity Beam." Exotica worthy of Les Baxter can be heard on the "Princess Salno" variations.

Also joining the giant reptile party in 1965 was *Daikaijû Gamera* (*Gamera*, or *The Giant Monster Gamera*). Tadashi Yamauchi scored the first film, as well as a few of its sequels. Kenjiro Hirose and Shunsuke Kikuchi scored several others, and Chuji Kinoshita also contributed music during the 1965–1971 period.

Ifukube's *Furankenshutain no kaiju: Sanda tai Gaira* (*War of the Gargantuas*, 1966) employs electronic enhancements and raspy, shrill brass. The composer takes advantage of the film's Frankenstein theme to amp up the sense of perverse horror. The soundtrack also features examples of Ifukube's take on easy listening ("Feel in My Heart").

Although others have scored Japanese sci-fi monster movies, Ifukube remains the king of the genre. He continued to contribute to the genre, with his final Godzilla score being *Gojira vs. Desutoroia* (*Godzilla vs. the Destroyer*, 1995), which fittingly had the tag line "Godzilla Dies!"—at least until his resurrection in 2000.

Sci-Fi on TV

Science fiction on TV began in 1949 with *Captain Video and His Video Rangers*, which ran until 1955. It was basically a show for kids, as was *Tom Corbett—Space Cadet* and the U.S version of *Space Patrol*. Among the other shows with a sci-fi bent were *The Adventures of Fu Manchu, The Adventures of Superman, Buck Rogers, Captain Midnight, Commando Cody: Sky Marshal of the Universe, Flash Gordon, Johnny Jupiter, Men Into Space, Out of this World, Operation Neptune, Rocky Jones—Space Ranger, Science Fiction Theater* and *Tales of Tomorrow* (among others).

The most famous sci-fi show of the pre–*Star Trek* era is *The Twilight Zone* (1959–1964), featuring music by Herrmann, Goldsmith, Marius Constant and others. The original Rod Serling–hosted show, which was less concerned with outer space than most sci-fi shows of the '50s, was one of the first of its kind to appeal as much, if not more, to adults as to children. Marius Constant's famous spiraling electric guitar figure has made the theme music identifiable to this day.

Herrmann's contributions to *The Twilight Zone* are up to his usual high standards. In fact, Herrmann played an important role in the development of sound libraries for TV productions to draw upon. He had his old radio scores recorded for use in TV shows, while he composed original scores for select shows. His original work for *The Twilight Zone* is particularly memorable. Here, as with his big-screen work, one hears Herrmann's distinctive approach to minimalism, using repetitive motifs and pulsing undercurrents to connote an air of mystery, lurking fear and imminent danger. Harp and vibraphone often provide this mood. And no one uses oboe to suggest dread as well as Herrmann. For passages of high anxiety and emotional catharsis, however, he relies on strings and brass. Herrmann uses small ensembles tailored to specific melodic ideas, such as the three-note figure in the show's pilot episode, "Where Is Everybody?" If one wished to demonstrate Herrmann's influence on latter-day minimalists they need only listen to the "Outer Space Suite." Its clockwork "Prelude" weaves a sinister spell as low brass and high woodwinds exchange foreboding asides over a chiming ostinato. And the pulsing polyrhythm of "Signals" anticipates longer works by such artists as Philip Glass and Steve Reich.

Goldsmith's suites for "Back There," "The Invaders" and other episodes are just as gripping as Herrmann's, though distinctly different. A self-pro-claimed serialist, Goldsmith brings symphonic complexity to everything he writes. He's said on more than one occasion that he tries for emotional penetration instead of simply describing the action. He manages to do both on *The Twilight Zone*. He also supplies some cool crime jazz themes that are complex in their own right. With its purring flutes and tick-tock guitar rhythm, the suite that most perfectly blends the symphonic and jazz sensibilities is "Nervous Man in a $4.00 Room."

Nathan Van Cleave, Nathan Scott, Rene Garriguenc, Fred Steiner, Leonard Rosenman, Jeff Alexander and Franz Waxman also contributed music to Serling's groundbreaking show.

While *The Twilight Zone* was a landmark for sci-fi TV in America, *Doctor Who* (1963-present) remains the ultimate example of British sci-fi on TV. Numerous composers have contributed to the series over the years, but Ron Grainer wrote the famous theme music for the show's premiere in 1963 (he later wrote the theme for another sci-fi influenced British show, *The Prisoner*). The *Doctor Who* theme, which has inspired more than its fair share of pop tributes over the years, is a classic example of early electronic scoring. Drop a thumping beat behind its throbbing electronic rhythm and squealing, chiming melody, and it's suitable for a discotheque. The actual sound of the recording was accomplished by the BBC Radiophonic Workshop, namely Delia Derbyshire and Dick Mills, whose pioneering experimentation with oscillators, wobbulators, filters and tape recorders frequently transformed the sounds made on refuse like scrap metal into futuristic sound effects. Amazingly, they managed to make dense electronic textures without the aid of synthesizers or samplers. In the booklet notes for the BBC Legends CD *Doctor Who at*

Delia Derbyshire and Dick Mills produced the early electronic soundtracks for the quirky *Doctor Who* (BBC, 1963–1989), who has been played by several actors, including Tom Baker (1974–1981).

the BBC Radiophonic Workshop, Volume One—The Early Years (1963–1969), producer Mark Ayres describes how the recording team created the sound of Doctor Who's TARDIS time/space travel machine materializing and dematerializing by "torturing the strings of a retired upright piano with a front-door key."

One of the best TV sci-fi shows of the '60s is *The Outer Limits* (1963–1965), featuring music by Dominic Frontiere. Next to Herrmann's work on *The Twilight Zone*, Frontiere's music for *The Outer Limits* is arguably the best TV sci-fi score of the '60s in the symphonic style. Taking inspiration from the work of Ravel and Bartók, the composer creates a lavish sound of shimmering, swirling strings, heavy brass and exotic accents. Theremin fans are sure to delight in the dense, futuristic soundscapes heard on tracks like "Probing the Galaxies" and "Spaceship Entering Atmosphere."

Voyage to the Bottom of the Sea (1964–1968), the longest running of the Irwin Allen–produced sci-fi series, was based on the hit 1961 theatrical release about deep sea adventures on a nuclear submarine. Among the composers who contributed original music were Herrmann, Riddle, Stevens, Goldsmith, Alexander Courage, Joseph Mullendore and Sawtell (who collaborated with Shefter on the movie's score). Instead of using the schmaltzy theme song from the movie, the TV show opts for a shimmering deep dive fanfare by Sawtell. Like the movie score, the show's music suggests a somewhat militaristic version of nautical impressionism (harp glissandi are never in short order, but they're frequently countered with a brassy flourish and a drum roll). Goldsmith's moody, dark score for the episode "Jonah and the Whale" is a highlight. Startling shifts in instrumentation keep a listener guessing, as the composer experiments with unexpected combinations. Electric keyboard and theremin embellish the orchestra, which stops intermittently, giving way to deep piano notes and bells, then raspy menacing brass. Goldsmith never settles into an easy groove. The "Jonah" score grows in intensity and inventiveness, dragging the listener further into its ominous depths with each passage. TV music rarely sounds as ominous as it does here. Even a lot of sci-fi movie scores pale in comparison.

Equally popular—or perhaps even more so—was Allen's production of *Lost in Space* (1965–1968), about a space colony family struggling for survival on an unknown planet. Williams, Courage, Richard LaSalle, Herman Stein, Hans Salter, Stevens and others contributed to the show. Regardless of the composer, the *Lost in Space* music suggests alien landscapes and encounters, with harp glissando, vibes, strings and brass creating shimmering layers of sound ("A Walk in Space"). Williams uses theremin for tried and true otherworldly effects on the episode "The Reluctant Stowaway." At other times the mood runs the gamut from playful ("A Weightless Waltz") to foreboding ("The Earthquake"). Williams' lively theme uses percussion, penny whistles and brass to describe robots and starships in action. The music has more in common with Williams' light romantic comedy work, and will surprise listeners who expect to hear an early version of his heroic fanfares (á la *Star Wars*). Regardless of expectations, the scores for *Lost in Space* are top shelf sci-fi music.

Williams also wrote the theme for Allen's *The Time Tunnel* (1966–1967). It is less catchy but just as dynamic as his theme for *Lost in Space*. Polyrhythmic percussion suggests that a very bewildering experience is about to unfold. Flutes and strings swirl as brass pulses through the rhythmically propelled spiral. A bit of reverb electric guitar and pulsing horns creep on "To the Tunnel," but most of the score eschews mod touches in favor of more traditionally dramatic scoring. Given the time traveling gimmick, it isn't surprising to hear an old-fashioned musical style on occasion; in the case of the episode "Rendezvous with Yesterday," Williams whips up a bit of ragtime. Another contributor, George Duning, who started scoring in the early '40s, brings a bit more old school bluster to his *Tunnel* sound on the episode "Death Merchant." His use of brass pummels relentlessly on tracks like "Doug Duels" and "Stand Back."

Last and perhaps least, depending on one's liking of *Voyage*, *Lost* and particularly *Tunnel*, is *Land of the Giants* (1968–1970), about a space flight that crashes on a version of Earth where the inhabitants are, you guessed it, supersized. Williams delivers another exciting, pulsating theme. His music for the first episode includes jazzy little riffs mixed in with passages that boast bombastic horns, and others where flutes and xylophones swirl, suggestive of chaotic misadventure. *Land* certainly has some of the most electrifying action cues to be heard in any Irwin Allen show.

With its campy dialogue, colorful pop art direction and zany comic energy, *Batman* (1966–1968) was a big hit for ABC, and was one of the first TV shows to inspire a theatrical release. The music for both the show and the original movie, starring Adam West, blends high-energy big band and early rock 'n' roll. Neal Hefti (who wrote the catchy surf rock theme music), Nelson Riddle, Warren Barker and Billy May contributed to the TV soundtrack. Riddle scored the less successful theatrical release (1966). Hefti took the "Dark Knight" into surf territory on a non-soundtrack release. Electric guitar, organ, brass, woodwinds, electric bass, and drums join forces to vanquish the boring and ordinary. Riddle's *Batman* movie soundtrack is a bit more sophisticated and more cinematic than Hefti's record. While the energy level is suitably cartoonish, Riddle finds room to explore moods ranging from romantic to suspenseful. The score has as much "pop" as the Technicolor set pieces they aurally depict.

Undoubtedly the most famous sci-fi TV show of all time is *Star Trek* (1966–1969), though its influence wasn't recognized until after the original show's premature cancellation when it gained a devoted audience through syndication. Eventually it spawned five TV spin-offs and ten major motion pictures. Part of the original show's appeal is its music. Several composers

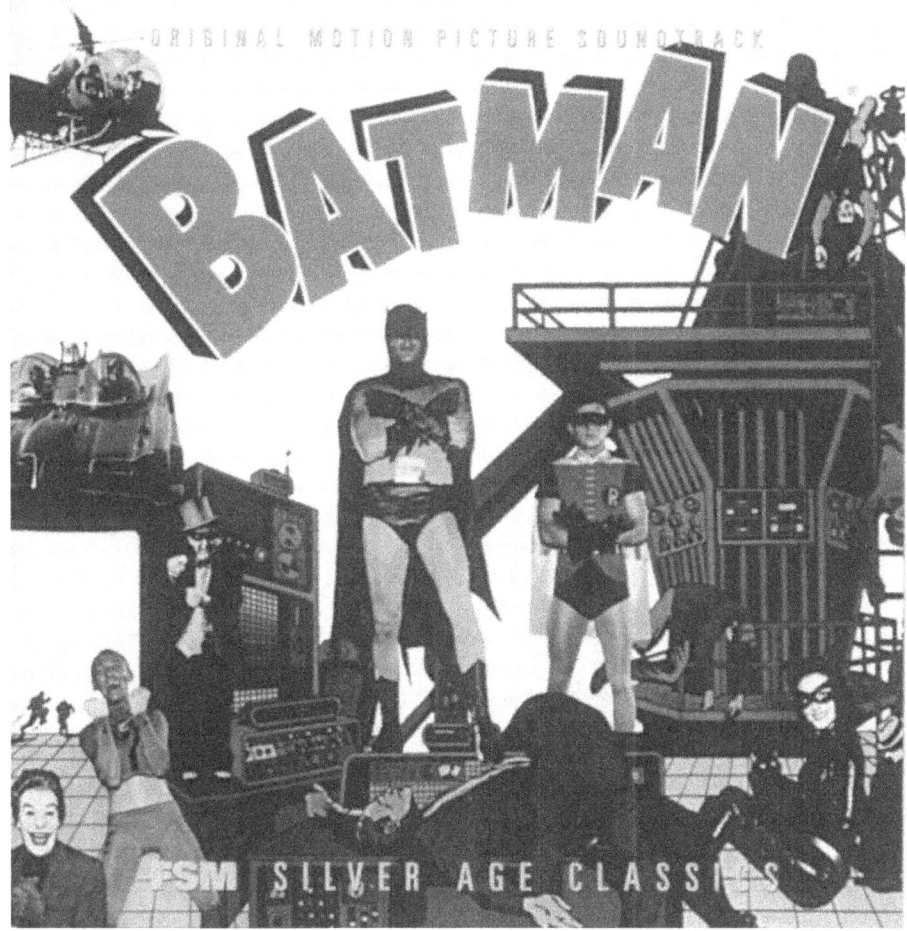

Nelson Riddle's score for *Batman: The Movie* (1966) captures the show's cartoonish crime-fighting sense of excitement. (CD cover appears courtesy of Film Score Monthly; graphic design by Joe Sikoryak.)

contributed during its three-year run, but most people naturally think of Alexander Courage's soaring theme music when the words "Star Trek" are mentioned. Over the opening fanfare we hear Captain James T. Kirk (William Shatner) speak the familiar lines about the "Starship Enterprise" and "going where no man has gone before." And then the piece takes off like a rocket into the wonders of deep space as stars flicker past. With buoyant optimism about space exploration, the theme ingrained itself in the collective conscious of all who heard it—notably at a time when Americans were riveted by stories of NASA's quest to put man on the moon.

Star Trek's scores are just as enthralling. The show owes part of its enduring success to the rich orchestral music that accompanies each far-flung episode. As *Star Trek* creator Gene Roddenberry recollected in the booklet notes for a Varese Sarabande compilation, the composers for the show were asked to emphasize the emotional components of the drama, not the science and gadgetry. As a result of Roddenberry's directive, the scores are primarily orchestral, with little to no electronic effects.

"Perhaps the most remarkable of music's mysteries is its power to transport us ... into other bodies and events and places, letting us magically overcome the limits of our own identities," Roddenberry noted.

Courage delivered exciting orchestral scores for the original pilots "The Cage" and "Where No Man Has Gone Before." Look to "The Cage" for the original appearance of mysterious and exotic "snake-charming" love themes that would be used in later episodes as well. The ominous Echoplex effects and other electronic accents were rarely heard in the series, but work very well.

Sol Kaplan's music for "The Doomsday Machine," and Gerald Fried's music for "Amok Time," are among the most powerful in the series. In particular, Fried's "Amok Time" score is one of many sci-fi scores that drew inspiration from Stravinsky's "The Rite of Spring." Tracks like "Mr. Spock" make effective use of electric bass to represent the brooding disposition of the Vulcan who assumes a trance to participate in a mating ritual and engage Kirk in battle.

"The music for 'Amok Time' was written to reflect [that] despite all the sophistication and intellectuality we may have accrued over the millennia, our species (and Vulcan off-shoots of the same) is essentially grounded in the same biological, primitive inheritance which controlled our ancient ancestors," said Fried in the booklet notes of a DRG CD compilation. "One way or another, all the episodes probed, or attempted to deal with, the internal, primal mysteries of our species in the guise of 'let's have an adventure' science fiction."

Fried's "Shore Leave," and Courage's "The Naked Time," explore extroverted emotional states and otherwise altered states of mind.

"'The Naked Time' was fun and a challenge to score because of the variety of the story," Courage said in the CD's booklet notes.

Fried added, "*Star Trek* once again astonishes us with yet another bold plunge into not just an unknown area of the possible physical universe, but also into a little-explored area into the minds of us Earthlings.... My job as composer was to help bring into reality both the various fears, and then, the resulting delights of having absorbed and mastered them."

Other composers who contributed to the original *Star Trek* include George Duning, Jerry Fielding, Samuel Matlovsky, Joseph Mullendore and Fred Steiner.

In 1970–1971, marionation kid's show creator Gerry Anderson launched the live-action *U.F.O.*, a short-lived series about the efforts of S.H.A.D.O. (Supreme Headquarters Alien Defense Organization) to combat an alien invasion. Barry Gray, who scored Anderson's marionation shows *Stingray* (1964), *Thunderbirds* (1965) and *Captain Scarlet and the Mysterons* (1967), provides groovy big band pop that wouldn't have sounded out of place in one of the '60s spy spoofs (or an *Austin Powers* movie). Occasionally, it gets "spacey" with Echoplex effects. It's likely to remind some of Peter Thomas' music for *Space Patrol*, and while it's enjoyable in its own right, it lacks Thomas' inventive arrangements.

Gray also scored Anderson's more successful series, *Space: 1999* (1975–1977). Other composers who contributed to the show were French sound library specialists Jack Arel and Pierre Dutour, Paul Bonneau and Serge Lancen, Giampera Boneschi, Robert Farnon and others. Aside from a disco rock theme, the tone is far more cinematic and serious than *U.F.O.* Slashing, swirling strings, harp glissandi, percussion runs, trilling woodwinds and stabbing brass replace the pop grooves heard on the earlier show. While the *U.F.O.* soundtrack has great kitsch appeal, the *Space: 1999* score is a purer sci-fi listening experience.

Laurence Rosenthal scored the pilot of the *Logan's Run* TV show (1977–1978). He wrote the theme and scored the first few episodes before Jeff Alexander, Jerrold Immel and Bruce Broughton were brought in for specific episodes. Unlike Goldsmith's partially electronic and somewhat atonal score, Rosenthal took a more melodic approach, using a 26-piece orchestra. The composer attributes this to the TV show's comparatively optimistic tone. Regardless of tone, Rosenthal also employed synths and wasn't shy about lending the series' score a certain "futuristic" feeling. Expertly orchestrated, the score delivers plenty of thrills, as tracks like "The Collectors" and "Fear Factor" describes the action. And the theme is rousing in the same way as the *Star Trek* TV theme.

Joe Harnell scored the pilot of *The Incredible Hulk* live action show (1978–1982). Charles R. Casey also contributed music during the series. Some listeners are likely to peg Harnell's theme music as crime show funk because of its slick electrified big band sound. Much of the soundtrack, however, will reassure sci-fi fans, as otherworldly electronic effects lend disquieting dissonance to the atmospheric underscore. "Gamma Ray Treatment" is a fine example of that effect. The music, sans electronics, is indeed reminiscent of Schifrin's *Dirty Harry* music, with strings veering into psychotic mood swings and piano tinkering with off-kilter harmonics. Add the electronics, and the effect mutates the show's contemporary setting into something ominous and unsettling. When a swift current of percussion is added (as on "Growing Anger"), it's like a ticking time bomb; Bruce Banner's transformation to the Hulk is palpable. Harnell at full tilt ("Hulk on the Rampage") calls for swirling strings, stabbing brass, smashing snares and a shrill climax.

A show that drew inspiration from *Star Wars* was *Battlestar Galactica* (1978–1980). A veteran of TV and film, Stu Phillips scored the series in the grand orchestral fashion, sans electronic gimmickry. He started with the three-part pilot, and that music was reworked for later episodes. It's clear that Phillips drew inspiration from Williams' tremendously popular symphonic *Star Wars*, which amounts to a revival of the Golden Age sound where themes are heroic and melodies are rarely dissonant (and quite often affirmative in their representation of good and evil). Phillips' action cues accomplish their clear-cut aims with economy of style and clear purpose in orchestration. The love themes display hints of exoticism.

Phillips went on to score *Buck Rogers in the 25th Century* (1979), which was meant to be a pilot for the TV show (1979–1981). *Buck Rogers* has a lot to offer fans of heroic scores. The mostly action-oriented arrangements combine traditional orchestration with keyboard accents that occasionally take center stage to provide "futuristic" effects on the more atmospheric tracks. Phillips' gift for melody is on display on such tracks as the exotic "Princess Ardala/Seduction" and the comical "Introducing: Twiki & Dr. Theo."

Imaginary Sci-Fi Soundtracks

During the '50s and early '60s film composers and adventurous orchestra leaders recorded a number of outer space-related concept albums that would be called "imaginary soundtracks" today. Among the best are *Exploring the Unknown* by Leith Stevens, featuring the Voices of Walter Schumann and narration by Paul Frees; Russ Garcia's *Fantastica*; Frank Comstock's *Project: Comstock—Music from Outer Space*; and Attilio "Art" Mineo's *Man in Space with Sounds* (for the 1962 World's Fair). In addition, there are numerous pop-oriented "space age" records by such artists as Juan Esquivel (e.g. *Other Worlds, Other Sounds*) and Ferrante & Teicher (e.g.

Joe Harnell's score for *The Incredible Hulk* (CBS/Marvel, 1978–1982), starring Lou Ferrigno, makes the character's violent transformation palpable through the use of swirling strings, stabbing brass, smashing snares and propulsive percussion.

Blast Off!), as well as the interstellar big band jazz of Sun Ra (e.g. *We Travel the Spaceways*). Many of these imaginary soundtracks outstrip legitimate sci-fi scores of the same era for sheer imagination.

Mineo's *Man in Space with Sounds* merits special attention since it served as a soundtrack for a futuristic exhibition at the 1962 World's Fair in Seattle, Washington. A limited edition album was sold at the event and later issued on CD. Mineo's far-out, electro-acoustic musical experiments are heard with and without narration about the exhibition's "Mile-a-Minute Monorail" and "Boeing Spacearium." The upbeat, optimistic narration describes "the unbelievable worlds that man is going to conquer" and "the most exciting glimpse of the future Americans have ever had." At other times, the antiquated and naïve language is unintentionally funny to 21st-century ears ("The fabulous gay way [to heaven] where you guide your own rocket..."). Heard without these musings, Mineo's music is sublimely futuristic, combining Stravinsky-esque orchestration with Barron-esque electronic effects.

Back to the Future

Sci-fi soundtracks strive to describe the unknown, which often means imaginative, experimental music. The genre, more than any other, encourages composers to explore unusual sound textures and otherworldly sonorities. Experimentation is the key to many artistically successful sci-fi scores, but hardly necessary. When the focus is on adventure, the outcome can be relatively traditional. However, when the focus is on the alien, the results can be beguiling and transporting. Unfortunately, sci-fi scores, like too many sci-fi movies and TV shows, frequently rely on Earth-bound ideas of what is "futuristic," and fail to make a major breakthrough. Whether the approach is old-school or avant-garde, however, the world of sci-fi soundtracks understandably remains a big draw for collectors who dream of going where no other music fan has gone before.

12 Essential Sci-Fi Soundtracks

The Day the Earth Stood Still (1951)—Bernard Herrmann
Godzilla (1954)—Akira Ifukube
Forbidden Planet (1956)—Louis and Bebe Barron
The Twilight Zone (1959–1964)—Various Artists
The Outer Limits (1963–1965)—Dimitri Tiomkin
Fahrenheit 451 (1966)—Bernard Herrmann
Star Trek: The Original Series (1966–1969)—Various Artists
Raumpatrouille (Space Patrol) (1966)—Peter Thomas
Planet of the Apes (1968)—Jerry Goldsmith
Close Encounters of the Third Kind (1977)—John Williams
Star Wars (1977)—John Williams
Star Trek: The Motion Picture (1979)—Jerry Goldsmith

Chapter 6

A Fearful Earful

What is the sound of terror? A piercing scream? Shrieking violins? In the annals of cinematic horror and suspense, it is both and so much more. The jolt of a minor key horn blast seizes your senses. The sinister web weaved on diabolical strings strikes fear in your heart. The discordant cacophony of a strident choir takes possession of your mind. In fact, many of us happily subject ourselves to "scary" viewing experiences, fully expecting the worst to transpire on the screen before us, waiting in grim anticipation for our eyes and ears to be assailed by the sights and sounds of terror. Perhaps it is a way for us to sensitize ourselves against the horrors we may personally endure in real life, or the possibility of a terrible death. Regardless of reason, horror and suspense films possess undeniable allure, and part of their fiendish power stems from their soundtracks. An effective horror or suspense score tells us to brace for a sudden startle, and then reinforces the shock on impact. It's an obvious tactic, employed repeatedly and sometimes teasingly so that when the opportunity for a scare passes without incident, the audience is left to fidget and chortle nervously, awaiting the next fearful encounter.

Horror, as a storytelling genre, has roots in both folklore and documented history. But horror as a performing art can be traced back to at least the 1890s when Grand Guignol horror plays were the rage in Paris. Featuring depictions of violence, murder, rape, ghostly apparitions and suicide, these plays introduced the now familiar scenario of mad doctors conducting wicked experiments on scantily clad young women.

The silent film era introduced movie audiences to man-made monsters (*Frankenstein*, 1910, and *Der Golem*, 1914), madmen (*The Cabinet of Dr. Caligari*, 1919), vampirism (*Nosferatu*, 1922) and other horrors (*The Hunchback of Notre Dame* and *The Phantom of the Opera*, 1925).

The "Golden Age" of Universal horror movies followed in the '30s with *Dracula* (1931), *Frankenstein* (1932), and *The Mummy* (1933). Other studios followed suit with such memorable entries as *Dr. Jekyll and Mr. Hyde* (Paramount, 1931) and *The Mystery of the Wax Museum* (Warner Brothers, 1933). During the '40s, Universal had great success with *The Wolf Man* (1941), and

Val Lewton produced a number of influential horror movies for RKO, such as *Cat People* (1942) and *I Walked with a Zombie* (1943).

Creature Features and Haunted Houses

By the '50s gothic horror became unfashionable as filmmakers and studios gravitated to sci-fi and horror/sci-fi hybrids such as *The Thing from Another World* (1951) and *Invasion of the Body Snatchers* (1956) (see Chapter 5 for more about the "hybrids"). Whether the horror climbed from a coffin or from a spaceship, however, the period proved to be fruitful.

Hans Salter's score for *Creature from the Black Lagoon* (1954) is just what one expects from a '50s creature feature. Shimmering strings and anxious woodwinds accompany the dreaded man-fish as he emerges from the watery depths to wreak havoc on adventurers.

For *The Vampire* (a.k.a. *Mark of the Vampire*, 1957), Gerald Fried uses bombastic brass, shivering winds, shrill strings and crashing cymbals that are typical of the era. For *The Return of Dracula* (1958), Fried repurposes the grim Latin hymn "Dies Irae," which has served many classical composers (Mozart, Verdi, Berlioz), stage musicals (Stephen Sondheim's *Sweeney Todd: The Demon Barber of Fleet Street*) and heavy metal bands, not to mention films including *The Shining* (1980), *The Night of the Hunter* (1955) and *Witchfinder General* (a.k.a. *The Conqueror Worm*, 1968). Along with a creepy vampire motif and rumbling percussion, Fried's theme lends a sinister and exciting atmosphere to what is a near-perfect example of B-movie horror scoring.

For *I Bury the Living* (1958), Fried takes advantage of the sinister sound of manic harpsichord trills alongside worried woodwinds and low strings that quote from a grim Volga Boatman folk song. For the remake of *The Cabinet of Caligari* (1962), Fried's sweeping strings nauseatingly vacillate from sweetly romantic to suspenseful. More manic moments can be heard on "The Rorshach Test," on which argumentative brass jostle alongside panicked piano, and on "House of Horrors" where frantic keys, woodwinds and brass feverishly repeat a hypnotic figure until dissipating into nervous strings.

Roger Corman—King of Low Budget Chills and Thrills

Prolific filmmaker Roger Corman is widely renowned for his contributions to the genre during the early to mid–1960s when major Hollywood studios were ignoring horror. Corman's first two entries were the horror lampoon *A Bucket of Blood* and the sci-fi monster movie *The Wasp Woman* (both 1959). Fred Katz, who scored about a dozen B-movies, filled *Bucket* with a jazzy beatnik vibe and *Wasp* with creepy xylophone. Always working economically, Corman recycled the *Wasp* score for *Little Shop of Horrors* (1960).

Corman is best known for his adaptations of Poe's classic horror stories,

Gerald Fried's score for *The Return of Dracula* (1958) features bombastic brass, shivering woodwinds, shrill strings and crashing cymbals that are more typical of the Golden Age than the Silver Age. (CD cover appears courtesy of Film Score Monthly; graphic design by Joe Sikoryak.)

beginning with *The Fall of the House of Usher* (1960), starring Vincent Price, who became a fixture in the Poe series and other releases by American International Pictures (AIP). Les Baxter, who is best known for his exotica lounge records of the '50s and '60s, provided music for *Usher* that is by turns romantic and ominous, underpinning the doomed love story. Additionally, Baxter's discordant piano music captures Roderick Usher's madness.

Three other Baxter scores for Corman's Poe series include *Pit and the Pendulum* (1961), *Tales of Terror* (1962) and *The Raven* (1963). Watch any of these films and one bears witness to Baxter's penchant for creating creepy and hallucinatory music through the use of echoing xylophone, booming gong, harp glissandi, shuddering violins and frightened brass.

When Baxter wasn't scoring for Corman, Ronald Stein was—notably for *The Premature Burial* (1962) and *The Haunted Palace* (1963). The music for the Poe-based *Burial* is chillingly effective, but its theme is less compelling than the one heard in *Palace*. On *Burial*, Stein employs the old sea chantey "Molly Malone" that haunts the main character, using it occasionally as an eerie lament. On the main title, the orchestra attacks with stormy bluster. The score's violent passages ("Three Murders") features dissonant brass, seesawing strings and cymbal crashes. The suspenseful music for the dream sequence contains subtle echo on low piano strokes, but overall the sound is less hallucinatory than one would expect from one of Corman's famously psychedelic dream sequences. Despite periodic lulls, *Burial* captures the film's gothic mood.

Stein's *Palace*, which is an H.P. Lovecraft adaptation (though the film was marketed as Poe-inspired), is stylistically consistent with his work on *Burial* but more impressive musically. Following Baxter's AIP fanfare, Stein's lushly romantic theme sends strings soaring and horns pulsating. The melody is quoted at an ominously low pitch on "Vicious Ward/Mutant Circle" before giving way to shivering violins and rumbling drums. The high 'winds on "Arkham" suggest the residue of ancient evil that haunts the movie's main character.

Stein also provided magnificent music for *The Terror* (a.k.a. *The Haunting* or *The Castle of Terror*, 1963). "Prologue: The Secret Passage" uses trilling flutes, organ glissandi, muted brass and low strings to suggest shadowy, subterranean haunts. The theme is brassy and brash, almost grandiose in its connotation of the evil afoot. Strings take over on quieter cues like "Meet Helaine," which is ethereal and mysterious, like a phantom floating down a corridor by candlelight.

For *The Masque of the Red Death* (1964), composer Mark Governor provided a blend of heavy-handed fatalistic theme music, a Stravinsky-esque underscore for the hallucinatory dream sequence and medieval madrigal pastiche.

Baxter also scored *An Evening with Edgar Allan Poe* (1970), an AIP-TV special featuring dramatizations of several stories. Combining complex symphonic arrangements with occasional bursts of discordant electronics, the composer displays a tremendous capacity for evoking supernatural horror, graveyard atmospherics and creeping fear.

Baxter's *Cry of the Banshee* (1970) is a riveting listening experience. Vigorous orchestra is accentuated by eerie electronics, and the mood is tense and ominous, but there are brief romantic passages that correspond to the film's ill-fated love story. *Banshee* demonstrates Baxter's horror scoring prowess, and stands to impress those who are tempted to write him off as merely an exotica specialist.

Mark Governor provided a heavy-handed fatalistic theme and a Stravinsky-esque score for the Edgar Allan Poe adaptation *The Masque of Red Death* (MGM/UA, 1964), starring Vincent Price. (Photograph courtesy of the John Monaghan Collection.)

Interestingly enough, Baxter noted on the cover of the *Banshee* LP that friends of his and others claimed that a section of the suite caused an apparition to materialize in their midst. Baxter admitted that he'd never noticed such a phenomenon, but that "every composer will write things he doesn't remember [writing], as if they come from an 'outside' source."

Baxter's wizardry also can be heard on *The Dunwich Horror* (1970), which is loosely based on Lovecraft as well. There is a stronger rock feel thanks to the occasional back beat, but the music still brims with mystery and suspense as brass, woodwinds and keyboards take center stage. Track titles such as "Black Mass," "Sensual Hallucinations" and "Cult Party" add to the allure for fans of occult-themed B-movies, which were fashionable at the time.

In the early '70s, AIP released *The Abominable Dr. Phibes* (1971) and its sequel *Dr. Phibes Rises Again* (1972). Basil Kirchin, a library music specialist who worked on only seven films, scored the former; John Gale scored the latter. *Abominable* (taking inspiration from *Phantom of the Opera*) concerns a hideously deformed, tortured genius who plays the pipe organ and wreaks

Basil Kirchin's score for *The Abominable Dr. Phibes* (1971) blends minimalist classical with jazzy chamber music. (CD cover appears courtesy of Perseverance Records; graphic design by Wolfgang Fenchel.)

vengeance upon others while holding a romantic torch for a young beauty. In place of an opera house, there is a medical operating theater. Kirchin's score blends minimalist classical with jazzy chamber music. Variations on the achingly romantic theme recur throughout. According to Paul Tonks and Chris Tunnah, who wrote the CD booklet notes, the film's director wasn't overly fond of Kirchin's contributions and opted to use library pieces and a piece by John Gale, who scored the sequel.

Gale's *Rises Again*, with its Latin track titles and choral sections, is far more grandiose. Using a full orchestra, Gale's score fleshes out the action and drama better than Kirchin's score, which focuses on interior emotion instead.

Plus, Gale uses a wider variety of melodies and music styles (classical, lounge, swing, bossa nova). While Kirchin's theme is gorgeous, Gale's approach is more cinematic.

David Whitaker's *Scream and Scream Again* (1970) is a good example of the direction that many films, horror and other genres, went in the late '60s and early '70s. The psychedelic jazz-rock sound must have sounded mod to the hip young audiences that went to see the picture. A little known group called the Amen Corner performs the rockin' title track and "When We Make Love."

Splatter Sinema and Mixed-Up Maniacs

Horror cinema took an incredibly strange turn when independent filmmakers such as Jack Hill, Ray Dennis Steckler, Herschell Gordon Lewis and others hit the scene, making low-budget blood and gore flicks typically screened as drive-in double features.

For *Dementia 13* (1963), Francis Ford Coppola's first movie (about an axe-wielding maniac), Ronald Stein delivered a fittingly edgy score. Frenetic harpsichord, angular xylophone lines and dissonant sonorities evoke dementia. There's a darkly comic and quirky quality to the theme, but the tone gets progressively darker. Sustained organ tones and low brass underpin violent brass stings on "He Lost His Head."

Stein's theme for the comedic freak fest *Spider Baby* (a.k.a. *Cannibal Orgy*, 1964) is a minor beat jazz masterpiece that captures the film's truly eccentric characters and their gruesome shenanigans. Piano, percussion and handclaps provide an insistent, pulsating rhythm for intermittent noir-like brass figures. "Spider Orgy" is a poor title for an oddly tender track. "Spider Stravinsky" may be blatantly suggestive of the frequently imitated European composer, but it isn't particularly evocative here. The vocal version of the theme boasts a vividly theatrical spoken word performance (complete with wolf howls) by the movie's star, Lon Chaney, Jr., the legendary Universal Pictures *Wolf Man*.

Working economically, Herschell Gordon Lewis scored several of his own films, including *Blood Feast*, the influential gore classic, which had a marketing campaign that repeatedly warned moviegoers of the film's stomach-turning, heart attack-inducing horror. The soundtrack, which features blood-curdling screams and creepy, nausea-inducing organ music, lives up to that warning thanks to its stylistically schizophrenic, lo-fidelity listening experience.

"I'll tell you one truth: I couldn't repeat those orchestrations," Lewis recollected for an interview for the author's website, ScoreBaby.com. "Yes, I wrote the theme music for *Blood Feast 2*, but that's a primitive accomplishment compared with the actual composition, orchestrating, and kettledrum-playing for *Blood Feast*. At no time did I consider myself a 'composer' but, rather, a lucky fellow who was able to escape both the gigantic cost of a professional composer and the triteness of standard pre-recorded music effects. Ego and that accursed 'auteur' syndrome were never factors."

Alfred Hitchcock—The Master of Suspense

The name for suspense during the '50s and early '60s was Alfred Hitchcock, a Brit who made 20-some movies in England before achieving fame and fortune in Hollywood. Hitchcock's *Strangers on a Train* (1951) was his first masterpiece of the decade. Dimitri Tiomkin's score is very much in the symphonic style of the Golden Age, where soaring strings, blaring brass and crashing percussion emphasize the profound drama taking place on screen, culminating in a calliope-driven climax. For the easily manipulated hero, Tiomkin provides a purposely weak motif, and for the conniving villain something sinister.

Hitchcock continued to make classics of big screen suspense with Golden Age–style scores, including *Dial "M" for Murder* (1954), *Rear Window* (1954) and *To Catch a Thief* (1955). Tiomkin scored *Murder*. Franz Waxman scored *Window*. And Lyn Murray scored *Thief*.

Joining those esteemed composers was Bernard Herrmann, who started his own storied film career scoring Orson Welles' masterpiece *Citizen Kane* (1941). Beginning with *The Trouble with Harry* (1955), Herrmann became Hitchcock's go-to composer until the director rejected the score for *Torn Curtain* (1966).

Herrmann is the most influential film composer of the mid-century, and some of his success is owed to his high-profile assignments for Hitchcock. Arguably, the creative apex of Hitchcock and Herrmann's work began on their third film together, *The Wrong Man* (1957). The composer created a score that is bleak, minimalist, claustrophobic and oppressive—a style he perfected on *Vertigo* (1958), *North by Northwest* (1959) and ultimately *Psycho* (1960), the most influential modern horror movie ever made.

In the Screencraft book *Film Music* (RotoVision, 1998), Mark Russell and James Young call attention to Herrmann's reliance on ostinato, which is any short, repeated pattern of notes (the term comes from the Italian word for obstinate): "In Herrmann's Hitchcock scores, ostinato figurations stubbornly refuse to transform themselves into conventional melodies: instead, the fragmentary repeating patterns are formed into kaleidoscopic musical textures that tread a precarious middle ground between stability and instability."

To create the sense of uneasiness that is critical to any suspenseful mood, Herrmann used dissonant harmonies that eschew comforting resolutions. What made Herrmann a master at manipulating audiences is the virtuosity at using nagging ostinatos and inconclusive harmonies to tweak their expectations while rarely providing the melodic reassurance. It's worth noting that Herrmann's ostinatos became a hallmark of the minimalist classical music movement of

Bernard Herrmann once said that film music expresses what the actor cannot show or tell. Herrmann's ability to impart psychological impressions through music was one of his greatest accomplishments. (CD cover appears courtesy of Silva Screen Records.)

the late 20th century with such composers as Philip Glass, Steve Reich and Terry Riley. Unlike his imitators, who excel in the technical but whose works are sometimes overly cold and clinical, Herrmann's melodies frequently carry emotional weight and psychological import without resorting to cloying pop song conventions.

The hypnotic, spiraling six-note ostinato that opens *Vertigo* (1958) is iconic Herrmann. Hearing the repeated string and vibraphone figures punctuated by blasts of ominous minor key brass, the audience can identify with the phobic fear and oppressive psychological troubles that plague the principle characters. This music is the sound of obsession. In fact, Herrmann's score for Brian De Palma's 1976 film *Obsession* is reminiscent of *Vertigo*, which is not surprising, given the later film's other similarities to the Hitchcock classic (more on that later). For all of the moments of dread, there are passages of aching romanticism too when weeping strings well up with emotion. For fans of suspense, however, the haunting moods of mystery are the real draw.

It's tempting to state that *Vertigo* is the Herrmann-Hitchcock score that belongs in every collection, but that would be misleading, since *North by Northwest* and *Psycho* are equally essential. Amazingly, none of them was nominated for an Academy Award.

Hitchcock's *North by Northwest* (1959) is a breezy entertainment compared to the obsessive moods of *Vertigo* and shocking horror of *Psycho*, but it's still a masterpiece of suspense with a riveting score by Herrmann. The composer started work on it right after scoring the pilot episode of TV's *The Twilight Zone*. As was his practice, he wrote the score by hand, from beginning to end, based on roughly-sketched motifs. The sinister fandango theme music that opens the film, and ends without resolution, is melodically memorable and rhythmically invigorating. According to musicologist Christopher Husted, who wrote the booklet notes for the Rhino Records edition of the soundtrack, Herrmann claimed to have been inspired to use Latin American rhythms by star Cary Grant's "Astaire-like agility." Elsewhere, Herrmann uses popular melodies ("In the Still of the Night" and "It's a Most Unusual Day") to reinforce the romantic undercurrent. The film's love theme—a lyrical duet between clarinet and oboe—uses propulsive rhythms played on strings to suggest the steady forward momentum of the train carrying Grant and Eva Marie Saint toward their shared destiny. The score has its share of ominous ("Kidnapped") and thrilling sections ("On the Rocks") wherein Herrmann combines swirling strings, stabbing winds and brass, and pulse-pounding percussion.

In scoring Hitchcock's *Psycho* (1960), which is generally considered the original "slasher" movie, Herrmann provided not only gripping cues for psychological and physical terror, but also deeply emotional underscoring for the plights facing Janet Leigh's character. As Jason Comerford wrote in *Film Score Monthly* of Joel McNeely's re-recording, Herrmann's score identifies with Leigh's character while commenting on her situation as a detached observer. This is hardly surprising, given Herrmann's gift for suggesting character traits of an almost subliminal nature. Unlike on his other work for Hitchcock, Herrmann works with an all-strings orchestra, as if to call attention to the horrible, almost incestuous intimacy of the story as well as its stark black and white cinematography. Although the score sounds starkly modern, it was actually an adaptation of a much earlier piece by the composer, "Sinfonietta for Strings" (1936). If the screeching, slithering violins of "The Murder" and "The Knife" don't put listeners on edge, nothing will. The sound of those stabbing violins

Alfred Hitchcock originally wanted no music to accompany the famous shower scene in *Psycho*, but Bernard Herrmann insisted—and the iconic cue of sudden terror was born. (CD cover appears courtesy of Silva Screen Records.)

remains to this day the unofficial sound effect for maniacal stabbing gestures made in jest. The only other movie cue that comes remotely close to it in universality is Williams' ostinato for "Bruce" in Steven Spielberg's *Jaws* (1975). Interestingly, Hitchcock originally wanted no music to accompany the "shower scene"—and even considered doing the film sans score—but, according to more than one source, the composer changed the filmmaker's mind. (Other famously misguided intentions on the director's part were his initial belief that the project would be better suited to TV and that it needed a jazz score.) In the end, Hitchcock liked the score so much he paid Herrmann twice his usual fee, and said "33 percent of the effect of *Psycho* was due to the music" (according to Kevin Mulhall's insightful booklet notes for McNeely's re-recording). *Psycho* may not be as lush as *Vertigo* and *North by Northwest*, but it is more effective for it. To this day, both the film and the score are among the most influential in cinematic history.

"[Herrmann] is still being ripped off," said Leonard Maltin in a radio interview heard on the Bernard Herrmann Society Website. "I don't think there is a more imitated score than *Psycho*."

Psycho also marked the beginning of the end of Herrmann's fruitful collaboration with Hitchcock.

For Hitchcock's *The Birds* (1963), the director and composer decided to dispense with a traditional score in favor of bird cries created by an electronic keyboard instrument known as the Studio Trautonium, co-designed by German avant-garde composer Remi Gassmann. Herrmann took the role of advisor. According to Steven C. Smith, author of the definitive Herrmann biography, *A Heart at Fire's Center* (University of California Press, 1991), Hitchcock and Herrmann were highly satisfied with the Trautonium's "bizarre, atonal squawks that sounded amazingly like actual bird calls." (p. 254)

"I just worked with [Gassmann] simply matching it with Hitchcock," Herrmann said in 1971, "but there was no attempt to create a score by electronic means."

Alastair Reid, a later Herrmann collaborator, later said that Herrmann regarded himself as "almost a co-director because of his role in creating the soundtrack." (*AHFC*, p. 254)

Next, Herrmann scored the coolly received *Marnie* (1964), a "suspenseful sex mystery" (as its movie poster promised). The film has since grown in stature, and Herrmann's score is well respected, if not celebrated with the same intensity as his scores for the earlier Hitchcock hits.

Notoriously, Hitchcock rejected Herrmann's score for his next film, *Torn Curtain* (1966). Hitchcock was under pressure from the studio to use a pop score that would presumably appeal to a younger audience; actually, Hitchcock had been under pressure for several films to include at least a pop song. The director publicly argued with the understandably resistant Herrmann, humiliating the composer in front of his orchestra by calling a halt to a recording session before it even began. John Addison replaced Herrmann on the project. Herrmann's rejected score, which Hitchcock never even heard, is intense and dark. His prelude features agitated flutes and emphatic, unyielding counterpoint between the trombones and trumpets. For the film's harrowing murder scene, which did not use music, Herrmann had written a five-note motif that combines a battery of hard-driving percussion with unruly piccolos and flutes that might have helped to emphasize the scene's sense of havoc.

It's been said that modern movie music came of age with Herrmann's contributions to the art form. More than 30 years after his death on Christmas Eve, 1975, after finishing work on Martin Scorsese's *Taxi Driver*, he is still a giant of film music.

Roman Polanski—On-Screen Suspense/ Off-Screen Horrors

In 1969, filmmaker and Holocaust survivor Roman Polanski experienced real-life horror when his wife, starlet Sharon Tate, who was pregnant with their child, was murdered by the Manson family. That same year Polanski lost his friend, film composer and Polish jazz legend Krzysztof Komeda, who scored several of Polanski's early films, including the drama *Knife in the Water* (1962), the comedy crime thriller *Cul-de-sac* (1966), the horror comedy *The Fearless Vampire Killers* (1967) and finally, and most importantly, *Rosemary's Baby* (1968), one of the most influential horror films of the period.

Komeda's *The Fearless Vampire Killers, or Pardon Me but Your Teeth Are in My Neck* (1967), which marked Tate's film debut and her introduction to her future husband, befits the film's 19th-century time period with clearly defined melodies, stately rhythms, serene woodwinds, classical guitar, harpsichord, strings and choir. The throbbing acoustic bass lines serve as one of the few reminders of Komeda's jazz background. The theme, with its Alessandroni-esque choir, is reminiscent of Morricone's spaghetti western music of the same period.

Komeda's *Rosemary's Baby* (1968) is a far darker affair, which is no surprise, given the film's satanic storyline. The double bass, harpsichord and strings are back, joined by wordless vocals from the movie's star, Mia Farrow. The theme, which can be hauntingly melancholic or balefully beautiful, depending on the treatment, serves many variations. Komeda also provides an unexpected "hoe-down" number ("Dream") and a Beach Boys–style pop number ("Lullaby, Part II"), in addition to short, creepily atmospheric cues and coven chants. The echoing vibes on "Expectancy, Part II," and the hideously laughing horn on "Through the Closet," are deliciously sinister. It is an essential horror score.

A notable exception among Polanski's '60s output is his psychological thriller *Repulsion* (1965), which features a post-bop jazz score by Chico Hamilton. His slashing drum solo when Catherine Deneuve's repressed delusional character attacks a man with a razor is nearly *en homage* to Herrmann's famous stabbing strings of *Psycho*'s shower scene.

The film Polanski made after his Hollywood crime drama *Chinatown* (1974) is the suspense cult classic *The Tenant* (1976), in which the director played the main character. Without Komeda around, Polanski turned to Philippe Sarde, who recalls one of their first meetings in the booklet notes for the Universal release of his scores for *The Tenant* and *Tess* (1979):

6. *A Fearful Earful*   235

Krzysztof Komeda's score for *Rosemary's Baby* (Paramount/William Castle, 1968) features wordless vocals by its star Mia Farrow. (Photograph courtesy of the John Monaghan Collection.)

> We were observing each other like china dogs, a bit shyly. During the meal, while he was talking, Roman dipped his forefinger into his glass and rubbed it round the inside of the rim. As if he wanted to make his glass sing. I didn't say anything, but it was a detail important enough to put me on the right track....

Having read the script, Sarde recognized that Polanski's character was obsessed with glass, as it factored in premonitions of his death. That is how he got the idea to use a glass harmonica, which he describes as a "large mahogany trough full of empty glasses that the musician causes to vibrate after wetting his fingers." In fact, he found a glass harmonica dated from the 16th century that Mozart had used as a solo instrument for several pieces. Soon after, Sarde enlisted a German musician, Bruno Hoffmann, who was well known for playing such an instrument on TV.

After Sarde delivered just the theme, Polanski gave him the go-ahead. "You've built a musical drama that melts into the picture," Sarde recalled the director saying.

In addition to using the distinctively eerie glass harmonica for one theme (substituting wooden contrabass flutes at times), Sarde supplies a second theme for clarinet, marimba and strings. In the Universal notes, Sarde explains that the glass harmonica represents the evil in the film and the omen of death, while the "ambiguous" clarinet represents the main character. String glissandi and spidery pizzicato effects add to the edgy atmosphere. Despite the orchestral effects, Sarde never loses the melodic touch, which makes *The Tenant* an enjoyable listen even when it means to be unnerving.

Other Mainstream Chillers

While Hitchcock and Herrmann are undeniably the masters of the suspense genre, they weren't alone in creating memorably chilling cinema. Still, during the '50s and '60s few major films came close to the standard set by H&H, with most horror and suspense films being B-movie fare.

Herrmann also scored *Cape Fear* (1962). The soundtrack is among the composer's very best. In fact, when Martin Scorsese hired Bernstein to score the 1992 remake, Bernstein wisely interpolated portions of Herrmann's score into his own (and added selections of Herrmann's *Torn Curtain* as well). All of the hallmarks of Herrmann's style can be heard here: a strong modernist aesthetic with a minimalist tendency, starkly stated and spacious melodies, grim ostinatos, swirling violins and stabbing brass. Bernstein, in an interview with Günther Kögebehn in June 2003, remarked that Herrmann's score overwhelmed the original film and proved to be better suited for Scorsese's harder hitting remake.

"That score is a monument and that first film was flimsy compared to what Scorsese did," Bernstein said (bernardherrmann.org, 2003), adding that his late old friend Bernard would have "killed" him for reusing the original score. Granted, it was Scorsese's intention to use the score in the first place, and Bernstein signed on to the 1992 project, in part, to "protect" his friend's work. Of course, Scorsese already had a deep respect for Herrmann, having employed the composer for *Taxi Driver* (1976), which proved to be Herrmann's last assignment. Regardless, *Cape Fear* (both the original and the remake) contains some of the greatest suspense music ever composed, and is essential listening.

A suspense thriller with a score on the jazz tip is Edward Dmytryk's *Mirage* (1965), featuring music by Quincy Jones, who was one of the busiest and hippest film composers of the decade. *Mirage*'s most suspenseful track is "Shoot to Kill," a two-and-a-half minute stop-and-go jam of hard-driving horns and frenzied percussion. "Dead Duck" uses a slow pulse, tension-building tick-tock piano and vibes, wailing free jazz soprano sax, and echoing flutes punctuated with brass bursts to create an atmosphere of imminent danger. The raucous and stream-of-conscious harpsichord solo on "Purple Prose" is stunning in its complexity. Other standout tracks include the scheming "Turtle's Last Lap," the pulse-pounding "A Shot in the Park" and the comically groovy "Kinda Scary."

Bernard Herrmann's score for *Cape Fear* (Universal Pictures, 1962), starring Gregory Peck and Robert Mitchum, was so strong that Elmer Bernstein simply adapted it for Martin Scorsese's 1991 remake.

Jerry Goldsmith scored many memorable horror and suspense films during the '70s, including *The Mephisto Waltz* (1971). With a plot that involves a concert pianist and satanic possession, Goldsmith surely had a ball scoring *Waltz*. Its theme is propulsive but abstract and fragmentary, with sawing, screeching violins mingling uneasily with gurgling electronics, echoing flutes, piano rumblings and percussion. Much of the score follows suit, never settling for ordinary suspense moods and always favoring angular, disorienting textures—earmarks of the composer's mastery of classical serialist conventions. It's hard to imagine a more effective use of electronics in an orchestral setting.

For *The Other* (1972), a film about an "evil twin," Goldsmith provides more passages of pure melody. Since the film revolves around children, there is a playful innocence and naiveté to the melodies; there is even a lively Chinese pastiche. It's not all sweetness and light, of course. Goldsmith finds plenty of moments to inject a subtle yet creepy undercurrent of dread and wrongdoing.

Two underappreciated horror scores of the '70s accompany the Andy

Warhol–produced *Flesh for Frankenstein* and *Blood for Dracula* (1973). Although these films are often maligned as over-the-top sex-and-gore camp fests rather than serious horror films, Claudio Gizzi's scores are memorably melodic, richly orchestrated and wonderfully atmospheric and suspenseful. *Flesh* and *Blood* both feature haunting themes, the former played by an all-strings ensemble and the latter on solo piano. The *Flesh* theme anticipates Goldsmith's theme for *Alien* (1979), with melancholy strings evoking a desolate corner where horror lurks. The *Blood* theme (a.k.a. "Old Age of Dracula") suggests a heartbreaking nostalgia for lost youth and unrequited love. In fact, a variation on the theme is called "Nostalgia." Elsewhere in both scores Gizzi does an excellent job of blending scraps of catchy folk melodies with skin-crawling spooky sections worthy of Herrmann. *Flesh* and *Blood* are exceptional scores that remain underappreciated due to the composer's relative obscurity.

One of the scariest movies ever made, *The Exorcist* (1973) was also one of the biggest blockbusters of its era, and won Oscars for screenplay and sound. The latter honor is significant, as the music that director William Friedkin decided to use is often mistaken for sound effects. Originally the Oscar-winning director (for *The French Connection*, 1971) wanted to hire Herrmann, but the two could not reach an agreement, so Friedkin turned to Lalo Schifrin. Friedkin wasn't satisfied with the Oscar-nominated and Grammy-winning composer's effort. The director characterized Schifrin's score at a 1974 American Film Institute seminar as being "big, loud, scary, wall-to-wall," and that the movie needs "very little music ... [that should be] subtle and small." Schifrin countered in *The Hollywood Reporter* that he was the victim of a power struggle between the director and screenwriter/producer William Peter Blatty, that he had followed Friedkin's directives, and that he stood by his score as "one of the best I've ever done."

Soundtrack producer Nick Redman maintains that Friedman was right not to use Schifrin's score, because it tends to prepare the viewer for the movie's shocking moments rather than blending in with them. "Schifrin's musical language was innovative," Redman noted. "[But] *The Exorcist* could play just as successfully without a note of music." (All quotes are from the Warner Bros. CD booklet notes of *The Exorcist* by Jon Burlingame.)

Being an avid classical music fan, Friedkin opted for a selection of modern and contemporary classical works. Among them are several percussive atonal pieces by Krzysztof Penderecki, as well as single pieces by Anton Webern, Harry Bee, Hans Werner Henze and George Crumb. Most memorably, the soundtrack features Mike Oldfield's transfixing "Tubular Bells," which proved influential in the genre; Goblin's *Suspiria* (1977) is a notable follower. In addition, Hollywood composer Jack Nitzsche composed short bits to fill in gaps. In fact, his experiments with vibrating crystal stemware provide the hypnotic howl that opens the re-released version of the film; it also accompanies Father Merrin's legendary arrival at the house.

"I wanted the overall effect to be like a cold hand on the back of the neck," Friedkin said of the soundtrack upon the film's theatrical re-release in 2000. "My feeling is that thanks to the work of people like Buzz Knudson [dubbing mixer] and Jack Nitzsche that's exactly what we got. A lot of it is almost imperceptible, with the 'music' blending into the sounds of the landscape. Never controlling a scene. I never planned to put music in any of the 'big moments,' because the so-called big scenes carry themselves in my view."

Although *The Exorcist* lacks a memorable melody or thematic development, and is little more than "needle drop" soundtrack—which rarely makes for a satisfyingly holistic listening experience—it is consistent in tone.

Brian De Palma's *Sisters* (1973), about a Siamese twin who takes on the personality of her deranged and dead sister, is a clear homage to Hitchcock (particularly *Psycho* and *Rear Window*). De Palma even listened to Herrmann's *Psycho* soundtrack while reviewing the rushes of his film, and soon decided to hire the composer to score *Sisters*. Herrmann delivered one of his most frighteningly effective scores, featuring chilling glockenspiel, demented Moog drones, taunting nursery melodic figures and psychotic major-minor horn arrangements. Royal S. Brown notes in the Southern Cross CD notes that Herrmann's fee was the most costly item on the film's budget. Although the film is rarely seen in comparison to De Palma's later work, the production certainly got its money's worth with this dark, bone-chilling score.

Herrmann and De Palma worked together again, with equally impressive results, on *Obsession* (1976), another Hitchcockian pastiche. The film concerns a widower who—15 years after his wife and daughter were presumed killed in a botched rescue from kidnappers—marries his dead wife's doppelganger, only to discover that he's married his daughter. Just as he provided a suitable Hitchcockian mystique to *Sisters*, Herrmann's *Obsession*—his second to last score—recalls his classic work on *Vertigo*. With deep romanticism coupled with dreamy detachment, the swirling strings, ethereal choir and ominous pipe organ create a deliriously fatalistic atmosphere. The effect is particularly haunting when "Valse Lente," which accompanies the film's early joyful flashbacks, is later used to underscore the film's bitterly ironic denouement. Despite its being derivative of *Vertigo*'s score, it is still highly effective and memorable.

De Palma intended to employ Herrmann again for his next film, *Carrie*, but the composer died just hours after completing work on *Taxi Driver* (1976) in December 1975. Luckily, the director's second choice, Pino Donaggio, was available. The composer provides a breezy, romantic sensibility to the early sections that establish the title character's sensitive side (including a couple of easy listening ballads sung by Katie Irving). Thankfully, the music accompanying the horrific scenes of the "blood bath" and the telekinetic maelstrom in the school gymnasium make up for the earlier soft moods. There is a Herrmann-esque quality to the music as Donaggio works with sustained spacious chords and subtle electronics to create a disquieting mood on such tracks as "Bucket of Blood" and "School in Flames."

While *Carrie* was hugely influential as a movie, its soundtrack was too soft and subtle to leave a lasting impression with moviegoers. For an influential and famous horror score one must backtrack one year to Stephen Spielberg's *Jaws* (1975) to hear the music that made Williams a household name. The movie, of course, was a blockbuster and made Spielberg the A-list director he is today. Before *Jaws*, Williams had transitioned from scoring second-rate romantic comedies of the '60s (as Johnny Williams) to providing first-rate disaster movie music for Irwin Allen. Williams went on to establish himself as a sort of neo–Golden Age-style composer given to thrilling melodies and grand orchestration, which made him something of an anomaly at a time when film soundtracks veered from avant-garde experimentalism to crowd-pleasing Top 40.

Williams' three-note motif for *Jaws* is so effective and memorable that one need only hear it briefly hummed to identify it. The theme has transcended its connection with the movie, having come to represent imminent danger of any kind. It is rare film music that carries that kind of cultural collateral. (Two others are Herrmann's shower scene music from *Psycho* and Morricone's "ay-e-yi-e-yi" theme from *The Good, the Bad and the Ugly*.) The odd thing about the *Jaws* score, however, is how most of it differs from typical horror movie music. Instead of atonal atmospherics of dread, one gets buoyant, melodic adventure music that hints at what Williams would provide to numerous later blockbusters by Spielberg and George Lucas. Only the three-note motif (perhaps lifted from Stravinsky's "The Rite of Spring") reminds one that it is a horror movie score, and legend has it that Spielberg didn't even care for it at first. But its primitive, single-minded forward momentum proved perfect for a man-eating shark. Later,

Pino Donaggio's score for *Carrie* (MGM/UA, 1976) has moments that are reminiscent of Bernard Herrmann's work. Director Brian De Palma originally intended to hire Herrmann for the film, but the composer died after finishing work on *Taxi Driver* (1976).

Spielberg reportedly acknowledged that the music contributed greatly to the film's success. Williams brought the same motif and more vigorously suspenseful music to *Jaws 2* (1978).

Another popular horror movie of the mid–1970s is *The Omen* (1976), about the Anti-Christ born into a powerful American family. For *The Omen*, Goldsmith won his first and only Oscar, and a "Best Song" Oscar nomination for "Ave Satani," which also earned a Grammy nod. Early on, the score melodically portrays the picture-perfect and privileged life of an ambassador and his wife. But as the darker aspects of the story unfold, Goldsmith's love theme adds an emotionally involving sentiment that accentuates the dramatic conflict and maintains a human dimension even as the supernatural elements take control of the story. The most influential element in the score is the use of chorus. These days no self-respecting movie studio puts out a horror movie trailer without music featuring a "demonic" choir (usually Carl Orff's "O Fortuna"). Goldsmith's *The Omen* arguably established that tradition with "Ave Satani." Somehow, nothing sounds as sinister as a brooding male and female choir chanting in Latin over a dark, minor key dirge. In the booklet notes of the Varese Sarabande CD, Goldsmith gives much of the credit for the choral parts to his friend and collaborator Arthur Morton, who orchestrated the score (Lionel Newman conducted). Said Goldsmith:

> I hadn't written that much chorus in the previous 25 years and I admit I was somewhat rusty. He made a tremendous contribution in that area alone. Arthur arranged at least 65 percent of the choral writing and he opened it up in a way that sounded much better than the way I wrote it. It's situations like that where a talented orchestrator is of great assistance.

Interestingly, the composer also noted that his initial ideas for the score stemmed from "hearing voices."

Goldsmith also wrote dynamic scores in the same vein (demonic choirs, riveting orchestral suspense) for the hit sequels *Damien: Omen II* (1978) and *The Final Conflict: Omen III* (1981).

Another demonic soundtrack of note is Jerry Fielding's *Demon Seed* (1977). Fielding's score is abstract and embraces avant-garde techniques that could be an extension of the fiendish supercomputer that rapes and kills in the movie. Fielding worked with keyboardist Ian Underwood (a close associate of Frank Zappa during the '60s and early '70s), as well as jazz session guitarist Lee Ritenour, both of whom are credited with electronic performances that enhance an otherwise atonal orchestral approach. As Lukas Kendall and Jeff Bond observe in the booklet notes for the *Film Score Monthly* CD, Fielding's score "hovers in 'trapped with a killer' territory," relying on dissonance to capture the film's claustrophobic story of technology run amok.

And the devilish hits just kept coming. *Exorcist 2: The Heretic* (1977) failed to live up to its predecessor, but the score by Morricone is a killer. The

Jerry Fielding's score for *Demon Seed* (1977) relies on dissonance to capture the film's claustrophobic story of technology run amok. (CD cover appears courtesy of Film Score Monthly; graphic design by Joe Sikoryak.)

opener is gentle and feminine, like a *giallo* theme, with strings, Spanish guitar and wordless female vocals establishing a mood that is anything but horrific or suspenseful. The main theme, "Pazuzu," befits the picture, with African percussion, tribal-style chants and angular counter-melodies creating a foreboding sinister exoticism. The poignant and meditative "Interrupted Melody" anticipates Morricone's later theme for *Once Upon a Time in America* (1984). Other tracks, like "Rite of Magic" and "Dark Revelation," reprise "Pazuzu" with more spacious atmospheric arrangements. A standout track is the psychedelic rock mini-masterpiece "Magic and Ecstasy," which combines the theme with diabolical keyboard runs, a heavy metal guitar riff and chanting choir.

After writing *Jaws*, Peter Benchley wrote another ocean-oriented suspense thriller about treasure hunters in over their heads that became *The Deep* (1977). John Barry scored the picture, bringing his distinctive lush orchestral sprawl (no one uses low brass as effectively as Barry) with more than a hint of nautical romanticism. Imagine the underwater or outer space cues used in Barry's 007 scores, add synthesizers and water bells, and one gets *The Deep*. It has gorgeously spectral sections, and some that are suspenseful. However, it remains an underrated, albeit non-essential, Barry score. (Notably, British recording artist Grantby sampled and looped a short cello section on the classic trip-hop CD *Coffee Table Music*.)

In the late '70s Goldsmith was on a serious creative hot streak. In 1978 alone he scored *The Boys from Brazil, Capricorn One, Coma, Damien: Omen II, Magic,* and *The Swarm*—all of which feature strong action and suspense elements (and he continued the amazing run in 1979 with *Alien*).

Goldsmith provided a suitably chilling atonal score for the conspiratorially suspenseful *Coma* (1978). It is Goldsmith at his most Bartók-esque. Disconcerting strings and staccato piano are enhanced by a metallic sheen of electronic accents that evoke the menace of surgical instruments and sinister conspiracies. Goldsmith used four prepared pianos to create disturbing textures and an echo effect to lend an air of mystery to the already alien sonic palette. Most film score fans will agree that not only was the late '70s a great period for this composer, but also that *Coma* is among his best from this era.

For *Magic* (1978), Goldsmith taps into the sick and twisted mind of a magician and ventriloquist who commits heinous crimes as directed by "Fats," his dummy. Goldsmith uses a stark, simplistic harmonica motif to represent Fats, which is a queasy reference to the crude humor of vaudeville. The lyrical, proud but melancholy melody for the Anthony Hopkins character is played on strings and recalls the early era of urban American entertainment. The piano notes sound out simple accents between the two dominant characteristics like a moral balance that is constantly in flux. *Magic* is a fine score, though it is overshadowed by Goldsmith's other work from the era.

Having enjoyed great success with paranormal horror with *Carrie*, De Palma made *The Fury* (1978), which failed to generate the same amount of box office success but does feature a fine Williams score. At the time, Williams was basking in the critical and commercial success of his collaborations with Spielberg and Lucas. Considering De Palma's history with Herrmann, Williams understandably pays subtle homage to the late master on *The Fury* without sacrificing his own distinct melodic and harmonic sensibilities. Swirling strings, cascading woodwinds and heavy, pulsating brass recalls classic Hitchcock scores, particularly *Vertigo*. The carousel organ, which gradually speeds up, reminds one of the climactic scene in Hitchcock's *Strangers on*

Jerry Goldsmith's score for *Coma* (1978) contains metallic electronic accents that evoke the menace of surgical instruments and sinister conspiracies. (CD cover appears courtesy of Film Score Monthly; graphic design by Joe Sikoryak.)

a Train, which Tiomkin scored. And the use of a theremin during the climax of *The Fury* is perhaps the ultimate nod to Herrmann (e.g. *The Day the Earth Stood Still*), as well as Hitchcock (e.g. *Spellbound*).

While supernatural thrillers dominated horror in the late '70s, other films set out to copy the success of *Jaws*. One such film is *Piranha* (1978), which features one of Pino Donnagio's more riveting scores. For a composer who tends to write a lot of soft, sunny ballads for flute, strings and acoustic guitar, it is refreshing to hear ominously gurgling synths and dark, edgy passages. At times the edgier material flashes on Williams' shark attack music, as well as Goblin's *giallo* soundtracks or John Carpenter's synth scores of the period.

When the orchestra is at full bore the effect is stunningly dramatic, calling to mind Herrmann at his grimmest. The final track—all gurgling electronics that suddenly become frenzied—is truly blood-chilling.

John Carpenter is one of the few film directors who also scores for his movies. One of his most successful works in both respects is the influential slasher flick *Halloween* (1978), about a maniac who stalks babysitters. Surely not a favorite of film score purists who prefer full orchestration and complex theme development, *Halloween* is nonetheless a minimalist masterpiece and a highly influential one at that. Working primarily with synthesizers, piano and drum machine, the composing filmmaker provides four basic motifs: the main theme, another for the main character, another for the haunted house, and the stalking theme. Although some sections offer little more than sprawling, sustained synth tones, the famous passages are quite exciting in terms of rhythm because Carpenter uses ⁵⁄₄ tempo to create a sense of panic. If the score has a weakness it is due to relentless thematic repetition. Regardless, *Halloween* is essential for horror fans. Carpenter's next effort, *The Fog* (1980), continues in the same stylistic vein, but is less memorable.

Possibly the best known horror movie of 1979 is *The Amityville Horror* (1979). After having his score for *The Exorcist* rejected, Schifrin took the opportunity to create an eerie and unsettling soundtrack, though it is important to note that *Amityville* is not *The Exorcist* rehashed. Using children's voices, harp, piano and complex string parts, the theme carries a creepy aura of heinous crime. Schifrin's use of two unusual instruments—the waterphone and crystallophone—lends spooky atmosphere to many of the tracks. Brilliantly, Schifrin takes a stylistic cue from Herrmann by extracting a two-note fragment from the theme for highly effective suspense passages. As critic Jon Burlingame later wrote, the soundtrack "not only frightened moviegoers but managed to convince them that the events being depicted were real." The soundtrack also features Bach's "Fifth Concerto for Harpsichord and Strings." *Amityville Horror* is in the same league as Goldsmith's *The Omen* and deserves a spot in every horror soundtrack collection.

The Studio That Dripped Blood

During the late '50s—after the big Hollywood studios abandoned gothic horror, and shortly before AIP plundered Poe's tomb—horror found new blood at Hammer Film Productions in Great Britain. Among the early Hammer releases was the mediocre thriller *The Mystery of the Mary Celeste* (a.k.a. *Phantom Ship*, 1935), starring Universal horror legend Bela Lugosi. The Hammer-Universal connection would prove more fruitful two decades later.

In 1955, Hammer started a new era of fantastical cinema with a sci-fi horror thriller, *The Quatermass Xperiment*. Based on a 1953 BBC mini-series, the film spawned two successful sequels, but more importantly spurred the studio to make more fantastical films—particularly in the gothic horror vein—between 1957 and 1976.

Hammer is best known for three series based on the classic Universal monsters: Frankenstein, Dracula and the Mummy. Many of the Hammer soundtracks are in the Golden Age tradition that uses an operatic leitmotif for distinctive character themes. But some are more modern in the way they simply strive to create a compelling atmosphere through modern orchestral techniques.

The first of many successful productions was *The Curse of Frankenstein* (1957), starring Peter Cushing as the mad doctor and Christopher Lee as his monster. The film was such a hit that the directing and acting teams were brought back for several Frankenstein sequels and other films. Another member of Hammer's esteemed creative team on *Curse* was composer James Bernard, who made his first Hammer appearance on *Quatermass*, replacing John Hotchkiss. Listen closely to the theme music and you'll swear the melody mimics the syllables of the title. Bernard did that on purpose, and Hammer's music director of the time, John Hollingsworth, is said to have encouraged him to use that tactic for later Hammer projects, most noticeably for the studio's first *Dracula* movie.

For *The Curse of Frankenstein* (Warner Bros./Hammer, 1957), starring Peter Cushing, composer James Bernard wrote a suitably gothic theme that melodically states the title—a technique he often employed on Hammer themes.

"I thought, why not treat it like the opening of a song?" said Bernard, as quoted in Marcus Hearn's booklet notes for *The Hammer Film Music Collection Vol. 1*. "Of course, I never intended it to be sung, but the outline of a tune seemed to present itself when I imagined how 'The-Curse-of-Frankenstein' might be sung."

Such a composing formula would prove helpful to Bernard, as Hammer typically gave composers only two to four weeks to complete scores. Still, Bernard commented later on, "Unlike other genres, I don't think themes for horror films lend themselves to catchy tunes."

Curse also marked Bernard's first opportunity to employ a full orchestra on a Hammer film. The mix of swirling strings, mysterious woodwinds, alarming brass and crashing percussion became Bernard's trademark sound for his Hammer scores, and those by other contributing composers.

The Horror of Dracula (a.k.a. *Dracula*, 1958) was an even bigger hit than Hammer's *Frankenstein* and spawned several sequels. Bernard again used the film's title (actually just "DRAC-u-la") to compose a theme. The orchestral sound is typical of Hammer. Strings swirl menacingly as brass blares with full-blooded passion. Woodwinds flutter like bat wings in the night, and thundering percussion punctuates the grim processional that promises inevitable doom. In other words, break out the crucifix and holy water—Count Dracula is on the prowl! Bernard's "Dracula" theme remains one of the most identifiable horror themes ever.

Bernard's use of motifs is particularly effective in the *Dracula* score. The theme always resolves itself as a reflection of the Count's prowess and control over his victims, except at the end when Dracula's demise is reflected by his unresolved theme.

Despite his penchant for employing motifs, Bernard told *Fantasmagoria* magazine in 1972 that he avoided giving every character in a movie a theme. "It would become much too complicated," he said. "Film music is, in my opinion, most effective when it is basically simple, even if it sometimes demands elaborate orchestration."

Looking for another hit, Hammer relied on the Universal monsters, this time *The Mummy* (1959). The film wasn't as successful as Hammer's *Dracula* and *Frankenstein* films, but inspired three sequels. The first film features a dynamic, vigorous score by German born concert pianist Franz Reizenstein. It features a tragic and ancient-sounding love theme for choir, brass and tympani, or, in variation, oboe, brass and bell-like organ chimes.

Hammer started the swinging '60s with *The Brides of Dracula* (1960), which isn't an official *Dracula* sequel, but rather a female vampire picture. Howard Maxford, author of *Hammer, House of Horror: Behind the Screams* (Overlook, 1996), called *Brides* "one of the studio's key films." Malcolm Williamson provided the thunderous score. The music favors dissonance, abrasive instrumentation and punishing volume to maintain a mood of horror, but is bereft of memorable melodies. In preparation, Williamson viewed Hammer films featuring scores by Bernard, who Williamson deemed "faultless."

"I only wish I could write horror scenes of that quality," Williamson told Sam Irvin of *Little Shoppe of Horrors* magazine in 1990 (No. 10/11). "Hammer was then, and still is, very circumscribed in its ideas of what horror music should be. They accept a certain modernity in the musical language, but as far as the orchestration is concerned, they tend to like things to be stereotyped and conventional."

Hammer continued to explore cinema's back catalogue of monsters in 1961 with *The Curse of the Werewolf*, and in 1962 with *The Phantom of the*

Opera, with bombastic scores by Benjamin Frankel and Edwin Astley, respectively.

In 1963, Hammer delivered one of its better non–*Dracula* vampire movies, *The Kiss of the Vampire*, featuring another powerful Bernard score. In the film, a member of the vampire sect performs the macabre "Vampire Rhapsody," a Franz Lizst–inspired piano piece, as a way of hypnotizing victims. The virulent, profanely romantic piece has drawn comparisons to Herrmann's gothic piano concerto for the crime drama *Hangover Square* (1945).

For *The Gorgon* (1964) Bernard delivered another atmospheric score that uses organ and soprano voice to chilling effect. It is one of his more complex efforts, featuring four themes. The orchestration is textbook Bernard, with woodwinds and strings supplying the softer passages, brass and tympani handling the horrific, and organ, voice and strings supporting suspenseful scenes. *The Gorgon* also marks one of the few occasions that the composer used an electronic instrument, namely the novachord, which Bernard paired with a soprano voice for the movie's Medusa figure (RDL, p. 36).

The Evil of Frankenstein (1964) benefits from a rousing score by Don Banks, who conductor Phillip Martell described as "brilliant—one of the most brilliant composers that ever lived." Although Banks is a Schönberg-inspired, 12-tone composer at heart, he wrote a highly melodic *Evil* that still manages to be dissonant and abrasive. Among Banks' other Hammer scores are *Hysteria* (1965), *The Reptile* (1966) and *Rasputin the Mad Monk* (1966).

For *Rasputin*, Banks conjured swirling, insidious strings, forceful brass, portentously tolling bells and a Russian-sounding melody that calls to mind the infamous mystic who mesmerized the Romanov aristocracy during the run-up to World War I.

Also made in 1966, *The Plague of the Zombies* features Bernard's frantic, brassy, thunderously percussive theme. He composed three major themes—for the film's zombies, investigators and villain. Primitive drums, strummed marimba, forlorn woodwinds and xylophone reverberations conjure the voodoo spirit of the story.

After several years delay between the second and third installments in the *Dracula* series, the rest of the series came almost yearly between 1966 and 1973. The fourth film, *Dracula Has Risen from the Grave* (1968), has a relatively atonal score in comparison to its predecessors. According to Marcus Hearn, who wrote the booklet notes for the GDI Hammer anthologies, the "discordant and cacophonous" score prompted Hammer producer Aida Young to request "something more tuneful on the next one," which turned out to be *Taste the Blood of Dracula* (1969). For *Risen*'s theme, Bernard used a motif first heard in the climactic chase sequence of the first *Dracula* film. Also familiar is the monsignor's theme, which is derivative of the Gregorian chant "Dies Irae" (Day of Wrath), adapted for the Catholic mass of the dead and a staple of many horror scores. Nonetheless, the famous *Dracula* theme was not used.

6. *A Fearful Earful* 249

One of the themes heard in James Bernard's score for *Dracula Has Risen from the Grave* (Warner Bros./Hammer, 1968), starring Christopher Lee, is based on the Gregorian chant "Dies Irae," which is the Catholic mass of the dead and a staple of many horror scores. (Photograph courtesy of the John Monaghan Collection.)

"The thing one has to decide is how much to repeat [the theme]," said Bernard, as quoted by Colin and Sue Cowie in "He Scribbles and I Wave the Wood" for *The Horror Elite* fanzine in 1978. "In one or two *Dracula* films where we haven't used it I always miss it. It's difficult to try not to repeat it and yet keep that mood that you've created in the previous ones."

Both *Taste the Blood* and *Scars of Dracula* (1970) make prominent use of the familiar *Dracula* theme. Both movies feature love themes that balance with the film's horrific passages.

"I admit this sounds unlikely but there are two young lovers in this story. As with *Taste the Blood of Dracula*, I was grateful for the chance of some tenderness amid the mayhem, even if there never seemed quite enough time before the horror struck again. But there is enough time now, so here is the tune without vampire intervention," wrote Bernard in the booklet notes for *Hammer—The Studio That Dripped Blood!*

"In *Taste the Blood*, Bernard's love theme is absolutely gorgeous," wrote

The Studio That Dripped Blood is one of many soundtrack compilations that collects themes from Hammer horror films. (CD cover appears courtesy of Silva Screen Records.)

Larson in his book about Hammer film music. "It's [his] prettiest melody.... The romantic theme in *Scars* is less lilting, [but] receives its prettiest variation during the end titles."

Bernard told Ed Mumma and Neil Leadbeater for an interview in *Fantasmagoria* No. 2 (1972) that he welcomed the opportunities to write love themes for Hammer. "Unrelieved tension and horror in the music can become a bore," he said.

Occult thrillers were highly fashionable between the late '60s and mid–1970s. Hammer's best entry in the genre is *The Devil Rides Out* (1968), which was poorly received upon release but has since become a classic, bolstered by Bernard's outstanding, feverish score. Bernard remembered the project fondly in that compilation's booklet notes:

> Like *Dracula* and *She*, this was another of my favorite books. I read it when I was 15. During the part about satanic orgies my teenage imagination ran riot, though I took serious note of Dennis Wheatley's warnings about meddling with dark forces. I have always believed strongly in the transcendental powers of good and evil and their eternal battle. So, it was easy for me to put my heart into the music.

Bernard recounted in a 1994 interview for *Little Shoppe of Horrors* (No. 12, p. 52) that he was allowed to use more percussion than usual, including conga drums, bongos, tom-toms, vibraphones, sundry percussion and "deep African drums in the orgy scene."

Devil's score is persistently dark until the forces of evil are vanquished. Only then does a heroic, uplifting theme take over. Of course, the best bits belong to the orgiastic pagan ritual scenes.

Williamson scored *The Horror of Frankenstein* (1970), a satirical jab at the genre, though selections by Bernard were recycled from earlier films in the series. Larson described Williamson's score as odd and seemingly ill-fitting (RDL, p. 79), but quoted the composer as saying: "It is an occupational hazard of any film composer that when he gets a good idea the convention-ridden pundits try to squash it." He added, "I was forced to add flutes and oboes ... the final effect was ludicrous. I did not enjoy it at all." (*Little Shoppe of Horrors* No. 10/11, 1990)

Another notable composer for Hammer was Harry Robinson, which is a pseudonym for Harry Robertson. Under another pseudonym, Lord Rockingham, the former music director for EMI and Decca had scored a number-one hit in 1958 with the manic "Hoots Mon." His first efforts for Hammer included the theme to the 1968 TV series "Journey to the Unknown." Known for working quickly under a deadline, he scored the Karnstein family vampire films: *The Vampire Lovers* (1970), *Lust for a Vampire* (1970) and *Twins of Evil* (1971), as well as *Countess Dracula* (1971).

Having scored the Poe adaptation *The Oblong Box* (1969) for AIP, Robertson was brought in to score the AIP/Hammer co-production of *The Vampire Lovers*. Robertson provided a lushly sensuous score, ripe with gothic atmosphere, built around three basic themes. "The *Vampire Lovers* was a brutal score to write," Robertson told Bruce Hallenbeck for *Little Shoppe of Horrors* magazine (No. 7, 1982). "There were about 75 minutes of music in the movie, and I did it in ten days."

Robertson—again working under the name Robinson—composed an even more complex score for *Lust for a Vampire*, the second in the Karnstein trilogy, using four themes. "I basically worked the same sort of formula for *Lust* as I had done on *The Vampire Lovers*, although I did attempt to make *Lust* sound more romantic," Robertson said in the booklet notes for GDI's *The Hammer Vampire Film Music Collection (HVFMC)*.

Robertson, who died in 1996, held *Lust* in low regard. "The other two movies in the Karnstein trilogy were for the most part very good, but *Lust* was the weakest of the three," he is quoted in GDI's Vampire compilation. "I regard *Lust for a Vampire* as one of Hammers' 'tits and bums' productions—it relied more on the uncovering of flesh than the unfolding of a story."

Robertson's experience on *Lust* also was marred by the fact that the producers asked him to provide a pop song for use during a love scene. "Strange Love" drew hoots and jeers from audiences, Robertson later claimed in an article in *Fandom's Film Gallery*, No. 3 (p. 163, 1978).

Next, Robertson simultaneously scored the third and final Karnstein film, *Twins of Evil*, and the "historical" vampire film *Countess Dracula*. According to Larson, the producer Harry Fine again requested a pop song for *Twins*, but the composer refused to oblige. Instead, Fine had words set to Robertson's powerful theme for an unsuccessful single performed by the group Essjay (RDL, p. 109–111). The theme has an almost Morricone-esque western feel, with Gatlin gun snare drum accents and an ascending strings-and-trumpet melody. "I always wanted to do a western score," Robertson told Bruce Hallendbeck for *Little Shoppe of Horrors* (No. 7, 1982). "*Twins of Evil* was a cowboy film in disguise."

For *Countess Dracula*, Robertson delivered a score befitting a "historical" vampire film. He made a quick study of ethnic Hungarian music and used instruments such as the cimbalom to create "an extremely sensual, rhythmically undulating motif" (RDL, p. 112). The theme is one of the loveliest in the Hammer catalogue.

For *Blood from the Mummy's Tomb* (1971), the fourth and final Hammer *Mummy* movie, Tristram Cary treated some of his score with subtle electronics. The film's dreamlike theme strives for atmosphere over character, and the remainder of the score follows suit, sometimes with slightly Oriental overtones. Cary still calls attention to charac-

Harry Robertson (a.k.a. Harry Robinson) provided a lushly sensuous score built around three basic themes for *The Vampire Lovers* (Hammer/AIP/MGM, 1970), starring the femme fatale Ingrid Pitt.

terization through orchestral textures and moods. In retrospect, the composer admits that his aim was simply to satisfy the needs of the film and its director.

"With most movies I would expect the director or possibly the producer to turn up at least at one recording session, but as far as I remember the Hammer people left [conductor] Philip [Martell] to get it right," Cary told Larson (RDL, p. 95).

Hammer attempted to appeal to fans of rock and pop by employing Mike Vickers, lead guitarist of Manfred Mann, to score *Dracula A.D. 1972*, along with a cameo by the little known group Stoneground.

The rock feel is also evident on *The Satanic Rites of Dracula* (1974), by John Cacavas, who brought a similar sound to *Horror Express* (1973), an English-Spanish co-production.

Fittingly, Hammer Studio's most productive period ended in the mid–1970s much as it had begun—with Bernard composing *Frankenstein and the Monster from Hell* (1973), the final installment in the series. It briefly resurrected the gothic era, albeit with a predominantly atonal score. "With that and *The Legend of the 7 Golden Vampires*, I could feel in my bones that things were winding down a bit," Bernard said in the booklet notes for *HFMC-2*, which also features the theme for *Monster from Hell*.

For his final feature score, *The Legend of the 7 Golden Vampires* (1974), a co-production between Hammer and the kung fu masters Shaw Brothers Films, Bernard blended his style with traditional Chinese music. He also recycled his "DRAC-u-la" theme and cues from *Taste the Blood of Dracula*. Although the Shaw Brothers originally intended to use library music for the movie, Hammer brought in Bernard, whose score outshines the film itself.

Other British Horror & Suspense Movies

Released three months before Hitchcock's *Psycho*, Michael Powell's *Peeping Tom* (1960) unflinchingly examines the relationship between violence and voyeurism. Critics greeted the film with intense disdain, ending Powell's career in England virtually overnight. Today, this portrait of perversity is recognized as an undisputed masterpiece. Brian Easdale's sensitive score features emotionally charged solo piano by Gordon Watson, a percussion number performed by Angela Morley (as Wally Stott), and hip dance floor jazz by Freddie Phillips. The solo piano pieces are particularly effective at capturing the central character's obsessive-compulsive behavior.

Goodbye Gemini (a.k.a. *Twinsanity*, 1970), a swinging '60s horror flick, features murder, incest and drug parties with transvestites and homosexuals. Christopher Gunning's mostly laid back score would indicate something a bit less extreme—say, a moody romance—if it weren't for tense tracks like "Ritual Murder" and "Jacki's Nightmare." Gunning rarely goes for the obvious

Christopher Gunning served as arranger for such artists as Shirley Bassey and Mel Torme before scoring his first film, *Goodbye Gemini* (a.k.a. *Twinsanity*, 1970). (CD cover appears courtesy of Harkit Records; graphic design by Tim Noel-Johnson.)

swinging London sounds, favoring instead subtle orchestration, delicate acoustic guitar and piano filigree, soaring strings and tasteful brass. The closest thing to swinging London is "Houseboat Party No. 3," which boasts a very sampleable groove. A former arranger for Shirley Bassey, Mel Torme and the Hollies, this was Gunning's first excursion into scoring.

Marc Wilkinson's excellent score for *Blood on Satan's Claw* (a.k.a. *Satan's Skin*, 1971) is hauntingly beautiful. It features a lyrical melody reminiscent of (but not based on) an old English folk song. However, the musical element that makes this an essential horror score is Wilkinson's use of the "Devil's

Interval," the descending chromatic scale that omits the perfect fifth and therefore highlights the diminished fifth to sinister effect. Wilkinson, a former music director for the British National Theatre, noted in the Trunk Records CD's booklet that he used mostly conventional classical orchestration, but—to his credit—the soundtrack never sounds conventional. Adding to the spookiness is the use of the eerie-sounding ondes martenot (like a theremin with additional keyboard) and the cimbalom, which lends an Eastern European/Turkish flavor to the film's occult content. It's impossible to listen to *Blood on Satan's Claw* without thinking of chilly October nights, spooky old graveyards and cackling crones. Simply put, it is a perfectly realized horror score.

Another memorable British horror is the bikers-from-hell flick *Psychomania* (a.k.a. *The Death Wheelers*, 1971), featuring music composed and performed by John Cameron and "Frog," with an additional track ("Riding Free") by David Whitaker and J. Worth, sung by Harvey Andrews. "*Psychomania* was the most bizarre [film I ever wrote music for]," Cameron wrote in the booklet notes for the Trunk CD release. "Jazz and session musicians playing pre-punk trash rock for a tale of supernatural gore and mayhem."

A prolific library session musician, Cameron recalled that a lot of studio tricks were employed to get strange sonorities: "Musser vibes played through phase and wah pedals, phased bowed bass, drumsticks inside a grand piano, electric harpsichord through a phase unit and Leslie speakers." *Psychomania* lives up to its title with dope bass lines, sleazy guitar licks, and disorienting passages of echoing dialogue over abstract noise.

An Italian-English co-production, *Don't Look Now* (1973) received an X rating for a soft-core sex scene that was added at the last minute to offset the many argumentative scenes. These days the film is better remembered for its murderous Venetian dwarf. Pino Donaggio's score is mostly gentle and romantic, given its piano, strings, flute, Spanish guitar and harp, with additional passages of atonal suspense. The climax of "Dead End" is a delicious bit of orchestration, with escalating strings, trilling flute, harp and guitar glissandi building to a shrill finish.

Horror Express (*Pánico en el Transiberiano*, 1973), an English-Spanish production, features a John Cacavas score that blends atmospheric suspense with diabolical keyboard textures and psychedelic touches, like fuzz-tone guitar and electronic effects. One of the film's victim's whistles the theme as he unwittingly opens a crate containing the movie's monster. The end credits put it to a funky beat.

The ultimate British cult horror movie is the occult mystery *The Wicker Man* (1973). Paul Giovanni's Celtic-styled pagan folk songs (performed by Magnet) give the soundtrack a unique vibe. The use of lyre, acoustic guitars, recorders and violins cast a powerful spell. Among the highlights are the medieval-sounding "Procession" and the bagpipe number "Chop Chop."

Terror Italian Style

The only national cinema that rivals the United States or Great Britain for quality and quantity of horror and suspense thrillers during the '60s and '70s was Italy. Whether one enjoys gothic, slasher, supernatural, zombie or cannibal pics, Italian filmmakers delivered thrills and chills.

The first Italian horror movie was *I vampiri* (*The Devil's Commandment*, or *Lust of a Vampire*, 1957), for which future master of the genre Mario Bava served as cinematographer and arguably co-director. Roman Vlad (and Franco Mannino) provided the melodramatic old-fashioned score for the modern day vampire movie about a mad scientist who drains blood from healthy young women to keep an ancient evil duchess alive (a concept later adapted by Hammer for *Countess Dracula*, among other films).

Next up was the Roberto Nicolosi–scored *Caltiki—il mostro immortale* (*Caltiki—The Immortal Monster*, 1959), which represents another baby step in the Italian horror moviemaking scene. Just as both movies' plots are derivative of classic Hollywood horror films, so too are the scores. Vlad and Nicolosi took stylistic cues from the works of Golden Age greats like Max Steiner, Franz Waxman and Hans Salter. Strings shudder, horns groan and woodwinds shiver through dark passages and sinister moods. Palpable evil seems to be edging nearer with each tense measure, each pregnant pause.

No one will claim *I vampiri* or *Caltiki* to be lost masterpieces of horror scoring. But there's no denying the composers' mastery of the form. Vlad finds dark magic in his monothematic symphonic score by employing eerie instrumentation—harp, celeste and organ bewitch the atmosphere around swirling strings of imminent terror. Nicolosi's score is even eerier and uses exotic instrumentation to summon the ancient Mayan evil wreaking havoc on archeologists. Harp, celeste and strings capture the unspeakable Lovecraftian horror, while brass evinces the resilience of the men who must do battle with it. Percussion and "tribal" chants work hard to cast a voodoo spell, but the best tracks are more reminiscent of Akira Ifukube's music for the early *Godzilla* films.

It's easy to see *Il vampiri* and *Caltiki* as practice runs for Bava, who soon after created his first masterpiece of horror, *La maschera del ccemonio* (*The Mask of Satan*, or *Black Sunday*, 1960). Like many films made in Italy during that period, *Black Sunday* used different scores for domestic and foreign markets. While Nicolosi tracked the Italian release, Les Baxter scored the AIP version released in the U.S. Nicolosi and Baxter's treatments of the material are not significantly different. There are passages that quietly build tension or provide an eerie ambience, followed by sections of cacophony for scenes of climactic horror. And both scores feature the aching beauty of the Romantic school of classical composers. However, AIP deemed Nicolosi's score underorchestrated and too romantic for AIP's mostly teen audience, and hired Baxter to rescore. Baxter and Nicolosi both delivered serviceable scores, but

Both Roberto Nicolosi and Les Baxter composed scores for *La maschera del demonio* (*The Mask of Satan*, or *Black Sunday*, 1960), the former heard in the European release and the latter heard in the U.S. (CD cover appears courtesy of Digitmovies Alternative Entertainment; graphic design by Claudio Fuiano.)

personal preference is obviously dependent on each person's original viewing experience. Simply put, both scores for *Black Sunday* are classic gothic horror listening experiences.

"To hear [Baxter's] stirring, sorcerous score is to see images from the film replayed in the cinema of one's own mind," noted critic Tim Lucas in the *Black Sunday* (Baxter version) CD insert.

Bava's next horror film proved phenomenally influential and historically important. *La ragazza che sapeva troppo* (*The Girl Who Knew Too Much*, or

The Evil Eye, 1963) was the first cinematic attempt at the *giallo*—a term coined in 1929 describing Italian mystery paperbacks published by Mondadori and featuring lurid yellow covers (*giallo* is Italian for yellow, which supposedly is the color of fear). In fact, the film's heroine is seen reading a *giallo* paperback on an airplane at the beginning of the film. Later, *giallo* pictures (beginning with Dario Argento's *L'uccello dalle piume di cristallo*, a.k.a. *The Bird with the Crystal Plumage*, 1970) would earn the genre a reputation for bloody violence, stylish cinematography and gripping soundtracks.

Nicolosi's *The Evil Eye* is predominantly atonal and sinister. There are brief respites from paranoia, however, where he provides sultry lounge jazz and light romantic moods. Those cues date the score, but most of it is suitably dark, with jazzy highlights, even during the orchestral sections. In final analysis, however, Nicolosi's score for *The Evil Eye* is less noteworthy than the film itself.

Also in 1963, Bava made a gothic anthology film, *I Tre Volti Della Paura* (*Black Sabbath*). Again Baxter scored the American version and Nicolosi scored the Italian release. Shimmering strings, low brass and booming kettledrums deliver the theme in Nicolosi's version. Low-down jazz moods and brassy big band numbers blend well with variations of the main theme, a tender love theme and sparely arranged suspense passages.

Carlo Rustichelli scored Bava's kinky gothic horror film, *La frusta e il corpo* (*The Whip and the Body*, 1963), and the *giallo* masterpiece *Sei Donne per L'assassino* (*Blood and Black Lace*, 1964). For *Whip*, Rustichelli composed a tragic love theme known as "The Windsor Concerto" for piano and orchestra. Turbulent, melodramatic and gorgeous, the theme's frequent reprise captures the film's story of unrequited love. There also is a strong supernatural element in the film that is bolstered by the composer's subtle orchestration and atonal atmospherics. Lone instruments like piano and organ flit in and out of the shadows before ensemble climaxes drive them out into the light.

If Bava's first attempt at a *giallo* is historically significant, his second effort in the fledgling cinematic genre was stylistically influential. *Blood and Black Lace* features the now familiar villain wearing a black trench coat and fedora, gorgeous damsels in distress and multiple bloody murders. Rustichelli's score offers both atmospheric orchestral moods and suave Latin jazz for the film's fashion house setting. Sometimes the styles overlap, with solo organ reprising the theme melody over shuddering strings and stealthy bass. Throughout, Rustichelli displays his penchant for spare orchestration that leaves plenty of room for solo "voices."

Italian horror really caught fire at the end of the '60s and blazed well into the '70s. Bava's *Rosso segno della folia* (*Hatchet for the Honeymoon*, 1969) features a score by Sante Maria Romitelli. Following the cheerful waltz are psychedelically tinged tracks that feature repetitive harpsichord lines, intermittent percussion fills, electric bass, effects-laden electric guitar, mysterious oboe and

Carlo Rustichelli's turbulently melodramatic score for Bava's kinky gothic horror film *La frusta e il corpo* (*The Whip and the Body*, 1963) captures the film's story of unrequited love. (CD cover appears courtesy of Digitmovies Alternative Entertainment; graphic design by Claudio Fuiano.)

flute melodies, and organ backdrops. There also are gentle, even pastoral passages that use acoustic guitar or xylophone or strings to deliver the sort of sweet melodies heard on the waltz. The blend of the edgy dissonant suspense cues and the pleasant sensual romantic pieces educe the dichotomy suggested by the movie's title. Falling in between the two moods is "Hatchet Shake," a dance rock number with a funky organ and jazz guitar solos, vibes, groovy bass line and booming drums.

A classic of 1969 is Riz Ortolani's *Così dolce ... così perversa* (*So Sweet, So

Perverse), directed by Umberto Lenzi. Much of the score is built around the stirring theme "Why," which is sung by J. Vincent Edward, who performed on the London cast recording of *Hair*. The soundtrack has the requisite nightclub dance music as well. "Shake in the Disco" boasts an irresistible groove, and, amazingly, seems to have escaped notice among those who compile psychedelic soundtrack funk. Speaking of psych, "Shadows in the Mind" features fuzz-toned guitar, and "The Best Pleasure" has a breezy flute loop heard through an Echoplex. Flute is the favored solo instrument on several groovy lounge tracks, like "So Soft" and "A Flute in the Night." Lenzi recycled the theme and its instrumental variations in *Sette Orchidee Macchiate Di Rosso* (*Seven Blood Stained Orchids*, 1972), which uses a different and almost funky instrumental for the theme.

Ortolani's *Una sull'altra* (*Perversion Story*, or *One on Top of the Other*, 1969) is another killer. *Perversion Story* offers the coolest crime jazz theme in Italian cinema. It opens with blaring brass and pounding drums before giving way to handclaps, a walking double bass, vocal percussive noises, solo flute, then solo sax over a fuzz-tone bass. Vamping brass soon underpin a brief high register trumpet-and-sax wrestling match. Highlights include the lush and lovely "Susan and Jane," the lowdown groovy "Lombard Street" and "Latin Quarter," the exquisitely psychedelic "Sitar in Blues" and the shake-adelic "The Roaring Twenties," among others.

Nicolai's *Femmine insaziabili* (*The Insatiables*, 1969) is another sleazy soundtrack gem. Vocalist Lara Saint Paul gives her all on "I Want It All," the ultimate theme for hedonists. The bustling jazz of "Autostrada per Los Angeles," and the erotic balladry of "Squardi Teneri," follow, along with a Latin jazz version of the theme. One of the best instrumental versions of the theme blends flanged electric guitar, harpsichord, a brisk rhythm and Dell'Orso's vocalisms. Between its lush lounge, sensual voices and jazzy interplay evocative of big city life, *Insatiables* satisfies in more ways than one. Above all, it is a showcase for Nicolai's imaginative orchestrations and catchy melodies.

Nora Orlandi's fetching *A doppia faccia* (*Double Face*, 1969), which was credited to "Joan Christian," is dominated by variations on the emotive theme. Arranged and conducted by Roby Poitevin, the theme can be heard as an extravagant grand piano solo, and as an exquisite and intricate jazz pop number (with and without vocals). The score also features the ballad "The Face of Love" and a frenzied Hammond organ–fueled shake titled "Soho." Orlandi's choir is nearly as well known as Alessandro Alessandroni's Il Cantori Moderni.

Gianni Ferrio's lively *La morte risale a ieri sera* (*Death Occurred Last Night*, 1970) boasts the classic nightclub number "Milano Rhythm and Blues," which features a catchy bass line, flaring brass and wah guitar. Harpsichord-led baroque pop ("Livia"), Hammond organ–drenched psych pop ("L'Inchiesta") and crime jazz workouts ("Il Duro Scappa") mix with melancholy jazz meditations ("Un Giorno, Ieri") to make *Death* a thoroughly engaging experience.

Baroque pop, psych rock, crime jazz and melancholy meditations make Gianni Ferrio's *La morte risale a ieri sera* (*Death Occurred Last Night*, 1970) a lively experience. (CD cover appears courtesy of Digitmovies Alternative Entertainment; graphic design by Claudio Fuiano.)

The same year, Umiliani delivered a thoroughly groovy score for *Cinque bambole per la luna d'agosto* (*Five Dolls for an August Moon*, 1970), by Bava. The movie presents a series of grisly murders in a story line similar to Agatha Christie's *Ten Little Indians*. Never before has a group of people been knocked off one by one to such an absurdly breezy, fun-loving musical backdrop. A combo featuring organ, harpsichord, harp, flute, choir, guitar, bass, percussion and drums keeps the mood so light it is tempting to think that Umiliani never even saw the film when he delivered the music. It even has whistling by

Alessandroni. The theme gets reworked over and over again, and while there isn't a lot of reinvention taking place, it's difficult not to be seduced by it.

The *giallo* genre hit its commercial stride in 1969, continuing into the early '70s. One of the most influential *gialli* is Dario Argento's directorial debut, *L'uccello dale piume di cristallo* (*The Bird with the Crystal Plumage*, 1969). Morricone scored *Bird*, as well as Argento's next two features, *Il gatto a nove code* (*The Cat O'Nine Tails*, 1971) and *Quattro mosche di velluto grigio* (*Four Flies on Grey Velvet*, 1972). By turns jazzy, avant-garde and memorably melodic, Morricone's *Crystal Plumage* is an outstanding example of the composer's work

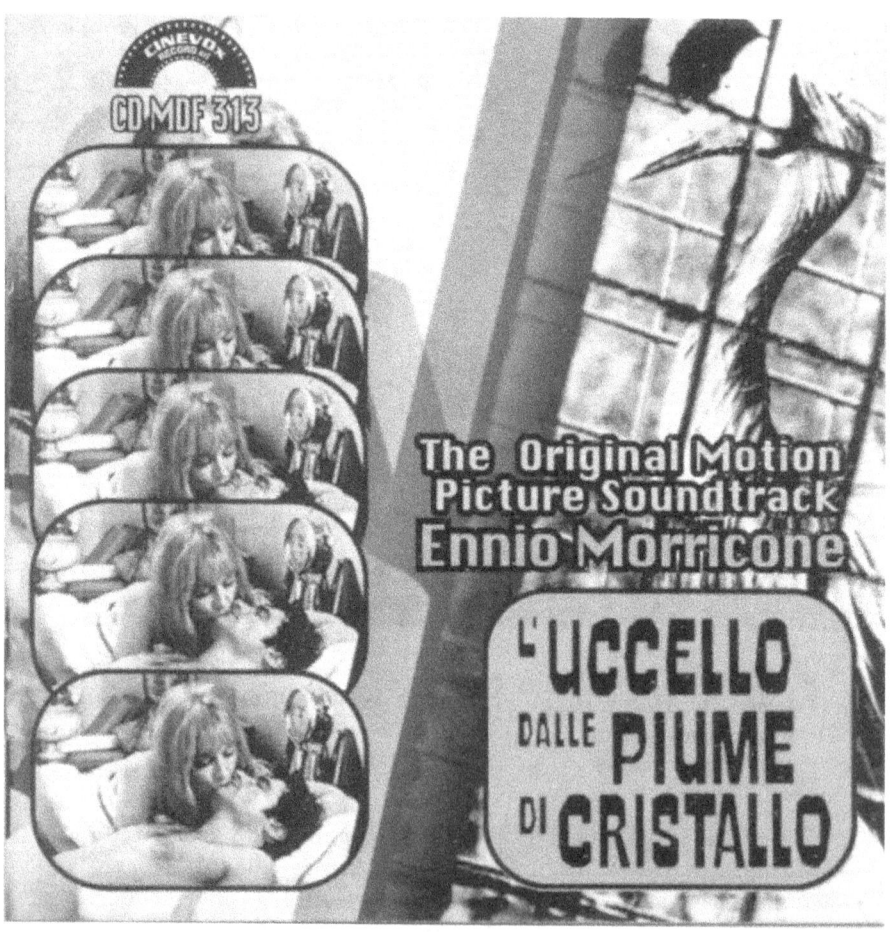

Ennio Morricone's score for *L'uccello dalle piume di cristallo* (a.k.a. *The Bird with the Crystal Plumage*, 1970) was the first of three the composer completed for filmmaker Dario Argento. (CD cover appears courtesy of Cinevox Records; graphic design by Fredrika Cao.)

in the genre, though in retrospect the composer and the director aren't ideally matched. By the time Argento hit his stylistic stride with *Profundo rosso* he opted for a more aggressive rock-oriented soundtrack, courtesy of Goblin (but more on that later). The *Crystal Plumage* theme opens with the tinkling of chimes and the sublime vocalism of Dell'Orso, evoking the titular glass bird. The effect is simultaneously gentle and creepy. When Alessandroni's choir replaces Dell'Orso, and gently plucked acoustic guitar joins the tuned percussion, the sound is tender and lovely. That mood is carried forth on the lilting Latin ballad "Non rimane più nessuno." Suspense enters the picture on "Corsa sui Tetti" when a malevolently groaning male voice pursues the frightened panting of a female voice over avant-garde jazz, with angular keyboard lines being taunted by frantic drums and spastic, sickly brass. That style persists through much of the score (and much of the genre). The only thing missing is a sinister fuzz-tone guitar ostinato that eventually became a staple of the *giallo* sound. While abrasive atonality is a perfect accompaniment for onscreen murder and mayhem, most record collectors will agree that it makes for a difficult and sometimes disconcerting listening experience. Women in particular are likely to find the almost erotic panting of a seemingly suffering female, which is set to an escalating heartbeat, a bit disturbing. Fans of Morricone's relentlessly experimental spirit, however, will appreciate the extremes on display on this soundtrack.

Morricone continued to strike a balance between pop and avant-garde sounds on *Le foto proibite di una signora per bene* (*Forbidden Photos of a Lady Above Suspicion*, 1970). The score, which contains one of Morricone's deeply involving Latin pop themes, features Dell'Orso's incomparable vocalisms. It's a fine example of the composer's gift for ear-catching melodies, and is nearly matched by the heartbreaking and lovely "Amore Come Dolore," which builds from a hypnotic three-note figure, jittery sustained piano textures and deep breathing strings. Morricone also rocks out on "Intermezzino Pop," an organ-drenched slab of '60s-style groove. The score favors disturbing moods—where sexual tension blends with fear—exhibiting considerable experimental flourish. Electronic disturbances and dissonant strings accompany hypnotic keyboard textures and mysterious unresolved counter melodies.

The fact that Morricone scored so many Italian thrillers, providing haunting themes as well as highly effective horror underscore, is awe-inspiring. In the CD booklet notes for *Forbidden Photos*, Morricone admits that he often went for days after viewing a film without writing a note of music to accompany it. "Then, suddenly, as I am on the way to pay the gas bill (as really happened once) the idea comes to me. And, the idea (luckily, I always carry a pen and paper) I write immediately; it's just an idea, not yet refined, a general idea, not even a melody...."

Morricone also acknowledged his great reliance on, and admiration for, Dell'Orso, whose singing he considers exceptional. "She sings, upon reading for the first time, extremely difficult things that I write for her," he says in the booklet notes. "Edda is an incredibly rare musical animal."

Another of the countless Morricone scores featuring Dell'Orso belongs to *La corta notte della bambole di vetro* (*Short Night of the Glass Dolls*, 1971). *Short Night* is predominantly dissonant. Through much of the score scraping violins are accompanied by heartbeat rhythms, repetitive keyboard textures and Dell'Orso's horrotic moans and sighs.

Morricone composed a memorable theme for Argento's *Il gatto a nove code* (*The Cat O'Nine Tails*, 1971). Its gently strummed guitar, plaintive flute, interlocking harpsichord and piano, understated strings and Dell'Orso vocal coalesce into something surprisingly tender for a film featuring a psycho killer. The remainder of the score explores stripped-down, electric bass-led experiments in tension and terror. *Nine Tails* is yet another brilliant slab of avant-garde film scoring from a *giallo* master.

John Bender, resident critic of European film music for *Film Score Monthly*, recognized the *Nine Tails* score as a metaphor for "the evil mind of an insane genius" in his booklet notes for DRG's Morricone set *The Thriller Collection*. "Each note represents a synaptic firing, every chord struck is a neuron relaying its fraction of a malignant thought through the wormy pathways of a brain. The music advances to a sinister pattern, and describes a cold, potentially virulent purpose."

Riz Ortolani scored *Nella stretta morsa del ragno* (*Web of the Spider*, 1971), a remake of *Danza Macabra* (*Castle of Blood*, 1964), which also features the composer's work. Both *Web* and *Castle* were falsely billed as Poe story adaptations, though both feature a character named after the writer. *Web* ranges from tense intrigue, featuring diabolical fuzz-toned guitar and violin lines, piano stings and percussion accents (main theme, "Hallucinations"), to sweetly serene strings ("Love Theme") to a stately waltz played by harpsichord and strings ("Ball at the Castle"). Diabolical moods dominate "Obsession," "Nightmares" and "In the Dark."

Alessandro Alessandroni's psychedelic *La notte più lunga del diavolo* (*The Devil's Nightmare*, 1971) boasts gloriously gothic pipe organ, fuzzy guitar stings and Dell'Orso's seductive vocals. "Dark Dreamer," "Demon Night," "Deadly Beauty," "Erotic Demon" and "Caressing" bewitch with organ swells, discordant strings, creepy percussion accents, throbbing bass and spooky whistling. Electronic effects and orchestral dissonance produce disturbing atmospheres that conjure evil winds and tortured felines. For a composer who rarely gets his due, Alessandroni sounds like a master of the genre on *The Devil's Nightmare*.

That's not to say *Nightmare* is Alessandroni's only horror or *giallo* soundtrack. He also scored *Lo strangolatore di Vienna* (*The Mad Butcher of Vienna*) and *Lady Frankenstein* (*La figlia di Frankenstein*), both in 1971.

The tongue-in-cheek *Mad Butcher* begins with a jaunty barroom piano piece that has a passing resemblance to Kurt Weill's "Mack the Knife." The theme is quoted throughout the score, sometimes by electric guitar amid discordant keyboard runs, or over simple acoustic guitar and piano rhythms. Set in Vienna, the score naturally includes waltz-style tracks, but also explores more acid-tinged suspenseful moods and bluesy jazz interludes.

Alessandroni's music for *Lady Frankenstein* coaxes creepy and sinister moods with strings, fuzz-toned guitar and piano. The strings connote the single-minded obsession of the female Frankenstein in her perverse quest to cre-

Alessandro Alessandroni's score for *Lo strangolatore di Vienna* (*The Mad Butcher of Vienna*, 1971) features waltz-style tracks, but also explores more acid-tinged suspenseful moods and bluesy jazz interludes. (CD cover appears courtesy of Beat Records; graphic design by Daniele De Gemini.)

ate a monster that "could satisfy her strange desires" (or so the movie's tagline promises). The most memorable bits use electronic feedback and a reverberating pulse, presumably for the film's monster. This modern style is distinctively different from Hammer's gothic *Frankenstein* scores.

After scoring *A doppia faccia*, Orlandi scored *Lo strano vizio della signora Wardh* (*The Strange Vice of Ms. Wardh*, or *Next!*, 1971). *Ms. Wardh*, which Paolo Ormi conducted, is another *giallo* classic. On the breezy lounge jazz theme, which figures prominently throughout the score, piano introduces the melancholy melody, joined by lush strings and choir over an insistent beat. Other tracks provide hazy intrigue ("Theme"), dreamy sensuality ("The Pleasure of Pleasure"), discothèque groove ("Shakin' with Edwige") and suspense ("Obscure Remembering"). "Bondage Suite" is comparatively abstract and atonal, using electric guitar, organ and congas on one part to suggest a sordid atmosphere, a choir and harp or zither to suggest something more sublime and ethereal on another. "Dies Irae," which Quentin Tarantino later used for the *Kill Bill Volume 2* (2004) trailer, also is heard in the suite.

A popular subject for European knife-wielding maniac movies is Jack the Ripper. Among the many examples is *Sette cadaveri per Scotland Yard* (*Seven Murders for Scotland Yard*, 1971), an Italian-Spanish production that turns Jack into a cannibal. Piccioni supplies the tense, propulsive score, which is drenched in corrosive fuzz guitar, thick horn and organ clusters. Most interesting are the jazzy Schifrin-esque drum and bass patterns with pulsing flute melodies, organ washes and punchy brass. Tracks like "The Investigation Starts" and "Suspecting" sound ripped from the soundtracks of *Bullitt* and *Dirty Harry*. It is interesting that Piccioni, who has his own distinctive style, would so brazenly imitate a Hollywood composer. In one way it is disappointing to hear something derivative coming from the composer of *The Tenth Victim* and *Colpo Rovente*, but it's still a terrific score, full of nail-biting tension and sinister atmosphere. Piccioni scored three other Italian-Spanish *gialli* in 1971—*El Ojo del huracán* (*La volpe dalla coda di velluto*, or *In the Eye of the Hurricane*), *Marta* (*...Dopo di che, uccide il maschio e lo divora*) and *Fieras sin Jaula* (*Due maschi per Alexa*, or *Two Masks for Alexa*).

The year 1971 also saw the release of several *gialli* featuring memorable Morricone scores. Arguably the best of the lot belongs to *Una lucertola con la pelle di donna* (*Lizard in a Woman's Skin*, or *Schzoid*), a favorite among genre fans for its lurid mix of LSD, psychedelic dream sequences, psychoanalysis, lesbianism and gore. The theme, featuring Dell'Orso's vocalisms, is hypnotic and gorgeous. Opening with reverberating piano and woodwind figures, and electronic cricket noise, it soon picks up a bouncing bass line and swelling orchestration, complete with muted trumpet and Dell'Orso's sublime voice. The theme's raspy electronic effects are a consistent feature through many of the atonal passages ("Legitimate Fear") and groovier psychedelic tracks ("Night of Day"). In the booklet notes for *The Thriller Collection* CD, critic John Bender called the score "dynamite ... it will seem to mutate and be different upon each successive listen—like a thing alive."

Morricone's *Giornata nera per l'arete* (*The Fifth Cord*, or *Evil Fingers*, 1971) has a dreamy but disquieting atmosphere not far removed from *Lizard*. Electronic "static" on some tracks reinforces the impression. Dell'Orso's sighs and gasps on "Fear and Assault" suggest both sexual ecstasy and nightmare. Sharp, shrieking violins on another cue quote Herrmann's stabbing music from *Psycho*. Cold, plodding electric bass notes evokes prowling menace on many tracks.

Morricone's *Gli occhi freddi della paura* (*Cold Eyes of Fear*, 1971) features Gruppo Di Improvvisazione Nuova Consonanza, an improvisation ensemble founded in 1964 and made up entirely of composers. It also explores dissonant sounds but displays a more aggressive avant-garde jazz style. On "Seguita," busy drums and walking bass provide an anchor for wah guitar and electronically enhanced trumpet interplay worthy of *Bitches' Brew*–era Miles Davis. Morricone may be the trumpeter. Elsewhere, one can hear such bizarre sounds as ashtrays in pianos, bowed cymbals, scraping metal alongside the more typical but still jarring jittery horns, and string drones. Although *Cold Eyes'* cacophonous and abstract sounds discourage casual listening, its strong jazz and psychedelic aspects will engage listeners who are more attuned to experimental, exploratory music genres. No self-respecting avant-garde music or Morricone fan should be without a copy.

On Morricone's *La tarantola dal ventre nero* (*Black Belly of the Tarantula*, 1971) high-pitched strings waft overhead like an ominous October wind as unresolved chords conjured on keyboards mingle poisonously with dissonant notes struck on vibraphone and guitar. On "Spirale Misteriosa" this disconcerting blend takes on a noir-esque character with the accompaniment of a cymbal ride. Again, Dell'Orso is featured on the more languid, feminine mood pieces.

Morricone's close associate Bruno Nicolai scored many Italian thrillers. Two of the classics from 1971 are *La coda dello scorpione* (*The Case of the Scorpion's Tail*) and *La notte che Evelyn usci' dalla tomba* (*The Night Evelyn Came Out of the Grave*).

Scorpion's Tail opens with a hypnotic acoustic guitar ostinato over throbbing electric bass accented by threatening electric guitar growls. It evinces the plot's vicious twists. However, the acoustic guitar element is sometimes more evocative of spaghetti westerns than *gialli*. Virtuoso piano fills and lush strings give other cues a more sophisticated feeling more in keeping with the movie's modern day setting. *Scorpion's Tail*'s dissonant suspense cues feature muted brass and shrill woodwinds that cry out over seesawing strings, rumbling bass and drums, keyboard abstractions and electronic textures. When the rhythm section locks into a groove underneath these sinister sound effects it is difficult to imagine a more perfect *giallo* soundtrack style. Nicolai's more conven-

Ennio Morricone has many fine *giallo* scores to his credit, including *La tarantola dal ventre nero* (*Black Belly of the Tarantula*, 1971). Another exceptional *giallo* composer, Bruno Nicolai, conducted. (CD cover appears courtesy of Digitmovies Alternative Entertainment; graphic design by Claudio Fuiano.)

tional themes—those that speak to the vulnerability of the heroine and caring sensitivity of the hero—are as memorably melodic as any heard in the genre.

The same can be said of Nicolai's *The Night Evelyn Came Out of the Grave*. Although the title suggests a "living dead" flick, *Evelyn* is a traditional *giallo*, complete with mysterious killer, macabre killings and a greedy scheme to drive a character insane. According to Tim Lucas of VideoWatchdog.com, the *Evelyn* soundtrack is believed to be a collection of library cues by Nicolai and not an original score. In Lucas' booklet notes for the DigitMovies soundtrack CD of Bava's *Bay of Blood*, which also came out in 1971, the Nicolai tracks might have replaced a rejected score by Stelvio Cipriani, whose *Bay* includes "Evelyn's Theme." A bit more upbeat is Nicolai's theme ("Evelyn's Ghost Theme"), which breezes along on swelling strings, acoustic guitar, solo trumpet, a rolling bass line and Dell'Orso's vocalisms. Elsewhere, Nicolai provides perfectly disturbing atonal atmospheres with screeching violins, bizarre electronic accents and ominous bass notes. He also cooks up groovy dance floor psychedelia on "Funeral Striptease" and "I Get You." The former, in particular, is memorable for its despondent dirge-like intro that morphs into acid blues before launching into dance rock.

Stelvio Cipriani scores Bava's *Ecologia del delitto* (*Bay of Blood*, or *Twitch of the Death Nerve*, 1971), an especially gory multiple murderfest that paved the way for Hollywood slasher fare like *Friday the 13th*. In addition to the aforementioned "Evelyn's Theme," a lovely, melancholy piece for piano and orchestra, there are dance grooves ("Shake Giradischi"). There are also multiple variations of the theme, which is a slow groove with prominent Latin American percussion (such as the guiro), organ and string drones, and guitar, harpsichord or sax phrases. Whether or not the score was originally intended—in part or in its entirety—for *The Night Evelyn Came Out of the Grave*, critic Tim Lucas notes that the *Bay* score resembles Cipriani's music for José Ramón Larraz's horror flick *Deviation* (1971). "Whatever its exact origins, Cipriani's *Ecologie del delitto* is one of the very best Bava soundtracks—brutal, ironic and sensuous, like the film itself," Lucas wrote.

Also in 1971, Cipriani scored *L'iguana dalla lingua di fuoco* (*The Iguana with the Tongue of Fire*), another filmic exercise in bloody cruelty by Riccardo Freda, the father of Italian Gothic horror. While the film's title certainly ranks among the genre's most bizarre, the original poster image used on the cover of this soundtrack captures the iconic act of violence found in nearly every *giallo*: a straight razor held by a black-gloved hand cutting the throat of a beautiful woman. By all appearances *Iguana* is an archetypal Italian thriller, and Cipriani's sensuous and sinister score only confirms it. *Iguana* opens with a theme that—typical to the genre—describes the carefree existence and ultimate vulnerability of the story's leading lady. Gentle guitar and keyboard figures sprinkle over swaying strings, swooning female vocalisms (care of Nora Orlandi) and a sexy Latin rhythm, suggesting sunny days of shopping on the plaza and nights of passionate love by a crackling fire. What she doesn't know is that her life soon will become a nightmare of sinister strangers, drug-induced hallucinations, raging paranoia and knife-wielding maniacs. Like clockwork, the second track introduces the idea of imminent danger through intricate minor key lines, plodding bass notes and mysterious oboe that suddenly succumbs to Herrmann-esque strings that jab with knife-like precision. Then, on another cue, devious piano lines give way to shrieking echo-drenched strings

Stelvio Cipriani's score for *L'iguana dalla lingua di fuoco* (*The Iguana with the Tongue of Fire*, 1971) features passages of frantic action and psychedelic fear alongside lush reprieves of tenderness. (CD cover appears courtesy of Digitmovies Alternative Entertainment; graphic design by Claudio Fuiano.)

and distorted guitar stings. Naturally, it progresses from there into even darker territory, with fragmented passages of frantic action and psychedelic fear alongside lush reprieves of surprising tenderness.

Cipriani's score for Bava's *Gli orrori del castello di norimberga* (*The Horrors of Nuremberg Castle*, or *Baron Blood*, 1972) starts with a light-hearted pop instrumental of soaring strings, "la-la" female vocals, Latin percussion and flirty trumpet and saxophone. Again, it's hardly the tone one expects to hear at the start of a movie about a sadistic murderer from beyond the grave. But the score predictably descends into dark and eerie territory thanks to instrumentation that emphasizes distorted guitar and heavy percussion.

Like other Bava films, *Baron Blood*'s U.S. distribution relied on American International Pictures. Not satisfied with Cipriani's uneven score, AIP enlisted horror specialist Les Baxter to compose a mostly brass orchestral score for the North American release of *Baron Blood* that is gothic and stirring. Dominated by brass and percussion, Baxter's music also relies on a chiming keyboard theme, organ stabs and mysterious flute solos. Although Cipriani's score has its merits, Baxter's is more consistent in tone, "launching a superbly spooky aural tour of the Baron's dungeon, full of bubbling cauldrons and web-infested torture devices," as Lucas wrote in the Citadel CD notes.

Cipriani also scored *La morte cammina con i tacchi alti* (*Death Walks on High Heels*, 1971). Like many *giallo* scores, *Death Walks on High Heels* blends light romantic themes with tense moods of terror. Orlandi lends her sensual vocalisms to the romantic tracks that float along on a gentle beat, piano chords and strings. Again, this music represents the carefree women who will be stalked and killed by a black clad, razor-wielding maniac. The suspense tracks employ creepy organ tones, a web of 12-string acoustic guitar, spidery keyboard figures and unsettling percussion accents. Oddly, the most riveting track here, a five-minute dramatic climax, sounds more appropriate for a western. With pounding clockwork rhythm, electric guitar stings, jangly acoustic guitar and tense staccato strings, it is more in keeping with Cipriani's *Blindman*, a western he scored the same year.

Much more experimental is Morricone's *Il diavolo nel cervello* (*Devil in the Brain*, 1972). Having delivered hard-hitting music for Sergio Sollima's crime drama *Città violenta* (*Violent City*, 1970), Morricone provided more sensual and feminine music for the director's *Devil*. Woodwinds and harpsichord engage in call and response during passages of quiet contemplation. Strings and Dell'Orso's vocalisms float over a gentle rhythm during the lush passages. Even the atonal sections—as on the meditative "Prima della Rivelazione"—are lovely, with a keyboard and glockenspiel quoting repeatedly the opening notes of Beethoven's "Für Elise" alongside overlapping and spacious counter phrases played on strings and brass. Like ambient music innovator Brian Eno's deconstruction of Pachebel's "Canon in D Major" (on *Discreet Music*, 1975), Morricone's post-modern take on Beethoven's theme is simultaneously familiar and inaccessible. Notably, Morricone also adapted "Für Elise" for the final gunfight in *La resa dei cconti* (*The Big Gundown*, 1966).

Another gripping Morricone score from 1972 belongs to *Quattro mosche di velluto grigio* (*Four Flies on Grey Velvet*), the composer's third and final effort for Argento. Opening with a frantic psych rock title track, the soundtrack promises to turn into an acid freak out. Rock is a primary influence in the soundtrack, in part because the plot revolves around a drummer who is blackmailed for killing a stalker. Tracks featuring rock drums, throbbing electric

Ennio Morricone's rock-influenced score for *Quattro mosche di velluto grigio* (*Four Flies on Grey Velvet*, 1972) reflects the film's plot about a drummer who is blackmailed for killing a stalker. (CD cover appears courtesy of Cinevox Records; graphic design by Fredrika Cao.)

bass, distorted electric guitar and wailing Hammond organ pepper the soundtrack. In fact, Argento originally wanted to hire the then popular heavy rock band Deep Purple for the soundtrack, but the band was unavailable due to a U.S. concert tour. Despite the rock elements, Morricone never lets you forget that this is a *giallo* soundtrack, as dissonant strings, stabbing piano chords, electronic noise and Dell'Orso's panicked panting create an atmosphere of dread and uncertainty. Morricone also supplies an odd slow motion madrigal as well as a bit of calliope organ music.

Chi l'ha vista morire? (*Who Saw Her Die?* 1972) also features a Morricone score. Morricone subverts the perverse premise of schoolgirl abductions with a score dominated by a children's choir that sings sublime modern/medieval melodies. Occasionally the melodies are reinforced with a throbbing bass line and back beat, but the choir's contribution is persistent through tracks that range from celebratory to reverent to inscrutable.

One of Bruno Nicolai's best belongs to *Tutti i colori del buio* (*All the Colors of the Dark, Day of the Maniac,* or *Demons of the Dead,* 1972). Several tracks feature Dell'Orso's softly erotic vocalism, including the theme ("Magico Incontro"), an entrancing melody played on oboe over lush strings, reverb guitar, chiming xylophone and a simple beat. The track repeats several times. Other cuts feature Alessandroni's chorus and his adept sitar playing. There are plenty of dissonant, skin-crawling pizzicato string passages, fraught with electronic textures and screeching violin stabs against aggressive piano and bass patterns. Some of the best are versions of "Insidia," where jazz drums kick up the tension while fuzz guitar, piano and harpsichord repeat a diabolically angular riff.

Nicolai was clearly on a roll with the genre and delivered another fascinating score for *La dame rossa uccide sette volte* (*Red Queen Kills Seven Times,* or *The Corpse Which Didn't Want to Die,* 1972). Starting with a little girl's solo voice, the theme unfolds like a nursery rhyme or folk melody played on harpsichord and guitar, with pop orchestra supplying a lift. It is yet another paradoxical example of a lovely, feminine melody for a brutally bloody film where violence against scantily clad women is a part of its entertainment value. Another winsome track is "In Automobile," a bossa nova that expresses sunny seaside drives. The suspenseful material also is top flight. Nicolai uses strings to create a veneer of tension, as lone instruments (harp, harpsichord, etc.) sound out figurative "bumps in the night." During the second half, a rock sensibility creeps into the rhythm section; frantic cymbals accompany insistent drums, forceful bass and the metallic texture of a jaggedly strummed electric guitar, while fast arpeggios race across this uneasy surface. This approach serves several tracks as the plot clearly reaches its climax. This is Nicolai at his most frantic, but even when he slows the orchestra and stops the rhythm section he never loses sight of the suspense.

Nicolai also scored *Perche' quelle strane gocce di sangue sul corpo di Jennifer* (*The Case of the Bloody Iris,* or *What Are Those Strange Drops of Blood Doing on Jennifer's Body,* 1972). The composer provides another drop-dead gorgeous theme using soaring strings, with countermelody played by harpsichord and xylophone. Naturally, *Bloody Iris* also has its fair share of suspenseful moods and tension builders where strings groan alongside hypnotic harp and harpsichord arpeggios backed by jazzy cymbal work, throbbing bass, guitar and piano underpinning. Nicolai delivers the thrills and chills like a virtuoso. He is easily Morricone's equal when it comes to *giallo,* yet he is comparatively neglected when it comes to CD retrospectives.

Gianni Ferrio's score for *La morte accarezza a mezzonotte* (*Death Walks at Midnight*, 1973) is a fine example of the *giallo* tradition, offering sensual themes, groovy nightclub numbers and suspenseful passages. (CD cover appears courtesy of Easy Tempo Records [ET902]; graphic design by Giulio "Jazzy Jules" Maini.)

Ferrio's exquisite *La morte accarezza a mezzonotte* (*Death Walks at Midnight*, 1973) features a breathy wordless vocal by period pop singer Mina on the sad and lovely tune "Valentina." More intriguing is the title track that rumbles forth on a thick bass line with Alessandroni's choir countering brass, woodwinds, organ and restless percussion that suggests criminal activity is afoot. Other themes provide a lighter party mood. Three takes of "Amanda Blues," with its Hammond organ solo and jazz guitar solo, calls forth a groovy striptease nightclub mood. "Ira Rhythm and Blues" is sassier yet, with brash brass blowing over trilling piano blue notes, followed by more note strangling on a Hammond. Last but not least is "Oliver Rhythm and Blues," featuring call and response brass, followed by piano and flute solos.

Morricone scored *Spasmo* (*The Death Dealer*, 1974), a surreal thriller with delightfully daft dialogue ("I have a razor in my room—big, sharp and sexy"). The music, which Nicolai conducted, favors heavy moods dominated by screeching strings and turgid pipe organ. Occasionally, Alessandroni's delicate acoustic guitar and chorus provides a respite from the insanity. *Spasmo*'s centerpiece is "Stress Infinito," a masterful slab of experimental suspense music. Dissonance and discord lead to disorientation in this diabolically designed labyrinth of despair. If that sentence seems overwrought you can blame it on the music, which is impressively single-minded in its mission to undermine sanity wherever it may be sequestered. At the onset of "Stress Infinito" Morricone summons jarring electronic sound effects that pierce the writhing orchestral discord before setting down a simple beat offset by angular bass and keyboard lines. Eventually the volume and tempo verge on hard rock, but in the least conventional sense possible. Easy listening it is not, but it also makes a lot of *giallo* music sound easygoing by comparison.

In 1973, Nicolai scored *Una vergine tra i morti viventi* (*A Virgin Among the Living Dead*, or *Christine—The Princess of Eroticism*, or *Zombi 4*, among other titles). Echoing harps crawl up the backside, screeching violins cut across the ears, forlorn voices (Dell'Orso, of course) haunt the thoughts, and electronic dissonance sears the brain. Nicolai also knows how to get a groove on— albeit a sinister groove where throbbing bass and funky drums are accosted by organ drones, piano calamity and relentless electronic disturbances. But not all is dark and sinister on *A Virgin*. There is a jaunty solo piano number, and Dell'Orso lends her sweet voice to an elegant orchestral bossa nova.

Everyone's favorite German cult movie star, Klaus Kinski, made his fair share of Italian horror movies. Among them are *La morte ha sorriso all'assassino* (*Death Smiled at Murder*, 1973), *La mano che nutre la morte* (*The Hand That Feeds the Dead*, 1974) and *Le amanti del mostro* (*Love of the Monster*, 1974), with scores by Berto Pisano (*Death Smiled*), and Stafano Liberati and Elio Maestosi (*The Hand* and *Love of the Monster*).

Pisano's *Death Smiled* opens with rattling percussion, electric guitar stings and eerie electronics. It's an effective way to start a horror movie, but there's more to the music than creepy atmospherics. Featuring strings, harpsichord, muted brass, lightly plucked acoustic guitar and Dell'Orso's lovely voice, Pisano's theme for the film is romantic and sad. The use of harpsichord befits the film's Victorian setting. Elsewhere, Pisano creates a mysterious, macabre atmosphere through the dissonant overlapping of fragmented melodic lines. *Death Smiled* isn't immediately gratifying as a listening experience—there aren't any big hook melodies—but it quite successfully captures the creepy decay of gothic horror.

Like Pisano's *Death Smiled*, Liberati and Maestosi's scores for *The Hand*

and *Love of the Monster* favor strings, harp, woodwinds and muted brass, befitting the gothic horror genre. The compositions are refined and delicate, evoking bouquets of shriveled flowers in gloomy parlors where dust hangs in the air like pestilence. Both films were shot at the same time, with the same cast and crew at the same locations, and the scores are nearly indistinguishable, and even share cues, such as "La Bambola di Vetro" and "Il Diario." Nonetheless, they elicit the macabre realm where tragic romance has taken a turn for the terrible.

An Italian horror soundtrack that wears its rock (and soul) influences in a more accessible manner is Franco Micalizzi's *Chi Sei?* (*Beyond the Door*, 1974), a film that brazenly rips off *The Exorcist* (1973) and *Rosemary's Baby* (1968). The theme song, "Bargain with the Devil," features soul singer Warren Wilson. With its sax solos, rock solid beats, busy drums, funky Rhodes keyboard and high synthesizer lines, the score is reminiscent of a blaxploitation soundtrack. By that standard it's outstanding, but as a horror soundtrack it fails to generate much suspense or inspire fear.

The Italian-Spanish co-production *No profanar el sueño de los muertos* (*The Living Dead at the Manchester Morgue*, or *Zombi 3*, or *Let Sleeping Corpses Lie*, 1974) sports an accessible score by Giuliano Sorgini. It begins with "John Dalton Street," an action theme featuring a spare, rock-influenced arrangement driven by crackerjack drumming, tympani rolls, rumbling bass line and shuddering string patterns. "Surreal" slows down the pace with an ominous woodwind line accompanied by groaning and moaning male and female voices, followed by a spacey organ texture that conjures a supernatural mood. Maniacal laughter and musical moaning dominate "Trance," and wind effects open "The Raised Dead." The rock instrumentation and creepy sound effects anticipate the zombie and cannibal soundtrack style that dominated Italian horror at the end of the decade. The otherworldly sounds on the most abstract cues ("The Death of the Dead" and "The Torment of the Dead") complement the film's supernatural element.

The rock influence also staked a place in *giallo* pictures beginning with Argento's genre masterpiece *Profundo rosso* (*Deep Red*, 1975), featuring music by Italian progressive rock band Goblin, and additional scoring by Giorgio Gaslini. The original release of the soundtrack on LP sold millions of copies, making it one of the best selling Italian horror soundtracks of all time. The director allegedly brought Goblin on board after a creative conflict with Gaslini. While the Gaslini tracks add plot-specific details, like the child singing the lullaby, it was Goblin's hard rock instrumentals that gave the film a modern touch and laid the groundwork for the band's other collaborations with Argento.

In an interview with *Fangoria* magazine (#127), keyboardist Claudio Simonetti described the band's trepidation going into the studio for the film. "At first we were caught off balance by Dario's interest in our music. He was

Franco Micalizzi's score for *Chi sei?* (*Beyond the Door*, 1974) is reminiscent of blaxploitation soundtracks. (CD cover appears courtesy of CAM Original Soundtracks; graphic designer unknown.)

a very hot name then and, of course, we were tremendously nervous. Hell, we had no idea how to score a film. *Deep Red* was a real challenge for us."

Guitarist Massimo Morante added that one of the challenges stemmed directly from Gaslini's rejected score. "Our musical approach was totally different, mostly because we had to interpret Giorgio's original score which had a jazz component that Dario didn't like much," he told *Fangoria* (#127).

In fact, up until their involvement with Argento, the band was known as Cherry Five, but changed it to Goblin for the *Deep Red* project.

The group's theme, which reached number one on the Italian charts, snatches the bass line from "Tubular Bells." In turn, Goblin's theme arguably influenced filmmaker/composer John Carpenter's soundtracks. The theme has been remixed for the dance floor as well.

Other outstanding tracks from *Deep Red* include "Death Dies," a frantic rhythmic exercise with funky drumming, jazzy piano and an angular guitar line; "Mad Puppet," a tense, atmospheric number built around a hypnotic guitar ostinato; and a plethora of variations on the theme of "Death Dies." Gaslini's contributions are numerous and often times resemble the Goblin tracks (particularly on the rock-oriented "Deep Shadows"). The composer also contributes the lullaby-like "School at Night," and the gentle and old-fashioned "Gianna." It remains one of the strongest and diverse Argento soundtracks.

Though *Deep Red* established Goblin as a horror soundtrack powerhouse, Argento's *Suspiria* (1977) remains their most focused and effective horror soundtrack, fittingly for the director's most innovative film. Like the film, it is a masterpiece of the genre. The hypnotic and sinister theme (clearly inspired by "Tubular Bells") uses celesta and bell sounds, along with synthesizer, organ, guitar, bass, drums and percussion, to create a spellbinding whirlwind of

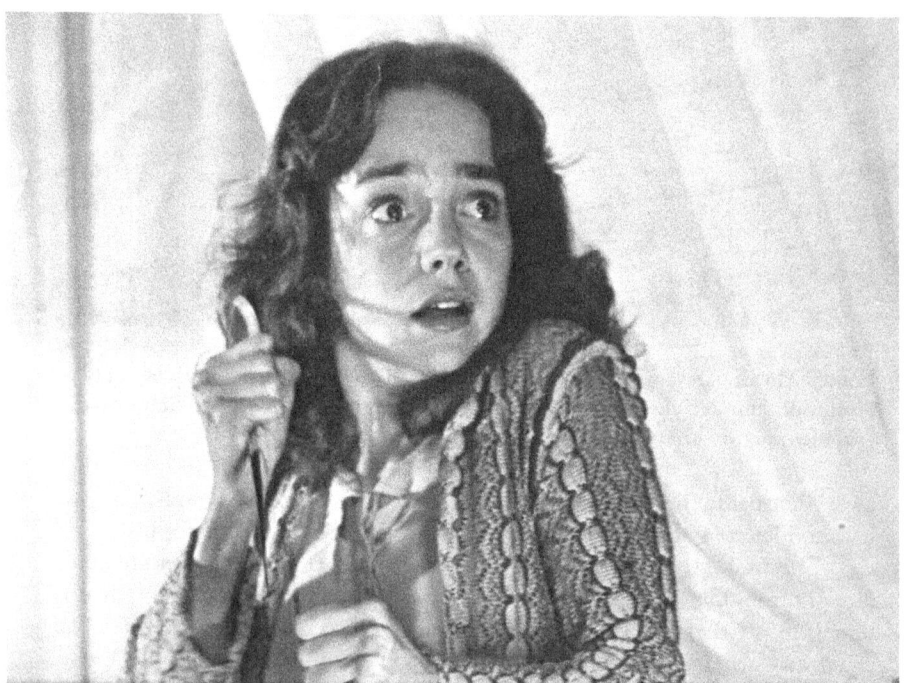

Goblin's *Exorcist*-inspired score for *Suspiria* (Seda Spettacoli, 1977), starring Jessica Harper, ratchets up the terror.

demonic rock. Further enveloping the listener in a hellish atmosphere throughout the score are the wheezing, wailing, screaming, groaning voices of the band members, sounding like evil spirits echoing up from the pits of hell. Most of the tracks use repetitive trancelike patterns overlaid with distorted free-form vocalisms to create a persistent atmosphere of fear and loathing that reinforces the plot concerning witches and curses. Like *Deep Red*'s theme, *Suspiria*'s theme has inspired a dance remix as well.

While *Suspiria* is not only a favorite with fans and critics, it also rates highly with the band members. Ironically, Morante also told *Fangoria* that he prefers Argento's earlier thrillers (like *Bird*, *Flies* and *Cat*) over the director's later, more violent fare. "He's gone a bit too far with the violence," Morante said.

After *Suspiria*, Goblin scored the crime thriller *La via della droga* (1977) and recorded a Kafka-inspired concept album, *Il fantastico viaggio del "Bagarozzo" Mark* (*The Fantastic Journey of "Beetle" Mark*, 1978), before scoring George Romero's *Dawn of the Dead* (*Zombi*, 1978), a U.S./Italian co-produced sequel to Romero's classic *Night of the Living Dead* (1968). The group continued to work the sinister prog rock style with aplomb, but instead of a *Suspiria*-like focus the band experimented with different sounds. *Zombi* boasts a dirge-like prologue ("L'alba dei Morti Viventi"), frenetic "news at 11" theme music, tribal drum chant ("Safari"), ragtime ("Torte in Faccia"), disco metal ("Zaratozom"), synth pop ("La Caccia"), country folk ("Tirassegno"), smoky jazz-rock balladry ("Oblio"), classically inspired solo piano ("Risveglio"), lounge jazz ("Zombi [Sexy]"), Tangerine Dream–style synth atmospheres ("Al Margini Della Follia" and alternates) and funky easy listening ("Zombi [Supermarket]"). While the overall effect is less intense or singularly brilliant as *Suspiria*, and few of the tracks live up to the standout cuts on *Deep Red*, the *Zombi* score shows Goblin's range.

Habitual Italian soundtrack recycler Quentin Tarantino used Bixio-Frizzi-Tempera's theme from *Sette Note In Nero* (*Seven Notes in Black*, or *The Psychic*, 1977) in *Kill Bill—Volume One* (2003). Indeed, the theme is well worth resurrection. It features a hypnotic ostinato played on carillon (tuned bells sounded by hammers controlled by a keyboard), accompanied by sighing strings, low synth and piano tones. It's simple, elegant and gravely beautiful. Arguably, it's Bixio-Frizzi-Tempera's greatest theme. Much of the score follows suit, with variations on the theme as well as similar cues that rely on slow, spacious moods full of tension and eerie dread ("Suicidio" and "Strane Visioni," for instance). Occasionally, throbbing bass and conga rhythms accompany the synth drones. The epilogue theme briefly flirts with rock. The only track that really breaks the mood comes early—the soft pop English-language ballad "With You," sung by Linda Lee. Unlike a lot of *giallo* scores, *Seven Notes in Black* generally steers clear of rampant atonality and shrieking strings. The score is relatively understated on the horror angle, but its subtly unnerving tone is well suited to the film's supernatural element.

Dawn of the Dead, a.k.a. *Zombi* (UFDC/Laurel Group, 1978), features music by Goblin that lends itself to the film's ironic subtext about people being mindless consumers. (Photograph courtesy of the John Monaghan Collection.)

Stelvio Cipriani's *Solamento nero* (*The Bloodstained Shadow*, 1978) has the rock influence (synths, guitars, rock drumming, electric bass), but the methods are experimental and darkly aggressive. If it sounds like Goblin there is good reason for it. According to an interview with the director on the movie DVD, Goblin was originally slated to score the picture, but due to a contractual disagreement Cipriani was enlisted to write music that Goblin in turn arranged and performed. That makes *Bloodstained Shadow* an unofficial Goblin soundtrack.

Occult horror—satanic orgies and séances—was a popular sub-genre during the late '70s in Italy. One of the less famous entries is *Un' ombra nell' ombra* (*Ring of Darkness*, 1979). It features an entrancing electronic rock score by Cipriani. By the late '70s film composers were increasingly using the era's advances in synthesizer technology to their advantage, allowing them to create densely layered music without hiring an orchestra. Again, there is a Cipriani-Goblin connection, as the composer hired Goblin's keyboardist, Claudio Simonetti, to perform on this standout example of the era's electronic horror scores.

By the late '70s, *gialli* went out of fashion and gothic horror was old hat.

Thanks in part to the international success of *Dawn of the Dead* (*Zombi*, 1978), the hot sub-genre was cannibal horror. Two examples are *Zombi 2* (*Zombie*, or *Zombie Flesheaters*, 1979), featuring a score by Fabio Frizzi and Giorio Cascio, and Ruggero Deodato's *Cannibal Holocaust* (1979), with music by Riz Ortolani.

While Frizzi and Cascio's keyboard-dominated *Zombi 2* occasionally hits the right nerve with frenzied electronic rhythms, tribal percussion, looped moans and screams, it proves inconsistent.

Ortolani's *Cannibal Holocaust* is by turns gently folksy (theme and "Love with Fun"), perversely beautiful ("Adulteress' Punishment"), cheekily funky ("Cameramen's Recreation" and "Relaxing in the Savana"), tense ("Massacre of the Troupe" and "Savage Rite"), achingly lovely ("Crucified Woman") and sexy ("Drinking Coco"). Ortolani frequently uses a synth sound that will remind more than a few listeners of vintage video games. The sound, used as an accent, adds a perverse cruelty to several tracks.

By the end of the decade horror scores were increasingly rock-influenced, with synthesizers often taking the place of traditional orchestration. With its most experimental years behind it, the genre became more formulaic and arguably less interesting.

12 Essential Horror and Suspense Soundtracks

Dracula (1958) — James Bernard
Vertigo (1958) / *Psycho* (1960) — Bernard Herrmann
Cape Fear (1962) — Bernard Herrmann
Rosemary's Baby (1968) — Krzysztof Komeda
The Bird with the Crystal Plumage (1970) — Ennio Morricone
La coda dello scorpione (1971) — Bruno Nicolai
Blood on Satan's Claw (1971) — Marc Wilkinson
Deep Red (1975) — Goblin and Giorgio Gaslini
Jaws (1975) — John Williams
The Omen (1976) — Jerry Goldsmith
Suspiria (1977) — Goblin
The Amityville Horror (1979) — Lalo Schifrin

Chapter 7

Rockin' Revolution

Rock 'n' roll rumbled into cinemas shortly after erupting onto the popular music scene in the '50s. By most accounts, *Rock Around the Clock* (1956), featuring Bill Haley & the Comets, was the first rock movie. The prototype for it came a decade earlier in *Beware* (1946) and *Look Out Sister* (1948), featuring rhythm 'n' blues legend and proto rocker Louis Jordan. Since those early shots in the rock revolution, the sound and fury of post-war youth culture has infused countless films with a rebellious attitude and sexually charged energy.

Perhaps the most obvious rock movies are those that showcase recording artists. Elvis Presley and the Beatles are the most famous examples, though artists as wide ranging as Chuck Berry, Bob Dylan, the Ramones and Frank Zappa have electrified the silver screen.

Movies starring rock stars typically fit into one of a few categories. In one type, the rock star plays a character similar to his public persona (e.g. Elvis as Vince Everett in *Jailhouse Rock*, 1957). Or, the rocker appears as himself in loosely linked vignettes, including musical performances (e.g. the Beatles in *A Hard Day's Night*, 1964, and *Help!* 1965). The rocker might appear in concert (e.g. the Rolling Stones in *Gimme Shelter*, 1970). Or, in an effort to break out of the "rock ghetto," rockers take dramatic roles that allow them to "stretch" (e.g. David Bowie as Thomas Jerome Newton in *The Man Who Fell to Earth*, 1976).

Naturally, the rock star that made the most movies was none other than "the King." Elvis Presley starred in 31 features playing characters that, while not all officially musicians, often display a musical side. These roles rarely required Elvis to "stretch" a great deal. From Clint Reno in *Love Me Tender* (1956) to Dr. John Carpenter in *Change of Habit* (1969), Elvis' onscreen personas typically hook up with a girl, overcome a few pesky conflicts and sing a few songs along the way. The King didn't win any awards for acting, but his fans were happy just to see their larger-than-life idol on the big screen. Despite the disposability of most Elvis movies, his loyal fans made him one of the few rock stars to become a bankable movie star.

Over the decades, the rock star as movie actor formula has achieved occasional critical kudos as well as box office prosperity. With the exception of Elvis and a handful of pop singers and rappers, however, musicians rarely endure as

Gimme Shelter (Maysles Films, 1970), starring Mick Jagger and Keith Richards, captures the tragic moment when lethal violence erupted during the Rolling Stones' performance of "Sympathy for the Devil" at Altamont Speedway in California. (Photograph courtesy of the John Monaghan Collection.)

onscreen talents. The key is believability, and the closer the onscreen persona is to the music persona the better.

Naturally, films that capture rock stars as themselves, doing what they do best, are often highly appealing. During the late '60s and especially during the '70s concert films were in vogue for rockers seeking big-screen cachet (and filmmakers seeking rock and roll notoriety). The early entries include *Monterey Pop* (1968), starring Jefferson Airplane, Jimi Hendrix and many others; the notorious *Gimme Shelter* (1970), with the Rolling Stones; the landmark *Woodstock* (1970), starring the Who, Santana and others; and the copycat *Wattstax* (1972), with Isaac Hayes, the Staples Singers and others. After the Beatles rockumentary *Let It Be* (1970), George and Ringo performed alongside Bob Dylan, Eric Clapton and others in *The Concert for Bangladesh* (1972). Then, the uninspired *Ziggy Stardust and the Spiders from Mars*, starring David Bowie, arrived—first as a truncated TV special in 1974 and later as a full-blown concert film in 1983. The most famous concert film of the decade is *The Song Remains the Same* (1976), starring Led Zeppelin, but *The Last Waltz* (1978), starring the Band, among others, received greater accolades. Most of the pre–MTV concert films look laughably dated now, due in part to relatively staid editing and the requisite audience shots; and since the birth of MTV and home video, the need for concert films has significantly diminished. Of the concert film soundtracks, perhaps *Woodstock* and *Wattstax* are the most essential, because they capture not only concerts but also the zeitgeist—the "soundtrack" of the era.

A sub-genre of the concert film is the so-called "rockumentary" that mixes interviews and other non-performance footage with in-studio rehearsals and isolated song performances. *A Hard Day's Night* and *Help!* are influential examples, as is *Don't Look Back* (1967), with Bob Dylan. *Head* (1968), starring the Monkees, takes the loopiness of the Beatles movies to absurd lengths. Maverick musician Frank Zappa made the zany rockumentary *200 Motels* (1971). *The Kids Are Alright* (1979) captures the Who on stage and off. The sub-genre even has notable parodies, including *The Rutles* (1979), a Beatles parody. Later, *This Is Spinal Tap* (1984) defined rock parodies for a new age of filmmaking.

Occasionally, rock musicians have used the big screen (and even the small screen) as a canvas for conceptual works. The Beatles directed themselves in the made-for-television psychedelic road picture *Magical Mystery Tour* (1967), but it's a poor example compared to the cinematic works of the Who. Pete Townsend's band brought two rock operas to the screen, the over-the-top *Tommy* (1975) and the mods-versus-rockers epic *Quadrophenia* (1979). Pink Floyd's monumental double album *The Wall* (1979) became an instant midnight movie classic in 1982.

Naturally, the soundtracks for such films favor the songs featured in the movies, and sometimes add non-movie songs deemed appropriate for the audience. If the film features additional underscore it is rarely heard on the soundtrack release.

That said, it is doubtful that any music fan actually thinks of an album like *Help!* as a soundtrack. Surely, only in the official sense. It's an album of Beatles songs to most who know it. And *The Song Remains the Same*? Technically a soundtrack, but if you're honest it's a mediocre Led Zeppelin concert album. And *Tommy* and *The Wall*? More like glorified concept albums, which is how they originated.

So, where does that leave this "rock 'n' roll" chapter—up Soundtrack Creek without a guitar? Absolutely not. In fact, there are a great number of rockin' movies that don't always rely on big name rock stars for their appeal, but still have the sound and fury. The inherent riotousness of the music has provided numerous rebel-themed movies featuring motorcyclists, hot-rodders, surfers, skateboarders, hippies and druggies with an outlaw sound.

Rebels and Rockers, Hoods and Hippies

Since the birth of rock 'n' roll there have been movies that depict rebellious youth and the music that drives them wild. A film of social consciousness such as *The Blackboard Jungle* (1955) examines the rise of juvenile delinquency and disaffected youth. Flicks such as *Rock Around the Clock* (1956) focus on the raucous appeal of the music. Both movies feature Bill Haley & the Comets' eponymous hit, though, ironically, *The Blackboard Jungle* used it first. Legend has it that the movie's producer selected the song from a stack of records owned by the young son of lead actor Glenn Ford. Originally recorded in 1954, the song was one of the first successful attempts to transform black rhythm 'n' blues into something marketable to young white record buyers.

The tune is heard three times in the musical *Rock Around the Clock* (1956), but, oddly, never as a full-blown performance number. A major box office success, the film co-stars the Platters and legendary radio disc jockey and rock champion Alan Freed. Aside from inspiring a slew of copy-cat pictures like *Twist Around the Clock* (1961), starring Chubby Checker, it also spawned a shoddy sequel from the same director and producer, called *Don't Knock the Rock* (1956), that also stars Haley & the Comets. Although its original release failed to climb higher than 33 on the charts, the song re-charted several times, like when George Lucas used it as the theme for *American Graffiti* (1973). Another version recorded by Haley was used as the theme for the first season of the *Graffiti*-inspired sitcom *Happy Days* (1974–1984).

In the wake of *Rock Around the Clock* were numerous mid-1950s films that banked on the box office appeal of rock and played up the rock content in the title. One such flick is *Rock, Pretty Baby* (1956), about aspiring rock musicians. The soundtrack features Bill Haley's "The Saints Rock 'n' Roll," alongside tunes by Sonny Burke and Rod McKuen, who later achieved considerable fame as a popular poet of the '60s. Most of the music is by Henry Mancini, who was on the verge of fame himself with his theme for the hit TV show *Peter Gunn* (1958–1961). Mancini takes a shot at rough and raucous on the rock numbers, but the sound is rooted in big band swing. Some hot tracks include "Rockin' the Boogie," "Juke Box Rock," "Teenage Pop"

Bill Haley & the Comets' hit "Rock Around the Clock" first appeared in *The Blackboard Jungle* (1955), then in *Rock Around the Clock* (1956), and later in *American Graffiti* (1973) and TV's *Happy Days* (1974–1984).

and "Hot Rod." He also lays down smoky rhythm 'n' blues on "Dark Blue," and lounge jazz on "Free and Easy" and "Young Love."

Mancini (and McKuen) also worked on *Baby*'s sequel, *Summer Love* (1958), this one set at a summer camp. Mancini wrote rockin' tunes with lyricist Bill Carey, including the theme song sung by Kip Tyler. Full of no-nonsense drums, smoldering sax solos, slightly bent guitar solos and the familiar ding-ding-ding of early rock piano, numbers like "Night Walk," "Beatin' on the Bongos" and "Boppin' at the Bash" get toes a-tappin'.

Some films of the era, like *The Girl Can't Help It*, starring Jayne Mansfield, present a broad range of musical styles that includes rock. In the film, popular rock acts perform (Little Richard, Fats Domino) back to back with lounge pop singers (Julie London) and big band leaders (Ray Anthony). Lionel Newman and Leigh Harline provided the underscore.

The same is true of Jack Arnold's *High School Confidential* (1958), which features opening and closing onscreen performances by Jerry Lee Lewis of the title track, which the fiery piano-banging rocker composed. The single reached 21 on the chart, but took a nosedive when Lewis married his 13-year-old cousin.

The loose sequel, *College Confidential* (1960), fittingly features a jazz soundtrack, because jazz was popular with college audiences at the time. The leader is Dean Elliott, who also worked on *Sex Kittens Go to College* (1960) and is famous for his space age pop album *Zounds! What Sounds?* (1963). *College Confidential*'s style is close to the crime jazz of Mancini or Bernstein on the title track and "Wild Ride." Several tracks feature a distinctive, percussively picked guitar motif.

Bikers and Other Motor Heads

Nothing says "rebel" like a leather jacket, and no one looks more rebellious in leather than a man or woman on a motorcycle. A leather-clad malcontent—fists forward, gripping handle bars, revving an exhaust that growls like a metallic pit bull—is rock at its most ornery and non-conformist.

The seminal biker flick is *The Wild One* (1953), in which the Black Rebels gang rumbles into all–American Wrightsville to terrorize the locals and face off against a rival gang. Composer Leith Stevens delivered the score, which isn't rock but hard-swinging big band jazz. The propulsive sound of motorcycle tailpipes opens the fast and free-flowing theme. Led by Rogers on trumpet, the band's horns converse eloquently in time to a Latinesque cymbal ride. "Black Rebel's Ride" is a boisterous track, full of crashing drum fills and argumentative horn blasts. "Prelude to a Rumble" is ruminative and bleak. "Drag for Beers" captures the rambunctious energy of thrill-seeking free spirits trying to intimidate each other. The aptly titled "Scramble" finds the brass going blow for hard-won blow with saxophones over a brisk tempo. While the film lacks pure rock music, it provided a template for the biker flicks to come.

It took four years for another biker flick to hit the drive-in circuit. American International Pictures (AIP), which went on to release a number of biker flicks, released *The Motorcycle Gang* (1957), featuring a score by Albert Glasser.

The next stab at the genre came from Russ Meyer, a former Playboy photographer turned exploitation filmmaker. Meyer made *Motor Psycho* (a.k.a. *Motor Mods and Rockers*, 1965) the same year he made his bitches-on-wheels masterpiece, *Faster Pussycat Kill! Kill!* If *The Wild One* provided the basic blueprint for the biker flicks that hit theaters during the late '60s and early '70s, *Motor Psycho* refined it for the Vietnam era with a rip-roaring story about three crazed bik-

The motorcycle revving on the main theme of *The Wild One* (Columbia, 1953), starring Marlon Brando, is a thoroughly modern soundtrack moment.

ers who brazenly rape and assault before getting their just desserts at the hands of their victims. Bert Shefter and Paul Sawtell's beat jazz score is one of their best. Shefter and Sawtell worked together frequently during the '60s, but rarely worked the jazz vein as well as they do here. The theme, "The Three Weirdos," with its motorcycle sounds, pulsing organ and acid-fried lead guitar, is pure rockin' biker movie bliss.

The real biker flick phenomenon began in earnest a year later with *The Wild Angels* (1966), starring genre icon Peter Fonda. With the tagline "their credo is violence and their god is hate," *Wild Angels* boasts most of the elements that turn up in the slew of copycat pictures that followed it: "authentic" members of the Hell's Angels, violence, rape, clashes with "the man," and an incendiary rock soundtrack. Produced by Mike Curb, *Wild Angels* is a showcase for the instrumental rock group Davie Allan & the Arrows (Bruce Wagner on bass guitar and David Winogrond on drums). Curb and the group worked together previously on the skateboard flick *Skaterdater* (1966) and continued to collaborate on several soundtracks; often times Curb gave the band a different name to create the illusion of having multiple groups in his stable.

Russ Meyer's *Faster Pussycat, Kill! KILL!* (Eve Productions, 1965), starring (rear to front) Haji, Lori Williams and Tura Satana, features raucous music worthy of the sleazy onscreen action.

On *Wild Angels*, Allan's snarling fuzz-toned guitar made the hard-driving "Blue's Theme" a Top-40 hit single—the group's biggest hit and a favorite of '60s instrumental rock compilers. The soundtrack also sold exceptionally well, reaching the Top 20 on the Billboard chart. The other seven tracks performed by the group range from the psychedelic drum workout "The Chase," the rambunctious blues number "Bongo Party," the upbeat and boisterous

The rock soundtrack for *The Wild Angels* (MGM/AIP, 1966), starring Peter Fonda (with guitar, right) and Nancy Sinatra (standing left), features plenty of rebellious fuzz-tone guitars. (Photograph courtesy of the John Monaghan Collection.)

theme, the go-go number "Rockin' Angel," the South-of-the-Border ballad "The Lonely Rider," the surf rock slide guitar showcase "The Unknown Rider" and a funeral dirge version of the theme.

At the center of it all was Curb—a songwriter, record producer, label owner and ultimately ironic figure in the biker and counterculture movie genres. A first-flush Baby Boomer (born in 1945), Curb went from college dropout to record label owner and cultural conservative, snagging the top job at MGM Records, where he proceeded to clean house. He cut druggie groups like the Velvet Underground in favor of family fare like the Osmonds. Eventually, Curb got into politics, becoming a major player among California's Republican elite. He rose to lieutenant governor of California in 1978 and acting governor for a year in the early '80s. What's fascinating about Curb is his seemingly contradictory role as a creative sparkplug in California's counterculture movement of the late '60s. *Wild Angels* was only one of numerous rock soundtracks—from *Angels from Hell* to *Zabriskie Point*—that bear his name and influence.

Curb and his maleable studio band followed up *Wild Angels* with *Devil's*

Angels (1967). Curb collaborated with Jerry Steiner (aka Jerry Styner) and Guy Hemric on the fuzz guitar anthem of a theme song. The Arrows delivered more raucous, rip-roaring rock. The freaked-out fuzz guitar and rumbling drums on "The Devil's Rumble" are more threatening than anything on *The Wild Angels*. Other highlights include the catchy "Cody's Theme," the anthem-like "Hell Rider," the free-wheeling stomper "Hole in the Wall," the Farfisa-driven "Devil's Carnival," and the psychedelic abstraction "The Ghost Story."

An even better biker soundtrack comes from *Hell's Angels on Wheels* (1967), which stars authentic Hell's Angels. The soundtrack boasts greater musical variety than usually found in biker flicks, thanks to Stu Phillips' flexibility as a writer and arranger. The theme pits shards of metallic guitar bursts and a heavy rock beat with catchy wordless pop vocals. It's biker rock at its most potently addictive. Next up is the languid sitar psychedelia of "Flowers" (which is also featured in *Finders Keepers, Lovers Weepers*, 1968). Another highlight is "Skip to My Mary J," which whips up more blistering fuzz-toned guitar against a pounding beat and spirited piano rhythm. The rollicking "Tea Party" picks up where the theme left off with "ba-ba-ba" pop vocals, but with a fresh melody. The similar "Sunday Arts and Football" adds sitar to the mix. "Poet" is haunting psychedelia featuring harpsichord, piano and reverb-effected guitar. With its sly walking bass line and vibes, "Poet Scores" is one of two jazzy tracks here, but still sounds psychedelic thanks to solo flute and "baroque" harpsichord. The other jazz number is "Four, Five, Sex," which wouldn't sound out of place in a French crime film of the same era. For sheer variety from a single composer, *Hells Angels on Wheels* is arguably the strongest of the '60s biker soundtracks.

"[Director Richard] Rush hated everything I wrote," Phillips noted in his autobiography *Stu Who?* (Cisum Press, 2003). "But fortunately for me, [producer] Joe [Solomon] liked the score.... [The movie] was quite raunchy.... I've scored worse, and I've scored better." (p. 170)

Phillips went on to score other biker flicks (*Angels from Hell*, 1968; *Run, Angel, Run*, 1969; and *The Losers*, 1970), as well as surf movies (*Follow Me*, 1969; and *Ride the Wild Surf*, 1964). He is best known for scoring *Beyond the Valley of the Dolls* and *Buck Rogers in the 25th Century* (1978), as well as the original *Battlestar Galactica* TV series (1978–1979).

Curb continued to be the most prolific musician associated with biker flicks. Around the time of *Devil's Angels*, Curb again hooked up with an uncredited Arrows (billed as the Sidewalk Sounds) for *Born Losers* (1967), a film that introduced director Tom Laughlin's politically charged character Billy Jack. The theme has a western flare, complete with mariachi-type brass. "The Born Loser's Theme" kicks into high gear like a buzz saw on a rampage. "The Loser's Bar" trades fuzz tone for echoing, chiming, reverb-laden slide guitar. Terry Stafford, an Elvis sound-alike, steps up to the microphone for "Forgive Me," a '50s style rock ballad. He later delivers "Alone, Never to Love Again," which is basically a vocal version of "Billy Jack's Theme." Sidewalk Sounds rumble through with "Gangrene's Fight." "Born Loser's Stripper" is a slow and raunchy striptease number. Legendary percussionist Hal Blaine is another featured performer.

The Sidewalk Sounds also contributed to *The Glory Stompers* (1968). The Moogy pop number "Mouth" and the soft, sentimental, string-laden "Casey's Theme" are so different from one another that it is hard to believe that the same musicians were used. (Perhaps Curb was up to his old creative attribution again.) Both of those tracks are named for a character played by American Top 40 legend Casey Kasem, who also served as the film's producer. In addition, "Black Souls" is an unintentionally funny spoken word showcase for Kasem, who was well used during subsequent years as voice-over talent for Saturday morning cartoons. The Arrows kick up the dust with the haunted funhouse romp "The Stompers and the Souls" and a handful of similar tracks, including the theme. Another bogus sounding contributor is Eddie & the Stompers, who are undoubtedly the Arrows again. Max Frost & the Troopers (featuring members of the Arrows) also is featured. The latter group is best known for its Top 40 hit "Shape of Things to Come," which Target stores later used in a TV advertisement. Here they provide a catchy slab of boogie with "There Is a Party Going On." Later they perform "You Might Want Me Baby," which anticipates both reggae and punk.

Stu Phillips scored several motorcycle movies during the '60s. (Photograph courtesy of the Stu Phillips Estate.)

One of the best biker soundtracks is *Hell's Belles* (1968) by Les Baxter. Although he is better known as one of the chief architects of the exotica sound, Baxter was highly active during the '60s as one of AIP's go-to composers for horror flicks. *Hell's Belles* proved to be one of his few soundtracks to favor pop or rock over orchestral sounds. Big back beats, swirling organ, thick bass lines, wailing harmonica, fuzz-toned guitar and brash brass pump up tracks like "Wheels," "Chain Fight" and "Hogin' Machine." The funky break beat on "Hot Wind" is attractive sample fodder for hip-hop deejays. There are two vocal tracks, but the instrumentals ("Soul Groove," "Wheels," etc.) are the real deal. Notably, Baxter also scored Dexter's *The Mini-Skirt Mob* (1968).

If Baxter was a bankable artist before he tracked *Hell's Belles*, imagine how revved up Curb and company must have been putting out *The Savage Seven* (1968), which Dick Clark produced. Featuring marquee names like Iron Butterfly and Cream, the soundtrack boasts more mainstream rock appeal than most biker flicks. The soundtrack recycles Cream's folksy music hall number "Anyone for Tennis" (originally featured on Cream's *Wheels of Fire*, 1968), as well as two tracks from Iron Butterfly's debut, *Heavy* (1968), including the ultra heavy "Iron Butterfly Theme" and the groovy psychedelic "Unconscious Power." Most of the soundtrack, however, belongs to Jerry Styner, who is only noted in the smallest print on the back cover. He provides atmospheric big band numbers ("Desert Love"), a few of which have a zany Benny Hill–like energy ("Here Comes the Fuzz"), and the occasional gritty rock number ("The Savage Struggle" and "Desert Ride"). Notably, the movie features twangy guitar legend Duane Eddy.

Styner also worked with Curb on *Five the Hard Way* (a.k.a. *The Sidehackers*, 1969), featuring the outstanding "Psychedelic Rape," as well as *The Cycle Savages* (1970), featuring the full-throttle bongo-driven theme music.

Any movie with a chain-wielding biker bitch wearing an eye patch needs a cool soundtrack, right? *The Hellcats* (1968) is a typical Curb production, with cheesy pop tunes and motoring buzz bomb surf rock. The Arrows kick up some dust on fuzz-buster garage rockers "Hell Cats" and "The Angry Mob." Most of the soundtrack is dominated by quasi-psychedelic pop tunes by the likes of Somebody's Chyldren, Davy Jones (not the Monkee), and the Dolphins. The latter group's "Hell Cats," with its cheesy organ solo, is laughably quaint. It's upbeat pop themes like this one that make a lot of the '60s biker flicks sound silly. The cheerfulness completely undermines any notion of rebellion. One version of "Hell Cats" isn't enough, though, as the Sunrays also deliver a version that is about as threatening as *Happy Days*. Still, *The Hellcats* has its highlights, including Davy Jones' daytime street scene reverie "Mass Confusion," with its hypnotic proto-techno outro, and Somebody's Chyldren's evening time street scene reverie "I'm Up," with its baroque guitar lick. Nonetheless, there's no doubt that *The Hellcats* is one of the weaker entries in the biker soundtrack genre.

A better, albeit atypical, biker soundtrack is heard in *Girl on a Motorcycle* (a.k.a. *Naked Under Leather*, 1968), starring Rolling Stones protégé Marianne Faithful. It's by Les Reed, who penned some 2,000 songs for artists like

Les Reed's main theme for *The Girl on a Motorcycle* (Warner Bros., 1968), starring Rolling Stones protégé Marianne Faithful, starts with revving motorcycle sounds.

Tom Jones ("It's Not Unusual") and Engelbert Humperdinck ("The Last Waltz"), and played keyboards with the John Barry Seven during the early '60s. His film work is limited to a handful of pictures, of which *Girl on a Motorcycle* is the most notable. Opening with a revving motorcycle, the title track (one of three character themes) is a classic slab of big band groove. The Hammond organ lays down a hook caught by the brass section before segueing to romantic strings and solo saxophone. "Dream" is an eerie trip of a track that bewilders with crowd noises and Echoplex-effected whip cracks mixing with demented Herrmann-esque orchestration. "Holiday with Raymond" is deluxe travelogue music, capturing the excitement of an afternoon on Alpen slopes under a carefree blue sky. "Take Me to My Lover" is another excellent big band groove number, complete with electric guitar revving high notes against a propulsive tempo; motorcycle noise provides an odd interlude. "Journey of Love" picks up the action mood, but uses full orchestra to add new dynamic twists. The mightiest groovedelic number to be found on *Girl* is "Big Bare Beat," which pushes Hammond organ and electric guitar against a wall of wailing brass and wild percussion. According to the RPM Records CD booklet notes, the film's producer, Ronan O'Rahilly, owner of the pirate radio station Radio Caroline, requested a rock score, but director Jack Cardiff requested a French-type, Francis Lai sound.

"I was very much enamored of Claude Lelouche's *A Man and a Woman*," Cardiff recalls in the notes. "I thought the music had a kind of sadness and fatality about it. And you don't get anything subtle with a rock score."

Reed struck a compromise by offsetting the high-energy rock sound of tracks like "Big Bare Beat" with more romantic moods like "Dawn Idyll." The theme captures both moods in one shot. "It actually worked in the film because the leather she wore sort of depicts the rock era of the time," Reed said, adding that the love affair needed beautiful music.

Among the featured players was Jimmy Page—one of the most in-demand session guitarists in London during the '60s, who was on the verge of forming the New Yardbirds (better known as Led Zeppelin). "I used Jimmy a lot in the early days," Reed said of the one-time session guitarist. "If we had anything special in to do we'd get Jimmy Page."

Despite Faithful's participation in the film, Reed didn't write anything for her to sing on the soundtrack, despite her burgeoning recording career, as he didn't want to encroach on her professional relationship with another writer.

To call *Girl on a Motorcycle* a great rock soundtrack is indeed a stretch, but fans of late '60s groove will want to seek it out.

Back on the L.A. biker scene Stu Phillips provided another gloriously psychedelic soundtrack for *Angels from Hell* (1968). It is front-loaded with California's Peanut Butter Conspiracy's bouncy anthem "No One Say a Word" (a.k.a. "No Communication"). From there, Phillips lays down the jazzy groove of a theme. He also contributes the upbeat, albeit episodic, "Propinquity," the brassy pop number "Walkin' In" and the mellow lounger "Amalgamation." Other highlights include the sitar-laced groove "4 O'Clock Tea," Ted Markland's folk rock anthem "Shake Off the Chains," the mystical folk of "Crystal Tear" and the raucous "Angels from Hell," which is melodically different from Phillips' theme. Another featured band is Lollipop Shoppe, a short-lived psych-punk group that contributes a couple of misanthropic rockers, "Who's It Gonna Be" and "Mr. Madison Avenue." Although it doesn't hang together as pleasingly as *Hells Angels on Wheels*, *Angels from Hell* ranks as one of the more diverse biker soundtracks, and one that holds up fairly well considering the obscurity of some of its featured artists.

Phillips also scored *Run, Angel, Run* (1969), featuring a vocal performance by Tammy Wynette, "the first lady of country music," on the theme, a mellow country western ballad. Phillips wrote in *Stu Who?* that getting the song recorded proved to be a fiasco. The song's co-composer, Billy Sherrill, kept the studio waiting until the eleventh hour for Wynette's rendition after Phillips composed his score around the song's melody. Then, adding insult to near injury, Sherrill allegedly demanded 100 percent of the publishing royalties. Later, Sherrill apologized for the incident, Phillips wrote, and in "a gesture of good will ... he put the song into *Tammy's Greatest Hits* album." (p. 174)

The rural vibe on *Run, Angel, Run* continues on the bluegrass banjo showcase "Up an Old Dirt Road" and the sleepy folk "True Believers." Just when a listener might be losing hope for some of Phillips' special magic, he busts out "Rescue," a madcap experimental funk number with electronic embellishments over a restless repetitive groove. "Friendly Fuzz" follows suit, pitting more fuzz-toned guitar and keyboard riffing against drum fills and flute accents. "Get It On" also carries the "Rescue" riffage, but adds Jew's harp accents and a frenzied rhythm guitar section. This is the stuff that makes Stu Phillips such an exciting soundtrack artist. There also is some prime southern boogie rock in the form of "Love and Admiration of the Brotherhood Society of South Napa County." Given its unlikely mix of country, folk and experimental funk rock, *Run, Angel, Run* offers a jarringly different take on the biker soundtrack, but that's what makes it so interesting.

Rock and folk also mix on *Easy Rider* (1969), the most famous and most popular motorcycle movie. The top-ten soundtrack features hard rockers Steppenwolf, the Jimi Hendrix Experience and the Electric Prunes, alongside folk rockers the Byrds and Roger McGuinn (a member of the Byrds). Legend has it that director and star Dennis Hopper had planned to hire folk rock super group Crosby, Stills, Nash & Young to score the entire film, but decided instead to use the tunes he'd been hearing on the radio, such as Steppenwolf's iconic motorhead anthem "Born to Be Wild" and the Band's "The Weight," which had to be covered by the group Smith due to licensing constraints. Another legend has it that the film studio insisted that the popular songs be used. By presenting an album of radio favorites alongside new tracks (like the two tracks that McGuinn wrote with Bob Dylan) and more obscure material (by the Holy Modal Rounders), *Easy Rider* helped pave the way for the mainstream "needle drop" soundtracks of today that tend to feature songs rather than original scores. *Easy Rider* sold very well, second only to Nino Rota's *Romeo & Joliet* in 1969. It offers songs that truly capture the spirit of the times. Between Fraternity of Man's comical ode to pot smoking etiquette, "Don't Bogart Me," and Steppenwolf's "The Pusher," one gets some hazy perspective on the drug culture of the time.

A less familiar biker film from 1969 is *Naked Angels*—the work of Jeff Simmons (guitar, bass, vocals), Al Malosky (drums) and Randy Steirling (producer). It was one of several notable releases on Herb Cohen and Frank Zappa's Straight Records that year, along with Captain Beefheart & His Magic Band's classic *Trout Mask Replica*, Alice Cooper's debut *Pretties for You*, and Tim Buckley's *Blue Afternoon*. In fact, Simmons frequently worked in later incarnations of Zappa's bands, and Zappa produced and wrote material for Simmons' other album for Straight, *Lucille Has Messed My Mind Up* (1969). *Naked*

Angels contains one of the greatest slabs of fuzz-toned title tracks in the genre. A machine-like rhythm propelled by chunky guitar chords sets up searing back-to-back solos, followed by overlapping solos. It's a hell of a ride, and it's tempting to dismiss the rest of the soundtrack as dispensable in comparison. *Naked Angels* is far from a bust. "Ride Into Vegas" quotes from Bobby Troup's "Route 66" during a spirited jam. Likewise, "Vegas Pickup," "Rat Grind" and "First Desert Ride" are sizzling tracks that show off not only Simmons' chops but also Malosky's funky drumming; he tackles time signature changes with more dexterity than one is used to hearing on a biker soundtrack. "Scots Breath" is the most unusual track, meshing the traditional Scottish folk of wheezing fiddles, flanged guitars and machine gun snare rolls with Southern boogie rock. "Bar Dream" is completely abstract, with backward tape trickery and echo effects that seem designed to make one feel drunk. Overall, *Naked Angels* is an unexpectedly solid soundtrack, but not because it contains great theme development or many memorable melodies. Rather, the musicianship on display is the real draw.

From the same year is *Hell's Angels '69*, featuring music by Tony Bruno and songs by the Stream of Consciousness, Sonny Valdez and Wendy Cole—an obscure line-up to say the least. The songs, such as Valdez' "What's His," Cole's "Say Girl" and Stream's "Til You're Through," fail to leave a lasting impression. Bruno's instrumentals are a bit more interesting. The tribal funk of "Chase of Death" boasts a riveting rhythm section, the flute solo is competent but aimless, and the rumbling motorcycle noises add interest. "Goofin'" gets started with a sneaky beat noir vibe until harpsichord and organ lay down a repeating melody punctuated by groaning brass. The motorcycles are back for the comically jaunty "Bass Lake Run," which features banjo and slide guitar. Bruno also contributed "Two of a Kind" to the surf and ski comedy *Wild, Wild Winter* (1966).

A better biker soundtrack comes from *Satan's Sadists* (1969). Harley Hatcher delivers one of the most memorable themes in the genre, simply called "Satan." The singer describes how he was "born mean" and even at the tender age of two had earned the nickname of "Satan." The lyrics describe a troubled childhood against a backdrop of stately soul. Other tracks, like the brassy and irrepressibly poppy "Gotta Stop That Feeling" and "Is It Better to Have Loved and Lost," make life with a biker gang sound pretty tame—even one led by a guy named Satan. The spaghetti western–inspired instrumental "Firewater" adds needed drama. The shake-it-don't-break-it soul shaker of "Can You Dig It" is another keeper. And "The Chase Is On" finally lets loose with the fuzz-toned guitar that every biker soundtrack needs. Finally, there's an upbeat reprise of the theme that makes the whole bad childhood and "Satan" complex sound like a blessing in disguise. Although, there isn't enough angry guitar and too many happy-go-lucky vocal numbers, *Satan's Sadists* has its share of pleasures.

This scene from *Easy Rider* (Columbia, 1969), starring Dennis Hopper (left) and Peter Fonda (with unidentified passenger), practically screams "get your motor running," the opening line from "Born to Be Wild"—Steppenwolf's iconic anthem of rockin' rebellion that is featured on the soundtrack.

At the start of the '70s Lenny Stack revved up funky rock for *C.C. and Company*. Star Ann-Margaret sings on the album, and the C.C. Riders make an onscreen appearance, performing a brassy rock song. The soundtrack also features Mitch Ryder and the Detroit Wheels' hit "Jenny Take a Ride."

Genre regular Phillips returned for *The Losers* (a.k.a. *Nam's Angels*, 1970), which is an unusual entry in the genre. The proto–*Rambo* storyline concerns a biker gang given a choice between jail time and a mission to Cambodia to rescue a presidential advisor who happens to be the brother of the gang's leader. Phillips' score differs significantly from his earlier psychedelic biker soundtracks, as it favors orchestral action cues and lyrical mood music. "Hogs Wild" blends swirling strings, terse brass and exotic percussion in a way that recalls Goldsmith's work on *Planet of the Apes* (1968). The rhythmically dense, exotic action number "Jungle Ride" has an exotica vibe, but is less romantic and more sweepingly cinematic. "Biker Romance" is harmonically rich in the impressionist style, gently evoking Asian ambience. "All Fall Dead" is frenetic action music that employs shrill strings and exotic percussion to create a ticking bomb tension. All told, *The Losers* transcends the biker soundtrack genre by embracing the film's foreign setting and using more complex orchestration to create a satisfyingly cinematic sound. It's far from rock, but, like Reed's *Girl on a Motorcycle*, it makes for a richer listening experience.

A biker soundtrack that's firmly on the rock tip is the one heard in *Angels Die Hard* (1970), featuring rough-and-ready bar tunes by East-West Pipeline and other obscure artists, including Richard Hieronymus, who went on to score *Angels Hard as They Come* (1971) and *Bury Me an Angel* (1972). Sylvanus performs a close cover of Sly & the Family Stone's classic raver "I Want to Take You Higher." The track was released as a single, backed with Rabbit Mackay's psych rocker "Tendency to Be Free," which originally appeared on Mackay's second album, *Passing Through* (1969). Medicine Ball performs the fierce blue-based rocker "Indian Child." Fever Tree, a Texas psychedelic band best known for their hit "San Francisco Girls," performs "Death Is the Dancer," which originally appeared on their second album, *Another Time, Another Place* (1968). Another featured performer is surfer-songwriter Mark Eric, whose "Night of the Lions"—a strings-bolstered sunshine pop-rocker—also appeared on his one and only LP, *A Midsummer's Day Dream* (1969). (Notably, Eric also appeared on TV's *The Partridge Family* as a pal to biker Snake, played by pre–Meathead Rob Reiner.) Most of the soundtrack belongs to East-West Pipeline, whose brand of boogie rock has a certain psych-glam charm, particularly in the catchy refrains. The multiple guitar attack and motoric bass lines, propulsive drumming and vocal harmonies are put to good use in unexpected ways on memorable tunes like the country-tinged "Kern County Line," the heavy metal stomper "You Could Be," and the brassy dance floor shaker "Angels Die Hard," the album's only instrumental. Reportedly, East-West Pipeline also recorded Hieronymus' music for *Bury Me an Angel*. Overall, *Angels Die Hard* is a very enjoyable rockin' biker soundtrack that falls just shy of essential.

Certainly not the last of its genre, but the last to be discussed here, is Randy Sparks' *Angel Unchained* (1970), featuring Jim Helms and the Drivers. Sparks' music isn't typical biker rock. He employs more brass than guitars, with organ providing a counterpoint over elaborate orchestra rock arrangements. "Borasca" exemplifies the sound. "Merrilee" pairs oboe with acoustic guitar for a gentle sound that segues into jazzy rock with a virtuoso electric bass solo, elaborate tympani runs and fast drum breaks. The bizarre vocal number "Chopper Charlie & Motorguzzi Molly" features more amazing bass playing and busy organ licks. With its slack-string wah guitar fills, "By Force" is action music befitting a '70s cop show—albeit a quirky one. "Following a Dream" is lovely and gentle, with acoustic guitar and piano stirring the heartstrings.

As the '70s kicked into gear, fewer cycle psycho pictures were made, as exploitation filmmakers turned to other genres such as blaxploitation and sexploitation. Before the genre ran out of gas in the mid–1970s, a handful of related pictures introduced new plot elements.

The comedy *Bunny O'Hare* (1971) features a few tasty tracks by top L.A. session guitarist and arranger Billy Strange. He scored only a few pictures during the period, including two Elvis flicks (*Live a Little, Love a Little* in 1968 and *The Trouble with Girls* in 1969) as well as *De Sade* (1969). "Put a Little Lead in Your Zeppelin" clearly recalls a certain chart topper, but aside from Strange's blistering solo, the sound is too brassy to be taken literally. With its throbbing bass line and busy brass and winds, "Run Away" is hard charging chase music and wouldn't sound out of place on any of the cop shows of the era. "Group Therapy," on the other hand, gets trippy with sitar and percussion fills that conjure the hippie mysticism that fueled popular interest in psychology at the time.

Associated only marginally with the biker genre is *Vanishing Point* (1971), because it famously features the shapely blonde Gilda Texter as the "nude rider" of a motorcycle. The movie actually centers on Kowalski, whose job is to deliver a 1970 Dodge Challenger from Denver to San Francisco. High on pep pills, he baits the police into a deadly cross-country chase. Radio deejay Super Soul provides cultural commentary. Fittingly, the soundtrack is a selection of tracks by a variety of rock and country artists. Along with *Easy Rider* and *Two-Lane Blacktop* (1971), *Vanishing Point* is one of the era's great "road movies." The soundtrack starts funky with the J.B. Pickers' good-time groove "Super Soul Theme," written by the soundtrack's producer and supervisor, Jimmy Bowen. Up next is Bobby Doyle's brassy boogie rocker "The Girl Done Got It Together" and Jimmy Walker's soul mover "Where Do We Go from Here?" Jerry Reed's country groove "Welcome to Nevada" rolls along effortlessly. Segarini & Bishop's country rock ballad "Dear Jesus God" features a hippie refrain about loving each other like brothers. The lightning fast bluegrass instrumental "Runaway Country" stampedes like a raging bull. Delaney & Bonnie & Friends bring the gospel on "You Got to Believe." Eva's mid-tempo soul rocker "So Tired" gets the groove back on track. The J.B. Pickers kick out the best track: the six-minute "Freedom of Expression," a hard-driving and tense instrumental full of fast drums and distorted guitar. The best familiar track, though, is Mountain's heavy-duty boogie "Mississippi Queen," which originally appeared on the band's debut album, *Climbing!* (1970). "Sing Out for Jesus," a Kim Carnes–penned gospel number (sung by Big Mama Thornton), is anticlimactic after the preceding heavy rock twosome. The blend of rock, soul, country, blues and gospel makes *Vanishing Point* a rootsy, rangy, rowdy listening experience.

Another unusual entry is the Oscar-nominated *On Any Sunday* (1971), the documentary about motorcycle racing narrated by rugged star Steve McQueen. Dominic Frontiere, who was head of Paramount's music department during the '70s, provided a suitably rockin' instrumental score for the film. Although the music is pure rock—it has a brassy Vegas character—there are energetic grooves with dueling horns (including Tom Scott on saxophone), wah guitar, sizzling solos, explosive drums and thick electric bass lines. Among the funky, fierce and full throttle highlights are "Stretchin' Out," "Sunday Drivin'," "Messin' Around," "Cross Country" and "Widow Maker"—all of which make up for the album's occasional easy listening tune, making this an essential listen.

Naturally, motorbikes aren't just for swastika-sporting cycle psychos; originally they were used by the police. One of the few contemporary films of that period to focus on the fuzz is James William Guercio's *Electra Glide in Blue* (1973). Guercio, who is better known as the L.A. session musician-turned-producer of such hit-making groups as Chicago and Blood, Sweat & Tears, also scored *Electra*—his only known soundtrack. *Electra* is an eclectic batch of vocal and instrumental tracks that run from funky ("The Chase") to easy groovin' ("Prelude") to country ("Song of Sad Bottles") to orchestral ("Overture"). The funky tracks are at least as cool as anything from a blaxploitation flick, which were peaking in popularity at the time.

Another cop-related biker flick is *Stone* (1974), an improbable Australian actioner about an undercover cop who infiltrates a gang of "bikies" to find out who is killing them off. Billy Green's psychedelic prog funk-rock score is among the most memorable of the genre, thanks to a relentless experimental streak and killer musicianship. Any psychedelic biker soundtrack that features French horn, zither, Moog and didgeridoo cross-wired with funky hard rock instrumentation is necessary listening. The most experimental tracks—"Pigs," "Toad," "Toadstrip" and "The Death of Doctor Death"—transport the listener into a hallucinogenic sonic space where electronic and acoustic noises mix in unexpected ways. Instead of sounding like interesting filler, these tracks compel close listening due to their complex arrangements. Even when Green takes a relatively melodic approach, the results are hardly conventional. The title track showcases electric and acoustic guitars backed by a locked-in rhythm section featuring funky electric piano. "Grave Diggers" is the ultimate Moog meets metal showdown, with guitar, keyboards, bass and drums playing lightning runs that would have made Mahavishnu Orchestra bow in appreciation. "Klaud Kool and the Kats" retrofits a '50s boogie with progressive chops. "Amanda" marries baroque strings to a steam-engine backbeat. "Septic" spills folk acoustic with strains of country and Irish jig. At more than seven-and-a-half minutes, "Cosmic Flash" explodes from pastoral strings into funky electric blues before fading into a gentle jazz guitar reverie. "Race" runs through a funky groove that gradually warps through ring modulation. "Do Not Go Gentle" turns a lyric inspired by the Dylan Thomas line into a growled rock anthem, complete with screaming guitar lead.

While biker flicks are the most identifiable genre where rock meets the motorway, another engine-revving breed of B-movie revolves around guys (and gals) who rebel by breaking the speed limit in souped-up hot rods. Like biker flicks, hot rod and racing movies don't always meet the rock soundtrack criteria, but the spirit of youthful rebellion is still there.

As early as the '40s, educational films documented the rampant juvenile delinquent problems that fueled hot rod culture in the U.S. *The Devil on Wheels* (1947) is believed to be one of the first non-documentary features. By the mid-century mark filmmakers were cashing in on the fad. There was *Hot Rod* (1950), *The Pace That Thrills* (1952), *The Fast and the Furious* (1954), *Hot Rod Girl* (1956), *Hot Rod Rumble* (1957), *Dragstrip Girl* (1957), *Dragstrip Riot* (1958), *Speed Crazy* (1959) and so on. Many of these films focus on the wicked lives of crime led by the hot rodders, using dragstrips and high-speed chases as climactic devices ("speed kills!" being the moral of the stories). Understandably, few if any of these films warranted a soundtrack release. It wasn't until the '60s that record companies began to see the marketing potential of rock album tie-ins—for almost any rock film, regardless of its hot rod quotient.

By the late '60s—when motorcycles were clearly the delinquent's vehicle of choice—hot rodders had given way to legitimate motor sports in stock car racing movies, like two of Elvis' vehicles—*Spinout* (1966) and *Speedway* (1968)—*Fireball 500* (1966), *Thunder Alley* (1967) and *The Wild Racers* (1968).

George Stoll is the credited songwriter for *Spinout*, but another dozen writers had their hands on the material. Despite featuring such rockin' tunes as "Stop, Look and Listen" and "I'll Be Back," *Spinout* doesn't boast any essential Elvis tracks.

Speedway features music and songs by Jeff Alexander, among others, including the late great Lee Hazlewood, who is best known for his idiosyncratic country western duets with Nancy Sinatra. Hazlewood also wrote songs for such '60s attractions as the spy spoof *The Last of the Secret Agents?* (1966), the go-go comedy *The Cool Ones* (a.k.a. *Cool Baby Cool*, 1967), the Frank Sinatra detective thriller *Tony Rome* (1967), and the surfing flick *The Sweet Ride* (1968). Despite the talent on hand, *Speedway* is a minor Elvis soundtrack. The single "Let Yourself Go" flopped out of the starting gate.

Elvis wasn't the only period icon getting in on the racing action in the late '60s. After playing "Dee Dee" in several "bikini beach party" movies, former Mickey Mouse Club sweetheart Annette Funicello hooked up with Fabian in *Thunder Alley*. The Mike Curb–produced soundtrack is a pop and rock affair designed for the young fans of the clean-cut stars. It features Curb's in-house band working under the name the Sidewalk Sounds, performing songs written by Guy Hemric and Jerry Styner; but fuzz rock guitar sounds are in short supply, as the soundtrack favors pop. Still, "Pete's Orgy" whips up some thrills, and "Calahan's Vision" is 20 seconds of ringing six-string riffage that is reprised on the Sidewalk Sounds' instrumental version of the theme. The Band Without a Name (undoubtedly another Arrows incarnation) performs the theme with revving engine noise and a pure pop vocal. Another track that will inter-

Elvis Presley, seen here with Diane McBain (left) and Shelley Fabares in *Spinout* **(MGM, 1966), plays a racecar driver who finds time to play the field and a few tunes at poolside.**

est rock fans is a mildly lysergic jam led by L.A.-based session drummer Eddie Beram that boasts sitar accents and a fierce tom-tom workout. Naturally, the soundtrack also features Funicello's modest vocal talent on "What's a Girl to Do" and "When You Get What You Want."

The instrumental rock sound is in greater evidence on *The Wild Racers* (1968), which stars Fabian. Knowing of Curb's penchant for creative band attribution, it is likely that the musicians featured here include a wider variety of session players than the original Arrows/Sidewalk Sounds, who were little more than a power trio. "The Checkered Flag" certainly sounds like the Arrows, but their "Love Theme" features a harpsichord, strings and woodwinds. Likewise, the Sidewalk Sounds' "Wild Racers' Theme" sounds like classic Arrows, but the group's "Bedroom Theme" and "The Train Station" are both horn showcases. One of the more interesting tracks here is "Dance Party," which incorporates cuckoo clock noises with rock instrumentation.

Fabian turned up the next year in a moonshine bootlegger movie, *The Devil's 8* (1969), featuring another Curb-produced soundtrack. Working again with Styner and Hemric, Curb cooked up a funky rock score with a couple of highlights. The theme song features a male chorus that sings the movie's story, with a catchy chorus about "angry young men" with a "mission to accomplish." More interesting is "Sam Escapes," an episodic piece that segues from pastoral reverie to chugging prog rock with blaring brass, trilling winds and shifting rhythms. "Chandler's Grenade Ride" and "Let's Go" reprise the theme, overlaying the funky guitar rhythms with sweeping strings and punchy brass.

Better yet is *Bug-In!* (1969), which features cover art depicting bikini-clad girls in a dune buggy, a vehicle closely associated with surf culture first and racing culture second. The ultra-obscure Inter-Urban Electric A&E Rhythm and Pit Crew Band perform blistering big band funk. On tracks like "Baja Boot" and "The Classic 2000," revving motor sounds mix with feisty horns and relentless chunk-a-funk electric rhythms. One would be hard pressed to serve up a more solidly entertaining motor-mania soundtrack.

Another movie featuring dune buggies is *Wild Wheels* (1969), which pits a biker gang (led by Casey Kasem) against a group of dune buggy-drivin' surfers. It is generally regarded as one of the most inept films in both the wheels and waves genres. The soundtrack itself is a bit too "fun" to appeal to fans of biker fuzz and hell fire. "Makin' Love" may be the catchiest number on this vocal-heavy platter of country and pop tunes.

Surfers and Skateboarders

Movies about wave riding emerged alongside the beach party movies of Avalon and Funicello. True surfing movies of the era are typically documentaries, arguably beginning with pioneering filmmaker Bud Browne's *Hawaiian Surfing Movie* (1953). "Barracuda" Browne—a legendary surfer in his own right—churned out countless flicks, such as *The Big Surf* (1957) and *Surf Happy* (1960).

Following in Browne's wake came another surfer-cum-filmmaker, Bruce Brown, who filmed a string of celebrated documentaries, starting with *Slippery When Wet* (1958) and culminating with his globetrotting hit *The Endless Summer* (1964). West Coast jazz saxophonist Bud Shank scored *Slippery*, as well as Brown's *Barefoot Adventure* (1961). The cool jazz sound is, perhaps, more apt for the improvisatory nature of surfing than rock or pop. Heard in the context of these laidback documentaries, the shimmering cymbal rides and crashes, jazz guitar curlicues and freewheeling horn solos capture the carefree spirit of fun in the sun, even if it fails to capture the headlong rush of a Banzai Pipeline wipeout.

The music most identified with surfing comes from the rock instrumental groups of the '60s whose distinctive sounding guitars sport an undistorted tone but exaggerated use of tremolo, sustain and vibrato. Such early '60s classics as the Surfaris' "Wipeout," The Ventures' "Diamond Head" and Dick

Dale and the Del-Tones' "Misirlou" would have been perfect for the surfer film genre. Ironically, these bands and their thrilling sounds went unused in the films of Browne, Brown and their contemporaries. The same can be said of surf culture's most popular rock group, the Beach Boys, whose early '60s hits "Surfin' Safari," "Surfin' USA," "Surfer Girl," and others didn't make the big screen until George Lucas used some of them in his ode to the era, *American Graffiti* (1973).

The first and possibly only surf rock group to score a movie was the Sandals, which was formed in California by two Belgian-born brothers, Walter and Gaston Georis (playing guitar and keyboards respectively). When the group—then dubbed the Twangs—was preparing to release its first single, "Out Front," on World Pacific Records, filmmaker Brown caught wind of their sound and decided it would be perfect for his next picture, *The Endless Summer*. Brown had already been using World Pacific recordings for his previous films (including the Bud Shank scores). Some of the music in the film is sophisticated orchestral pop and probably from library sessions licensed by World Pacific. Of course the most memorable tracks are by the Sandals. The theme breezes along on strummed acoustic guitar at a relaxed tempo, with bass guitar, harmonica and clean electric guitar fills. "Out Front" is classic up-tempo surf rock with a cheerful hook. Although this is surf rock, don't be surprised to hear revving engines mixed in, as is the case on "Scrambler" and "TR-6."

A jazzier surf soundtrack can be heard on *Gone with the Wave* (1965). It's another West Coast–style session featuring seasoned players like Shelly Manne (drums), Paul Horn (saxophone and flute) and Howard Roberts (guitar), but this time the leader is none other than Lalo Schifrin, who sits in on piano. "A Taste of Bamboo" is one of the more imaginative tracks, with tuned percussion and piano ringing out an "oriental" melody over a quick, slippery groove of guitar trills. "Breaks" is a bit more conventional, but grooves even harder, with Manne's drums crashing like waves behind Roberts' nimble fretwork, Schifrin's chomping piano chords and Horn's liquid sax solo. "Aqua Blues" is another up-tempo ride that wouldn't sound out of place on Schifrin's *Bullitt* (1968). Another highlight is "Breaks Bossa Nova," an outstanding showcase for the soloists, this time working it out over a sweet Latin groove.

Long before the 2001 documentary *Dogtown and Z-Boys* explained the cultural connection between surfing and skateboarding, a little film called *Skaterdater* (1965) made a similar link. *Skaterdater*'s Curb-produced soundtrack is rife with surf rock that wouldn't sound out of place in *The Endless Summer*. Chiming, vibrato-laden guitars jangle over no-nonsense rock rhythms and Hammond organ tones on tracks like "Skateboard Safari" and "Skaterdater." Davie Allan's fuzz-toned guitar takes the lead on "Skaterdater Rock," making it sound more like a biker soundtrack. The rousing theme is reprised again and again, but variations on a gentler melody also make the scene on "Together" and "Missy's Theme." Simply put, *Skaterdater* is the best surf soundtrack that doesn't actually belong to a surf film.

Another classic Curb-produced surf rock soundtrack, introducing the dubiously dubbed Back-Wash Rhythm Band, comes from *Golden Breed* (1968), a legitimate surf flick. Like any Curb soundtrack, it features a dopey theme song that sentimentalizes the surf lifestyle. The instrumental tracks are better. "Hawaiian Circus" features lively marimba trills over chirping guitar and an easy-flowing groove. "In the Curl" uses frantic bongo patterns to create mounting excitement. There are instrumental and vocal versions of the hooky "What Turns You On," which uses the classic combination of minor-key verses and major-key choruses. Davie Allan's chiming surf guitar echoes over a soulful horn vamp. "High Rise" and "Surfer Paradise" are iconic wave-riding anthems on par with anything in the Dick Dale songbook. "Over the Falls" and "Golden Time" use brass for Technicolor widescreen appeal. "Waimea Bay" features groovy electric piano that throws in jazzy turns of phrase over blues changes. The album ends with a reprise of the cheesy pop dreck about "following the sun and following your dreams." Despite its trite theme song, *Golden Breed* remains one of the best surf soundtracks.

Lalo Schifrin frequently plays the piano on his soundtracks, including the surfer flick *Gone with the Wave* (1965). (Photograph courtesy of the Lalo Schifrin Estate.)

Also released in 1968 is *The Sweet Ride*, a sexy drama set in Malibu at a beachfront bachelor pad where surfer dudes entertain their bikini babes. Pete Rugolo, veteran arranger for Stan Kenton and occasional film and television composer, provides one of his best jazzy orchestral pop scores. Dusty Springfield gives her all on the brassy, Motown-type theme song written by Lee Hazlewood. Next up is the stately "Vicky Meets Denny," which matches do-do-la-la chorus to staccato keyboard rhythms and tame surf guitar. Jazzy vibes, Hammond organ and husky flute tones color "Collier's Riff," "Thumper" and "Lost Wages Brash." Nothing beats "My Name Is Mister Clean," a swaggering sexy groove with fuzz-toned guitars and punchy brass. "Sock Me Choo

Choo" picks up a few lines from the theme for a zany, zippy instrumental version that qualifies as surf rock, especially when the electric guitars dual wildly over the frantic beat. "Where's the Melody" is fast and frantic as well, but the fireworks come from the pianist and jazz guitarist. The bubbly "Swing Me Lightly" closes out this classic '60s bachelor pad soundtrack that happens to take place in a surfer's paradise.

Another jazzy cool surf soundtrack belongs to the documentary *The Fantastic Plastic Machine* (1969), a title later adopted by Japanese DJ-producer Tomoyuki Tanaka for a string of albums released during the lounge revival. The original soundtrack is by Harry Betts, a West Coast jazz musician whose most known recording as a leader is *The Jazz Soul of Doctor Kildare* (1962). Betts also scored Richard Benedict's beach party movie *Winter a-Go-Go* (1965), but *The Fantastic Plastic Machine* is his best effort. The theme races along on fast drums, bongo fills, wailing organ solo, ringing chimes and heavily processed guitars and strings. It flies by with an urgency that would leave most surf rock groups gasping. "Endless Bummer" slows things down considerably with a stately rhythm, smooth brass and strings with acoustic guitar filigree and harmonica. Betts kicks it up a notch for the spirited jet-set rockers "Night Flight" and "Green O" before launching "Day Groovin,'" a soulful up-tempo blues number that showcases fleet-fingered Hammond organ and guitar soloists. Boasting a crackerjack rhythm section and top-shelf musicianship, the group proves positively electric, even on Bacharach-esque easy listening like "Straight Ahead" and "Rock Slide." One of the best tracks on an otherwise strong album is "Green Grotto," which borders on psychedelic with its wild chime glissandi and repetitive motifs. The album closer, "Long Reef," is less ambitious but nearly as impressive; it's simply surf rock played by the best session musicians L.A. had to offer. Overall, Betts' group pushes the envelope stylistically without losing the essential vibe of the genre.

Stu Phillips delivered the most romantic and melodically rich surf soundtrack of the period for the documentary *Follow Me* (1969). The lush, exotic score makes use of scene-specific sounds such as elephant trumpet, India's Ranee Express and Hawaiian boat whistle. Like a psychedelic symphonic suite, *Follow Me* takes in the sights of Portugal, Morocco, Ceylon, India, Hong Kong and Hawaii. Just close your eyes and listen, and Phillips' music takes one on a Technicolor journey. The film's kaleidoscopic theme song, "Thru Spray Colored Glasses," is a lovely sunshine pop tune sung by the short-lived trio Dino, Desi and Billy, who enjoyed some brief success due to having powerful parents, namely Dean Martin, Lucille Ball and Desi Arnaz, as well as a connection to the Beach Boys. Surf rock it certainly is not, but Phillips' stirring theme song and imaginative musical ideas make *Follow Me* the greatest jet-setter travelogue soundtrack of its era. (Notably, Japan's Fantastic Plastic Machine sampled a keyboard riff from the *Follow Me* track "Guincho.")

While documentaries and occasional adult-themed features are respon-

The pop music heard on *Gidget* (ABC, 1965–1966), starring Sally Field, reflected the character's perky innocence.

sible for the best surf soundtracks, a string of youth-oriented flicks also exploited surf 'n' sand culture. *Gidget* (1959), a comedy about a surfer girl whose on-board skills make up for her lack of bodacious bodily curves, was among the first to make a splash, inspiring the eponymously titled TV show (1965–1966). Fred Karger and Stanley Styne composed the movie's song, "The

Next Best Thing to Love," a sappy ballad crooned by co-star James Darren. The movie also spawned several sequels.

Several beach party rock 'n' pop musicals followed, starring Funicello, Avalon and others, including *Beach Party* (1963), *Bikini Beach* (1964), *Muscle Beach Party* (1964), *Beach Blanket Bingo* (1965) and *How to Stuff a Wild Bikini* (1965). AIP's go-to composer, Les Baxter, worked on all of these films, alongside songwriters such as Guy Hemric, Jerry Styner and others. The original soundtrack LPs ignored Baxter's contributions to focus on Funicello's vocal performances, often including songs unrelated to the movies in question. Also, they often tack her first name before the movie title to cash in on her pop appeal. While these records are highly collectible due to the vocal presence of the onscreen personalities, the lack of Baxter underscore is a potential deterrent for soundtrack fans.

Musicians in Focus

From the beginning, rock cinema has been, first and foremost, about showing performing musicians on screen. The bigger the stars (think Elvis or the Beatles) the bigger the box office. Naturally, such projects often merit soundtrack releases, but since they tend to feature songs instead of score they have somewhat dubious appeal for traditional soundtrack collectors. However, the considerable influence that "songtracks" have had on the marketability of the soundtrack genre justifies a closer look.

As mentioned earlier, Elvis Presley's 30-plus feature films provided the singer with high profile opportunities to introduce new songs to his immense fan base. His early soundtracks were solid sellers for RCA, particularly *Blue Hawaii* (1961), which reached number one on the album charts, where it remained for 20 weeks. With sales of two million, *Blue Hawaii* was Presley's best-selling album up until that time. But, as Presley devoted the bulk of his creative energy to moviemaking during the '60s, the quality of his music suffered. In fact, his '60s soundtracks are often padded with outtakes from much earlier sessions and rarely feature more than one or two memorable tracks. Having originally made his big splash on the small screen (most famously on *The Ed Sullivan Show*), it seems apt that after squandering his talent on half-baked theatrical releases the King had to retake his throne with a "comeback" TV special in 1968. After that, he made a few more forgettable films (along with equally dispensable song-oriented soundtracks) before turning his focus to live performance during his waning years. Even so, Presley's recordings continue to be featured in films made since his death in 1977.

The staying power of rock, both as a popular music genre and as a cinematic subject matter, was made even more viable with the arrival of the "Fab Four," not to mention the entire British Invasion. At the forefront were the Beatles. *A Hard Day's Night* (1964) and *Help!* (1965) were commercially suc-

Elvis Presley and Ann-Margret put on a show in *Viva Las Vegas* (MGM/UA, 1964). As in other movies, the "King" plays a racecar driver who does a bit of singing on the side.

cessful and innovative films, but those titles are more likely to bring to mind their accompanying albums and hit singles. The original U.S. releases of both albums contain the songs featured in their respective films, while the equivalent U.K. releases contain additional tunes. When the Beatles' catalogue made the transition from LP to CD during the '80s the U.K. versions replaced the domestic versions. Rehashing the merits of music contained on these albums would be an exercise is pop cultural redundancy. Suffice it to say they're packed with some of the biggest hits of the band's early era, including the title tracks, "Can't Buy Me Love" and "Ticket to Ride." The U.S. versions also include instrumental versions of some hits, like "And I Love Her" and "This Boy," and *Help!* has some movie-only instrumentals, such as "From Me to You Fantasy," "The Chase" and "In the Tyrol."

Later, the band made the inferior British TV special *Magical Mystery Tour* (1967). The U.S.-released soundtrack LP (an expansion of the U.K.-released six-song EP) features some of the band's best psychedelic songs ("I Am the Walrus," "A Fool on the Hill") plus period singles like "Strawberry Fields Forever" and "Penny Lane." Compared to the band's watershed concept album *Sgt. Pepper's Lonely Hearts Club Band* (1967), which was released just a few months earlier, *Magical Mystery Tour* is often dismissed as "Sgt. Pepper Junior." And while it fails to deliver a true soundtrack experience, it's still a classic collection from the band's most experimental period.

The most unusual Beatles soundtrack is for the animated fantasy feature *Yellow Submarine* (1968). Unlike the soundtracks for their previous movies, *Yellow Submarine* features Beatles songs (the title track, "All Together Now," etc.) as well as underscore by their longtime producer George Martin. Tracks like "Pepperland," "Sea of Time" and "March of the Meanies" were especially recorded for the soundtrack release. Lushly orchestrated by Martin himself, these classical-inspired pieces are far removed from the Beatles songs of the era and, in comparison, far less memorable. That said, the best Beatles songs on the soundtrack were already familiar from previous Beatles releases. The title track originated on *Revolver* (1966), and "All You Need Is Love" appeared on *Magical Mystery Tour*. The Beatles side of the original LP is padded with throwaway tunes like "Hey Bulldog" and "All Together Now." Seemingly slapped together with disparate material, *Yellow Submarine* doesn't make for a coherent or satisfying soundtrack listening experience and is more of a collector's item than a must have. In 1999, Apple/Capitol released an alternate "songtrack" containing the songs originally featured on the original soundtrack release plus other Beatles songs featured in the movie ("Eleanor Rigby," "Lucy in the Sky with Diamonds," etc.) For hardcore Beatles fans, the songtrack is even less necessary, as there is nothing here that wasn't released on an earlier album.

The final Beatles movie, *Let It Be* (1970), marks the demise of the band. Its "songtrack" contains classic cuts ("Across the Universe," "The Long and Winding Road," "Get Back" and the title track), but as an album it pales in comparison to the band's latter-day masterpieces *The Beatles* (1968) and *Abbey Road* (1969). Although, the film and soundtrack were the Beatles' final release, the documented sessions actually preceded the recording of *Abbey Road*. Controversially, "Wall of Sound" producer Phil Spector was brought in for post-

7. Rockin' Revolution 311

Yellow Submarine (United Artists, 1968) is a colorful showcase for many great Beatles songs, as well as additional scoring by their producer George Martin. (Photograph courtesy of the John Monaghan Collection.)

production tweaking, including lush string sections. In 2003, an alternate version of the soundtrack, *Let It Be ... Naked*, mixed out Spector's contributions and added snippets of studio dialogue. As a "soundtrack" for a band's demise, there can hardly be a more famous example than *Let It Be*. But like the group's earlier "songtracks," its tunes are so well known in their own right as to make their association with a movie a mere footnote in an otherwise chart-topping career.

When Beatle-mania first swept the States, TV producers fabricated another foursome in order to cash in on the mop-top craze—namely, the Monkees. After two years of wacky, mildly surrealistic TV comedy and hit singles ("I'm a Believer," "Last Train to Clarksville," etc.), Davy Jones, Micky Dolenz, Michael Nesmith and Peter Tork made the trippy feature *Head* (1968). Notably, the group's usual composers, Tommy Boyce and Bobby Hart, are absent from this project. The first song on *Head* is the ethereal and psychedelic "Porpoise Song" (written by Carole King and Gerry Goffin). Next up is Michael Nesmith's souped-up country rocker "Circle Sky." Peter Tork also contributes

After two years of NBC-TV comedy and a string of hit singles ("I'm a Believer," "Last Train to Clarksville," etc.), the Monkees made the trippy feature *Head* (Columbia Pictures, 1968).

original material, the Eastern-tinged "Can You Dig It?" and the acid-rock rant "Long Title: Do I Have to Do This All Over Again." The group embraces its folk side on Toni Stern's "As We Go Along" and its music hall flair on Henry Nillson's "Daddy Song." Overall, the songs account for about half of the material, with absurd dialogue taking up the rest. While the songs are often catchy they aren't the Monkees' most famous or accessible material.

One of the bit players in *Head* is Frank Zappa, whose group the Mothers of Invention recorded such psychedelic classics as *Freak Out!* (1966) and *We're Only in It for the Money* (1968). Zappa made two movies of his own, the mockumentary *200 Motels* (1971) and the concert film (with clay animation sequences) *Baby Snakes* (1979). Actually, he'd intended to make a sci-fi film in the late '60s, *Uncle Meat*, but ended up releasing its would-be soundtrack as just another (albeit excellent) Mothers album in 1969. *200 Motels* was Zappa's twelfth album in half as many years, and it's a double. Zappa recorded *200 Motels* with his band, as well as the Royal Philharmonic Orchestra, in England at the filming at Pinewood Studios. Only 24 of the 34 tracks featured on the soundtrack appear in the film, and several other tracks appear only in brief or truncated form. On it, one hears the wildly talented composer-bandleader exploring amped-up rock ("Magic Fingers"), grand filmic orchestration with choir ("Semi-Fraudulent/Direct from Hollywood Overture"), country western pastiche ("Lonesome Cowboy Burt"), loads of avant-garde orchestral passages ("Motorhead's Midnight Ranch"), Zappa's trademark raunch ("Penis Dimension") and absurd skits about traveling musicians (regarding the temptation of stealing hotel towels, the mysteries of catered food and, most humorously, the compulsion to quit the band and go solo). Ideas for the film/soundtrack began to gestate as soon as Zappa and company signed with United Artists to make the movie. In fact, the prodigious musician wrote in the booklet notes of his album *Chunga's Revenge* (1970) that all of the vocals on the album provide a preview of the story of *200 Motels*—not that the film has a strong storyline, but the basic concept is in place on *Chunga's* tracks like "Road Ladies." It would be stretch to categorize a lot of the music heard on *200 Motels* as rock. Zappa's astonishing gift for complex orchestral arrangements makes even the most progressive rock bands sound pedestrian. Clearly, had Zappa been born even 20 years earlier he would have written "serious music" all of the time. But, as destiny would have it, he split his genius between rock and classical forms. *200 Motels* may not be Zappa's greatest album, but it's an excellent example of his astounding musical gifts.

Another ambitious rock group of the era with cinematic aspirations was the Who. Part of the first wave of British Invasion groups, the Who racked up several smash hits ("My Generation," "I Can See for Miles," "I Can't Explain," etc.) before making their groundbreaking album, *Tommy* (1969). This rock opera about a "deaf, dumb and blind kid who sure plays a mean pinball" ushered in the era of the story-driven con-

Roger Daltrey, the singer of the Who, played the title role in the band's tremendously successful rock opera *Tommy* (Columbia Pictures, 1975).

cept album, bolstered by the hit single "Pinball Wizard." It was re-recorded in 1972 as an all-star production on Ode Records with the London Symphony Orchestra and Chamber Choir, starring the Who's Roger Daltrey and John Entwistle, along with Rod Stewart, Stevie Winwood, Ringo Starr, and other singers and actors. Packaged like a classical opera with a full libretto, the orchestral version of *Tommy* is overblown and lacks the raw energy of the original on MCA. Still, the extravagant production is suggestive of the piece's dramatic possibility, which was finally realized by the over-the-top film in 1975. Naturally, the film warranted a soundtrack release on Polydor, this time featuring members of the Who. As if three versions of *Tommy* weren't enough, the 1992 Broadway production is available on RCA. All things considered, the original 1969 recording is the definitive version.

As it turns out, Pete Townsend had more than one rock opera in him. The original *Tommy* album was such a monster success that expectations were exceedingly high for its follow-up—especially from Townsend's perspective. He set out to create another rock opera, *Lifehouse*, about a dystopian society that is eventually redeemed by music. The plan entailed an album, live performances and a movie. Universal Pictures even expressed interest and allegedly promised upfront funding of a million dollars. After about six months in development hell, Townsend shelved the project and used several of its songs ("Baba O'Riley," "Won't Get Fooled Again" and "Behind Blue Eyes" among them) to make the group's next album, *Who's Next* (1971), which is now considered one of the group's best. Thirty years later, Townsend released a six-disc set, *The Lifehouse Chronicles*, featuring original demos.

Before long, Townsend came up with another rock opera that would result in another double album and, by decade's end, a movie, too. *Quadrophenia* is a coming of age story about a young mod in England during the early '60s. More autobiographical than *Tommy*, it features such classic Who tracks as "The Real Me" and "Love, Reign o'er Me." The original album came out in 1973. The soundtrack for the 1979 film (featuring the acting debut of Gordon "Sting" Sumner) revisits some of the album's best tracks and adds period material by the Kingsmen ("Louie, Louie"), James Brown ("Night Train") and Booker T and the MGs ("Green Onions"), among others. The Who also recorded three new songs for the soundtrack ("Get Out and Stay Out," "Four Faces" and "Joker James") to flesh out the plot. Unlike the orchestral and film versions of *Tommy*, *Quadrophenia* (the album, film and soundtrack) is down to earth. Like *Tommy*, the original *Quadrophenia* album remains the essential document, with the soundtrack being of secondary interest.

That same year saw the release of the Who documentary *The Kids Are Alright*, featuring live and TV performances of the band's classic songs.

Another band of the era with cinematic aspirations was Pink Floyd. Originally a psychedelic space rock band, Pink Floyd is best known for a run of bleak but beautifully executed albums in the '70s. Long before the landmark album and film *The Wall*, the group recorded two soundtracks for filmmaker Barbet Schroeder: *More* (1969) and *Obscured by Clouds* (for *The Valley*, 1972). The films are trippy hippie affairs that are rarely seen today, though the director went on to work in Hollywood.

Pink Floyd's third album overall, *More* reached the top ten in Britain, but is generally overshadowed by the group's earlier, Syd Barrett–era albums *The Piper at the Gates of Dawn* (1967) and *A Saucerful of Secrets* (1968). Stylistically, it's a transitional album containing full throttle rock ("The Nile Song") and psychedelia ("Quicksilver"), as well as gentle folk ("Green Is the Colour") and blues ("More Blues"). Like a lot of the group's music, there is a strong cinematic grandeur in *More*'s atmospheric soundscapes, but in the end the whole is less memorable than some of Pink Floyd's non-soundtrack albums.

Obscured by Clouds also suffers in comparison to the albums that came immediately before and after its release (namely, *Meddle*, 1971, and particularly *Dark Side of the Moon*, 1973). Again, it modestly presents various sides of the group, from space rock (the title track) to pastoral folk ("Wots ... uh the Deal"), but never quite catches fire. Interestingly, the tracks "Burning Bridges" and "Childhood's End" sound like prototypes for "Breathe" and "Time," two classic tracks from the band's best-selling *Dark Side of the Moon*. In the end, both Pink Floyd soundtracks have remained in print (on Capitol) due to the band's popularity and not because *More* or *Obscured* are particularly great. Although they could hardly be deemed essential Floyd albums, they remain fascinating entries in the psychedelic soundtrack genre.

Pink Floyd's Roger Waters also teamed up with Ron Geesin on the documentary/art film *The Body* (1970). Geesin's name will be familiar to hardcore fans of Floyd, as he co-wrote the sidelong suite on the band's *Atom Heart Mother* (1970). Geesin's classical-styled cello melody for "Breast Milky" provides ill preparation for his work on *The Body*, which is far more experimental and displays his mastery of tape manipulation. Geesin dominates *The Body*, claiming sole compositional credit for 14 of the 22 tracks. Four of the tracks are collaborations and three are quiet acoustic numbers by Waters alone. The collaborations and Geesin's tracks are arrestingly experimental and display a strong penchant for tape manipulation and sound collage, as well as avant-garde music. This was typical of Geesin's recorded work starting in 1967, which undoubtedly influenced Waters' similarly styled "Several Species of Furry Animals Gathered Together in a Cave and Grooving with a Pict" from Pink Floyd's *Ummagumma* (1969). Listening to *The Body* isn't likely to leave a lasting melodic impression, but on several tracks Geesin and Waters memorably exploit the sounds of the human body, from breathing, burping, farting, skin slapping, coughing, grunting, and so on. One imagines that hearing this "body music" within the movie's context is the preferred way to experience its outré sounds.

Pink Floyd also contributed to *Zabriskie Point* (1970), performing three tracks on the soundtrack, though Rhino's extended two-disc set adds four more tracks. The first track, "Heart Beat, Pig Meat," is experimental and abstract, with echoing voices, a heartbeat drum and ominous organ. "Crumbling Land" finds Floyd in an up-tempo folksy mood, with vocal harmonies, acoustic guitars and shimmering cymbal work. "Come in Number 51, Your Time Is Up" starts spacey and slow motion but then rips into an acid rock death spiral with screams like the band's classic "Careful with That Axe, Eugene."

Pink Floyd wasn't the only band contributing to films of the psychedelic rock era. On *Zabriskie Point* they are joined by the Grateful Dead and solo work of the Dead's late leader Jerry Garcia. There is an excerpt of the band's classic track "Dark Star" and a serene guitar solo by Garcia on "Love Scene." Also featured are country rockers the Youngbloods ("Sugar Babe") and Kaleidoscope ("Brother Mary," "Mickey's Tune"). More country and bluegrass flavor comes courtesy of John Fahey ("Dance of Death") and Roscoe Holcomb ("I Wish I Was a Single Girl Again"). Then, for an unexpected bit of nostalgia there's Patti Page's rendition of "Tennessee Waltz." Overall, it's an odd combination: classic country, modern country, country rock, the Dead and Pink Floyd. It makes about as much sense as Antonioni's notoriously oblique homage to American hippies.

Zabriskie Point is hardly the only example of a late '60s anti-establishment soundtrack. Among the many trippy movies of the late '60s and early '70s a few had soundtrack releases featuring groups of the era.

One of the earliest and best examples is *The Trip* (1967). The film is one of the better "head" movies of the period. *The Trip* marked the debut of the San Francisco–based psychedelic rock band the Electric Flag. Founded by blues-rock guitarist Mike Bloomfield, the Electric Flag made the album before they even performed a gig (their debut gig ended up being the Monterey Pop Festival in 1967). The lead off track, "Peter's Trip," is Beatle-esque in its elegant approach to psychedelica. From there, the soundtrack is mystical ("Joint Passing"), nostalgic ("Senior Citizen"), whimsical ("Hobbit"), druggy ("Synesthesia"), carnival-esque ("Green and Gold"), jazzy ("Peter Gets Off"), groovy ("Practice Music"), funky ("Fine Jung Thing") and bluesy ("Getting Hard"). *The Trip* is one of the best rock soundtracks of the era.

Another soundtrack released in 1967 belongs to *Riot on Sunset Strip* (1967). Sam Katzman, who also produced *Rock Around the Clock*, billed *Riot* as "the most shocking film of our generation." The L.A. garage rock band the Standells (best known for their Stones-ish single "Dirty Water") perform the punkish title track. Even more punk is the Chocolate Watchband, who performs the ornery "Don't Need Your Lovin'" and the ripping "Sitting There Standing." Both L.A. bands appear in the film, miming songs from the soundtrack in the Pandora's Box nightclub (actually a Paramount soundstage). The Mugwumps (not Mama Cass' group) perform the rollicking country rocker

"Sunset Sally." And what would a Curb production be without his favorite session band, the Sidewalk Sounds, who perform the surf rocker "The Sunset Theme" and the bubblegum popper "Make the Music Pretty." Also on tap are Debra Travis for a sensitive folk number, "Old Country" (which was cut from the film), and the Mom's Boys for a typical sunny '60s psychedelic rocker.

Also released in 1967 was the documentary that aimed to tell "the truth about the 'Now' generation," *Teenage Rebellion* (a.k.a. *Mondo Teeno* in Italy). The soundtrack by Curb, Hollywood session trumpeter Bob Summers and the Arrows' guitarist Allan ranges from propulsive power pop (the title track) to sunny surf sounds ("The French Kiss"), from fuzz-buster biker rock ("The Young World") to proto-noise rock ("Make Love Not War"). While those tracks offer pure rock thrills, *Teenage Rebellion* also boasts a handful of unintentionally funny spoken word tracks with titles like "Pot Party," "The Call Girl" and "The Gay Teenager." Narrator Burt Topper walks a fine line between objectivity and moral objection as psychedelia and beatnik vibes provide musical counterpoint; it's funny how the hallucinogenic crime jazz that accompanies Topper's indictment of drug culture only serves to make that culture more attractive. With music like that, why would you resist "the crazy acid," as Topper refers to LSD. The only disappointment on this otherwise strong soundtrack is "Orgy Around the World," which comes off like music for an eccentric square dance.

Speaking of pot parties, future Republican politician Curb also scored *Maryjane* (1968), starring teen idol Fabian. Curb gets the job done with help from surf rock drummer Larry Brown, Allan and the Arrows, long forgotten vocalist Mike Clifford and golden-throated Mrs. Miller of *Incredibly Strange Music* notoriety. Irrepressibly cheerful, with double entendre lyrics and woozy horns, the title track must be among the funniest odes to marijuana use in the history of pop music. Clifford's straight-faced vocal and the giddily catchy melody will hook on first listen. Mrs. Miller also gives the tune a whirl, but hearing her wince-inducing vibrato is too much to take. The instrumentals range from faux-Parisian ("Ellie's Theme") to freewheeling ("The Fun Zone"), from folksy ("Jerry's Theme") to jazzy ("Store Stealing"), from abstract and trippy ("Grass Party") to acid rockin' ("Bay City Boys"). There are showcases for electric harpsichord ("Gas Hassle") and surf guitar ("Pursuit"). *Maryjane* isn't likely to blow any minds, but it is among Curb's most satisfyingly diverse soundtracks.

Another Curb-related soundtrack of the era belongs to *Psych-Out* (1968), another counterculture film produced by Dick Clark. The soundtrack features music by Strawberry Alarm Clock and the Seeds, among others. Being an AIP release, house composer Ronald Stein is credited with original music and adaptation, but session band the Storybook performs the material. The serene sitar number "Psych-Out Sanctorum," the kaleidoscopic "Beads of Innocence," the groovy "The Love Children" and the darkly abrasive title track fit in alongside the tracks contributed by the established groups. In fact, the Storybook even performs a track written by S.A. Clock, a.k.a. Strawberry Alarm Clock ("The Pretty Song from Psych-Out"). Naturally, Strawberry Alarm Clock gets more than a single writing credit. The SoCal group also performs the hit title track and "Rainy Day Mushroom Pillow" from their breakout album *Incense and Peppermints* (1967), as well as "The World's on Fire," which is original to *Psych-Out*. Fellow SoCal psychedelic band the Seeds contribute "Two Fingers Pointing on You" (lifted from their third album, *Future*, 1967). The tune resembles their hit "Pushin' Too Hard." Also on the bill is the Denver group Boenzee Cryque, which delivers a derivative of Jimi Hendrix's "Purple Haze" with a touch of Vanilla Fudge's "You Keep Me Hanging On." In the film, Jack Nicholson's band is seen performing it in a psychedelic nightclub, but in a very lackadaisical manner; just seeing Jack (with pony tail) sleepwalking through a blistering guitar solo is one of the more absurd moments in this loopy movie. Overall, *Psych-Out* is a fun trip down Haight-Ashbury lane, but falls short of the bar set by the Electric Flag's *The Trip*.

While *The Trip* and *Psych-Out* present a fictionalized version of California hippie culture, *Mondo Hollywood* (1967) takes the documentary approach. The Curb-produced *Mondo Hollywood* features Allan and the Arrows, along with less familiar acts like Mugwump Establishment, the Riptides, God Pan and 18th Century Concepts. Allan and the Arrows rip through "Moonfire," an outstanding showcase for the band's drummer, presumably David Winogrond. The Riptides' "Last Wave of the Day" is typical surf pop with Beach Boys–style harmonies. God Pan's "Great God Pan" is like a kiddie novelty number that surely only flower children would enjoy. Mugwump Establishment (one of a few '60s bands named for William S. Burroughs' beat generation anti-novel *Naked Lunch*) performs two psychedelic numbers: the vocal theme "Mondo Hollywood (City of Dreams)" and the instrumental jam "Mondo Hollywood Freakout." 18th Century Concepts drums up a lively brass band "Magic Night March." Also featured are singers Mike Clifford (the hard-charging "The Magic Night"), Bobby Jameson (the blues shooter "Vietnam"), Darrell Dee (the limp ballad "You're Beautiful") and, most memorably, Teddy and Darrell (the monster masher "Beast of Sunset Strip").

A cast member of *Mondo Hollywood*, Bobby Beausoleil (as "Cupid"), went on to incarceration due to his involvement as a member of Charles Manson's infamous family. While he was doing time he scored Kenneth Anger's experimental film *Lucifer Rising* (1972). On first listen, Beausoleil's soundtrack seems little more than an intriguing bit of space rock. On the other hand, read the extensive booklet notes for this two-CD soundtrack reissue and the project becomes more fascinating. For one thing, Beausoleil's group the Freedom Orchestra recorded it in prison (nice bit of irony there). Consider also that Anger fired Aleister Crowley aficionado and Led Zeppelin ringmaster Jimmy

Page as the musical contributor for *Lucifer Rising* when the filmmaker first heard Beausoleil's creation, which is stately, spacey and hypnotic.

Another late '60s documentary soundtrack, *Revolution* (1968), features somewhat better known B-grade groups of the period, namely Quicksilver Messenger Service, Steve Miller Band and Mother Earth. QMS performs the rootsy, acid-drenched "Codeine" and "Babe, I'm Gonna Leave You" (the same as the Led Zeppelin tune, but sounding remarkably different). Meanwhile, Steve Miller—long before his days as a Top 40 "space cowboy"—kicks up a bit of country blues on "Mercury Blues," "Superbyrd" and "Your Old Lady." More bluesy rock comes courtesy of Nashville's Mother Earth, performing the title track and "Without Love." Overall, *Revolution* is a lesser entry in the genre, but the day-glo cover art is worth framing.

Speaking of trippy documentaries of 1967, who can forget Timothy Leary's *Turn On, Tune In, Drop Out*? Probably a lot of people, actually, considering the brain cells destroyed during the "Summer of Love." The soundtrack features Leary talking about "electric penetration" and "endless ecstasies of couples." Maryvonne Giecarz, Lars Eric and Richard Bond are credited with the soundtrack, which underlies the acid ramblings with "mystical" temple gongs and sitars.

Possibly one of the freakier soundtracks of the era belongs to *Angel Angel Down We Go* (a.k.a. *Cult of the Damned*, 1969), which is pretty weird in its own right. The sitar psychedelia, funky acid rock, country and folk numbers come courtesy of Fred Karger who worked on several rock films, including the Chubby Checker vehicle *Twist Around the Clock* (1961), three starring Elvis, and various hippie flicks (*Hot Rods to Hell*, *The Love-Ins*, *Riot on Sunset Strip*, 1967). *Angel* has some twisted songs celebrating obesity ("The Fat Song") and incest ("Mother Love"). The movie has drug-fueled scenes of ritual murder, cannibalism, flagellation, kinky sex and Satanism (fun for the whole family, perhaps, if your last name is Manson).

For every hippie flick with a rock soundtrack there are others—usually mainstream studio pictures with big stars—featuring jazzy pop scores that occasionally flirt with rock when a scene calls for it. Movies like Hy Averback's *I Love You Alice B. Toklas* (a.k.a. *Kiss My Butterfly*, 1968) and Gene Saks' *Cactus Flower* (1969) are a bit like that. Interestingly, both films concern men who, in the throes of a mid-life crisis, hook up with exciting, free-spirited hippie chicks.

Averback's film features music by Bernstein, a well-established Hollywood composer with a string of successful scores behind him, ranging from jazzy (*The Man with the Golden Arm*, 1955) to epic (*The Ten Commandments*, 1956) to action packed (*The Great Escape*, 1963). Clearly, there was no pinning down this mercurial and legendary talent. For this Peter Sellers comedy, Bernstein contributes a light, satirical pop sound, complete with mystical sitar, exotic tabla, kitchen sink percussion and trippy production effects. Jazzy flute, strutting brass and a bit of back beat add attitude to this repetitive, but charming, score. The title song is a mere ditty with only a handful of lyrics.

Cactus Flower, another mid-life crisis comedy, features a groovy but laid back score by Quincy Jones. *Cactus Flower* was among a whopping eight movies that "Q" scored in 1969, and while it isn't as colorful as *The Italian Job* or as funky as *The Lost Man*, it has some appealing tracks. The theme, "The Time for Love Is Any Time," is elegant easy listening sung by the incomparable Sarah Vaughan. Things quickly get groovy on "To Sir with Love," and soulful on "I Needs to Be Bee'd With," a showcase for singer Johnny Wesley. Q's take on Neil Diamond's and the Monkees' "I'm a Believer" features a nice round bass guitar tone, but the arrangement sticks too close to the song's bubble gum origins. Following a lush piano rendition of the theme, Q gets back into the groove on "She Hangs Out (Doin' the Dentist)." The vibe gets easy on "The Spell You Spin" before flirting with rock on Tommy Boyce and Bobby Hart's up-tempo "I Wonder What She's Doin' Tonight."

No one is likely to mistake the music on these two classic hippie-era movie soundtracks for rock, but that just goes to show how mainstream Hollywood softened the counterculture scene for Middle American audiences.

While some mainstream films relied on studio regulars like Mancini, Bernstein and Jones, others turned to popular songwriters. One of the most famous examples is the soundtrack for the award-winning blockbuster *The Graduate* (1967). With songs by Paul Simon (and performed by Simon & Garfunkel), and additional music by jazz pianist Dave Grusin, the film struck a big chord with audiences and record buyers. As a portrait of anti-establishment disillusionment and promiscuous sex, the film was a massive success. The soundtrack also enjoyed immense popularity, hitting number one on Billboard. It was the first modern soundtrack to repackage previously released pop songs that the filmmaker appropriated to fit certain scenes in the movie. This is a common practice today, and a regrettable one at that, as it tends to coerce music fans into purchasing music they may already own in a context that has nothing to do with the musical artist's original vision. With all due respect to Grusin (whose incidental music is excellent), the fans that purchased *The Graduate* soundtrack did so to get "Mrs. Robinson," the only Simon & Garfunkel track on the soundtrack not already available on one of the duo's albums. While director Mike Nichols' use of Simon's songs is spot on, the practice of pop song appropriation has become little more than a marketing strategy for albums that feature "music from and inspired by" the latest formulaic flick in lieu of an actual soundtrack release that features the original score.

Arlo Guthrie penned another notable folk-flavored anti-establishment soundtrack for the comedy-drama *Alice's Restaurant* (1969), in which the son of Woody Guthrie plays the leading role. *Alice's Restaurant* should not be confused with Guthrie's classic debut album of the same name released two years earlier. Although both albums feature versions of "Alice's Restaurant Mas-

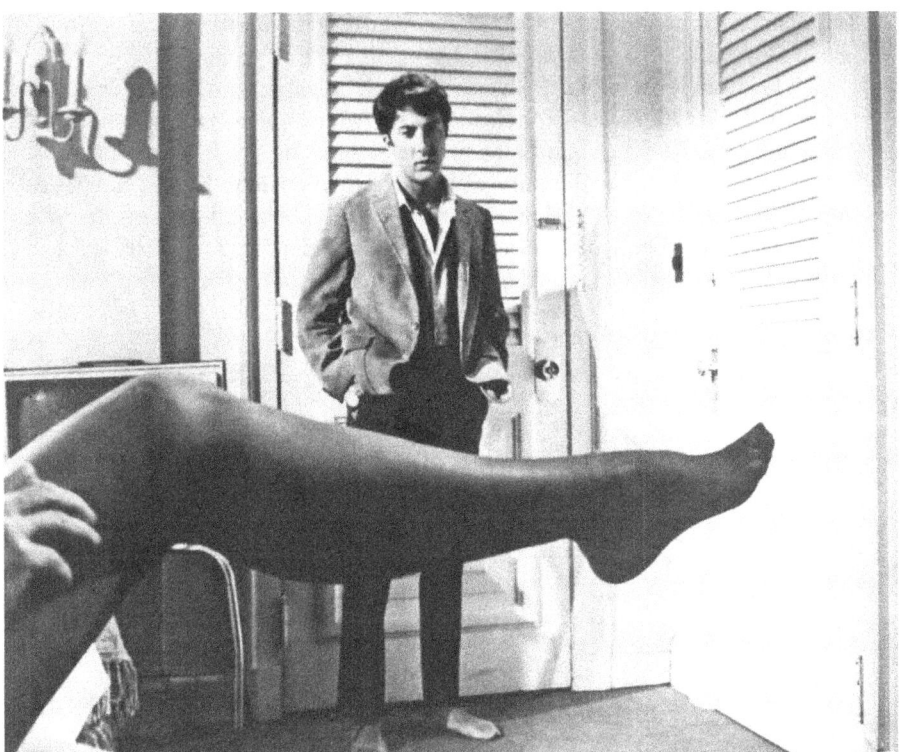

Anne Bancroft seduces Dustin Hoffman in *The Graduate* (MGM/Embassy, 1967). The use of Simon & Garfunkel's folk-rock songs captures Benjamin Braddock's uncertainty, while Dave Grusin's jazz-lounge source music evokes Mrs. Robinson's easy sophistication.

sacre," the original sidelong version is superior to the two-part near-parody recorded for the soundtrack. The rest of the soundtrack consists of folk instrumentals by Guthrie or producer Garry Sherman, plus an a cappella version of "Amazing Grace," a country-fried honky tonk sung by Al Shackton, a mediocre Joni Mitchell song sung by an impersonator (Tigger Outlaw), and a guitar solo on "Crash Pad Improvs." *Alice's Restaurant*, like many counter-culture film soundtracks of the late '60s, remains a product of its time, a bit dated in its style and attractive to collectors only.

There is one more notable folk-oriented "songtrack" of the era—the free-spirited *Harold & Maude* (1971), featuring tunes by Cat Stevens. Songs such as "Don't Be Shy," "If You Want to Sing Out, Sing Out" and "Trouble" work beautifully within the film and remain cult favorites by the popular singer-songwriter who later converted to Islam.

In the history of popular soundtracks, however, folk and singer-songwriters constitute a mere supporting act in the comparative concert extravaganza of rock.

The ultimate example of the late '60s rock movie is, without a doubt, Russ Meyer's *Beyond the Valley of the Dolls* (a.k.a. *Hollywood Vixens*), even though it came out in 1970. The soundtrack features a score by Stu Phillips and additional music by psychedelic pop groups Strawberry Alarm Clock, the Sandpipers and the Carrie Nations. The latter group—an all-girl outfit—was invented for the film, which documents the sex-and-drugs rock party scene in psychedelic L.A. in all its seedy, depraved glory.

Stu Phillips' soundtrack for *Beyond the Valley of the Dolls* (1970) features performances by the psych pop groups Strawberry Alarm Clock, the Sandpipers and the Carrie Nations. (CD cover appears courtesy of Harkit Records; graphic design by Taiga Grebe.)

In the booklet notes for Harkit Records' CD of the *BVD* soundtrack, Phillips recollects that he composed under "the Svengali spell of Russ Meyer":

> Meyer liked his musical scores to have as little continuity as possible. A dash of this; a touch of that; some far-out reference to a theme that has nothing whatsoever to do with the scene—but strange as it all seemed, it somehow magically jelled into a Russ Meyer classic.... Every frame and foot of a Russ Meyer film bore his personal signature.... [Meyer] was prone to finding little open spaces between the dialogue to squeeze in some little odd and completely unnecessary piece of library music.

Sadly, Phillips notes, the original soundtrack LP release did not feature actress Lynn Carey's powerful vocals for the Carrie Nations material due to a contract stipulation. Phillips was forced to use the "adequate" replacement Ami Rushes. "For more than 30 years, many fans tried in vain to find recordings of Lynn's original vocals, but with little or no success," he notes. Thankfully, the Harkit reissue restores Carey's original vocal renditions.

Rife with sex, drugs and rock 'n' roll, the UK film *Groupie Girl* (a.k.a. *I Am a Groupie*) also boasts a psychedelic soundtrack, this one featuring Opal Butterfly, English Rose, Salon Band, Billy Boyle and Virgin Stigma.

Perhaps the most commercial hippie-era soundtracks belong to the musicals *Godspell* (1971), *Jesus Christ Superstar* (1973), and *Hair* (1979). *Hair* premiered off–Broadway in 1967 and became an on–Broadway smash the following year. Oddly, the movie didn't appear until 1979, long after hippie culture had lost its relevance. Astonishingly, there are at least 29 different versions of the score by James Rado and Jerome Ragni (lyrics), and Galt MacDermot (music). The soundtrack spawned such hit songs as "Aquarius." (MacDermot also scored the classic and influential blaxploitation movie *Cotton Comes to Harlem*, 1970).

Godspell is based on the Gospel of Saint Matthew, with music and lyrics by Stephen Schwartz. It first appeared off–Broadway in 1971 and spawned a hit single, "Day by Day," in 1972. The film appeared in 1973. Understandably, the storyline isn't about hippie culture, but the art direction and music owe a considerable debt to psychedelic pop culture.

The same is basically true of *Jesus Christ Superstar*, which originated as a rock opera album by composer Andrew Lloyd Webber and lyricist Tim Rice. The show appeared on Broadway in 1971 and on the big screen in 1973. There are numerous recorded versions of *JCS*. The original features Ian Gillian, lead singer of Deep Purple, in the title role. Glam pan-flasher Gary Glitter also had a role, albeit a minor one.

Enjoyment of all three musicals really depends on one's taste for wall-to-wall singing. For that reason, show tunes aren't of primary interest for most soundtrack collectors. On the other hand, if one thinks of them as rock operas as opposed to soundtracks it is easy to see how *Hair*, *Godspell* and

Jesus Christ Superstar stack up nicely alongside an album like *Tommy* by the Who.

The subject of rock musicals isn't complete without a mention of *The Rocky Horror Picture Show* (1975). The brainchild of Jim Sharman (director, screenwriter) and Richard O'Brien (screenwriter, play author, songwriter), *Rocky Horror* remains a popular "midnight movie" experience for audiences everywhere, even three-plus decades after its release. Its manic blend of Broadway musical, Frankenstein-inspired horror story and shameless sexuality—both gay and straight—is unique in the annals of film. As anyone who has seen the movie knows—and that would be many—the movie's "sweet transvestite," Dr. Frank N. Furter, not only creates a beefcake "monster" for his own carnal amusement, but also seduces reluctant male and female guests. Those plot points alone warrant its inclusion here, but Tim Curry's performance as the lecherous, leering, lingerie-clad "transsexual from Transylvania" makes this musical movie a must see and a must hear. There are numerous stage and screen versions of the soundtrack, but the original 1975 soundtrack is the most popular choice.

The rock musical *The Rocky Horror Picture Show* (20th Century–Fox, 1975) became a favorite with participatory audiences at midnight movie showings. (Photograph courtesy of the John Monaghan Collection.)

While hippie culture is a suitable frame of reference for shows like *Hair* and *Godspell*, it also provides a provocative context for *Joe* (1970), starring Peter Boyle as an outspoken, gun-toting hippie hater and bigot. *Joe* is just one of two films scored by jazz multi-instrumentalist Bobby Scott (his other belongs to Herbert Biberman's *Slaves*, 1969). The style favored for *Joe* is pure crime jazz. Horns prowl like police cars through the city at night, headlights flashing around corners catching furtive figures that race down alleyways to the quick pace of drums and repetitive keyboard patterns. "The Expiration of Frank" is an excellent example of Scott's mastery of the crime jazz idiom. One might even mistake it for a Quincy Jones soundtrack, like *The Lost Man*, which was released a year earlier. "Compton's Hangout" is big band blues for a dimly lit lounge, featuring a sly piano solo; coy, muted horns; and a bit of bongo. "It's a Crock" goes back out on the streets—the dirty streets of New York in the tawdry era of *Midnight Cowboy*. "When in Rome" inexplicably introduces sitar to the mix. It's a solo piece that is thankfully less than two minutes long. Scott's final entry is another quick blast of crime jazz, "Send the Hippies to Hell." Scott's score is book-ended by super-smooth Jerry "The Ice Man" Butler who sings the drowsy ballad "Where Are You Goin'?" The former leader of the Impressions draws on his church choir background for the gospel-tinged soul number "You Can Fly." Bahamian folksinger Exuma contributes the biting yet uplifting "You Don't Know What's Goin' On."

The soundtrack actually spawned a companion album full of *Joe*'s incendiary dialogue that rips on hippies, blacks, etc. Most of it is dialogue, except for Dean Michaels' "Hey Joe" tune, which has nothing in common with the song popularized by Jimi Hendrix. Butler's "You Can Fly" makes a repeat appearance.

Naturally, movies of social consciousness with rock soundtracks weren't limited to the U.S. Making the cut are *Here We Go 'Round the Mulberry Bush* (1967), *Up the Junction* (1968) and *Bronco Bullfrog* (1969).

Here We Go 'Round the Mulberry Bush (1967) is a swinging London coming-of-age sex comedy. Director Clive Donner commissioned tracks by British bands Traffic (featuring Stevie Winwood) and the Spencer Davis Group. The theme song, by Traffic, hit the Top 10, and the album was a best seller. Nearly every track is a catchy, energetic rock vocal number with a groovy high '60s vibe. The notable exception is the spectacular Hammond organ showcase "Waltz for Caroline." The Rykodisc reissue features daft incidental dialogue, colorful film stills and poster art reproduction, and nostalgic booklet notes by Hunter Davies, who wrote the original book *Here We Go, 'Round the Mulberry Bush* (Davies' comma). He also is the writer of the only authorized Beatles biography.

Manfred Mann's score for *Up the Junction* (1968) mixes jazzy instrumentals and Brit pop. There's even the single version of the title track and its original B-side, "Sleepy Hollow." The band had previously appeared on the *What's*

Manfred Mann's theme song for *Up the Junction* (Paramount Pictures, 1968) makes observations about a working class neighborhood from the point of view of "Polly" (Suzy Kendall, fourth from left), a rich girl who chooses to work in a factory.

New Pussycat? soundtrack, performing Burt Bacharach's "My Little Red Book." By the time keyboardist Mike Hugg and Mann had composed and recorded several TV themes and commercial jingles, the group was primed to deliver a full score. *Up the Junction*'s theme song sets the scene, shifting between leisurely tempo on the verse and a more upbeat tempo on the chorus. The rest of the vocal tracks—such as "Sing Songs of Love" and "Walking Round"—share the theme's penchant for harmonized vocals, acoustic guitars and piano. The style certainly would not be mistaken for any period but the late '60s. The instrumentals show more of an R'n'B flare, using organ and horns to carry the melodies. "Sheila's Dance" features some rousing piano by Hugg and some backward psychedelic horn effects. "Belgravia" is the jazziest of the lot, and certainly doesn't fit Manfred Mann's profile. And "Wailing Horn" boasts a cool echoing drum break. Manfred Mann went on to score (and perform in) Jess Franco's sleazy psychedelic psychodrama *Venus in Furs* (1970).

Bronco Bullfrog is a neo-realistic film that depicts the East End youth scene after the Mods embraced flower power. Its screenplay won the Cannes Carte d'Or. The soundtrack, by the underrated band Audience, mixes psychedelic rock with folk and R&B. Singer/guitarist Howard Werth, saxophonist Keith Gemmell, bassist Trevor Williams and percussionist Tony Connor keep things lively with several well-arranged, up-tempo tunes that wouldn't sound out of place on an early Jethro Tull record. Werth sometimes sounds like a young Peter Gabriel, and other members contribute pleasing backup harmonies.

The Beat Goes On

The seeds of rock were sown in cinema during the '50s, flowered during the '60s, and pollinated the diverse world of cinema during the '70s. In the dark days of the early '70s, as the Vietnam War droned on and the Watergate scandal rocked America's collective psyche, Baby Boomers began their nostalgia trip for the relatively innocent '50s. Filmmaker George Lucas exploited America's need for a sentimental journey with *American Graffiti* (1973), which inspired the nostalgic hit TV show *Happy Days*. Later, the animated feature *American Hot Wax* (1978) served up more early rock 'n' roll. Both films had best-selling needle-drop soundtracks featuring artists like Chuck Berry and Jerry Lee Lewis.

On the flipside, the increasing self-importance of rock music during the early '70s ("album-oriented rock") manifested itself in rock operas like *Tommy* and bloated concert films like *The Song Remains the Same* (complete with fantasy sequences).

While concert films rocked cineplexes, disco took over urban nightclubs in the mid–1970s. It wasn't until the release of *Saturday Night Fever* (1977), starring John Travolta, that disco briefly overtook rock as the pop music of choice for soundtracks. Ironically, by the time the movie came out the disco fad had mostly blown over. Still, the soundtrack hit number one on Billboard, featured several number one singles by the Bee Gees ("How Deep Is Your Love," "Night Fever," "If I Can't Have You"), and almost immediately became the best-selling soundtrack of all time (a whopping 25 million copies—of a double album, no less). Though it was hardly the first soundtrack to exploit audience interest in popular song, *Saturday Night Fever*'s success made song-oriented soundtracks an ever-more-popular gimmick for movie studios and record labels that continues today.

But, as most rock fans contend, disco sucks. The last word in rock cinema of the '70s is, without a doubt, *Rock 'n' Roll High School* (1979), starring the legendary punk band the Ramones in a supporting roll. Although some of the songs featured on the soundtrack ("Blitzkrieg Bop," "Teenage Lobotomy") come from previously released Ramones albums, the title track made its premiere in the movie (and later turned up on the band's *End of the Century*, (1980). It's another tight, fast punk classic from the band that practically invented the form. Joining the Ramones on the soundtrack are Nick Lowe,

The blockbuster success of *Saturday Night Fever* (Paramount Pictures, 1977), starring John Travolta (seen here with Karen Lynn Gorney), was propelled by its popular disco soundtrack—the most successful "songtrack" of the Silver Age.

Chuck Berry, Devo, Brian Eno, Eddie & the Hot Rods, Brownsville Station, Todd Rundgren, Alice Cooper and others. Although many of the songs on this soundtrack previously appeared elsewhere, *Rock 'n' Roll High School* remains an essential rock soundtrack. More than any other movie of the era, it demonstrates through its soundtrack and its story about teenage rebellion that rock music is an unstoppable force—in life and in cinema.

12* Essential Rock 'n' Roll Soundtracks

Rock Around the Clock (1956)—Various Artists
The Endless Summer (1966)—The Sandals
The Wild Angels (1966)—Davie Allan and the Arrows
Hells Angels on Wheels (1967)—Stu Phillips
The Trip (1967)—The Electric Flag
The Graduate (1967)—Simon & Garfunkel and David Grusin
Easy Rider (1969)—Various Artists
Beyond the Valley of the Dolls (1970)—Stu Phillips and Others
Stone (1974)—Billy Green
The Rocky Horror Picture Show (1975)—Richard O'Brien
Saturday Night Fever (1977)—Various Artists
Rock 'n' Roll High School (1979)—The Ramones and Others

**Other essential rock soundtracks, such as* Candy, Barbarella, Vampyros Lesbos *and* Schoolgirl Report, *appear in Chapter 3's list of "12 Essential Sexy Soundtracks."*

Epilogue

THE RESURGENT INTEREST IN SILVER AGE SOUNDTRACKS

The Silver Age soundtrack legacy is as far reaching as it is stylistically broad. In fact, interest in Silver Age soundtracks, which were originally released on LP or another pre-digital format, has flourished in recent years thanks to CD reissues and compilations.

In the late '90s, there came a resurgent interest in Silver Age soundtracks, thanks in part to pre-millennial popular fascination with all things "retro," including swing, lounge and exotica musics, as well as fashion, style, and cinema of the '50s, '60s and '70s. The audience largely responsible for bringing about the retro revolution, including interest in Silver Age soundtracks, was Generation X. Born between 1964 and 1979 (coincidentally the most protean part of the Silver Age), members of Gen X reveled in retro style throughout the latter half of the '90s, leading up to the millennium and the beginning of a new century.

Along the way, many record companies released retro mix CDs featuring "groovy" or "swingin'" music of the '50s, '60s and '70s. These collections sometimes compiled cover versions of movie and television themes that appeared on orchestral pop albums of the same era, or production library recordings done in the style of the period's soundtracks, which record companies also reissued to cash in on popular interest. An example of a retro movie/TV music CD marketed during the go-go '90s is *Spy Magazine Presents Spy Music*, featuring such themes as Henry Mancini's "Peter Gunn" and John Barry's "Goldfinger." Another is the two-volume *Crime Jazz* compilation released by Rhino Records, featuring Shorty Rogers' recording of Leith Stevens' theme for *The Wild One*, and Lalo Schifrin's "The Killer" from *The Liquidator*. By the time *Mojo* music magazine released its 2002 retro movie-themed issue with a CD of "20 ultra-cool soundtracks," including Johnny Pate and Adam Wade's *Brother on the Run*, and Roy Budd's *Get Carter*, popular interest in Silver Age soundtracks was waning. Today, record companies continue to reissue soundtracks and soundtrack compilations from the era, but primarily for the collector market, not for fad followers.

The retro soundtrack fad also introduced many American music fans to the groovy psychedelica heard in European cult films of the '60s and '70s. Compilations such as *Vampyros lesbos*, *Schoolgirl Report* and the *Easy Tempo* series ushered in Euro soundtrack revival that has continued well into the current decade.

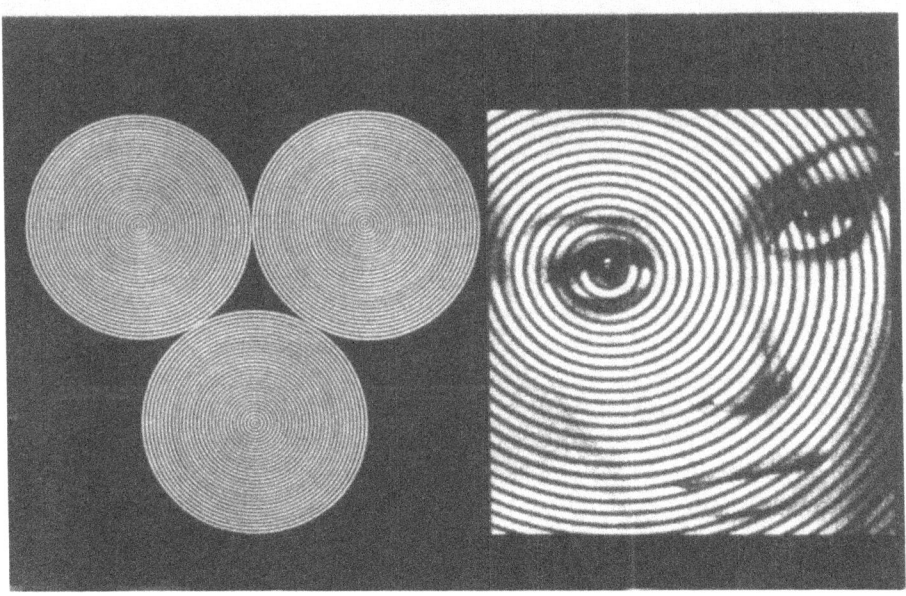

The *Easy Tempo* series, which compiled Italian soundtrack music of the late '60s and early '70s, fueled the lounge revival of the '90s, spurred interest in retro soundtracks and inspired several remix projects. (CD cover appears courtesy of Easy Tempo/ Right Tempo [ET913]; graphic design by Giulio "Jazzy Jules" Maini.)

The Silver Age influence can be heard in the soundtracks of the '90s and 2000s. The groovy psychedelia of *Vampyros* is evident in David Holmes' scores for *Ocean's Eleven, Twelve* and *Thirteen*. George Clinton's scores for the *Austin Powers* trilogy, and Michael Giacchino's score for *The Incredibles*, pay homage to John Barry's 007 scores. But when it came time to score his *Kill Bill* films, Quentin Tarantino went directly to his inspirational source by repurposing his favorite Italian soundtracks of the '70s.

An important byproduct of the retro soundtrack revival has been its influence on modern musicians. During the '90s, sampler technology—a common tool of hip-hop producers and electronic dance music DJs—made it possible for musicians of varying (and often marginal) musical ability to create cinema-inspired music by sampling portions (perhaps just a few seconds) of soundtracks. Listen to Portishead's 1994 trip-hop hit "Sour Times" and one hears Lalo Schifrin's "Danube Incident" from TV's *Mission: Impossible*. Listen to British singer Robbie Williams' Top 40 hit "Millennium" from 1998 and one hears John Barry's theme to *You Only Live Twice*. Listen to big beat recording artist Propellerheads' 1998 hit single "History Repeating" and one not only hears 007 diva Shirley Bassey on vocals but also a swinging sample from William Loose's soundtrack for Russ Meyer's *Finders Keepers Losers Weepers*, a late '60s sexploitation flick. When it comes to famous soundtrack samples, that's only scratching the surface.

Additionally, record companies have recognized the interest in film music and its influence on modern musicians by producing remix compilations wherein electronic musicians use sophisticated mixing techniques to reimagine the work of the masters (Morricone, Mancini, et al.). While compilations such as *Pussy Galore* (1996), *Serialement Vôtre* (1997), *Coffee Table Music* (1998), *Mancini Beats* (1999), *Morricone RMX* (2001), *Ennio Morricone Remixes* (2003) and *Cinematic* (2007) are merely an interesting diversion for film music purists, they also make vintage film music accessible for digital age ears.

Some contemporary recording artists have displayed great affection for Silver Age soundtracks in their music. British hip-hop collective the Herbaliser have recorded several albums for Ninja Tune, a record label that practically specialized in quasi-cinematic electronica and hip-hop during the peak years of the revival (1995–2000) with noteworthy releases by DJ Food, Cinematic Orchestra and Amon Tobin. Likewise, each of the Herbaliser's albums, which are masterminded by Ollie Teeba and Jake Wherry, contain several instrumentals that deftly explore spy jazz and crime funk sounds reminiscent of Silver Age soundtracks by Quincy Jones, Lalo Schifrin, David Shire, Roy Budd and Bernard Herrmann.

"We always tried to emulate those sounds," Wherry told the author. "Tracks like 'Shorty's Judgment' and 'Theme from Control Centre' from *Blow Your Headphones* were the results of us trying to make music for imaginary films."

The prototypical "imaginary soundtrack" is Barry Adamson's *Moss Side Story* (1988), but the fad's brief heyday accompanied the soundtrack revival of the '90s and early 2000s with such releases as the James Taylor Quartet's *The Money Spyder* (1996), Roger Joseph Manning Jr. and Brian Reitzell's *Logan's Sanctuary* (2000), and Chris Joss' *The Man with a Suitcase* (1999), among many others.

"'The Man with a Suitcase' just came along naturally and I thought it sounded like a theme for a series, so I did the arrangements in a late '60s style," Joss said of the title track for his first album. "After a while I managed to

Chris Joss' *The Man with a Suitcase* is one of many "imaginary soundtracks" or film music-inspired albums of the late '90s and early 2000s. (CD cover appears courtesy of Vadim Music/Pulp Flavor Records.)

gather eight tracks that had a soundtrack vibe. It really is an instinctive and un-mastered homage to 'The Avengers' and 'Mission: Impossible.'"

Joss added that the soundtracks of the '60s and '70s in particular are inspirational because they mix pop, rock, funk and jazz elements in creative arrangements, played by top session musicians. "I find it very inspiring to listen to their work. I'm tempted to recreate the feeling I get while listening to it," Joss explained, adding that samplers and computers have enabled modern musicians like himself to "have a go at arranging for virtual orchestras."

Adam Dorn, a.k.a. Mocean Worker, an electronic music artist with a jazz background, insists that soundtracks are "begging to be sampled." "It may have something to do with the emotive nature of a soundtrack," Dorn told the author. "The composers are trying to glean certain feelings or reactions from the audience, a mood maybe expressed succinctly."

Strictly Kev, of DJ Food, agrees. "They're full of sparse, solo sounds that make them ideal sample fodder. When you want strings, incidental solos and evocative pads, then soundtracks are where it's at."

In addition to vintage soundtracks, modern day imaginary soundtrack composers also look back to the original imaginary soundtracks: production library music of the '60s and '70s. Library music has been around since the beginning of cinema, originating as sheet music for sale to silent film accompanists. Once sound recording technology came into being, music publishers on both sides of the Atlantic began to record mood music for sale to film and radio productions, and eventually television shows. Just as the late '60s and early '70s proved to be an exceptionally creative period for film composers and musicians in the mainstream, the period also proved fruitful for library composers. They recorded a wealth of cinematically inspired mood music that also tapped into the psychedelic and progressive sounds coming from the rock scene, as well as the new electronic instruments heard on experimental and avant-garde recordings. Moreover, film composers such as Morricone, Bruno Nicolai and Vladmir Cosma also recorded many library sessions. The Silver Age library music albums released by such labels as De Wolfe, Chappell, Bosworth and KPM (to name a few), which were never sold in record stores, have become highly collectible in recent years.

"Current interest in old library music may have been started by hip-hop producers looking for a breakbeat or a loop, and post-rare groovers or acid jazzers searching for that full length funky track," wrote Jerry Dammers, founder of the Specials and 2 Tone, in the authoritative illustrated guide *The Music Library* (Fuel Publishing, 2005).

Contemporary musicians Shawn Lee (a.k.a. Ping Pong Orchestra) and Mark Pritchard of Harmonic 33 have recorded several albums' worth of faux library music—music that wouldn't sound out of place on a vintage De Wolfe record or, for that matter, a Silver Age soundtrack.

"I'm influenced by soundtracks and library music both on a conscious and unconscious level," Lee told the author. "TV cop music of the '70s really is in my blood."

For Pritchard, the fascination that he and other modern musicians have for soundtracks and library music is simply an extension of their inexhaustible musical curiosity and desire to make evocative music that doesn't require a vocalist to connect with listeners.

"To make music like that is such a freeing experience," Pritchard told the author. "I think soundtracks and library music will always be there as a form of inspiration."

Bibliography

AllMovies.com [for film production information].

AllMusic.com [for CD release information].

Ayres, Mark. *Doctor Who at the BBC Radiophonic Workshop, Volume One—The Early Years (1963–1969)* [CD booklet notes]. London: BBC Legends Records, 2005.

Bender, John. *Spaghetti Westerns, Volume 3–4* [CD booklet notes]. New York: DRG Records, 1999–2001.

_____. *The Thriller Collection* [CD booklet notes]. New York: DRG Records, 1999.

BernardHerrmann.org

Bernstein, Elmer. *Movie & TV Themes* [LP cover notes]. Los Angeles: Choreo, 1962.

Brown, Royal S. *Sisters* [CD booklet notes]. Australia: Southern Cross Records, 2001.

Burlingame, Jon. *The Exorcist* [CD booklet notes]. France: Warner Music, 2001.

_____. *The Fugitive* [CD booklet notes]. New York: Silva Screen Records, 2000.

_____. *Sound and Vision: 60 Years of Motion Picture Soundtracks*. New York: Billboard Books, 2000.

Cameron, John. *Psychomania* [CD booklet notes]. London: Trunk Records, 2003.

Cirillo, Luca, and Maurizio Mansueti. "An Interview with Goblin," *Il Giaguaro*, No. 5, Spring 2001.

Cowie, Colin, and Sue Cowie. "He Scribbles and I Wave the Wood," *The Horror Elite* [fanzine], 1968.

Curci, Loris. "To Score the Gore," Interview with Goblin, *Fangoria* magazine (#127).

Dassin, Jules. *Up Tight* [CD booklet notes]. Berkeley, California: Stax Records, 1992.

Davies, Hunter. *Here We Go 'Round the Mulberry Bush* [CD booklet notes]. Salem, Massachusetts: Rykodisc Records, 1998.

De Gemini, Franco. *From Beat to Beat*. Rome: Beat Records, 2006.

Deutsch, Didier. *Ennio Morricone—The Legendary Italian Westerns: The Film Composers Series, Volume II* [CD booklet notes]. New York: RCA Records, 1990.

_____. *Spaghetti Westerns, Volume 1–2* [CD booklet notes]. New York: DRG Records, 1995.

_____ (ed.). *MusicHound Soundtracks—The Essential Album Guide to Film, Television and Stage Music*. Detroit: Visible Ink Press, 2000.

Fagen, Donald. "Mancini's Anomie Deluxe," *Premiere Magazine*, Oct. 1987.

Fiegel, Eddi. *John Barry: A Sixties Theme*. London: Pan Macmillan, 1998.

FilmScoreMonthly.com

Fishman, Paul. *The Black Windmill* [CD booklet notes]. London: Castle Music, 1999.

Hallenbeck, Bruce G. Interview with Harry Robertson, cited by Larson, *Little Shoppe of Horrors*, No. 7, 1982.

_____. Interview with James Bernard cited by Larson, *Little Shoppe of Horrors*, No. 12, 1994.

Hearn, Marcus. *The Hammer Film Music Collection Vol. 1* [CD booklet notes]. London: GDI Records, 1999.

_____. *The Hammer Film Music Collection Vol. 2* [CD booklet notes]. London: GDI Records, 2000.

Heller, Skip. *Crime Jazz: Murder in the Second Degree* [CD booklet notes]. Los Angeles: Rhino Records, 1997.

Hildebrand, Lee. *The Blackbyrds & Charles Earland at the Movies* [CD booklet notes]. Berkeley, California: Prestige Records, 2001.

Hoffman, Eric, and Ted Newsom. *Not of This Earth* [CD booklet notes]. Los Angeles: Varese Sarabande, 1995.

Hughes, Howard. *Once Upon a Time in the Italian West: A Filmgoer's Guide to Spaghetti Westerns*. I.B. Tauris, 2004.

Husted, Christopher. *North by Northwest* [CD booklet notes]. Los Angeles: Rhino Records, 1995.

IMDB.com — The Internet Movie Database [for film and TV production information].

Irvin, Sam. Interview with Malcolm Williamson, cited by Larson, *Little Shoppe of Horrors*, No. 10/11, 1990.

Jones, Quincy. *Q: The Autobiography of Quincy Jones*. New York: Doubleday, 2001.

Kendall, Lukas. *Conquest of the Planet of the Apes* [CD booklet notes]. Los Angeles: Film Score Monthly, 2001.

_____. *The Liquidator* [CD booklet notes]. Los Angeles: Film Score Monthly, 2006.

_____, and Jeff Bond. *Soylent Green/Demon Seed* [CD booklet notes]. Los Angeles: Film Score Monthly, 2003.

Klemensen, Richard. "An Old Favorite Censored," Harry Robertson quote, cited by Larson, *Fandom's Film Gallery*, No. 3, Hove, Belgium: Jan Van Genechten, 1978.

Konjoyan, David. *What's New, Pussycat?* [CD booklet notes]. Salem, Massachusetts: Rykodisc Records, 1998.

Lappen, John. *Cotton Comes to Harlem* [CD booklet notes]. Los Angeles: Beyond Music, 2001.

Larson, Randall D. *Music from the House of Hammer: Music in the Hammer Horror Films, 1950–1980*. London: Scarecrow Press, 1996.

Lucas, Tim. *Black Sunday/Baron Blood* [CD booklet notes]. Los Angeles: Citadel Records, 1997.

_____. *Ecologia del delitto* [CD booklet notes]. Rome: Digitmovies Alternative Entertainment, 2005.

Mancini, Henry. *Did They Mention the Music?* Chicago: Contemporary Books, 1989.

Mansell, John, and Marcus Hearn. *The Hammer Vampire Film Music Collection* [CD booklet notes]. London: GDI Records, 2001.

Maxford, Howard. *Hammer, House of Horror: Behind the Screams*. New York: Overlook Press, 1996.

McCabe, Bob. *Girl on a Motorcycle* [CD booklet notes]. London: RPM Records, 1996.

McGilligan, Patrick. *I Want to Live!* [CD booklet notes] London: Rykodisc Records, 1999.

Meyer, Nicholas. *Time After Time* [LP cover notes]. San Francisco: Entr'acte Records, 1979.

Morgan, David. *Knowing the Score*. New York: Harper Entertainment, 2000.

Moynihan, Michael. *Lucifer Rising* [CD booklet notes]. Aumsville, Oregon: White Dog Music, 2004.

Mulhall, Kevin. *The Alien Trilogy* [CD booklet notes]. Los Angeles: Varese Sarabande, 1996.

_____. *The Omen* [CD booklet notes]. Los Angeles: Varese Sarabande, 1990.

_____. *Psycho* [CD booklet notes]. Los Angeles: Varese Sarabande, 1997.

_____. *Touch of Evil* [CD booklet notes]. Los Angeles: Varese Sarabande, 1993.

Mumma, Ed, and Neil Leadbeater. Interview with James Bernard, cited by Larson, *Fantasmagoria* No. 2, 1972.

Pending, Patrick. *200 Motels* [CD booklet notes]. Salem, Massachusetts: Rykodisc Records, 1997.

Phillips, Stu. "*Stu Who?*" Los Angeles: Cisum Press, 2003.

_____, and Alex Patterson. *Beyond the Valley of the Dolls* [CD booklet notes]. London: Harkit Records, 2003.

Pujol, Jordi. *Jazz en el cine negro espanol, 1958–1964* [CD booklet notes]. Spain: Fresh Sound Records, 2006.

Raworth, Ben. *The Italian Job* [CD booklet notes]. London: MCA Music UK, 2000.

Roddenberry, Gene. *Star Trek* [LP cover notes]. Los Angeles: Varese Sarabande, 1985–86.

Russell, Mark, and James Young. *Screencraft: Film Music*. London: RotoVision, 2000.

Saada, Nicolas. *The Fox* [CD booklet notes]. Los Angeles: Aleph Records, 2000.

Sarde, Philippe. *The Tenant* [CD booklet notes]. Paris: Universal France, 2000.

Smith, Steven C. *A Heart at Fire's Center:*

The Life and Music of Bernard Herrmann. Los Angeles: University of California Press, 1991.
SoundtrackCollector.com [for LP and CD release information].
Thomas, Peter. *Peter Scores* [CD booklet notes]. Cologne: Diggler Records, 2002.
Thomas, Tony. *Music for the Movies*. Los Angeles: Silman-James Press, 1997.
Tonks, Paul, and Chris Tunnah. *The Abominable Dr. Phibes* [CD booklet notes]. Los Angeles: Perseverance Records, 2003.
____, and Denny Zeitlin. *Invasion of the Body Snatchers* [CD booklet notes]. Los Angeles: Perseverance Records, 2003.
Trunk, Jonny. *The Music Library*. London: Fuel Publishing, 2005.

Vian, Boris. *Ascenseur pour l'échafaud (Lift to the Scaffold*, 1958) [CD booklet notes]. Paris: Fontana Records, 1988.
Warshow, Robert. "Movie Chronicle: The Westerner," New York: Partisan Review, April 1954.
Wilkenson, Marc. *Blood on Satan's Claw* [CD booklet notes]. London: Trunk Records, 2007.
Wishart, David, James Fitzpatrick and David Stoner. *Hammer—The Studio That Dripped Blood!* [CD booklet notes]. New York: Silva Screen Records, 2002.
Zamori, Roberto. *Le foto proibite di una signora per bene* [CD booklet notes]. Rome: Dagored Records, 1999.

Index

A doppia faccia 260, 266
A Sangre Fria 46
Abbey Road 310
The Abominable Dr. Phibes 226, 227
Abril, Anton Garcia 206, 207
Ace High 148, 149
Across 110th Street 26–27, 28, 34
Adams, John 170
Adamson, Barry 333
Addison, John 233
Adios Gringo 140
Adolescenza perversa 120
The Adventures of Fu Manchu 213
The Adventures of Superman 213
Aelita: The Revolt of the Robots 167
Aerial Ballet 99
L'Affaire Crazy Capo 43
After the Fox 48
Agente 077—dall'oriente con furore 78
Agente speciale LK 78, 79
Ahlberg, Mac 113, 114
The Alamo 128
Albinoni, Tomaso 197
Aleph Records 97, 98
Alessandrini, Raymond 83
Alessandroni, Alessandro 48, 50, 80, 81, 112, 117, 133, 135, 136, 137, 140, 144, 145, 148, 150, 151, 158, 234, 260, 262, 263, 264, 265, 273, 275
Alessandroni, Giulia 110
Alessandroni, Sandro 110
Alexander, Jeff 214, 219, 301
Alfie 107
Alguero, Augusto 46
Alice's Restaurant 320–321
Alien 56, 168, 186, 202–203, 204, 238, 243
The Alien Trilogy 202
Alistair Maclean's Puppet on a Chain 82
All Score Media 131, 208
All the Colors of the Dark 273
"All Things Bright and Beautiful" (hymn) 189
Allan & the Arrows, Davie (or Arrows) 287, 290, 291, 292, 301, 302, 304, 305, 317, 318, 329

Allen, Irwin 182, 198, 215, 216, 240
Allen, Steve 74
Alpert, Herb & the Tijuana Brass 73
Alraune 167
"Also Sprach Zarathustra" 185, 186
Altman, Robert 187
Le amanti del mostro 275–276
The Ambushers 73
Amen Corner 228
American Film Institute 91, 238
American Graffiti 285, 304, 327
American Hot Wax 327
American International Pictures (AIP) 224, 225, 226, 245, 251, 256, 271, 287, 291, 308, 317
L'amica di mia madre 119–120
The Amityville Horror 245, 281
Ammazzali tutti e torno solo 145
Amore piombe e furore 160–161
Amram, David 13, 15
Anatomy of a Murder 11–12
Ancor dollari per i MacGregor 152
And God Created Woman 104
Anderson, Gerry 218, 219
Anderson, Ian 144
Andress, Ursula 179
Andrews, Harvey 255
Andrews, Julie 103
The Andromeda Strain 191, 193
Angel Angel Down We Go 319
Angel Unchained 298
Angeli bianchi angeli neri 110–112, 126
Angels Die Hard 298
Angels from Hell 289, 290, 294
Angels Hard as They Come 298
Anger, Kenneth 318, 319
Ann-Margret 82, 297, 309
Another Time, Another Place 298
Anthony, Ray 286
Anthony, Richard 81
Antonioni, Michelangelo 19, 316
"Appalachian Spring" 37
Arabesque 10, 18
Araya, Zeudi 117
Arel, Jack 60, 87, 219

341

Argento, Dario 258, 262, 263, 264, 271, 272, 276, 277, 278, 279
Armstrong, Louis 65, 99
Arnaz, Desi 306
Arne, Thomas 179
Arnold, Jack 286
Arsan, Emmanuelle 121
Art of Noise 7
Ascenseur pour l'echafaud 12
The Asphalt Jungle 6, 47
L'assoluto naturale 116–117
Astley, Edwin 58, 59, 60, 248
Atlantis, the Lost Continent 179
"Atmospheres"
Atom Heart Mother 315
Atragon 212
Attack of the Crab Monsters 174
Attack of the 50-Foot Woman 174
Attack of the Mushroom People 212
Attanasio, Maurizio 138
Audience 326
Aulin, Ewa 108
Austin Powers 48, 57, 64, 219, 332
Autry, Gene 127
Avalon, Frankie 183, 303, 308
The Avengers 42, 60, 183, 334
Averback, Hy 319
Avison, Charles 179
Axelrod, David 189
Ayers, Roy 28, 29
Ayres, Mark 215

The B-52s 106
Baadasssss! 20
Babb, Kroger 86
Baby Doll 15, 90, 94
Baby Snakes 312
Bacall, Lauren 89
Bacalov, Luis 82, 140, 141, 142, 151, 153, 156, 165
Bach, Johan Sebastian 112, 156, 194, 197, 245
Bacharach, Burt 32, 48, 57, 73, 96, 99, 107, 123, 126, 166, 326
Bachelet, Pierre 121
Bachelor in Paradise 92–93
Background Studio Groupies 123
Backwash Rhythm Band 305
Badder Than Evil 32
Baez, Joan 193
Le Bain 85
Bakaleinikoff, Mischa 173
Baker, Chet 35
Baker, Tom 213
Bakshi, Ralph 188, 199
Baldan Bembo, Alberto 119, 120
Ball, Lucille 306
The Ballad of Cable Hogue 164–165
Bancroft, Anne 321
The Band 283, 295

The Band Without a Name 301
La banda del gobbo 45
Bandoleros 163
Banks, Don 248
Barbarella 108, 109, 126, 209, 329
Barbieri, Gato 100, 101, 110
Bardot, Brigitte 104, 105, 106, 122
Bardotti, Sergio 205
The Barefoot Adventure 303
Baretta 19
Barker, Lex 132
Barker, Warren 9, 216
Baron Blood 270–271
Barrett, Syd 315
Barrons, Bebe 168, 173, 204, 221
Barrons, Louis 168, 173, 204, 221
Barry, John 18, 36, 37, 49, 50, 51, 57, 61, 62, 63, 64, 65, 66, 69, 70, 71, 72, 73, 74, 77, 79, 83, 84, 87, 99, 100, 106, 146, 147, 197, 203, 210, 243, 330, 332
Bart, Lionel 62
Bartók, Béla 187, 205, 215, 243
Basie, Count 21, 26
Bassey, Shirley 50, 62, 64, 65, 66, 89, 254, 332
Batman 13, 49, 167, 216, 217
Battista D'Amario, Bruno 158
Battle for the Planet of the Apes 187, 189
Battlestar Galactica (1978–1980) 219–220, 290
Bava, Mario 50, 152, 204, 256, 257, 258, 259, 261, 269, 270, 271
Baxter, Les 204, 212, 224, 225, 226, 256, 257, 258, 271, 291, 292, 308
Bay of Blood 269
Bayer Segar, Carole 66
BBC 176, 245
Beach Blanket Bingo 308
The Beach Boys 234, 304, 306
Beach Party 308
The Beast from 20,000 Fathoms 172
Beat Girl 61, 106
Beat Records 45, 49, 119, 150, 265
The Beatles 3, 4, 62, 65, 282, 283, 284, 308, 309, 310, 311, 325
"The Beatles" (album) 310
Beausoleil, Bobby 318, 319
Bech, Bertrand 113
Bedazzled 109
Bee, Henry 238
The Bee Gees 327
Beethoven, Ludwig van 112, 186, 191, 271
Bekku Sadao 212
Bells of Atlantis 173
Ben-Hur 1, 204
Benchley, Peter 243
Bender, John 144, 145, 147, 264, 266, 267
Beneath the Planet of the Apes 187, 188
Beneath the Valley of the Ultra Vixens 89
Benedict, Richard 306

Benkö, Anita 123
Bennett, Richard Rodney 71
The Benny Hill Show 105
Beram, Eddie 302
Berigan, Bunny 39
Berlioz, Hector 223
Bernard, James 13, 176, 179, 246, 247, 248, 249, 250, 251, 253, 281
Bernard Herrmann Society Website 233
Bernstein, Elmer 2, 6, 7, 9, 18, 56, 57, 58, 60, 71, 82, 84, 93, 128, 129, 130, 132, 134, 135, 162, 163, 165, 166, 171, 236, 237, 286, 319, 320
Berry, Chuck 282, 327, 329
Bertolazzi, Mario 119
The Best of Shaft 27
Betts, Harry 306
Beware 282
Beyond the Valley of the Dolls 89, 290, 322–323, 329
Biberman, Herbert 325
The Big Boss 36
The Big Country 127, 129, 165, 166
The Big Gundown 144–145, 148, 271
The Big Silence 145
The Big Surf 303
The Biggest Bundle of Them All 51–52
Bikini Beach 308
Bilitis 124
Bill Haley & the Comets 282, 285
Billboard 288, 320
Billion Dollar Brain 71
Billy the Kid 37
The Bird with the Crystal Plumage 258, 262, 279, 281
The Birds 233
Birds Do It 124
Birkin, Jane 106, 122
Birth of a Nation 85
Bitches Brew 189, 267
Bixio, Franco 141, 159, 160, 161, 279
Bizet, Georges 60
Black, Don 64, 65, 66
Black Belly of the Tarantula 267, 268
Black Belt Jones 36
Black Caesar 30
Black Emanuelle 122
The Black Hole 203
Black Sabbath 258
Black Sunday 256, 257
The Black Windmill 42, 75–76, 77
The Blackboard Jungle 285
The Blackbyrds 34
Blaine, Hal 291
Blakey, Art 105
Blast Off! 221
Blatty, William Peter 238
Blindman 157–158, 271
The Blob 96
Blood and Black Lace 258

Blood Feast 228
Blood Feast 2 228
Blood for Dracula 238
Blood from the Mummy's Tomb 252–253
Blood on Satan's Claw 254–255, 281
Blood, Sweat and Tears 300
The Bloodstained Shadow 280
Bloomfield, Mike 316
Blow Up 19
Blow Your Headphones 332
Blue Afternoon 295
"The Blue Danube" 185, 186
The Blue Flamingos 32
Blue Hawaii 308
Blume, David 40
Blutsbrüder 132
Bob & Carol & Ted & Alice 98–99, 116
Bob Crewe Generation Orchestra 108, 209
Bob le flambeur 43
Bobby Womack & Peace 26, 27
The Body 315
Boenzee Cryque 318
Bogart, Humphrey 89, 90
"Bolero" 79, 103
Bolling, Claude 83
Bonanza 130
Bond, Jeff 197, 241
Bond, Richard 319
Boneschi, Giampera 219
Bonneau, Paul 219
Bonnie and Clyde 37
Booker T and the MG's 314
Boot Hill 148, 149
Booth, Harry 58
Born Free 64
Born Losers 290
Bosch, Juan 46
Bosworth Recorded Music Library 334
Böttcher, Martin 46, 132
Bowen, Jimmy 299
Bowie, David 156, 282, 283
Boyce, Tommy 311, 320
Boyle, Billy 323
Boyle, Peter 325
The Boys from Brazil 187, 200, 243
Bradbury, Ray 185, 186
Brando, Marlon 100, 101, 287
Brandt, Carl 68
Brannigan 19
Branucci, Maria Cristina 144
Brass, Tinto 125
The Bravados 127
Brer Soul 23
Bricusse, Leslie 62
The Brides of Dracula 247
Bring Me the Head of Alfredo Garcia 55
British Agent 57
British Invasion 313
British National Theatre 255
Broccoli, Albert 61, 62

Bronco Bullfrog 325–327
Bronson, Charles 19, 151
Brother on the Run 30, 32, 330
Broughton, Bruce 219
Brown, Alex 34
Brown, Bruce 303, 304
Brown, James 23, 26, 30, 314
Brown, Larry 317
Brown, Royal S. 239
Browne, Bud 303, 304
Brownsville Station 329
Bruno, Tony 296
Bruton Music Library 42
Brynner, Yul 130
Buck Rogers 167, 199, 213
Buck Rogers in the 25th Century 220, 290
Buckaroo 147
A Bucket of Blood 223
Buckley, Tim 295
Budd, Roy 18, 40, 41, 42, 55, 56, 75, 76, 77, 177, 330, 332
Büdinger, Matthias 181
Bug-In! 303
Bullitt 16, 56, 82, 162, 266, 304
Bunny O'Hare 299
Buon funerale amigos, paga Sartana 154, 158
Il buono, il brutto, il cattivo see *The Good, the Bad and the Ugly*
Burgess, Anthony 191
Burke, Sonny 285
Burlingame, Jon 238
Burrell, Kenny 107
Burroughs, William S. 318
Burton, Richard 95
Burton, Tim 55
Bury Me an Angel 298
Butler, Artie 100, 103
Butler, Jerry 325
Buttolph, David 172
Byrd, Donald 34
The Byrds 108, 295

The Cabinet of Dr. Caligari (1919) 222
The Cabinet of Dr. Caligari (1962) 223
Cacavas, John 253, 255
Cactus Flower 319, 320
Cage, John 173
Caine, Michael 41, 54, 76, 107
The Caine Mutiny 1
Caligula 125
Caltiki—il mostro immortale 256
CAM Original Soundtracks 121, 138, 142, 277
Cameron, John 255
Cameron, Nevil 144
Camille 2000 113
Campbell, Glen 163
Candy 108, 126, 329
Cannes International Film Festival 106
Cannibal Holocaust 281

"Canon in D Major" 271
I Cantori Moderni 50, 81, 112, 117, 136, 137, 138, 144, 148, 152, 158, 260
Cape Fear 236, 237, 281
The Caper of the Golden Bulls 48
Caprice, June 85
Capricorn One 200–201, 202, 243
Captain Beefheart & His Magic Band 295
Captain Midnight 213
Captain Scarlet and the Mysterons 219
Captain Video and His Video Rangers 213
Carambola 159
Carambola filotto tutti in buca 159
Cardiff, Jack 294
Carey, Bill 286
Carey, Lynn 323
Carlos, Wendy (or Walter) 186, 191, 192
Carmen Baby 112
Carnes, Kim 299
Carpenter, John 168, 244, 245, 278
Carr, Vicki 71
Carrie 239–240, 243
The Carrie Nations 322, 323
Cary, Tristram 176, 252, 253
Casablanca 1
Cascio, Giorio 281
The Case of the Bloody Iris 273
The Case of the Scorpion's Tail 267–268, 281
Casey, Charles R. 219
Casino Royale 57, 58, 73, 123
Cass, Mama 316
Castle of Blood 264
Cat Ballou 130
The Cat O'Nine Tails 262, 279
Cat People 223
Cat Women of the Moon 171
Catholic Church's Legion of Decency 89, 90
CBS Radio Symphony 179
CBS Records 191
C.C. and Company 297
C'è Sartana, vendi la pistola e comprati la bara 154
Centomila dollari per Ringo 139
C'era una volta il west 149
Chan, Jackie 36
Chandler, Ward L. 35
Chaney, Lon, Jr. 228
Change of Habit 282
Chappell Recorded Music Library 42, 60, 334
Charade 10
Charles, Ray 22
Charteris, Leslie 60
Chaumont, Jaques 81, 84
Checker, Chubby 285, 319
Cherry Five 277
Chi l'ha vista morire? 272–273
Chi sei? 276, 277
Lo chiamavano King 156

Lo chiamavano Tresette, giocava sempre col morto 158–159
Chicago (band) 300
Chimenti, Silvano 158
Chinatown 38–39
Chocolate Watchband 316
Choderlos de Laclos, Pierre 105
Christie, Agatha 261
Christy 81, 144
Chunga's Revenge 313
El Cid 204
The Cincinnati Kid 55
Cinematic 332
The Cinematic Orchestra 332
Cinesoundz 131, 207, 208
Cinevox Records 153, 155, 160, 262, 272
Cipriani, Stelvio 114, 141, 142, 157, 158, 269, 270, 271, 280
Citadel Records 271
Citizen Kane 229
Città violenta 271
Il cittadino si ribella 45
Le Clan des siciliens 44
Clapton, Eric 283
Clark, Dick 292, 317
Clause, Robert 36
Cleland, John 114
Clemente, Paul 125
Cleopatra Jones 29, 31, 34
Cleopatra Jones and the Casino of Gold 29
Cleveland, Jimmy 107
Clifford, Mike 317, 318
Climbing! 299
Clinton, George S. 57, 64, 332
A Clockwork Orange 119, 186, 191, 192
Close Encounters of the Third Kind 197, 198, 199, 221
Cochran, Eddie 90
Coffee Table Music 71, 243, 332
Coffey, Dennis 36
Coffy 28–29
Cohen, Herb 295
Cohen, Larry 30
Cold Eyes of Fear 267
Cole, Wendy 296
Coll, Julio 46
College Confidential 286
La collera del vento 152
Collin, Ann 156
La collina degli stivali 148
Collins, Lyn 30
Colombier, Michel 193
Il colosso di Rodi 135
Colossus: The Forbin Project 193
Colpo grosso a Galata Bridge 81
Colpo maestro al servizio di Sua Maesta britannica 50
Colpo rovente 147, 266
Una Colt in mano al diavolo 158
Una Colt in pugno al diavolo 143

Coma 243, 244
The Comancheros 128
Come Back, Charleston Blue 26
Come Spy with Me 68
Comerford, Jason 231
Commando Cody: Sky Marshal of the Universe 213
Il commissario di ferro 45
Compartiment tueurs 43
Comstock, Frank 220
Conan the Barbarian 177
The Concert for Bangladesh 283
Connery, Neil 80, 81
Connery, Sean 62, 63, 64, 65, 80, 81
Connor, Tony 327
The Conquerer Worm see *Witchfinder General*
Conquest of the Planet of the Apes 187, 189
Conrad, Jack 35
Constant, Marius 213
Constantin Film 46
Contempt 105
Coogan's Bluff 162,
Cook, Peter 109
Cook & Benjamin Franklin Group 159
The Cool Ones 301
Cooper, Alice 295, 329
Copland, Aaron 37, 128, 165
Coppola, Carmine 38
Coppola, Francis Ford 228
Corliss, Richard 149
Corman, Roger 223, 224, 225
Cornbread, Earl and Me 34
Il corpo 117–118
The Corporation 30
Cosma, Vladimir 43, 334
Cosmic Equation 194
Cotton Comes to Harlem 23, 26, 323
Countdown 187
Countess Dracula 251, 252, 256
Courage, Alexander 183, 203, 215, 217, 218
Coward, Noel 52
Cowie, Colin 249
Cowie, Sue 249
Craig Huxdley's Blaster Beam 203
Crawford, Joan 85
Cream 292
Creature from the Black Lagoon 172, 223
Creatures the World Forgot 179, 180
Crewe, Bob 108, 109, 126, 209
Crime Jazz 330
Crime Jazz—Murder in the Second Degree 6
Cripple Creek Bar Room 127
Crippled Dick Hot Wax 78, 115
Crosby, Stills, Nash & Young 295
Crowley, Aleister 318
I crudeli 137
Crumb, George 238
Cry of the Banshee 225, 226
Cushing, Peter 246
Cul-de-sac 234

Curb, Mike 287, 289, 290, 291, 292, 301, 302, 303, 304, 305, 317, 318
Curry, Tim 324
The Curse of Frankenstein 246, 247, 266
Curse of the Fly 174, 176
The Curse of the Sinister One 206
The Curse of the Werewolf 247
Curtis, Tony 7, 60, 61, 91
Curtom Records 27
The Cycle Savages 292
Cypress Hill 35
The Cyrkle 100

Da uomo a uomo 144
Dale, Dick 305
Dallas (movie) 127
Daltrey, Roger 313, 314
Damaged Goods 85
Damiano, Gerrard 101
Damien: Omen II 241, 243
Dammers, Jerry 334
Dance, Fools, Dance 85
Danger Diabolik 49–50, 56
Danger Girl 87
Danger Man 42, 58, 60
Dankworth, John 60, 73, 74
Dark Side of the Moon 81, 315
Darren, James 308
Dassin, Jules 23, 47
Daughter of the Gods 85
David & Jonathan 73
David, Hal 66, 95, 99, 107
David, Mark 112
David Copperfield 185
Davies, Hunter 325
Davis, Carl 108
Davis, Miles 12, 42, 267
Davis, Sammy, Jr. 14, 73
Dawn of the Dead 279, 280, 281
Day, Doris 91, 92
The Day the Earth Stood Still 168, 170, 171, 173, 177, 221, 244
The Day the World Ended 173
Dead Men Don't Wear Plaid 6
The Dead Pool 16
Deadfall 50, 51
The Deadly Affair 21
De Angelis, Guido 43, 44, 45
De Angelis, Maurizio 43, 44, 45
De Angelis, Peter 103
Death of a Salesman 6
Death Walks at Midnight 274
Death Walks in High Heels 271
Death Wish 19
Debussy, Claude 60, 98, 183
Decca 251
La decima vittima see *The Tenth Victim*
Dee, Darrell 318
The Deep 243
Deep Purple 272, 323

Deep Red 263, 276–278, 279, 281
Deep Throat 20, 86, 100–102, 125
De Filippo, Eduardo 38
De Gemini, Franco 145, 147, 148, 150, 151
Dein Kind, das Unbekannte Wesen 124
De Jesus, Luchi 30, 34, 35
Delaney & Bonnie & Friends 299
De La Part Des Compains 43
De Laurentis, Dino 197
Delerue, Georges 105, 108
De Little, Johnny 106
Dell'Orso, Edda 81, 110, 116, 117. 119, 120, 137, 148, 149, 151, 155, 210, 260, 263, 264, 266, 267, 269, 271, 272, 273, 275
De Masi, Francesco 43, 45, 50, 81, 145, 146, 147, 154
Dementia 13 228
Demon Seed 197, 241, 242
Deneuve, Catherine 234
De Niro, Robert 40
Deodato, Ruggero 281
De Palma, Brian 231, 239, 240, 243
Derbyshire, Delia 214
Derek, Bo 103
Derek Flint 68, 72, 83
De Sade 299
Destination Moon 168
Detroit 9000 34
Deutsch, Adolph 91, 126
Deutsch, Didier 136
Deutsche Film-Aktiengesellschaft (DEFA) 132
Deviation 269
The Devil Came from Akasava 116
The Devil in Miss Jones 101–103, 126
The Devil on Wheels 301
The Devil Rides Out 250–251
Devil's Angels 289–290
The Devil's 8 302–303
The Devil's Nightmare 264
Devo 329
De Vol, Frank 92
De Wolfe Recorded Music Library 42, 334
Diabolik (comic book) 48
Dial "M" for Murder 229
Diamond, Neil 320
Diamonds 55–56, 77
Diamonds Are Forever 50, 61, 63, 65, 84
Il diavolo nel cervello 271
Dick Dale and the Del-Tones 304
Dick Smart 2.007 82
Did They Talk About the Music? 7
Dieci bianchi eccisi da un piccolo indiano 159
"Dies Irae" 223, 248, 249, 266
Diggler Records 124, 207
Digitmovies 80, 143, 146, 157, 161, 178, 257, 259, 261, 268, 269, 270
Dino, Desi & Billy 306
Dio perdona... il no! 143
Il dio serpente 117

The Dirty Girls 112
Dirty Harry 16, 44, 56, 162, 190, 193, 219, 266
Disco Godfather 35
Discreet Music 271
Disney, Walt 182, 183
DJ Food 332, 334
Django 141, 165
Django Kill 141
Django, Prepare a Coffin 141
Django Shoots First 141
Django the Bastard 162
Django, the Last Gunfighter 141
Dmytryk, Edward 236
Dobson, Tamara 29, 31
Dr. Jekyl and Mr. Hyde (1931) 167, 222
Dr. No 58, 61
Dr. Phibes Rises Again 226, 227–228
Doctor Who 60, 176, 192, 214, 215
Doctor Who at the BBC Radiophonic Workshop, Vol. 1—The Early Years 214–215
Dogtown and Z Boys 304
Dolenz, Micky 311
Un dollaro bucato 139
Un dollaro tra i denti 140
Dollar$ 55
The Dollars Trilogy 135, 137, 141, 162, 163
The Dolphins 292
Domino, Fats 90, 286
Donaggio, Pino 160, 239, 240, 244, 255
Donner, Clive 107, 325
Don't Knock the Rock 285
Don't Look Back 284
Don't Look Now 255
Dorn, Adam 334
Double Face 46
Double Indemnity 6
"007" 62, 65, 210
Douglas, Gordon 14
Down with Love 96
Doyle, Bobby 299
Dracula (book) 251
Dracula (1931) 222
Dracula (1958) 179, 246, 249, 281
Dracula A.D. 1972 253
Dracula Has Risen from the Grave 248
Dragon, Carmen 173
Dragstrip Girl 301
Dragstrip Riot 301
Drasnin, Robert 68
Drei Bayern in Bangkok 123
Drei Schwedinnen auf der Reeperbahn 123
DRG 218, 264
The Drifters 95
Drummer of Vengeance 138
Dual in the Sun 127
Duck You Sucker 155–156
Duclos, Jean-Pierre 82
Due mafiosi contro Al Capone 79
Due mafiosi contro Goldginger 78

I due Ringos del Texas 141
Duello nel Texas 135
Duning, George 216, 218
Dunlap, Paul 177
The Dunwich Horror 226
Dutour, Pierre 219
The Dynamite Brothers 34
Dylan, Bob 282, 283, 284, 295

Earland, Charles 34
Earp, Wyatt 162
Earth vs. the Flying Saucers 173
Earth, Wind and Fire 23, 24
Easdale, Brian 253
East–West Pipeline 298
Eastside Digital 191, 192
Eastwood, Clint 16, 133, 134, 162, 165
Easy Rider 4, 295, 297, 299, 329
Easy Tempo (series) 331
Easy Tempo Records 111, 113, 118, 205, 274, 331
Ecce Homo 210
Eckstine, Billy 21
Ecstasy 85, 86, 104
The Ed Sullivan Show 308
Eddie & the Hot Rods 329
Eddie & the Stompers 291
Eddy, Duane 292
Edison, Thomas 127
Edward J. Vincent 260
Edwards, Blake 7
Eidelman, Cliff 202
18th Century Concepts 318
Electra Glide in Blue 300
The Electric Flag 316, 318, 329
The Electric Prunes 295
Elephant's Memory 100
Elfers, Konrad 71
Elfman, Danny 55
Elgar, Sir Edward 191
Elkind, Rachel 191
Ellington, Duke 11, 12
Elliott, Dean 286
Ellis, Don 17, 56
Ellis, Steve 54
Elms, Alfred 60
Emanuelle 121
Emanuelle in Africa 122
Emanuelle nera see Black Emanuelle
EMI 251
Emmanuelle 120–121, 122
The Endless Summer 303, 304, 329
The Enforcer 16
Engel, die ihre Flügel verbrennen 123
English Rose 323
Ennio Morricone Remixes 332
Eno, Brian 271, 329
Enter the Dragon 22, 36
Enter the Wu Tang 36
Entwistle, John 314

Eolomea 207
Eric, Lars 319
Eric, Mark 298
Eric Burden and the Animals 52
Ernst-Sasse, Karl 132
Escape from the Planet of the Apes 187
Escobar, Enrique 46
Esper, Dwain 86
Esquivel, Juan 46, 220
Essjay 252
Eugenie 116
Europa—Operation Striptease 110
Eva 299
Evans, Robert 39
Eve & the Handyman 88
An Evening with Edgar Allan Poe 225
Evidence Records 194
The Evil Eye 257–258
The Evil of Frankenstein 248
The Exorcist 238–239, 245, 276, 278
Exorcist 2: The Heretic 241–243
Experiment in Terror 10
Exploring the Unknown 220
Exuma 325

Fabares, Shelley 302
Fabian 301, 302, 317
Faccia a faccia 148
Fagen, Donald 9
Fahey, John 316
Fahrenheit 451 184, 185, 221
Faith, Adam 106
Faith, Russell 183
Faithful, Marianne 107, 292, 293, 294
The Fall of the House of Usher 224
Fandom's Film Gallery 252
Fangoria 276, 277, 279
Fanny Hill 114
Fantasmagoria 247, 250
Fantastic Planet 210
The Fantastic Plastic Machine 306
Fantastic Voyage 183–184, 187, 188
Fantastica 179, 220
Il fantastico viaggio del "Bagarazzo" Mark 279
Fantasy Island 66
Fantasy Records 34
Fantomas 83
Farber, Mitch 34
Farmer, Art 11
Farnon, Robert 60, 87, 219
Farrow, Mia 234, 235
The Fast and the Furious 301
Faster Pussycat! Kill! Kill! 89, 287, 288
Fathom 73
Fear Is the Key 41, 42
The Fearless Vampire Killers 234
The Female Animal 114
Femina Ridens 114
Femmine insaziabili 260

Fender Stratocaster 133
Ferrante & Teicher 220
Ferrigno, Lou 220
Ferrio, Gianni 44, 139, 144, 152, 260, 261, 274
Fever Tree 298
Fia, Roberto 141
Fidenco, Nico 122
Fiegel, Edie 62
Field, Sally 307
Fielding, Jerry 16, 38, 55, 162, 165, 166, 197, 218, 241, 242
Fieras sin jaula 266
The Fifth Cord 267
Film Music Screencraft 39, 61, 99–100, 128, 185, 229
Film Score Monthly 51, 55, 67, 69, 72, 73, 92, 94, 129, 164, 168, 180, 182, 188, 189, 195, 196, 197, 217, 224, 231, 241, 242, 244, 264
The Final Conflict: Omen III 241
Finders Keepers, Lovers Weepers 89, 290, 332
Fine, Harry 252
Fireball 500 301
First Men on the Moon 183
First Spaceship on Venus 207
Fischer, Günther 132, 208
Fishman, Jack 76
Fishman, Paul 76
A Fistful of Dollars 133, 134, 135, 137, 138, 166
A Fistful of Dynamite 155–156
Fists of Fury 36
Five Dolls for an August Moon 261
Five the Hard Way 292
Flack, Roberta 26, 55
Flash Gordon 167, 199, 213
Flash Gordon's Trip to Mars 167
Fleischer, Mark 200
Fleming, Ian 61, 66, 73
Flesh for Frankenstein 238
Flick, Vic 60, 61, 106
"Flight of the Bumble Bee" 5, 174
"Flight of the Valkyries" 158
The Fly 174, 175, 176, 183
The Fog 245
Follow Me 290, 306
Fonda, Henry 151, 158
Fonda, Jane 108
Fonda, Peter 287, 289, 297
For a Few Dollars More 133, 134, 135, 136, 135, 166
Forbidden Photos of a Lady Above Suspicion 263
Forbidden Planet 168, 173, 204, 221
Ford, Glenn 285
Ford, Harrison 198
Ford, John 127
Fortunella 38
Four Flies on Grey Velvet 262, 271, 272, 279

Four in the Morning 106
4...3...2...1... Morte 206, 207
The Four Tops 31
The Fox 97–98, 107
Fox, Charles 108, 209
Fox Films Corporation 85
Foxbat 77
Foxy Brown 29, 33–34
Franco, Jess 46, 114, 115, 116, 326
Frankel, Benjamin 95, 248
Frankenstein (1910) 167, 222
Frankenstein (1931) 167, 222
Frankenstein and the Monster from Hell 253
Frankenstein Meets the Wolf Man 167
Franklin, Aretha 64
Fraternity of Man 295
Freak Out! 312
Freda, Riccardo 269
Free Love 152, 153
A Free Ride 85
Freed, Alan 285
Freedom Orchestra 318
Frees, Paul 220
The French Connection 17, 44, 56, 238
Fresh Sound Records 46
Freud 202
Friday Foster 34
Friday the 13th 269
Fried, Gerald 68, 194, 218, 223, 224
Friedhofer, Hugo 68
Friedkin, William 238, 239
Friedman, David 86
The Frightened Woman 114
Frizzi, Fabio 141, 159, 160, 161, 279, 281
Frog (band) 255
From Beat to Beat 150–151
From Here to Eternity 90
From Russia with Love 61, 62
Frontiere, Dominic 19, 29, 162, 163, 215, 299
Fu Manchu 46
Fuel Publishing 334
The Fugitive 13
The Fugitive Kind 15
Funeral in Berlin 71
Funicello, Annette 301, 302, 303, 308
"Für Elise" 271
The Fury 243, 244
Future 318
Futureworld 195

Gabriel, Peter 327
Gainsbourg, Serge 122, 126, 210
Gale, John 226, 227, 228
Galloway, A. Scott 27
Game of Death 36, 37
Gamera 212
Garay, Val Christian 34
Garcia, Jerry 316
Garcia, Russ (or Russell) 179, 180, 181, 220

Gardner, Ava 95
Garriguenc, Rene 214
Garvarentz, George 52, 53, 81
Gaslini, Giorgio 276, 277, 278, 281
Gassmann, Remi 233
La gatta in calore 117
The Gauntlet 16
"Gayane Ballet Suite" 185
Gaye, Marvin 27, 28, 32
GDI 248, 252
Geesin, Ron 315
Gemmell, Keith 327
Gemser, Laura 121, 122
The Genteels 86
Georis, Walter and Gaston 304
Gershenson, Joseph 9
Gertz, Irving 171
Get Carter 41, 75, 77, 330
Get Mean 141
Get Smart 66
The Getaway 55
Ghidorah, the Three-Headed Monster 212
Ghiglia, Benedetto 140, 141
Giacchino, Michael 64, 332
Gibson, Mel 203
Gidget 307–308
Giecarz, Maryvonne 319
Gielgud, John 125
Gillespie, Dizzy 21, 61
Gillette, Steve 38
Gillian, Ian 323
Gillis, Richard 165
Gilligan's Island 212
Gimme Shelter 282
Giombini, Marcello 206, 207
Giovanni, Paul 255
The Girl Can't Help It 90, 286
The Girl from U.N.C.L.E. 67
Girl on a Motorcycle 292–294, 298
The Girl Who Knew Too Much 257–258
Giù la testa 155–156
Gizzi, Claudio 238
Glass, Philip 170, 213, 230
Glasser, Albert 287
Gleeson, Patrick 34
Gli fumavano le colt, lo chiamavano camposanto 156
Gli specialisti 151
Glitter, Gary 323
Glitterhouse 108, 209
The Glory Stompers 291
Goblin 45, 238, 244, 263, 276, 277, 278, 279, 280, 281
God Pan 318
The Godfather 38
The Godfather of Soul 35
Godspell 323, 325
Godzilla (Gojira) 168, 210, 211, 221, 256
Godzilla vs. the Destroyer 213
Goffin, Gerry 311

The Golden Breed 305
The Golden Voyage of Sinbad 177
Goldfinger 61, 62–63, 65, 84
"Goldfinger" 330
Goldsmith, Jerry 2, 19, 38, 39, 56, 57, 67, 68, 71, 83, 84, 93, 94, 129, 162, 163, 164, 165, 168, 183, 186, 187, 188, 189, 190, 193, 195, 196, 197, 200, 201, 202, 203, 213, 214, 215, 219, 221, 237, 238, 241, 243, 244, 245, 281, 297
Der Golem 222
Gone with the Wave 304
Goodbye Emmanuelle 122
Goodbye Gemini 253–254
The Good, the Bad, and the Ugly (*GBU*) 134, 135, 137, 138, 161, 162, 166, 240
Goraguer, Alain 210
Gorath 212
Gordon's War 32
Gordy, Barry 30
The Gorgon 248
Gori, Lallo (Coriolano) 45, 147
Gorney, Karen Lynn 328
Gould, Glenn 194
Governor, Mark 225, 226
Gowers, Patrick 108
The Graduate 4, 109, 320, 321, 329
Graf, Maurizio 138
Grainer, Ron 59, 192 193, 214
"Grand Canyon Suite" 168
Grand Guignol 222
Il grande colpo dei sette uomini d'oro 48
Il grande duello 151
Il grande silenzio 145
Grant, Cary 231
Grantby 64, 71, 243
Grateful Dead 316
Gray, Barry 219
The Great Escape 319
The Great Train Robbery 52, 56
The Great Train Robbery (silent film) 127
Green, Billy 300, 329
The Green Hornet 13
Greene, Joe 97
Grier, Pam 28, 29, 34
Grofé, Ferde, Sr. 168
The Groop 100
Groupie Girl 323
Gruppo di Improvvisazione Nuova Consonanza 267
Grusin, Dave 75, 108, 109, 320, 321, 329
Guccioni, Bob 125
Guercio, James William 300
Guess Who's Coming to Dinner? 21
Gugusse et l'automate 167
A Guide for a Married Man 97
Guitar Player (magazine) 71
Gunfight at Red Sands 135
Gunn... Number One 9
Gunning, Christopher 253, 254

Guns Don't Argue 135
Guns for San Sebastian 148
Gunsmoke 130
Guthrie, Arlo 320, 321
Guthrie, Woody 133, 320
Gyldmark, Sven 113

The H-Man 211
Hackman, Gene 17, 199
Hadjidakis, Manos 47, 48, 105
Hagen, Earle 68
Haggard, H. Rider 167
Hair 23, 260, 323, 325
Haji 288
Hallendbeck, Bruce 251, 252
Halletz, Erwin 132
Halloween 245
Hamilton, Chico 7, 234
Hamilton, David 124
Hamilton, Guy 62, 63
Hamlisch, Marvin 66
Hammer, Shirley 111, 112
The Hammer Film Music Collection, Vol. 1 (*HFMC-1*) 246
The Hammer Film Music Collection, Vol. 2 (*HFMC-2*) 253
Hammer, House of Horror: Behind the Screams 247
Hammer Studios 13, 176, 179, 245–253, 256, 266
Hammer—The Studio That Dripped Blood! 249, 250
The Hammer Vampire Film Music Collection 252
Hampton, Lionel 21
Hancock, Herbie 19
Handel, George Frideric 98, 99
Hang 'Em High 162, 163
The Hanged Man 43
Hangover Square 248
Hanson, Howard 202
Happening in White 123
Happy Days 285, 292, 327
A Hard Day's Night 3, 62, 282, 284, 308–310
Harkit Records 52, 53, 74, 209, 322, 323
Harline, Leigh 286
Harmonic 33, 334
Harnell, Joe 219, 220
Harold & Maude 321
Harper, Jessica 278
Harrad Summer 103
The Harrad Experiment 100, 103
Harris, Bob 95
Harrison, George 283
Harrison, Noel 50
Harrison, Rex 50
Harryhausen, Ray 177
Harvey, Lawrence 117
Harvey, Richard 108
Hart, Bobby 311, 320

Hatcher, Harley 296
Hatchet for the Honeymoon 258–259
Hathaway, Donny 26
The Haunted Palace 225
Hausfrauen-Report International 124
Haven, Alan 106
Hawaii Five-0 19
Hawaiian Surfing Movie 303
Hawks, Howard 127
Hawksworth, Johnny 42, 60, 87, 107
Hayes, Isaac 22, 25, 26, 27, 32, 33, 56, 82, 283
Hays Code 85, 86
Hazlewood, Lee 301, 305
Head 284, 311–312
Hearn, Marcus 246, 248
A Heart at Fire's Center: The Life and Music of Bernard Herrmann 40, 233
Heavy 292
Hefner, Hugh 86
Hefti, Neal 15, 49, 96, 216
Heindorf, Ray 90
Heinz, Gerhard 123
Hell Up in Harlem 30
The Hellbenders 137
The Hellcats 292
Heller, Skip 6
Hell's Angels on Wheels 290, 293, 329
Hell's Angels '69 296
Hell's Belles 291, 292
Help! 282, 284, 308–310
Hemric, Guy 290, 301, 303, 308
Hendrix, Jimi 283, 318, 325
Henze, Hans Werner 238
The Herbaliser 332
Hercules 177
Hercules in the Haunted World 177
Hercules Unchained 177
Here We Go Round the Mulberry Bush 107, 325
Herrmann, Bernard 2, 28, 40, 55, 71, 98, 168, 170, 171, 173, 174, 177, 178, 179, 184, 185, 211, 213, 215, 221, 229, 230, 231, 232, 233, 234, 236, 238, 239, 240, 243, 244, 245, 248, 267, 281, 332
Heston, Charlton 10, 192, 194
Hewitt, Sandi 103
Hieronymus, Richard 298
Higgins, Monk 34
High Noon 127, 128
High Plains Drifter 162
High School Confidential 286
Hill, Jack 228
Hill, Terence 148, 149
Hilliard Stern, Steven 103
Himes, Chester 23
Hirose, Kenjiro 212
Histoire de Melody Nelson 122
Histoire d'O 121
Hitchcock, Alfred 55, 170, 184, 185, 229, 230, 231, 232, 233, 236, 239, 243, 244, 253
Hoffman, Dustin 321
Hoffman, Eric 174
Hoffmann, Bruno 235
Holcomb, Roscoe 316
Hold-Up—istantanea di una rapina 45
The Hollies 48, 254
Hollingsworth, John 246
The Hollywood Reporter 238
Holmes, David 55, 330
Holmes, Leroy 58
Holocaust 234
Holst, Gustav 5, 168, 204
Holy Modal Rounders 295
Honda, Ishirô 211
Hooks, Robert 28
Hope, Bob 92
Hopkins, Anthony 243
Hopkins, Kenyon 13, 15, 90
Hopper, Dennis 295, 297
Horn, Paul 304
Horner, James 203
The Horror Elite 249
Horror Express 253, 255
Horror of Dracula see *Dracula* (1958)
The Horror of Frankenstein 251
Hosalla, Hans-Dieter 132
The Hot Rock 55
Hot Rod 301
Hot Rod Girl 301
Hot Rod Rumble 301
Hot Rods to Hell 319
Hotchkiss, John 246
The Hound of Blackwood Castle 46
Hour of the Gun 162
How the West Was Won 127
How to Stuff a Wild Bikini 308
Hubbard, Freddie 27
Hübler, Manfred 115
Hudson, Rock 91, 92
Hugg, Mike 116, 326
Hughes, Howard 148
Hula 85
The Human Vapor 211
Humperdinck, Engelbert 293
The Hunchback of Notre Dame 222
The Hunchback of Soho 206
Husted, Christopher 231
The Hustler 15
Hutch, Willie 26, 29, 33, 34
Hysteria 248

I, a Woman I, II, and III 113–114
I Am Legend (book) 183, 192
I Bury the Living 223
I Love You, Alice B. Toklas 319–320
I Spy 66, 68, 69
I Told You Not to Cry 46
I Walked with a Zombie 223

I Want to Live 6, 10–11, 56
Ifukube, Akira 210, 211, 212, 213, 221, 256
The Iguana with the Tongue of Fire 269–270
Ikeno, Sei 211
I'll Never Forget What's'isname 107
The Illustrated Man 186, 193
Im Staub der Sterne 207, 208
Immel, Jerrold 219
The Immoral Mr. Teas 88
The Impressions 27, 30, 325
In Like Flint 57, 71, 84
In the Heat of the Night 22, 52
Incense and Peppermints 318
The Incredible Hulk 219, 220
The Incredibles 64, 332
Incredibly Strange Music 317
Inside of the White Slave Trade 85
International Detective 57–58
International Spy Museum 57
The Internecine Project 77
Inter-Urban Electric A&E Rhythm and Pit Crew Band 303
Intolerance 85
Intrada Records 190, 202
Invasion of the Astro-Monster 211
Invasion of the Body Snatchers (1956) 173, 223
Invasion of the Body Snatchers (1978) 200, 201
Invasion of the Saucer Men 174
The Invisible Man 167
The Invisible Man's Revenge 167
The Ipcress File 61, 69–71, 84, 106
Ireson, John 152
Irma La Douce 93
Iron Butterfly 292
Irvin, Sam 247
Irving, Katie 239
Ishii, Ken 212
It Came from Beneath the Sea 173
It Came from Outer Space 171, 172
It Conquered the World 173–174
It! The Terror from Beyond Space 174
Italia a mano armata 45
The Italian Job 52, 54, 320
Ivanhoe 204

Jackie Brown 20
Jackson, Millie 29
Jackson, Peter 151, 199
Jackson Five 30
Jacopetti, Gualtiero 109, 110
Jaeckin, Just 120, 121
Jagger, Mick 282
Jailhouse Rock 282
James, Bob 38
James Bond 27, 36, 57, 58, 60, 61–66, 68, 69, 73, 81, 83, 89, 99, 197, 203, 210
"The James Bond Theme" 60, 61, 74, 81, 106, 134, 137, 210

Jameson, Bobby 318
Jane Birkin et Serge Gainsbourg 122
Jansen, David 13
Jason and the Argonauts 177
Jaws 137, 198, 232, 240, 243, 244, 281
Jaws 2 241
Jazz en el cine negro espanol 1958–1964 46–47
Jazz Messengers 105
The Jazz Soul of Doctor Kildare 306
Jazz Track 13
Je t'aime moi non plus 122, 126
Jefferson Airplane 283
Jeffries, Fran 96
Jerry Cotton 46, 77–78
Jesus Christ Superstar 323, 324
Jethro Tull 144, 327
Jewison, Norman 197
Jim Helms and the Drivers 298
Jimi Hendrix Experience 295
Joe 325
John Barry: A Sixties Theme 62
The John Barry Seven 61, 106, 293
John Golfarb, Please Come Home 97
Johnny Banco 43
Johnny Cool 13–14
Johnny Jupiter 213
Johnny West il mancino 140
Johns, William 11
Johnson, Don 103
Johnson, J.J. 26, 27, 28, 29, 31, 34, 107
Johnson, Laurie 60, 183
Jolly, Pete 11
Jones, Booker T. 22
Jones, Davy (Monkee) 311
Jones, Davy (non-Monkee) 292
Jones, Quincy 7, 21, 22, 25, 26, 52, 54, 55, 56, 57, 98, 99, 236, 320, 325, 332
Jones, Tom 64, 96, 293
Joplin, Scott 103
Jordan, Duke 105
Jordan, Louis 282
Josephs, William 60
Joss, Chris 333, 334
Journey to the Center of the Earth 178–179
Journey to the Unknown (TV series) 251
Journeyman 40
Joy, Nick 171
Juice People Unlimited 35
Julian, Don 32
Jungle Exotica 86
Jungle Girl 87
Junior Bonner 55
Juvet, Patrick 124, 125

Kaempfert, Bert 75
Kaleidoscope 316
Kantor, Igo 88, 89
Kaper, Bronislau 172
Kaplan, Sol 69, 218

Karan, Chris 77
Karger, Fred 307, 319
Karlin, Fred 194, 195
Karnstein trilogy 251, 252
Kasem, Casey 291, 303
Katz, Fred 223
Katzman, Sam 316
Kaufman, Philip 200
Kaun, Bernhard 57
Kaye, Buddy 81
Kazan, Elia 6, 90
Keeping the Score 185
Kellaway, Roger 200
Kellermann, Annette 85
Kelly, Jim 36
Kelly's Heroes 52–53
Kendall, Lukas 189, 197, 241
Kendall, Suzy 326
Kenton, Stan 61, 305
Kerr, Deborah 90
Kershaw, Doug 55
Khachaturian, Aram 125, 185
The Kids Are Alright 284, 314
Kikuchi, Shunsuke 212
Kill! 78, 81–82, 84
Kill Bill, Vol. 1 32, 144, 151, 279
Kill Bill, Vol. 2 266
Kilmer, Val 60
King, Carole 311
King Kong 167, 197
King Rat 106
The Kingsmen 314
Kinoshita, Chuji 212
"Kinsey Report" 86
Kinski, Klaus 275
Kirchin, Basil 226, 227, 228
Kiss Kiss Bang Bang 78, 79
The Kiss of the Vampire 248
Kit & Co. 132
Klute 18
The Knack ... and How to Get It 106
Knife in the Water 234
Knotts, Don 48
Knudson, Buzz 239
Kögebehn, Günther 236
Kojak 19
Kojucharov, Vasco Vassil 147
Kolle, Oswalt 124
Komeda, Krzysztof 18, 234, 235, 281
Koo, Joseph 36
Korngold, Erich Wolfgang 1
Koscina, Sylva 117
Koseki, Yuji 211
Kosma, Joseph 108
Kosmos 206
Kovac, Roland 46
KPM Recorded Music Library 42, 334
Krafft-Ebing 97
Kraftwerk 122
Kriminal 48–49

Kristofferson, Kris 108
Kronos 174
Krupa, Gene 11
Kubrick, Stanley 94, 95, 185, 186, 191, 192
Kurosawa, Akira 133

Lady Chatterley's Lover 104, 108
Lady Frankenstein 264, 265
Lady in Cement 14
The Lady Vanishes 57
Lai, Francis 107, 124, 294
Lamarr, Hedy 86
Lambert, Dennis 31
Lancaster, Burt 7, 90
Lancen, Serge 219
Land of the Giants 216
Larraz, José Ramón 269
Larson, Randall D. 176, 181, 250, 251, 252, 253
The Las Vegas Grind 86
LaSalle, Richard 215
The Last Man on Earth 183, 192
The Last of the Secret Agents 301
Last Tango in Paris 100, 101, 110, 126
The Last Waltz 283
Laughlin, Tom 290
Laura 124
Lauren, Ralph 99
Lavagnino, Angelo 133, 135, 140, 151, 204
Lawford, Peter 13, 14, 73
Lawrence, D.H. 97, 104, 107, 108
Lazenby, George 65
Leadbeater, Neil 250
Leary, Timoth 319
Led Zeppelin 123, 283, 284, 294, 318, 319
Lee, Bernard 81
Lee, Bruce 36, 37
Lee, Christopher 66, 246, 249
Lee, Linda 279
Lee, Shawn 334, 335
The Legend of the 7 Golden Vampires 253
The Legendary Italian Westerns 136
La legge dei gangsters 44
Legrand, Michel 50
Leigh, Janet 231
Lelouche, Claude 294
Lem, Stanislaw 206
Lemmon, Jack 91, 93
Lennon, John 100
Lenzi, Umberto 260
Leone, Sergio 133, 134, 136, 137, 138, 145, 149, 150, 155, 162
Lester, Richard 106
Let It Be 283, 310–311
Let It Be... Naked 311
Let's Get It On 27
Leuter, Cecil 87
Lewis, Herschell Gordon 228
Lewis, Jerry 95

Lewis, Jerry Lee 286, 327
Lewis, Smiley 90
Lewton, Val 223
Les Liaisons dangereuses 105
Lialeh 103
Liberati, Stafano 275
The Libertine 114
The Lickerish Quartet 112
Liebe in Drei Dimension 124
Liebespiele Junger Mädchen 123
Lifehouse 314
The Lifehouse Chronicles 314
Ligeti, Gyorgy 185, 186
Light in the Attic Records 102
Lindsay, Mark 100
Lingua d'argento 120
The Lion in Winter 65
Lipman, Berry 206, 208
The Liquidator 72–73, 330
Liszt, Franz 41, 248
Little Shop of Horrors (1960) 223
Little Shoppe of Horrors (magazine) 247, 251, 252
Live a Little, Love a Little 299
Live and Let Die 20, 60, 65–66
The Living Daylights 61, 66
The Living Dead at the Manchester Morgue 276
Lizard in a Woman's Skin 266
Lloyd Webber, Andrew 323
Logan's Run 186, 195, 196
Logan's Run (TV series 219
London, Julie 286
London Symphony Orchestra and Chamber Choir 314
Lonelyville 15
Lolita 90, 94–95, 122, 126
Lollipop Shoppe 294
Look Out Sister 282
Looney Tunes 144, 174
Loose, William 88, 332
Loot 54
The Lord of the Rings 3, 151, 177
The Lord of the Rings (1978) 188, 199
Loren, Sophia 105
The Losers 290, 297, 298
The Lost Continent 177
Lost in Space 215–216
The Lost Man 22, 320, 325
The Lost World 167
Louie's Limbo Lounge 86
Love 96
Love Affair 54
Love in Outer Space 194
The Love Machine 100
Love Me Tender 282
Love Moods 86
"Love to Love You, Baby" 119
Lovecraft, H.P. 225, 226
The Love-Ins 319

Lovelace, Linda 102
Lover Come Back 96
The Lovers 104
Lover's Island 85
Lowe, Nick 327
Loy, Mino 112
Lucas, George 55, 193, 197, 198, 240, 243, 285, 304, 327
Lucas, Tim 257, 268, 269, 271
Lugosi, Bela 245
Lulu 66
Lucifer Rising 318–319
Lucille Has Messed My Mind Up 295
La lune à un mètre 167
Una lunga fila di croci 147
I lunghi giorni della vendetta 140
The Lushes 86
Lust for a Vampire 251, 252
Lust for Life 1
Lyon, Sue 95

M Squad 9
MacDermot, Galt 23, 323
MacDonald, Lydia 78, 79, 110, 140
The Mack 29–30, 33–34
"Mack the Knife" 265
Mackay, Rabbit 298
MacLaine, Shirley 93
Maclean, Alistair 41
The Mad Butcher of Vienna 264–265
Mad Max 203
Madame Claude 122
Mademoiselle Striptease 104
Maestosi, Elio 275
Magic 243
Magical Mystery Tour 284, 310
Magne, Michel 43, 83, 108, 209
Magnet 255
The Magnificent Seven (M7) 3, 128–129, 130, 132, 133, 135, 165, 166
The Magnificent Stranger 133
Le Magnifique 83
Magnum Force 16
Mahavishnu Orchestra 300
Mahler, Gustav 149
"Mah Na' Mah Na'" 110, 111, 112
Maidenhead Studios 206
Malle, Louis 12, 13
Malosky, Al 295, 296
Maltin, Leonard 232
A Man and a Woman 293
A Man Called Dagger 74
A Man Could Get Killed 75
The Man from U.N.C.L.E. 14, 66–68, 84
The Man with the Golden Arm 2–3, 6–7, 56, 58, 71, 93, 319
The Man with the Golden Gun 61, 66
Man in Space with Sounds 194, 220, 221
The Man Who Fell to Earth 282
The Man Who Shot Liberty Valance 130

The Man with a Suitcase 333
The Manchurian Candidate 15
Mancini Beats 332
Mancini, Henry 2, 6, 7, 8, 9, 10, 18, 19, 52, 56, 60, 74, 89, 92, 93, 96, 103, 134, 171, 172, 198, 285, 286, 320, 330, 332
Mancuso, Elsio 147
Mandel, Johnny 6, 10, 11, 37, 38, 56, 108
Manfred Mann 96, 116, 253, 325, 326
Manne, Shelly 11, 13, 71, 304
Manning, Roger Joseph, Jr. 333
Mannino, Franco 256
Mannix 16
Mansell, John 136, 137
Mansfield, Jayne 90, 110, 286
Mansfield, Keith 42, 54
Manson Family 234, 318
La mano che nutre la morte 275–276
Margheriti, Antonio 204
Marinacci, Gino 81
Marinuzzi, Gino, Jr. 204
Marjorie Morningstar 1
Markland, Ted 293
Markowski, Anrzej 207
Marnie 233
Marquis de Sade's Justine 116
Marquis de Sade's Philosophy in the Boudoir 116
The Marseille Contract 42, 76–77, 84
Martell, Phillip 248, 253
Martelli, Augusto 117, 152
Martelli, Carlo 176
Martha and the Vandellas 34
Martin, Dean 15, 71, 306
Martin, George 65, 66, 310, 311
Martinez, Rafael 180
Martinez Tudo, Federico 47
The Mary Tyler Moore Show 103
Maryjane 317
Masetti, Enzo 177
M*A*S*H 53
Mason, Barbara 34
The Masque of Red Death 225, 226
Matalo 154, 166
Matheson, Richard 183, 192
Mathis, Johnny 52
Matlovsky, Samuel 218
Matt Helm 68, 71, 73
Max Frost & the Troopers 291
Maxford, Howard 247
Maxwell, Lois 81
May, Billy 13, 14, 216
May, Brian 203
May, Karl 131
Mayfield, Curtis 26, 27, 30, 32, 35, 56
The May-Irwin Kiss 85
MCA 52, 314
McBain, Diane 302
McCartney, Paul 65, 66
McDowell, Malcolm 125, 191
McGilligan, Patrick 11

McGinnis, Robert 23, 27
McGoohan, Patrick 58, 59, 60
McGuinn, Roger 295
McGraw, Ali 55
McKuen, Rod 285, 286
McNeely, Joel 231, 233
McQ 18–19
McQueen, Steve 16, 55, 162, 299
McRitchie, Greig 200
The Meadowlarks 32
Meddle 315
Medical Center 16
Medicine Ball 298
Meier, Wolfgang 132
Méliès, Georges 167
Melle, Gil 193
Melodies in Love 123
Men into Space 213
The Mephisto Waltz 237
La Mer 183
Il mercenario 148
Mercer, Johnny 96
Mercouri, Melina 105
Metropolis 167
Metti una sera a cena 116–117
Metzger, Radley 112, 113
Meyer, Nicholas 204
Meyer, Russ 88, 89, 287, 288, 322, 323, 332
MGM 93, 134, 173
MGM Records 289
Miami Vice 103
Micalizzi, Franco 43, 45, 120, 149, 276, 277
Michaels, Dean 325
Mickey Mouse Club 301
Midnight Cowboy 65, 99–100, 325
Midnight Express 200
The Midsummer's Day Dream 298
Migliardi, Mario 154, 166
Mike Curb Congregation 54
Mike Hammer 9, 68
Milano trema: la polizia vuole giustizia 44–45
Milano Violenta 45
Miller, Mrs. 317
Miller, Steve (Band) 319
Mills, Dick 214
Mina 205, 274
Mineo, Art (Attillio) 194, 220, 221
The Mini-Skirt Mob 292
The Minx 100
Il mio nome e Nessuno 158
Il mio nome e Shanghai Joe 158
Mirage 21, 236
Miramagic 173
Miranda, Soledad 116
Mirren, Helen 125
Mishima, Yukio 108
Misraki, Paul 104
The Mission 148
Mission: Impossible 15, 66, 72, 84, 193, 332, 334

Missione morte molo 83 78
Mister Buddwing 15
Mr. Moses 106
Mitch Ryder and the Detroit Wheels 297
Mitchell, Joni 321
Mitchell, Red 11, 13, 71
Mitchum, Robert 237
Mix, Tom 127
Miyauchi, Kunio 211
Mizell, Fonce 30
Mizzy, Vic 48
Mocean Worker 334
The Mod Squad 13
Modesty Blaise 68, 73, 74
Mojo (magazine) 330
Mom's Boys 317
Mondadori 258
Mondo caldo di notte 110
Mondo cane 109–110
Mondo Hollywood 318
Mondo Topless 125
The Money Spyder 333
The Monkonious 105
The Monkees 284, 311, 312, 320
The Monkey Hu$tle 35
Monro, Matt 42, 62
Monroe, Marilyn 90, 91
Monster from Hell 253
The Monster of Soho 46
Monta in sella, figlio di... 156
Montenegro, Hugo 13, 14, 15, 67, 68, 73, 135, 162
Monterey Pop 283
Moonraker 61, 66, 203
Moore, Dudley 103, 109
Moore, Roger 60, 61, 65
Moore, Rudy Ray 35
Morante, Massimo 277, 279
More 315
Moreau, Jeanne 12, 104
Morgan, David 185
Morley, Angela 253
Moroder, Giorgio 122, 200
Moross, Jerome 129, 165, 166
Morricone, Ennio 14, 18, 43, 44, 49, 54, 56, 79, 80, 81, 84, 116, 117, 133, 134, 135, 136, 137, 138, 139, 140, 141, 144, 145, 147, 148, 149, 150, 151, 152, 154, 155, 156, 158, 160, 162, 163, 165, 210, 234, 241, 242, 252, 262, 263, 264, 266, 267, 268, 271, 272, 273, 275, 281, 332, 334
Morricone RMX 332
Morselli, Franco 147
La morte ha sorriso all'assassino 275
La morte risale a ieri sera 260–261
Morton, Arthur 241
Morton, "Jelly Roll" 103
Moss Side Story 333
Mother Earth 319
The Mothers of Invention 312

Mothra 211
Motor Psycho 89, 287
The Motorcycle Gang 287
Motown 26, 29, 30, 33, 305
Mountain 299
Movie & TV Themes 7
Mozart, Wolfgang Amadeus 156, 202, 223, 235
MTV 283, 284
Mugwump Establishment 318
The Mugwumps 316
Mulhall, Kevin 233
Mullendore, Joseph 215, 218
Mulligan, Gerry 11
Mumma, Ed 250
The Mummy (1933) 222
The Mummy (1959) 247
Murderer's Row 72, 73
Murray, Lyn 229
Muscle Beach Party 308
Music for the Movies 185
Music from the House of Hammer 176
Music from the Movies (magazine) 171
The Music Library 334
Music to Read James Bond By 68
Music to Spy By 57
Mussolini, Romano 48, 49
Mussorgsky, Modest 5, 172
Myers, Stanley 42, 108
My Name Is Nobody 158
My Name Is Shanghai Joe 158
Myrow, Fred 194
Mysterious Island (1929) 167
Mysterious Island (1951) 177
Mysterious Island (1961) 179
The Mystery of Mary Celeste 245
The Mystery of the Wax Museum 222

Nabokov, Vladimir 94
Naked Angels 295–296
Naked City 9, 13
Naked Lunch (movie) 3
Naked Lunch (book) 318
Napoli Spara 45
Nardini, Nino 87
Nascimbene, Mario 82, 108, 179, 180, 181
Nash, Dick 71
National Hijinx 40
National Philharmonic Orchestra 186, 202
Navajo Joe 138
NBC-TV 312
Neal, Patricia 171
Neef, Wilhelm 132
Nel Nome del Padre, del Figlio e della Colt 158
Nelson, Oliver 107
Nesmith, Michael 311
Never on Sunday 92, 105
The New Yardbirds 294

Newley, Anthony 62
Newman, Alfred 90, 127
Newman, Lionel 90, 241, 286
Newsom, Ted 174
Nichols, Leo (Ennio Morricone alias) 133, 137, 138
Nichols, Mike 320
Nicholson, Jack 39, 318
Die Nichte der O 123
Nicolai, Bruno 18, 49, 79, 80, 82, 84, 116, 117, 125, 138, 139, 141, 144, 148, 149, 154, 156, 158, 210, 260, 267, 268, 269, 273, 275, 281, 334
Nicolosi, Roberto 256, 257, 258
The Night Evelyn Came Out of the Grave 267, 268
The Night of the Hunter 223
The Night of the Iguana 95
Night of the Living Dead 183, 279
"Night on Bald Mountain" 5
The Night Porter 120
Nightmare! 15
The Nights of Cabiria 93, 105
Nilsson, Harry 99, 100, 312
Nina 65
Ninja Tune 332
Nitzsche, Jack 238, 239
Normal Records 87, 88
Norman, Monty 61, 134, 210
North, Alex 1, 2, 3, 6, 90, 185, 186
North by Northwest 229, 231, 233
Nosferatu (1922) 222
Not of This Earth 174
Not with My Wife 95–96
La notte dei serpenti 151

"O Fortuna" 241
The Oblong Box 251
O'Brien, Richard 324, 329
Obscured by Clouds 315
Obsession 231, 239
Ocean's Eleven 55, 332
Ocean's Thirteen 55, 332
Ocean's Twelve 55, 332
Octopussy 61, 66
The Odd Couple 96
Ode Records 314
O'Donnell, Peter 73
El ojo del huracán 266
OK Connery 80–81, 84
Oklahoma 152
Oldfield, Mike 238
Oliviero, Nino 109, 110
Un' ombra nell'ombra 280
The Omega Man 183, 191, 192–193
The Omen 241, 245, 281
On Any Sunday 299–300
On Her Majesty's Secret Service 50, 61, 64–65, 99
Once Upon a Time in America 242

Once Upon a Time in the Italian West: A Filmgoer's Guide to Spaghetti Westerns 148
Once Upon a Time in the West 132, 149–151, 161, 162, 166
Ondes Martenot 255
100 Rifles 163, 164, 166
One Million Years B.C. 179–180, 181
One More Time 74
Opal Butterfly 323
The Opening of Misty Beethoven 112
Operazione paradiso 82
Operation Neptune 213
O'Rahilly, Ronan 294
Orff, Carl 241
Orlandi, Nora 46, 111, 157, 260, 266, 269, 271
Ormi, Paolo 266
L'oro dei bravados 153
Ortolani, Riz 52, 109, 110, 151, 260, 264, 281
Orton, Joe 54
Osibasa 32
The Osmonds 289
OSS 117 82–83
The Other 237
Other Worlds, Other Sounds 220
O'Toole, Peter 125
Ott, Horace 103
Our Man Flint 71, 84
Out of this World 213
The Outer Limits 215, 221
The Outfit 38
The Outlaw Josey Wales 162, 165
Outlaw, Tigger 321
Owens, Frank 102

The Pace That Thrills 301
Pachelbel, Johann 271
Page, Bettie (Betty) 86, 87, 88
Page, Jimmy 294, 318, 319
Page, Patti 316
Paint Your Wagon 162
Pal, George 179, 181
Pale Rider 165
Palmer, Christopher 40
Panic! 15
Paolo, Gino 138
Papillon 93, 187
Paramount Pictures 326, 328
Parham, Wayne 152
Paris Blues 12
Paris, Danièle 120
Paris, Harry (Henry) 112
Parks, Gordon 24, 25, 27
The Partridge Family 298
Passion Flower Hotel 106
Pate, Johnny 27, 30, 32, 330
Patton 93, 187
The Pawnbroker 21
The Payback 30

Peaches & Herb 35
Peanut Butter Conspiracy 294
Peanuts 211
Peck, Gregory 237
Peckinpah, Sam 55, 163, 164
Peeping Tom 253
Penderecki, Krzysztof 238
Penelope 97
Penthouse (magazine) 125
The Penthouse 107
Percepto Records 175
Per qualche dollaro in più see *For a Few Dollars More*
Per un pugno di dollari see *A Fistful of Dollars*
Per una valigia piena di donne 110
Perren, Freddie 30
Perry Mason 9
Perry Rhodan—S.O.S. aus dem Weltall 206, 207
The Persuaders 60
Perseverance Records 200, 201, 227
Perversion Story 260
Peter Gunn 7, 8, 9, 10, 13, 46, 56, 74, 285
"Peter Gunn Theme" 134, 330
Peter Scores 123
Peyton Place 2, 90
The Phantom of the Opera 222, 226
The Phantom of the Opera (1962) 247–248
Phillips, Freddie 253
Phillips, Stu 88, 89, 219, 220, 290, 291, 294, 295, 297, 306, 322, 323, 329
Piccioni, Piero 48, 78, 79, 82, 105, 112, 147, 158, 205, 266
Pickers, J.B. 299
Pillow Talk 91, 96
Pinewood Studios 313
Ping Pong Orchestra 334
Pink Flamingos 90
Pink Floyd 81, 122, 284, 314, 315, 316
The Pink Panther 10
The Piper at the Gates of Dawn 315
Pippi Longstocking 114
Piranha 244–245
Pisano, Berto 81, 84, 275
Le pistola non discutono 135
Il pistolero cieco 157–158
Los pistoleros de Arizona 135
Una pistoli per Ringo 138
Pit and the Pendulum 224
Pitt, Ingrid 252
Pitts, Clay 114
La più grande rapina del west 141–142
The Plague of Zombies 248
Planet of the Apes (movie) 16, 93, 165, 173, 183, 186, 187, 200, 221, 297
Planet of the Apes (TV show) 187, 189–190, 193
Planet of the Vampires 204–5
Planet on the Prowl 204

La Planète sauvage 210
The Planets 5, 168, 204
The Patters 285
Playboy 86, 88, 287
Playgirl '70 147
Plenizio, Gianfranco 117
Poe, Edgar Allan 223, 224, 225, 226, 245, 251, 264
Point Blank 37–38
Poitevin, Roby 260
Poitier, Sidney 21
Poker at Dawson City 127
Polanski, Roman 234, 235
Police Story 19
Police Woman 19
La polizia incrimina la legge assolve 44
Pop Fiction 64
Porno Pop 104
Porter, Edwin 127
Portishead 68, 332
The Poseidon Adventure 198
Post, Mike 19
Potter, Brian 31
Powell, Michael 253
Pregadio, Roberto 48, 49, 141
The Premature Burial 225
Presley, Elvis ("The King" or Elvis) 4, 86, 282, 299, 301, 302, 308, 309, 319
Prestige Records 34
Pretties for You 295
Pretty Baby 103, 104
Previn, Andre 93, 97, 197
Previn, Dory 97
Price, Vincent 224, 226
Primitive Love 110
The Prisoner 42, 59–60, 192, 214
Pritchard, Mark 334, 335
The Private Afternoons of Pamela Mann 112
Private Girl 87–88
Procol Harem 107
Il profeta 114
Profundo rosso see *Deep Red*
Project: Comstock—Music from Outer Space 220
Prokofiev, Sergei 125
Promise Her Anything 96
Propellerheads 332
Prosperi, Franco 109, 110
Psych-Out 317–318
Psychedelic Dance Party 115
Psychedelic Sexualis 97
Psycho 179, 211, 229, 231, 231–232, 233, 234, 239, 240, 253, 267, 281
Psychomania 255
Pulp 206
Il punto 119
Puppet on a Chain see *Alistair Maclean's Puppet on a Chain*
Purcell, Henry 179, 191

Purdie, Bernard "Pretty" 103
Pussy Galore 332
QDK Media 87, 88
Quadrophenia 284, 314
Quanto costa morire 145–146
Quatermass & the Pit 176
Quatermass II 176
The Quatermass Xperiment 176, 179, 245, 246
I quattro dell'apocalisse 159, 160
I quattro dell'ave maria 148
I quattro del pater noster 151
Queen 203
Quel caldo maledetto giorno di fuoco 147
Quella sporca storia nel west 147
Questo sporco mondo meraviglioso 112
Quicksilver Messenger Service 319
Quien sabe? 140
The Quiller Memorandum 69
Quine, Robert 96

Rachmaninov, Sergey 41, 176
Radetski 60
Radio Caroline 294
Rado, James 323
La ragazza dalla pelle di luna 117–118
La ragazza fuori strada 117–118
The Ragged Princess 85
Ragni, Jerome 323
The Rainbow 108
Rambo 297
The Ramones 282, 327, 329
Rampling, Charlotte 117, 120
Randall, Tony 91, 92
Randazzo, Teddy 67
Ranieri, Katina 151
Raoul 81, 144, 145, 146
Rasputin the Mad Monk 248
Ratner, Brett 36
Raumpatrouille 206, 221
Ravel, Maurice 103, 215
The Raven 224
Rawhide 133
Raworth, Ben 52
Les Rayons Roentgen 167
RCA 67, 135, 162, 308
Rear Window 2, 229, 239
Rebus 82
Red Queen Kills Seven Times 273
Red River 127
Redman, Nick 238
Reed, Dean 147
Reed, Jerry 299
Reed, Les 292, 293, 294, 298
Reems, Harry 101
Reeves, Martha 234
Regan 42
Reich, Steve 170, 213, 230
Reid, Alastair 233
Reiner, Rob 298

Reitzel, Brian 333
Reizenstein, Franz 247
Rennie Michael 171
La resa dei conti 144–145
Reno, Peter 42
The Reptile 248
Repulsion 234
Requiem per un agente segreto 79
The Return of Dracula 223
The Return of the Dragon 36
The Return of the Fly 174, 175, 176, 183
The Revenge of Mister Mopoji 35
Reverberi, Gian Piero (G.P.) and Gianfranco (G.F.) 116, 141, 143
Revolution 319
Rhino Records 27, 231, 316, 330
Rice, Tim 323
Rich, Buddy 11
Richard, Little 55, 90, 286
Richard Diamond 13
Richards, Deke 30
Richards, Emil 193
Richards, Keith 283
Riddle, Nelson 68, 94, 95, 126, 183, 215, 216, 217
Ride the High Country 130
Ride the Wild Surf 290
Riedel, Georg 114
Rififi 43, 47
Riley, Terry 230
Rimsky-Korsakov, Nicolai 5, 191, 192
Ringo movies 138, 139
Ringo il cavaliere solitario 146
Rio Bravo 127, 128
Rio Conchos 129–130, 166
Rio Lobo 165
Riot on Sunset Strip 316–317, 319
The Riptides 318
Ritenour, Lee 197, 241
The Rite of Spring see *Le Sacre du Printemps*
Ritornano Quelli della Calibro 38, 45
Il ritorno di Ringo 138
Rivers, Johnny 58, 59
Rizzati, Walter 141
RKO 223
The Road Warrior 203
Roberts, Howard 304
Roberts, Rocky 156
Robertson, Bob (Sergio Leone alias) 133
Robinson, Harry (aka Henry Robinson and Lord Rockingham) 251, 252
Robot Monster 171
Rock Around the Clock 282, 285, 316, 329
Rock 'n' Roll High School 327, 329
Rock, Pretty Baby 285, 286
Rocketship X-M 168
The Rockford Files 19
The Rocky Horror Picture Show 324, 329
Rocky Jones—Space Ranger 213
Rodan, the Flying Monster 211

Roddenberry, Gene 218
Rodrigo, Joaquín 148
Roemheld, Heinz 57
Roger Roger 60, 87
Rogers, Roy 127
Rogers, Shorty 330
Rollerball 197
The Rolling Stones 282, 283, 292
Rollins, Sonny 107
Roma drogata 45
Roma violenta 45
Romanov aristocracy 248
"Romeo and Juliet" (classical work) 125
Romeo & Juliet (movie) 295
Romero, George 279
Romitelli, Sante Marie 258
Rose, David 93
Rosemary's Baby 18, 234, 235, 276, 281
Rosenberger, Raimund 132
Rosenman, Leonard 183, 184, 187, 188, 199, 200, 214
Rosenthal, Laurence 219
Rosolino, Frank 11
Rossini, Gioacchino 119, 191
Rósza, Miklos 1, 6, 162, 177, 204
Rota, Nino 38, 105, 295
Roy, Herve 121
Roy Colt & Winchester Jack 152, 153, 159
Royal Philharmonic Orchestra 312
RPM Records 294
Rugolo, Pete 13, 14, 305
Run, Angel, Run 290, 294, 295
Rundgren, Todd 329
Rush, Merrilee 99
Rush, Richard 290
Rush Hour 36
Rushes, Ami 323
Russell, Mark 39, 128, 185, 229
Rustichelli, Carlo 142, 143, 148, 149, 159, 258, 259
The Rutles 284
Rykodisc 11, 96, 325

Saada, Nicolas 97
Sacher-Masoch, Leopold von 116
Le Sacre du Printemps 71, 156, 168, 183, 210, 218, 240
Sad Sack 96
The Sailor Who Fell from Grace with the Sea 108
The Saint 58, 60, 61
Saint, Eva Marie 231
Saint Cyr, Lili 86
Saint Paul, Lara 81, 260
Saint Pauli Affairs 46
Sakata, Harold 63
Saks, Gene 319
Salon Band 323
Salt & Pepper 73–74
Salter, Hans 207, 215, 223, 256

Saltzman, Harry 61, 62, 65
San Antonio 127
San Francisco Chronicle 200
The Sandals 304, 329
The Sandpiper 11
The Sandpipers 96, 322
Santana 283
Santucci, Cicci 81
Sarde, Philippe 234, 235, 236
Sartana movies 152, 153, 154
Sartana nella valle degli avvoltoi 152
Sasse, Karl-Ernst 207, 208, 209
The Satan Bug 183
Satana, Tura 288
The Satanic Rites of Dracula 253
Satanik 48–49
Satan's Sadists 296
Satôh, Masaru 211
Saturday Night Fever 4, 327, 328, 329
The Savage Seven 292
Savage Super Soul 32
Savina, Carlo 141
Savio, Dan (Ennio Morricone alias) 133
The Saucerful of Secrets 315
Sawtell, Paul 88, 89, 174, 175, 176, 182, 183, 215, 287
Saxon, John 36
Scars of Dracula 249, 250
Scattini, Luigi 110, 117
Schaffner, Frank 93, 187
Scharf, Walter 67
"Scheherazade" 192
Scheikl, Michael 123
Schickele, Peter "PDQ Bach" 193
Schifrin, Lalo 15,16, 21, 36, 53, 56, 67, 68, 72, 75, 84, 97, 98, 147, 162, 187, 189, 190, 193, 219, 238, 245, 266, 281, 304, 305, 330, 332
Schirmann, Peter 46
Schneer, Charles 177
Schneider, Maria 101
Schönberg, Arnold 19, 200, 248
Schoolgirl Report 123, 126, 329, 331
Schroeder, Barbet 315
Die Schulmädchen vom Treffpunkt Zoo 123
Schüsse aus dem Geigenkasten 77
Schwab, Siegfried 115
Schwarz, Stephen 323
Sciascia, Armando 110
Science Fiction Theater 213
ScoreBaby.com 228
Scorsese, Martin 40, 234, 236, 237
Scott, Bobby 325
Scott, Nathan 189, 214
Scott, Ridley 202
Scott, Tom 187, 189, 300
Scream and Scream Again 228
Screencraft (publisher) 229
The Sea Around Us 182
The Searchers 127–128

Seberg, Jean 82
Secret Agent 42, 58–60
Secret of the Telegian 211
The Seeds 317
Segarini & Bishop 299
Sekizawa, Shinichi 211
Self Preservation Society 52, 54
Sella d'argento 159–160, 161
Sellers, Peter 48, 319
Send Me No Flowers 96
Sentenza di morte 144
Sgt. Pepper's Lonely Hearts Club Band 310
Sergio, Nilo 48
Serialement Vôtre 332
Serling, Rod 213, 214
Il serpente 81
Serpico 38
Sesame Street 110, 111
Sesso matto 118, 119
Sette note in nero 279
7 pistoli per i MacGregor 138–139
Sette uomini d'oro 48
Sette Winchester per un massacro 145
Seven Blood Stained Orchids 260
Seven Murders for Scotland Yard 266
The Seventh Voyage of Sinbad 177
77 Sunset Strip 9
Severino 132
Sex and the Single Girl 96
Sex Kittens Go to College 286
Sex Pervers 124
Sex-Shop 122
Sexadelic 115
Die Sexuellen Wünsche der Deutschen 124
Sexy 110
Sexy ad Alta Tensione 110
Sexy Magico 110
The Seven Year Itch 90
La sfida dei McKenna 154
Shackton, Al 321
"The Shadow of Your Smile" 38
Shaft 22, 25, 26, 33, 35, 36, 56
Shaft in Africa 27, 30, 32
Shaft's Big Score 27
Shank, Bud 11, 13, 303, 304
Sharman, Jim 324
Shatner, William 217
Shaw Brothers Films 253
Shaw, Sidney 58
She (book) 167, 251
She (1965) 179
She Killed in Ecstasy 116
Sheba Baby 34
Shefter, Bert 88, 89, 174, 175, 176, 182, 183, 215, 287
The Sheriff of Fractured Jaw 133
Sherman, Garry 321
Sherrill, Billy 294, 295
Shields, Brooke 103, 104
The Shining 192, 223

Shire, David 19, 20, 56, 332
The Shirelles 95
The Shootist 165
Shore, Howard 3, 151, 199, 200
Shores, Richard 68
Short Eyes 35
Short Night of the Glass Dolls 264
Shorty the Pimp 32
Shuman, Alden 102, 126
Si può fare ... amigo! 156
The Sidewalk Sounds 290, 291, 301, 302, 317
Siegel, Don 76
Signale—Ein Weltraumabenteuer 207, 208
The Silencers 57, 71, 84
Silent Running 193
Silva Screen 13, 59, 230, 250
Silver Saddle 159–160, 161
Silvestri, Alan 30
Simmons, Jeff 295
Simon and Garfunkel 159, 320, 321, 329
Simon, Carly 66
Simon, Joe 29
Simon, Paul 320
Simon Templar 60, 61
Simonetti, Claudio 276 280
Sinatra, Frank 13, 14, 15, 21, 109, 301
Sinatra, Nancy 14, 64, 99, 289, 301
Sinbad and the Eye of the Tiger 177
Sisters 239
Sisters Love 29
Sitting Target 42
Skaterdater 287, 304–305
Slalom 80
Slaughter 34
Slaughter's Big Rip-Off 30
Slaughterhouse Five 194
Slaves 325
Slippery When Wet 303
Sly and the Family Stone 26, 298
Small, Michael 18
Smith, Ellen 165
Smith, O.C. 27
Smith, Steven C. 40, 184, 233
Snow Devils 204
So Sweet... So Perverse 259–260
Sodom and Gomorrah 1
Sola, Jose 46
Solaris 206
Solie, John 27
Sollima, Sergio 148
Solo, Bobby 139
Solomon, Joe 290
Som Hon Bäddar Får Han Ligga 123
Some Like It Hot 91, 125, 126
Somebody's Chyldren 292
Something to Hide 41
Sondheim, Stephen 223
The Song Remains the Same 283, 284, 327
Sons and Lovers 108

Sorgini, Giuliano 276
Soul Ecstasy 35
Soundtrack! (magazine) 181
South, Harry 43
Southern Cross 239
Soylent Green 194, 197
Space: 1999 219
Space Is the Place 194
Space Patrol (German) 206, 208, 219, 221
Space Patrol (U.S.) 213
Stafford, Terry 290
Spaghetti Westerns, Vol. 1 140
Spaghetti Westerns, Vol. 4 147
Spagnolo, Gianna 138
Sparks, Randy 298
Spartacus (movie) 3, 185
"Spartacus" (classical work) 125
Spasmo 275
Specials 334
Spector, Phil 310, 311
Speed Crazy 301
Speedway 301
Spellbound 6, 244
The Spell of the Sinister One 46
Spelvin, Georgina 101
Spencer, Bud 148, 149
Spencer Davis Group 107, 325
Spider Baby 228
Spielberg, Steven 55, 197, 232, 240, 241, 243
Spillane, Mickey 68
Spinout 301, 302
Springfield, Dusty 73, 305
Spy Magazine 57, 330
Spy Music 57, 330
The Spy Who Came In from the Cold 69
The Spy Who Loved Me 66
Staccato 9, 46
Stack, Lenny 297
Stalker 206
Stalling, Carl 144, 174
The Standells 316
The Staples Singers 283
Star Maidens 206, 208
Star Trek (the original TV series) 203, 211, 213, 216–218, 219, 221
Star Trek: The Motion Picture 56, 202, 221
Star Trek: The Next Generation 203
Star Trek IV: The Voyage Home 200
Star Wars 3, 193, 196, 197, 198, 199, 216, 219, 220, 221
Starr, Edwin 30
Starr, Ringo 157, 283, 314
Starsky and Hutch 16
Stax Records 33
Steckler, Ray Dennis 228
Steely Dan 9
Stein, Herman 171, 172, 215
Stein, Ronald 75, 173, 174, 225, 228, 317
Steiner, Fred 214, 218

Steiner, Jerry 290, 292, 301, 303, 308
Steiner, Max 1, 3, 127, 128, 162, 197, 256
Steirling, Randy 295
Steppenwolf 108, 295, 297
Stereolab 158
Stern, Toni 312
Stevens, Cat 149, 321
Stevens, Leith 6, 168, 170, 173, 174, 207, 215, 220, 286, 330
Stevens, Morton 19, 67, 183
Stewart, Gloria 47
Stewart, Rod 314
Stingray 219
Stoll, George 301
Stone 300, 329
The Stone Killer 42
Stoneground 253
Storm, Tempest 86
The Story of O 121
The Storybook 317
Stott, Wally *see* Morley, Angela
Straight Records 295
Straigis, Ron 103
Strange, Billy 299
The Strange Vice of Ms. Wardh 266
Stranger movies 141
The Stranger Returns 141
Strangers on a Train 229, 243–244
Lo straniero di silenzio 141
Strauss, Johann 185
Strauss, Richard 185
Stravinsky, Igor 71, 156, 168, 172, 183, 187, 205, 210, 218, 221, 225, 228, 240
Straw Dogs 55
Strawberry Alarm Clock (S.A. Clock) 317, 318, 322
Stream of Consciousness 296
A Streetcar Named Desire 1, 3, 6, 90
Streets of San Francisco 19
Strictly Kev 334
The Stripper 93–94
Strip-tease 122
Strouse, Charles 37
Stu Who? 290, 294
Studio Trautonium 233
Styne, Stanley 307
Styner, Jerry *see* Steiner, Jerry
Succubus 114–115
Sudden Impact 16
Sugar Colt 141
Summer, Donna 119, 122
Summer Love 286
"Summer of Love" (1967) 319
Summers, Bob 317
Sumner, Gordon "Sting" 314
Sun Ra and His Intergalactic Solar Arkestra (or Sun Ra) 194, 221
Super Chase 35
Supercolpo de sette miliardi 78
Superfly 27, 32, 35, 52, 56

Superfly T.N.T. 32
Superman 167, 199
Surf Happy 303
The Surfaris 303
Susann, Jacqueline 97, 100
Suspiria 238, 278–279, 281
Sutherland, Donald 200
The Swarm 243
S.W.A.T. 19
Sweden, Heaven and Hell 110, 111, 112, 126
The Sweeney 42–43
Sweeney Todd: The Demon Barber of Fleet Street 223
The Sweet Ride 301, 305–306
Sweet Smell of Success 7
Sweet Sweetback's Baadasssss Song 23–24
Switched on Bach 191
Sylvanus 298
Synanon 15

Take Five 7
The Taking of Pelham, One, Two, Three 19, 20, 56
Take It Off: Striptease Classics 86
Tales of Terror 224
Tales of Tomorrow 213
Tammy's Greatest Hits 295
Tanaka, Tomoyuki 211, 306
Tangerine Dream 279
Tarantino, Quentin 32, 144, 151, 266, 279, 332
La tarantola dal ventre nero 267, 268
Tarantula 172
Taras Bulba 2
Tarkowskij, Andrej 206
Tarrago, Renato 50, 51
Taste the Blood of Dracula 248, 249, 253
Tate, Sharon 234
Taxi Driver 40, 234, 236, 239, 240
Taylor, Creed 15
Taylor, James (Quartet) 333
Tchaikovsky, Peter 41, 71, 197
Teasarama 86
Tecumseh 132
Teddy and Darrell 318
Teeba, Ollie 332
Teenage Rebellion 317
Tempera, Vince 141, 159, 160, 161, 279
The Temptations 32
10 103
The Ten Commandments 171, 319
Ten Little Indians 261
The Tenant 234–236
Tendres Cousines 124
The Tenth Victim 205–206, 266
Tepepa 147
The Terror 225
Terry, Lilian 152
Tess 234
Tessari, Duccio 138

Tevis, Peter 133
Tew, Alan 43
Texter, Gilda 299
Thank God It's Friday 122
That Man in Istanbul 81
Them! 172
Themes International 43
Theodorakis, Mikis 38, 105
Theremin 71, 168, 169, 170, 171, 215, 244, 255
They Call Me Mister Tibbs 22, 25, 55, 56
They Call Me Trinity 149
They Came to Rob Las Vegas 52, 53
The Thief of Badhdad 204
The Thing from Another World 168, 169–170, 223
Things to Come 167
The Third Man 70
The 39 Steps 57
This Is Hardcore 206
This Is Spinal Tap 284
Thomas, Dylan 300
Thomas, Peter 46, 77, 78, 84, 123, 124, 132, 206, 208, 219, 221
Thomas, Tony 185
The Thomas Crown Affair 50
Thornton, Big Mama 299
Three Days of the Condor 75
Three Degrees 56
Three Tough Guys 32–33
The 3 Worlds of Gulliver 179
The Thriller Collection 264, 266
Thunder Alley 301–302
Thunderball 49, 61, 62, 63, 66, 69, 70, 84, 106
Thunderbirds 219
THX 1138 191, 193
Time After Time 204
The Time Machine 173, 179, 180, 181
The Time Tunnel 216
Tiomkin, Dimitri 127, 128, 132, 134, 135, 162, 168, 169, 170, 221, 229, 244
Tipton, George 23
'Tis Pity, She's a Whore 117
To Catch a Thief 229
To Have and Have Not 90
Tobias, Ken 159
Tobin, Amon 332
Der Tod im Roten Jaguar 77
Tödlicher Irrtum 132
Toho Studios 211
Tom Corbett—Space Cadet 213
Tomorrow Never Comes 42
Tommy 284, 313–314, 324, 327
Tonks, Paul 227
Tony Arzenta 44
Tony Rome 14, 301
Topkapi 47
Topper, Burt 317
Tork, Peter 311

Tormé, Mel 254
Torn Curtain 184, 229, 233, 236
Touch of Evil 9–10, 46, 52, 89
The Towering Inferno 198
Townsend, Pete 284, 314
Townson, Robert 185
Traffic 107, 325
Travis, Debra 317
Travolta, John 327, 328
The Treasure of Silver Lake 131
The Trip 316, 318, 329
Troppo per vivere ... poco per morire 81
Trouble Man 27–28
The Trouble with Girls 299
The Trouble with Harry 229
Troup, Bobby 90, 296
Trout Mask Replica 295
Trovaioli, Armando 48, 105, 114, 118, 119, 140, 177, 178
Troy, Doris 81
Truck Turner 32–33
True Grit 163, 166
Truffaut, François 184, 185
Trumbull, Douglas 193
Trunk Records 255
"Tubular Bells" 238, 278
Tucker, Chris 36
Tucker, Terry 192
Tunnah, Chris 227
Turn On, Tune In, Drop Out 319
Tutti per uno, botte per tutti 159
The Twangs 304
20th Century-Fox 89, 171, 187
Twenty Million Miles to Earth 173
20,000 Leagues Under the Sea 182
The Twilight Zone 189, 213, 214, 215, 221, 231
Twins of Evil 251, 252
Twist Around the Clock 285, 319
200 Motels 284, 312–313
Two Lane Blacktop 299
Two Mules for Sister Sara 162
2001: A Space Odyssey 185–186, 191, 193, 197, 208
2 Tone 334
Tyler, Kip 286

U.F.O. 218, 219
L'ultimo killer 141
Umiliani, Piero 44, 79, 82, 110, 111, 112, 117, 118, 126, 147, 152, 153, 159, 261
Ummagumma 315
Una sull'altra see *Perversion Story*
Una vergine tra i morti viventi 275
Uncle Meat 312
Underwood, Ian 197, 241
Unforgiven 165
United Artists 313
Universal Pictures 222, 228, 234, 236, 245, 246, 247, 314

Un uomo chiamato Apocalisse Joe 154
L'uomo, l'orgoglio, la vendetta 148
Un uomo, un cavallo, una pistola 141, 142
Up! Mega Vixens 89
Up the Junction 325–326
Upperseven 79
Uptight 22

Vadim, Roger 104, 108
Vado, l'ammazzo e torno 145
Valdez, Sonny 296
The Valley 315
Valley of the Dolls 97
Vamos a matar, companeros 152–153
The Vampire 223
The Vampire Lovers 251, 252
The Vampires Sound Unlimited 115
I vampiri 256
Vampyros lesbos 115, 116, 122, 126, 329, 331, 332
Van Cleave, Nathan 68, 214
Van Cleef, Lee 136
Vandor, Ivan 141
Van Peebles, Melvin 23, 24, 26
Van Rooyen, Jerry 115
Vanilla Fudge 318
Vanishing Point 299
Varese Sarabande 186, 202, 218, 241
Un vaso de whisky 46
Vaughn, Robert 130
Vaughan, Sarah 21, 35, 99, 320
Velvet Underground 289
The Ventures 303
Venus in Furs 116, 326
Venus in Furs (*Le malizie di Venere*) 116
Verdi, Giuseppe 223
Verne, Jules 179, 182
Verrecchia, Albert 45
Vertigo 229, 230–231, 233, 239, 243, 281
La via della droga 45, 279
Vickers, Mike 253
Vidal, Gore 125
VideoWatchdog.com 268
A View to a Kill 61, 66
Villechaize, Herve 66
Vincent, Gene 90
Vinjak, Steffi 123
The Virgin and the Gypsy 108
Virgin Stigma 323
Viva Las Vegas 309
Vivaldi, Antonio 60
Vivi o preferibilmente morti 152
Vixen 89
Vlad, Roman 256
Voices of Walter Schumann 220
Voight, Jon 99
Vonnegut, Kurt 194
Voyage to the Bottom of the Sea 182–183, 215, 216

Wade, Adam 32, 330
Wagoner, Bruce 287
Wakeman, Rick 122
Walk on the Wild Side 93
Walker, Jimmy 299
The Wall 284, 315
Wallace, Edgar 46, 206
Warner Bros. 174
War of the Gargantuas 212
War of the Planets 204
The War of the Worlds 168, 170, 181
Warhol, Andy 237, 238
Warner Bros. 238
Warshow, Robert 127
Warwick, Dionne 64, 96, 97, 100
Washington, Dinah 21
The Wasp Woman 223
Wasserman, John 200
Watermelon Man 23
Waters, John 90
Waters, Roger 315
Watson, Gordon 253
Wattstax 283, 284
Waxman, Franz 1, 90, 214, 229, 256
Wayne, John ("Duke") 18, 19, 128, 129, 162, 163, 165
We Travel the Space Ways 194, 221
Web of the Spider 264
Webern, Anton 238
Weil, Kurt 144, 264
Weisse Wölfe 132
Welch, Raquel 52, 179, 181
Welles, Orson 9, 229
Wells, Brian 100
Wells, H.G. 170, 181, 183, 204
Wendy Carlos's Clockwork Orange 191
We're Only in It for the Money 312
Werth, Howard 327
Wesley, Fred 30
Wesley, Johnny 320
West, Adam 216
West, Mae 85
Westlake, Donald 37, 38
Westworld 194–195
Wexler, Jerry 103
Whale, James 167
What's Going On 27
What's New, Pussycat? 48, 96, 126, 325–326
Wheatley, Dennis 251
Wheels of Fire 292
When Dinosaurs Ruled the Earth 179, 180
When Worlds Collide 168, 170
Where the Spies Are 82
Wherry, Jake 332
The Whip and the Body 258, 259
The Whips 86
Whitaker, David 228, 255
The Who 283, 284, 313, 314, 324
Who's Next 314
The Wicker Man 255

The Wild Angels 287–289, 329
The Wild Bunch 55, 162, 163–164, 166
The Wild Gals of the Naked West 88
The Wild One 6, 286, 287
The Wild Racers 301, 302
The Wild Rovers 165
Wild Wheels 303
Wild Wild Planet 204
Wild Wild Winter 296
Wilden, Gert 46, 123
Wilder, Billy 91, 93
The Wilder Brothers 152
Wilkinson, Marc 254, 255, 281
Will Success Spoil Rock Hunter? 90
Williams, Hank, Jr. 54
Williams, John 2, 3, 55, 198, 204, 215, 216, 220, 221, 232, 240, 241, 243, 244, 281
Williams, Johnny 96, 97, 240
Williams, Lori 288
Williams, Pat 103
Williams, Robbie 64, 332
Williams, Tennessee 90, 95
Williams, Trevor 327
Williamson, Fred 32
Williamson, Malcolm 247, 251
Willie Dynamite 29, 34
Willy, Louise 85
Wilson, Warren 276
Il Winchester che non perdona 147
"The Windmills of Your Mind" 50
Wings 66
Winnetou 132
Winnetou the Warrior 132
Winogrond, David 287, 318
Winter a-Go-Go 306
Winwood, Stevie 314, 325
Witchcraft 176
Witchfinder General 223
The Wolf Man 222, 228
Women in Love 108
Wonder, Stevie 32
Woodstock 283, 284
World Pacific 304
World War I 248
World Without End 173
Worth, J. 255
The Wrecking Crew 73
The Wrong Man 229
Das Wunder der Liebe 2 124
Wu Tang Clan 35, 36
Wynette, Tammy 294

X the Unknown 176

Yamauchi, Tadashi 212
Yellow Submarine 310, 311
Yesterday, Today and Tomorrow 105
Yojimbo 133
You Only Live Twice 50, 61, 64, 65, 84, 99, 332

Young, Aida 179, 248
Young, James 39, 128, 185, 229
Young, Terence 77
The Young Savages 15
The Youngbloods 316

Zabriskie Point 289, 315–316
Zappa, Frank 197, 241, 282 284, 295, 312–313

Zatoichi 157
Zeitlin, Denny 200, 201
Ziggy Stardust and the Spiders from Mars 283
Zorba the Greek 38, 105
Zombi see *Dawn of the Dead*
Zombi 2 281
Zorn, John 145
Zounds! What Sounds? 286

www.ingramcontent.com/pod-product-compliance
Lightning Source LLC
Chambersburg PA
CBHW061343300426
44116CB00011B/1964